GENDERING THE RECESSION

GENDERING THE RECESSION

Media and Culture in an Age of Austerity

Diane Negra and Yvonne Tasker, editors

Duke University Press / Durham and London / 2014

© 2014 Duke University Press
All rights reserved
Printed in the United States of America on acid-free paper ∞
Typeset in Quadraat and Meta by Tseng Information Systems, Inc.

Library of Congress Cataloging-in-Publication Data
Gendering the recession : media and culture in an age of austerity /
Diane Negra and Yvonne Tasker, editors.
pages cm
Includes bibliographical references and index.
ISBN 978-0-8223-5687-5 (cloth : alk. paper)
ISBN 978-0-8223-5696-7 (pbk. : alk. paper)
1. Sex role—Economic aspects. 2. Global Financial Crisis, 2008–
2009. 3. Women—Employment. 4. Women in development.
I. Negra, Diane, 1966– II. Tasker, Yvonne, 1964–
HQ1075.G463 2014
331.4—dc23   2013042832

CONTENTS

ACKNOWLEDGMENTS

The editors would like to thank Shelley Cobb, Monica Cullinan of the James Joyce Library at University College Dublin, Nick Daly, Tamara Falicov, Paula Gilligan, Debbie Ging, Aisling Jackman, Karen Jackman, Liam Kennedy and the Clinton Institute for American Studies at University College Dublin, Anthony McIntyre, Gerardine Meaney and the UCD Humanities Institute, Moya Luckett, Christopher Holmes Smith, Ciaran Toner, and Erica Wetter. For help in assembling the final manuscript we particularly thank Elizabeth Rawitsch and Rachel Hall. Working with Courtney Berger, Liz Smith, Heather Hensley, and Willa Armstrong at Duke University Press has been a pleasure.

The editors gratefully acknowledge the permission of Oxford University Press to partially reprint material by Sarah Banet-Weiser first published in *Aftermath: The Cultures of the Economic Crisis*, edited by Manuel Castells, João Caraça, and Gustavo Cardoso.

Gender and Recessionary Culture

After a decade and a half of frenetic economic activity in the West, now often remembered as a boom period, the semicollapse of the global financial system in 2007–8 inaugurated a set of profound cultural shifts. During the boom the celebration of a market mind-set overarching all aspects of life coincided with an intensification of polarized gender norming that we and others have written about under the aegis of postfeminism. Postfeminist culture's key tropes—a preoccupation with self-fashioning and the makeover; women's seeming "choice" not to occupy high-status public roles; the celebration of sexual expression and affluent femininities—are enabled by the optimism and opportunity of prosperity (or the perception of it). Framed by what commentators have dubbed the Great Recession, this book asks whether and to what extent the conceptual and theoretical accounts of gender developed in an earlier and distinctly different economic era still apply.

While fields ranging from economics to sociology to equality studies have much to contribute in analyzing the recession's social character, media studies offers a unique disciplinary pathway for interpreting recession culture given its focus on the analysis of collective symbolic environments that hold enormous sway in shaping public views. Indeed, we contend here that our economic lives are both shaped by and embedded within popular and representational culture. As a consequence, any account of the economic conditions of the global recession will be incomplete without taking into consideration the cultural storytelling associated with the mass media. Crucially, popular culture helps to mobilize emotion and to allocate blame, frequently redirecting resentment and anger at structural problems away from elites and toward class peer groups who are imagined to retain the "privileges" of earlier eras. Media culture involves hegemonic processes of sense making; stitching together at times contradictory modes of conventional wisdom, media formats from financial journalism to reality television offer an understanding of the operations of power. In line with accounts of neoliberalism, we theorize this process as one in which media texts work to bridge the private and the public. Just as postfeminist culture suggests that it is individual women (rather than systems of gender hierarchy) that require modification, recessionary media culture implies that management of the self can effect positive change. Though governments seem increasingly unable to act in the interests of citizens, media texts offer reassuring vignettes of individual agency as compensation to the ill-defined yet intensely valorized power of the market.

Many features of what we characterize here as the gendering of the recession are operative at the level of everyday life, expressed in a media environment that performs cultural agenda setting in ways that are still too often taken for granted. It has become commonplace within journalism and political rhetoric, for instance, to employ terminology that caricatures state actions through reference to "female" qualities of nurturance; we do this reflexively when we use expressions such as "nanny state." Conversely, the need for action to counter the economic crisis has consistently been framed in terms of a language of toughness and austerity premised on supposed masculine virtues.[1] In an era in which accounts of economic decline frequently privilege male subjectivity (through such buzzwords as "mancession" and invitations to "man up"), it is instructive to consider the renewal of long-established tropes of masculinity in "crisis" (of which feminist scholars have rightly been skeptical). Underpinning the compelling rhetoric of masculine crisis is not only the suggestion that men are the primary victims of recession — a thread within the reporting of unemployment figures — but also that equality is a concern to be reserved for times of plenty. Recessionary conditions, we argue, have fortified a paradox well captured by Deborah Tudor, who notes that neo-liberalization "revoked but also reinvigorated white patriarchy."[2]

Aware of the need for critical studies in the humanities to generate theoretical and social accounts that keep pace with the rapid economic and social changes brought on by the recession, this book seeks to map the gendered impact of the recent unraveling of seemingly stable financial rubrics and institutions. Accordingly, it is particularly concerned to synthesize feminist theories with the critical study of consumerism. Wanting to pinpoint the ways that public culture genders our producing and consuming roles, we invoke and extend the historical feminist commitment to redressing social and economic inequities. Henry Giroux has written, "The survival-of-the-fittest ethic and its mantra of doing just about anything to increase profits now reach into every aspect of society and are widely dispersed as a form of public pedagogy in the dominant and new media."[3] In the context of the normalization of a socially damaging fixation on profit, the essays here are framed to examine how patterns of intense wealth concentration and the transfer of risk from cultural and financial elites to the public at large (and particularly to those at lower income levels) interact with and impact cultural conceptualizations of both femininity and masculinity.

Thus this book is shaped to provide a series of responses to the following questions:

- In an ever more convergent media landscape, what notions and narratives of recession recur across media forms too often studied in isolation from one another?
- How do media texts naturalize gender inequality at a moment when a range of social inequalities threaten to rise to the surface?

Part of a project of scholarly dissent, our work here is informed by an awareness of the current system of financial institutions and relations as facilitating the saving of the rich and the indebtedness of other classes. *Gendering the Recession* scrutinizes a contemporary public culture in which expressions of critique and protest are often muted by sophisticated forms of state and corporate suppression. The assembled essays largely explore media forms that trade in the repression of the socially destructive aspects of Western global capitalism, bid for affective normalcy, and commit themselves to strained fantasies of rejuvenated individualist enterprise, in particular demonstrating an inability to meaningfully critique the privileged male. In their analyses of reality TV, ads, blogs, vlogs, genre films, popular novels, documentaries, and sitcoms the authors turn to some of the most taken-for-granted popular culture forms to root an analysis of everyday recessionary culture and a preliminary mapping of what the cultural geographer Ruth Wilson Gilmore would term an "infrastructure of feeling."[4] In this way, *Gendering the Recession* addresses a corpus of texts with high cultural profiles that generate significant commentary but little full-fledged analysis.

In a moment characterized by widespread public anger at and lack of trust in corporations and governments, we argue that political questions about equality are deservedly acquiring a new centrality.[5] In exploring the diverse ways in which postfeminist popular culture acknowledges and evades these questions, this project offers a feminist response to a complex and contested economic crisis, noting that crisis discourse can promote the rollback of opportunities for women under the rhetorical cover of necessity. Indeed, a key development with which this project is concerned is the placement of intense economic austerity as an overriding priority that nullifies the interests of gender equity. Scholarly scrutiny shows that the gender dynamics of the recession are in fact discursively prominent, yet up to this point they have been little addressed by academics.

We argue not that these questions are new but rather that they are increasingly compelling. The weight of postfeminist cultural formation and retrograde political actions meant that prior to the recession women were already precariously placed even in contexts of comparative national privilege. In 2007 Michaele L. Ferguson and Lori Jo Marso wrote that "the constellation of an eviscerated liberal feminism, a hierarchical gender ideology, and a neoconservative security strategy articulated by the Bush presidency represents a new configuration of gender politics whose significance and impact will extend far beyond Bush's two terms in office."[6] More recently, feeble progress toward financial reform (thus ensuring ongoing inequality) coupled with efforts to reduce U.S. women to a diminished status through a set of rightwing political initiatives often referred to as the "war on women" have spelled further exacerbation of existing gender inequalities.

The postfeminist popular culture of recent decades has tended to suggest that gender equality has been achieved, rallying around images of success and "empowerment" in such forms as the cinematic action heroine, the female lawyer of television drama, and the spectacularly sexually assertive pop star. Recessionary culture maintains these celebratory discourses of course but, we argue, they are underwritten or more precisely contextualized by a perception that equality is a luxury that can no longer be afforded. Within this formulation, the postfeminist female consumer is placed as an icon of excess as much as admiration, an emblem of the boom and a symptom of its short-term financialism. Other current narratives and tropes situate the recession as an opportunity to recover from a disordered work culture (*The Company Men* [2010], for example; a flurry of journalistic accounts early in the recession of once-harried now-downsized corporate employees using savings to travel) or to reconstitute and refresh existing consumer paradigms such as the female hyperconsumer (thus the emergence of the term "recessionista" to designate the budget-conscious yet highly fashion-forward woman; see figures intro.1 and intro.2).[7]

Though there are notable exceptions (some of which we mention here), the popular culture of the ongoing recession has most often cast women as

FIGURES INTRO.1 AND INTRO.2. Responsiveness to recession conditions is heavily gendered, with films like *The Company Men* dramatizing the plight of male corporate workers and popular terms like "recessionista" recuperating female consumerism.

passive and personal responders to the economic downturn, stressing positive thinking and visualization techniques (as in Rhonda Byrne's blockbuster book *The Secret*), the cultivation of smart relationship skills (through the lessons of best-selling advice literature like Steve Harvey's *Act Like a Lady, Think Like a Man*) and the tutelage of male life coaches (centralized in "rescue reality" genres where participants' health, job, and life predicaments are therapeutically addressed, as in NBC's *Breakthrough with Tony Robbins*).[8] Such appeals take place in the context of a complex cultural politics of happiness and self-responsibilization detailed by Sara Ahmed, among others, who usefully invites us to think about "how claims to happiness make certain forms of personhood valuable."[9]

Labor, Corporatism, and Equality in Recessionary Popular Culture

Postfeminism has shown itself to be significantly related (if not reducible) to the "bubble culture" of the twenty-first century's first decade, a period marked, according to Christopher Holmes Smith, by "a successive series of asset bubbles that have ranged from property and credit to commodities and emerging market equities."[10] In continuity with this association, the upscale female consumer became one of the defining archetypes of postfeminism in the 2000s. Her purchases and the celebration of her self-production effectively masked or at least deflected attention from the low-paid workers whose labor serviced and supported that self-fashioning. On one hand, the post-boom period has arguably brought a new visibility to the inequalities that the pervasive rhetoric of empowerment previously belied. Thus austerity measures across Europe and growing economic inequalities in the United States have triggered highly visible forms of public protest. Yet, as in previous periods of economic uncertainty, a surge in traditionalist discourses of gender and labor is equally evident in nostalgic evocations of, for example, maternal (but also fashionable) thrift.[11] In this context the material trappings that define female success in postfeminist culture can easily seem inauthentic as much as desirable. Such a perception of the inauthenticity of material goods already informed retreatist postfeminist fantasies, although the scenarios of downsizing that have typically circulated in popular culture remain premised on affluence and even luxury.[12] Given that these very trappings served as popular culture's primary manner of gesturing toward a gender equality it assumed was achieved (an assumption that we would of course contest), to what extent does recession-era gender representation acknowledge persistent economic and cultural inequalities?

Put simply, postfeminist culture's emphasis on choice—the freedom to consume and self-fashion rather than the economic necessities that underpin women's working lives—has not disappeared but reads differently now that the economic bubble has burst. Recessionary popular culture has latched onto the commodification of domestic femininities in ways continuous with but also distinct from previous eras, with female consumer resourcefulness becoming a new theme on many fronts. In the TLC television series *Extreme Couponing*, for instance, female thrift is shown to work for an era of adjusted economic realities. A number of the series' first-season profile subjects in 2011 were women who had lost a male breadwinner's salary (through either unemployment or divorce); they are invariably such assiduous and adept coupon clippers that they get their groceries for free. These women are seen to step into the income breach without deviating from their domestic roles, and the series sustains a mixed discourse of praise and pathologization around figures inscribed on the one hand as bravura postfeminist housekeepers but on the other as intense overconsumers who speak of "stockpiling." *Extreme Couponing* illustrates how popular culture's commitment to consumption remains largely intact, if suitably qualified, in the recession. Indeed, recessionary images of female resourcefulness have proliferated in forms that seek to retain traditionalist femininity under conditions of financial exigency, leading to phenomena like the privileging of the female cupcake baker (widespread in media discourse) as the exemplar of adaptive economy and safe female entrepreneurialism.[13]

Recovery rhetoric in the recession often suppresses both the reality of ongoing gender inequalities and postfeminism's status as an accessory discourse to neoliberal corporatism. In chapter 4, Pamela Thoma maintains that the recession-era chick flick, often considered a throwaway genre, urges women to accommodate their wage labor to domestic and emotional labor in order to mitigate the economic crisis; chick flicks are thus revealing of a process in which all labor is becoming feminized—which is to say insecure, flexible, invisible, and/or poorly paid. An interesting correlative in this regard is a turn toward female-oriented rural fantasy work that would appear to be thriving in the recession, in the process raising the premium on postfeminist retreatism. Female domesticity is attributed a more functionalist character in digital domains such as the social network game Farmville (played more by women than by men) or the growing Pioneer Woman franchise.[14] In 2011, Ree Drummond's blog under that name, a chronicle of daily ranch life in Oklahoma, created a significant stir, becoming one of the most widely read among U.S. women, a development that seems indicative of the repositioning of the retreatist woman in a recession context of pragmatism and functionality. Such dynamics are also at work in the large number of female-oriented fashion blogs premised on the belief that fashion can turn female consumers into producers, which Elizabeth Nathanson explores in her essay (chapter 5), as well as in the proliferation of "mommy blogs" in recent years.[15] Broadly speaking, the new domestic economies of recessionary media showcase a permutation of postfeminism in which women adeptly monetize domestic skills and resources.

Film, television, and digital culture increasingly compensate for broad vulnerabilities of economic citizenship with gendered rhetorics of power, success, and family or community membership. *Gendering the Recession* thus scrutinizes postfeminism in the cultural context of a recession era that activates particular vocabularies of gender while suppressing others. While the book builds on the proliferating scholarship concerned with postfeminist femininities, it also aims to shift emphasis toward questions of masculinity, noting both that this area has received less attention and the centrality of discourses of masculinity and male crisis to recessionary culture.[16] Postfeminist culture generated and mediated new male types such as the metrosexual, figures as tied to consumption practices as the postfeminist woman it also imagined. If dedication to consumption defined the postfeminist woman of popular media culture, how has that culture made sense of the male financial worker/executive? How, for example, do reports of extravagant bonuses—and the conspicuous consumption this fuels—figure within the gendered discourses that circulate around and define the world of finance? And how do "financialized" male citizens more broadly negotiate social terrain in which the definitional power of earning and providing roles functions as a neoliberal credo? Significantly, it is the failing male finance worker that is typically centralized within popular films and fictions, with successful financiers demonized, marginal figures. "The epic proportions of this crisis invited melodrama," notes Kirby Farrell, and indeed that is one form the recession took, specifically, via corporate melodrama, a formula we discuss further below that customarily assesses the plight of former "masters of the universe" in straitened circumstances.[17] In his essay (chapter 8), Hamilton Carroll reads two male-centered, postcorporate recession-era novels, finding that the protagonists of *The Financial Lives of the Poets* and *The Ask* operate in a mode of recuperative failure to ultimately retrieve a kind of success from experiences of personal and financial loss.[18]

In chapter 3, Sarah Banet-Weiser explores advertising as a form that has effectively branded the economic crisis as a challenge to U.S. masculinity, appealing to the image of physical rather than white-collar labor.[19] More broadly, the financial crisis promulgates cultural themes of male infantilism and underdevelopment, circulates tropes of male injury in which white men are positioned as both sign and symptom of economic contraction, and generates a strange sort of zero-sum thinking when it comes to the experiences of men and women in recession (e.g., if women are gaining, men must be losing). Commentary that positions men as privileged subjects of recessionary exigency is regular, routine, and runs across a spectrum of publication forms. In one example among many, Don Peck asserts that "the weight of this recession has fallen most heavily upon men" and provides this vivid characterization of the social consequences of the recession: "a slowly sinking generation; *a remorseless assault on the identity of many men*; the dissolution of families and the collapse of neighborhoods; a thinning veneer of national amity."[20] As these examples suggest, the discursive trope of failing males and coping females (which predates the recession) has been given significant impetus and inflection.

This book's interrogation of gender within recessionary culture is throughout informed by what Purnima Bose and Laura E. Lyons have termed a "critical corporate studies." As they note, state intervention in response to the global financial crisis has tended to buttress "existing social inequalities by propping up institutions that benefit the wealthy and which precipitated the financial crisis in the first place."[21] In continuity with the intellectual traditions of cultural studies, we insist upon a "destabilization of the category of the 'economic' as clearly distinguishable from other social phenomena."[22] The analyses in *Gendering the Recession* are set against a material landscape of intense financialization in which the policies, practices, and performance of Wall Street in the United States and the City in Britain have moved to a position of historically unprecedented cultural centrality. While astute critics such as Randy Martin have tracked the "financialization of daily life" in the contemporary United States, few assessments have considered the gendered dynamics of this shift.[23] With (male) risk in the high-flying domains of Wall Street culturally juxtaposed with the castigation of risk by the (often feminized) poor, two additional elements to consider are the increasing frequency of unpaid work and the broad phenomenon of wage theft. John Harris is among a number of U.K. commentators who have highlighted the rise of work programs and training courses that require those out of work to undertake unpaid work for private firms in order to maintain their unemployment compensation.[24] Documenting the variety of ways in which U.S. workers go under- (or un)paid for their labor, Kim Bobo has drawn attention to the limitation of using employment statistics as a gauge for standard of living. At a time when gross overpayment and tax breaks for the wealthy have drawn scrutiny, few examinations of underpayment to the middle and service classes have been undertaken. Yet from flouting the minimum wage to the neglect of overtime pay, American employers use a variety of means to reduce wage payments and underfund the tax system. Some of the most egregious wage theft is congregated in industries such as construction or nursing home care dominated by immigrant and female workers.[25]

Sites and Signs of Gender in Recession Culture

In the main, recessionary popular culture is marked by an impoverished public discourse and a deep political complacency implied in rhetorical formulations like "it is what it is" and the ubiquitous "it's going to get worse before it gets better" that often substitute for meaningful analysis. In popular culture the recession has largely factored as an opportunity to reboot established, enduring ideological precepts about class, race, consumerism, individualism, work, and (as is the particular concern of this book) gender. Yet even as a slew of revanchist economic and social policies have been installed in recession, issues of inequality have played a significant part in high-profile fiction films (*The Dark Knight Rises* [2012], *The Hunger Games* [2012], *Les Miserables* [2012]) and documentaries (*Inside Job* [2010], *Queen of Versailles* [2012]) alike.[26] The contributors to this book share an interest in the role media representations may play in both highlighting such inequalities and perpetuating "magical thinking" around issues of economic security and mobility.

It is apparent that a range of the most high-profile media products in recent years highlight particularly charged themes of empowerment at a time when a sense of our powers and rights as citizens is greatly diminished. The culture of gaming is especially noteworthy in offering symbolic alternative experiences of control that sidestep overt national and cultural allegiances. High-profile Hollywood superhero films work through some of these themes too, dramatizing fantasies of benevolent paternalistic power. Meanwhile, "tycoon television" trains our gaze on CEOs in series like *The Apprentice* and *Secret Millionaire* and a renewed fascination with aristocratic elites underscores media events from the U.K. royal wedding to the phenomenon of *Downton Abbey*. The context of recession clearly underpins these diverse images and formats, with wealth and inequality emerging as key themes across numerous media genres and modes.

The vaporization of public resources, the rupturing of the social contract, and the disappearance of forms of health and safety protection long understood to be intrinsic to the working lives of citizens in Western democracies have accompanied the emergence of extraordinary new protocols of preference for corporations.[27] Karen Ho has noted that "what is clearly unique in the recent history of capitalism in the United States is the complete divorce of what is perceived as the best interests of the corporation from the interests of most employees."[28] Popular forms make cultural sense—and entertainment—out of such complex developments. This book's concern with the thematization of downsizing, unemployment, thrift, austerity, poverty, and other recession-related phenomena in popular media is set in the broader context of the explosion of financial media and an ongoing commitment to the presentation of global financial markets as embodying a charismatic public authority. The financial industries at the heart of the economic crisis have been characterized by a clear masculinization of risk and a feminization of back office functions. Meanwhile, U.S. financial news is delivered by emphatically gendered figures ranging from CNBC's hyperbolic Jim Cramer to such so-called money honeys as Maria Bartiromo and Erin Burnett.[29] This financialized mind-set is built in part through the familiarity of media representation and indeed, celebrity economists and finance gurus such as Cramer, who have proved durable features of the recessionary media landscape (figures intro.3 and intro.4).

In an era in which the free market is frequently presented as naturally and inevitably meritocratic and capable of resolving all diversity concerns, it is surely noteworthy that a number of national and global television franchises in the recession are highlighting the theme of unruly employees and benevolent bosses. Exemplary in this regard is *Undercover Boss*, a reality series originating in the U.K. that has been rapidly globalized with U.S., Australian, German, Norwegian, and Canadian versions produced and Danish, Spanish, Swedish, Dutch, and Belgian versions being developed. Generating a timely fantasy for an era of downsizing and multitasking, *Undercover Boss* is based on the idea that if the boss only knew how hard you were working, things would be different. Each episode involves a boss disguising his or (very occasionally) her identity and secretly mingling with low-level workers before a closing reveal sequence has him rewarding selected workers for the fine performances clandestinely observed. The series presents its corporate CEOs as benefactors and the workplace as a purely meritocratic space where no collective bargaining is necessary.

Unpacking the formula of *Undercover Boss* in a little more detail, it is apparent that viewers are invited to follow the CEOs of enterprises and corporations negatively impacted by the recession. Framed as responsive to straitened commercial circumstances, these business leaders and managers go undercover (following a "make-under") with a camera crew, posing as prospective entry-level employees, in order to identify at a grassroots level work and employment practices in need of improvement. Their subsequent investigations allow these benevolent figures to reward examples of good practice with isolated gestures of generosity and disingenuous good will. In this way the CEOs profiled, in the face of recessionary contextual forces, maintain a

FIGURES INTRO.3 AND INTRO.4. Themes of charismatic male financial and corporate authority predominate on television, as exemplified by cable news personality Jim Cramer and the global reality franchise *Undercover Boss*.

neoliberal ethos of individual empowerment and the credo of self-managing one's way out of crisis. They positively reframe themselves, ameliorating their own images to convey paternalistic benevolence at a time when the figure of the greedy, self-interested corporate CEO-financier is being demonized elsewhere in media culture. Operating as a form of "advertainment" for those corporations it profiles, Undercover Boss also offers a rich case study of the key links in place between entertainment and economics; in the series' first U.S. season, all of the companies featured saw a rise in their stock prices. Undercover Boss's highly sympathetic presentation of corporate CEOs helps to naturalize a business climate in which the downsizing of the public sector often stands as an unquestioned value, a return to the paternalistic philanthropy of the robber baron era appears unproblematic, and the idea that corporations are good citizens whom individuals can emulate is received as credible. Since female CEOs are rarely presented, the series predictably genders corporate authority in line with a familiar, masculine-coded paternalism.

Any comprehensive mapping of the complex media ecology of the recession is of course impossible; the spectrum of representational responses to the recession is vast and this book could not possibly do justice to them all. However, it is clear that across media forms as diverse as reality television, financial journalism, lifestyle blogs, popular cinema, and advertising some tropes recur as meaningful responses to the global financial crisis. The representational dynamics discussed in this book are framed against a backdrop of broader cultural keynotes that include the dyad of the failing man and the adaptive/coping woman; the positioning of home and community as sites of crisis and new figurations of labor; the contrast of hyped-up capitalist empowerment fantasies anchored through terminology such as "wealth creators" with the casting of those in economic distress as "dependent" recipients of government "entitlement programs"; the abstract figuring of bankers as hate figures and entrepreneurs as saviors; and the careful placement of social others, whether Latinos in the U.S. context or gypsies in the European one, so as not to disrupt gendered myths of capitalist enterprise and social and familial integrity.[30]

The complex interrelation of discourses of ethnicity, nation, and gender are touched on by several of the contributors to this volume. While mass cultural fictions tend to eschew the explicit racism currently being played out in right-wing political activism across Europe, suspicion of migrant workers (who epitomize those forms of mobility that resist conventional valorization) frames recessionary discourse, and television and other media forms in Europe interpret a social context in which an aspirational individualism centered on consumption remains dominant yet unachievable. Mobility and migration emerge as key media themes in this context: whether movements of populations in pursuit of the lifestyles popular media encourage us to desire, or the move to identify groups whose symbolic (and in some cases actual) expulsion it is imagined will secure European prosperity. In the United Kingdom and Ireland, the media preoccupation with "gypsies" (to some extent a codified reference to migration from Eastern European nations such as Romania and Bulgaria) activates ambivalent spectatorial engagement with notions of subcultural apartness and alternate economies while potentially serving as grist for conservative political arguments about minoritarian over-entitlement. In the Netherlands, *Weg van Nederlands* (2011) has employed a quiz show format to ideologically manage the volatile issue of national inclusivity in recession, as rejected asylum seekers vie to prove their knowledge of Dutch culture, with the winner obtaining a small sum of cash to take along upon expulsion.

Such nationally particular forms of recessionary media include a steady output of post–Celtic Tiger horror films in Ireland, U.K. reality series that offer comparative experiences of state benefit (Channel 4's *Go Greek for a Week*, in which British families temporarily take on the tax obligations, pension benefits, and work practices normative to Greece), and insensitive or mistimed adaptations of global media franchises to national environments (*The Real Housewives of Athens*). German television has demonstrated a particular proclivity in the recession for material that tests the promises and perils of mobility with series like *Die Auswanderer, Mein Neuer Job,* and *Auf und Davon,* depicting Germans emigrating or returning from emigration. U.S. television has generated a spate of "girl"-centered series in which young urban women make their way socially while coping with financial duress (2 *Broke Girls, Girls, Whitney, New Girl*). Writing about *Girls* specifically but generating a characterization that applies to most of these series, Lauren J. DeCarvalho has noted, "When televisual feminism collides with recession anxiety, not only are both trivialized, but male authority is reinforced for good measure."[31]

The past decades have seen postindustrial Western societies embrace various formulations of consumption-led growth. Postfeminist culture has supported and celebrated such economic ideals, glossing over the increasing degrees of indebtedness that came to constitute full citizenship. Though crisis-ridden European economies increasingly appeal to austerity—suggesting an end to the mantra of spending one's way out of crisis—popular culture's commitment to consumption remains (unsurprisingly) largely intact, if suitably qualified and downsized. Aware that visits to the cinema are an expensive luxury for many, marketing early in the recession for the critically derided *Sex and the City 2* (2010) emphasized a sense of occasion, while responses to it were framed by an uneasy sense of the film's affluent hedonism in the context of its release.[32] Such tone-deaf efforts have been followed by releases like *Tower Heist* (2011), an acutely recession-conscious (and far less commercially successful) film that casts Matthew Broderick and Eddie Murphy and symbolically places a red sports car as a zealously guarded icon of (male) achievement and agency to recall 1980s films like *Beverly Hills Cop* (1984) and *Ferris Bueller's Day Off* (1986) and generate a critique of the capitalist boy-wonder narratives of that era perceptively analyzed by Elizabeth Traube.[33] Recourse to the imagery of the 1980s is charged in a recessionary context and notably invested with a masculinized sense of defensive aggression; this sensibility is showcased, for instance, in a set of television and radio ads for Snickers candy that resuscitate 1980s icon Mr. T. The "Get Some Nuts" campaign broadcast in the U.K. and Ireland suggests that instead of directing anger at any of the structural causes of the recession, "the so-called men of Ireland" (as Mr. T puts it in one of the ads) should use it to toughen themselves. If national audiences in recession-beset nations like Ireland are being exhorted by U.S. figures of aggressive agency to "man up," such appeals clearly play within a broader cultural matrix that presupposes the experience of recession as feminization. In her essay (chapter 7), Sinéad Molony reads the gender dynamics of three post–Celtic Tiger documentaries and finds that nationalist myths of the risk-taking male rebel that flourished in the Irish boom have given way more lately to re-idealizations of maternal domesticity.

Genres of Inequality: The Recessionary Chick Flick and the Corporate Melodrama

Making sense of the recessionary cultural moment requires an acknowledgment of the contradictions between political rhetoric and popular culture, between diverse screen fantasies and lived realities. While we may identify particular trends, the postboom period is a complex one, involving competing discourses of anger, nostalgia, denial, and loss. These discourses are in turn complexly gendered, mediating shifting patterns of male employment through long-standing associations between consumption, mass culture, and femininity. The conjunction of women's increasing legal, educational, and economic assertiveness on one hand and the availability of cheap female labor on the other ensures that economic change is repeatedly framed in terms of shifting gender norms. Thus, for example, the supposed feminization of the white-collar male centralized in both art house and popular culture texts of the 1990s and 2000s. *Fight Club* (1999) has been much analyzed in this regard, but we might equally consider a less hyperbolic instance such as *Michael Clayton* (2007) in which the eponymous hero, played by George Clooney, flounders in a corporate environment in which he is an invisible yet necessary fixer.[34] The opposition of Clayton and icy, neurotic company executive Karen Crowder (Tilda Swinton) maps male disempowerment against the figure of (undeserved) female success in familiar ways. Clayton's gambling debts render him financially vulnerable, casting him as both corporate insider and sympathetic economic outsider. Clooney's subsequent role as Ryan Bingham, a dismissal specialist, in *Up in the Air* (2009) is a fascinating extension of this double discourse, one explicitly located within the context of economic recession. Initially cast as a tragic figure, with his relevance called into question by an upstart young female colleague, Natalie Keener (Anna Kendrick), Bingham's way of working is ambivalently reinstated at the film's conclusion. In this way the triumph of the corporate male is typically rendered melancholic, a result of the social and economic dilemmas that such genre films cannot resolve.

Amid austerity-driven welfare reform programs and the rampant privatization of state resources, these fictions exemplify Henry Giroux's insightful point that within discourses of privatization "there are no public or systemic problems, only individual troubles with no trace or connection to larger social forces."[35] With its consistent commitment to symbolic resolution of collective concerns via the depiction of individual experience, genre filmmaking has been well positioned to privatize the recession. Epitomic of this tendency has been the corporate melodrama (exemplified by films like *The Company Men*, *Up in the Air*, *Cosmopolis* [2012], and *Arbitrage* [2012]), which in recent years has come to represent Hollywood cinema's most persuasive articulation of workplace frustration.[36] In corporate melodrama, anxieties about recession are displaced onto and articulated through contradictory gendered discourses which suggest that the corporate environment is both a site of power and authority and fundamentally incompatible with American manhood. Corporate melodramas present scenarios of victimized men — whether via corporate corruption, conspiracy, or the more mundane scenario of redundancy. Like the fantastic (and equally melodramatic) form of action cinema, this cinematic category situates a hard-working male hero against forces that stand for a ruthlessly unyielding economic context.

Significantly, while films such as *The Social Network* (2010) and *Margin Call* (2011) suggest that the corporate world is unfulfilling for or uninteresting to men, these scenarios remain unwilling to cede positions of authority to women. Thus it is female executive Sarah Robertson, rather than her male counterpart Jared Cohen, who is sacrificed in a reckoning with the markets in *Margin Call*.[37] In the cinematic corporate melodramas of the recession, a surface plot about the travails of the male professional is accompanied by an underlying misogyny. At their most extreme these narratives expose a deep fund of rage against women who don't play the part of accessory figures in the white male identity quest. This is expressed in *The Company Men* by Bobby Walker's vitriolic phone messages to H R executive Sally Wilcox, whom he blames personally for the loss of his job, and in an extraordinary scene where Bobby rails against a black female H R recruiter, both of which stand in stark contrast to his forbearance with male cronies. Such discourses play out somewhat differently in *The Social Network*, wherein Mark Zuckerberg's ambition is marked by a seeming maverick indifference to the Harvard business model while remaining underpinned by a casual misogyny.[38] The film's final scene conveys both vast personal wealth and personal isolation as Zuckerberg is imagined obsessively refreshing his ex-girlfriend's Facebook page, indecisively hovering over the action of sending her a friend request. Such a double position, suggesting both a desire for material success and dissatisfaction with the terms of the corporate world, comes to define corporate melodrama with its evocation of, in Linda Williams's phrase, "a hero who is also a victim."[39]

In contrast to these cinematic assertions of masculine authority, one of the most discernible shifts in recessionary postfeminist culture is the transference of some of the anxieties and obligations once attached only to female subjects to male ones. Popular culture couples now often comprise male and female subjects who are equally uncertain about their roles, goals, and commitments. The most recurrent narrative formula for staging male anxieties about intimacy is the "bromance," in which male characters awkwardly navigate under new obligations to understand their emotional relationships to others and to the world at large. Recessionary culture thus seems to be both reenergizing and critiquing male breadwinner roles. One consequence of this is a heightened passivity in the male leads of romantic comedy; another is a succession of films in which high-profile female stars play single mothers (Jennifer Garner in *Juno* [2007], Jennifer Lopez in *The Back-Up Plan* [2010], Jennifer Aniston in *The Switch* [2010]). *The Back-Up Plan*'s Zoe, a former corporate high flyer moved by a disabled dog to cash in her stock options and open a pet shop, is affluent enough to purchase fertility when she finds herself unpartnered in her late thirties. Her subsequent romance with Stan, an artisanal cheese maker struggling to make his way through night school, is marked both by Stan's acceptance of fatherhood and his uncertainty about the couple's discrepant cultural and economic capital levels. Meanwhile, Zoe's inability to give full credence to Stan's commitment generates a late-stage (and short-lived) crisis before the predictable close. This scenario of esoteric entrepreneurs whimsically underlines the way in which movies continue to register male anxiety in terms of female empowerment, both economic and reproductive.[40]

As the recession came in, depictions of female consumerism seemed to reach a higher and higher pitch, with films like *Bride Wars* (2009) and *Confessions of a Shopaholic* (2009) pathologizing competitive female consumerism. Behaviors once deemed praiseworthy come to be inscribed as frenzied, mindless, antisocial, and out of control. Meanwhile, high-profile films chronicling the (real-life or fictional) exploits of male tycoons are lavishly promoted and even critically celebrated (*The Social Network, Wall Street: Money Never Sleeps* [2010]).[41] We might equally note that stylish films based on displays of unreconstructed misogynist rage have hardly faded from the scene. Michael Winterbottom's 2010 *The Killer Inside Me* (which includes the on-screen battering to death of female characters played by Jessica Alba and Kate Hudson) enjoyed largely respectful reviews upon its release, with feminist critiques decidedly shifted to the margins.[42]

In the midst of the recession, the indefatigable "chick flick" certainly continues to factor in both U.S. and overseas box office takings, but its tone is shifting. Recent romantic comedies appear to be significantly less lighthearted, marked by a (relative) loss of subtlety and lacking the sense of play and pleasure that many postfeminist texts bid for. Many are weighted down by conditions of open, structurally central misogyny (witness Gerard Butler's role as a nominal romantic lead in such films as *The Ugly Truth* [2009] and *The Bounty Hunter* [2010]). If female-centered genres are undergoing an affective transformation that leads away from (plausible) romantic comedy toward other kinds of texts such as moody vampire dramas, this may be part of a broader tonal shift that sees postfeminist popular culture becoming blunter in its approach, its ideological investments laid bare in new ways.

Disrupted Domesticities and Public Femininities

A small set of female-centered independent films, notably *Wendy and Lucy* (2009) and *Winter's Bone* (2010), showcases the impact of financial exigency in desolate working-class settings. Another alternative response to recession is seen in *Made in Dagenham* (2010), a film that celebrates a historical campaign for gender-equal pay as if the issue has been resolved in the contemporary era. In other ways, the cultures of the recession are giving license to new expressions of female anger and resentment in a trend that evokes the early 1990s films of an earlier recession like *Thelma and Louise* (1991) and *Basic Instinct* (1992). Such anger is evident in the unheralded 2009 indie hit *Paranormal Activity*, a horror film in which a male day trader and his English graduate student partner find themselves terrorized in their condo by a malevolent entity. The film's delayed distribution (made in 2007, it was released two years later) enabled it to act as a potent critique of boom-era norms, and as the film progresses it exposes deep rage at the heart of the couple's seemingly tranquil domesticity. Katie's brutal murder of her partner Micah at the close of the film stunned audiences and culminated a burgeoning textual critique of Micah's technophilic, dispassionate, and controlling response to Katie's disclosure that she has been haunted since childhood. The couple's unequal economic partnership, which privileges Micah's superiority over Katie, comes to constitute an intolerable unbalance and the film's conclusion thus stages a violent overthrow of the preferred postfeminist domestic arrangement and its accompanying masculinizations of the market and feminizations of art and culture. In this way, *Paranormal Activity* renders supernatural rather prosaic fears about female anger and violence in response to hegemonic gender regimes. As such it also offers a marked contrast to the more popular and pervasive romantic characterization of the male undead in television shows such as *True Blood* and the teen franchise *Twilight*.[43] In his essay for this volume (chapter 6), Tim Snelson considers the horror genre in greater depth, reading "the new paranormal dramas" against the popping of the housing bubble, noting that these films exhibit a timely and "morbid fascination . . . with the disruption, takeover and abandonment of homes."

Such new, sometimes uncertain, evocations of home are matched by an increasing anxiety about the nation-state and its ability to provide a home for its citizens. A pronounced feature of political rhetoric in both recessionary Europe and the United States is an antipathy toward immigrant laborers and ethnic minorities. In the U.S. context, Isabel Molina-Guzmán explores the presentation of unruly Latina motherhood and the retrenching of whiteness in the ABC sitcom *Modern Family* (chapter 2). Anikó Imre's contribution reads the politics of minoritization at work in "austerity Europe" through an analysis of the reality hit *My Big Fat Gypsy Wedding* (chapter 10). As she shows, such programming works to generate a privileged, postfeminist consensus in relation to the spectacle of a racialized underclass; in the process excessive consumption is disavowed as tasteless, feminized, and ethnically other.

As these examples suggest, this book asks how certain media forms and popular culture more generally are responding to the uncertain citizenship (of individuals) in postboom culture. It is concerned with examining both nationally specific representational repertoires and transnational developments. We concentrate primarily on U.S. representations, in part because they remain so globally influential, yet also seek to foster comparative perspectives as often as possible.[44] Two essays in the book in particular (Sinéad Molony's study of post–Celtic Tiger Ireland and Anikó Imre's account of a fracturing Europe) consider national and regional circumstances in considerable detail.

Reality TV has particularly thrived in the long-lasting and multidimensional global financial crisis, and so it is a subject of inquiry for several contributors. Moreover, the rightward moves and explicit racial hostility underpinning much recent political discourse registers most obviously in such formats. As Anna McCarthy writes, "the reality program—produced (unlike fiction TV) without union labor and proposing the makeover (rather than state assistance) as the key to social mobility, stability, and civic empowerment—is an important arena in which to observe the vernacular diffusion of neoliberal common sense."[45] This televisual mode, more than any other, starkly demonstrates Jennifer M. Silva's contention that "without a broad, shared vision of economic justice, race, class, and gender have become sites of resentment and division rather than a coalition among the working class." For Silva "young men and women inhabit a *mood economy* in which legitimacy and self-worth are purchased not with traditional currencies such as work or marriage or class solidarity but instead through the ability to organize their emotions into a narrative of self-transformation."[46] In chapter 9, Hannah Hamad demonstrates reality television's rather smooth adjustment to an altered economic climate. Her discussion of recessionary themes centers upon the striking case of U.K. series *The Fairy Jobmother* (subsequently adapted for the U.S.), which undertakes the transformation of its makeover subjects into modes of job readiness that comply with conventional gender norms. McCarthy couples the concept of governmentality—prominent in analyses of reality formats—with that of trauma. Citing Nikolas Rose's framing of welfare as abjection, McCarthy notes that modern subjects must negotiate a world in which "neoliberal rule and trauma go well together." As Hamad notes, the work of a series such as *The Fairy Jobmother* is to extend reality television's logic of the makeover to the unemployed, focusing on individuals who seek not so much to escape their situation—and the implicitly shameful culture of welfare—but rather to reinvent the self as productive subject.

The popular culture of the recession tends to treat the conjoint problems of economic uncertainty and persistent gender inequality evasively and disingenuously. While there are established cultural protocols for mourning male job loss, there are seemingly no such protocols for women.[47] Indeed, many current cultural texts elide female job loss altogether, preferring instead to privilege a narrative of unequally gendered economic impact that is contiguous with postfeminist rhetorics of female agency and choice. On August 10, 2010, NBC's *Today Show* featured a segment titled "Alpha Moms and Stay-at-Home Dads" profiling the "phenomenon" of trophy wives who morphed into family breadwinners. In an interview accompanying the piece, Joanna Coles, editor of *Marie Claire* magazine, opined, "Clearly, a lot of dads have fared much worse than women in this economy" while questioning by the journalist Matt Lauer ludicrously sought to centralize the question of whether "having a stay-at-home husband is the ultimate status symbol for the professional power mom." Operating under similar assumptions about gendered disproportion when it comes to the economic consequences of recession, a December 22, 2010, "Minding Your Business" segment on CNN's *American Morning* titled "Recession Recovery" trumpeted that "women will recover faster than men when the economy rebounds." A male newsreader, in responding to the piece and transitioning to the next segment, feigned comic misery, saying, "You're making it sound very sad for me."

In her essay (chapter 1), Suzanne Leonard establishes the pervasiveness of the recessionary discursive paradigm in which women are seen to be surging ahead and men falling back. As she shows, a wide range of cultural products including trend pieces, sitcoms, and popular books with titles like *The Richer Sex* cumulatively sound a theme of disadvantage and vulnerability for men and boys in certain regions and industries or certain generational cohorts or (most often) simply at large. The inverse development, according to the paradigm, is a sharp rise in women's economic and cultural power. The journalist Hanna Rosin galvanized a public conversation along these lines with her 2010 *Atlantic* article and TED talk "The End of Men," now adapted into a book titled *The End of Men: And the Rise of Women*. For Rosin, "our vast and struggling middle class, where the disparities between men and women are the greatest, is slowly turning into a matriarchy, with men increasingly absent from the workforce and from home, and women making all the decisions."[48] Rosin's account, which has been rightly critiqued for its inaccuracies, nevertheless seeks to position itself in a discursive "sensible center" that targets readers steeped in postfeminist cultural ideation, which consistently censures "feminist judgment."[49] Indeed, the book's marketing blurb emphasizes exactly such positioning, promising analysis marked by "wide-ranging curiosity and insight unhampered by assumptions or ideology." Following on from Rosin's account, in 2013 Facebook billionaire Sheryl Sandberg weighed in with her efforts to spearhead a "Lean In" movement in which women are cued to transcend structural disadvantages and assert their professional ambition. The intense press bombardment that accompanied the publication of Sandberg's *Lean In: Women, Work and the Will to Lead* was telling of a recessionary discursive environment in which class tensions are consistently processed as gender conflict.

One critique that should be made of accounts such as Rosin's is that in lamenting men's losses, they neglect the ongoing exclusion of women from key realms of power. Other commentators stress the persistent underrepresentation of women at executive political and economic levels, a phenomenon that runs across the political spectrum as the putatively liberal government of Barack Obama has hardly distinguished itself in its inclusion of women. Chrystia Freeland compellingly writes, "What's especially striking about this absence of women at the top is that it runs so strongly counter to the trend in the rest of society. . . . As the 99 percent has become steadily pinker, the 1 percent has remained an all boys club. One way to understand that gap between the 1 percent and the rest is as a division of the world into a vast female-dominated middle class ruled by a male elite at the top."[50]

While popular culture forms disseminate a conventional wisdom suggesting that the recession has had its most acute effects on men, a wealth of scholarly evidence suggests that such understandings may well invert actual economic realities.[51] Generally speaking, women have more fraught and contingent financial arrangements, lower amounts of savings and more dependent obligations, and their more vulnerable economic position prior to the recession has been well documented. In the United States, for instance, as Heidi Hartmann observes, "women, especially women of color, took out a disproportionate share of mortgage loans at subprime rates."[52] There is evidence that women's cultural organizations and economic initiatives directed toward women are being disproportionately negatively impacted by governmental cuts. In the U.K. context, for instance, Shadow Home Secretary Yvette Cooper has cited research results indicating that more than 70 percent of revenue derived from tax and benefit changes instituted under the Tory-led government will come from female taxpayers.[53] In February 2011, Denise Marshal, chief executive of a group dedicated to helping abused and trafficked women, returned the OBE she had received in recognition of this work to register a protest against cuts that would decimate the group's budget.[54] Equality studies scholars maintain that the active campaigns against public service workers that have marked national politics in the United States, U.K., and Ireland in recent years are in effect attacks against women. Kathleen Lynch has argued this position, showing that public sector work, particularly at lower echelons, is disproportionately female.[55]

Running alongside the positioning of economic crisis as an opportunity to obscure or delegitimate the concerns of gender equity and to defund women's advocacy organizations has been the heightening profile of right-wing female politicians. Contextually important for the analyses undertaken in this book is the seeming emergence of new, rhetorically sophisticated forms of political tokenism that have led some commentators to detect signs of a "separate spheres" mentality and to pinpoint representational recidivism in the current political culture. In the United States, such analyses have emphasized the relegation of high-profile women to the judiciary and the state department while the president's inner circle contains few women and at least one major advisor (Lawrence Summers) who is famously on record questioning the inherent abilities of women.

In a similar vein, we may point to the 2010 scrutiny of then–U.S. Supreme Court nominee Elena Kagan, whose single status was ruminated about at length and interpreted through one of two rubrics, the tragic "spinster" or the unacknowledged lesbian. The public mystification about and suspicion of Kagan's unpartnered situation bespeaks the refusal to accept that such a state could be chosen (it is deemed instead to inevitably represent either failure or cover-up) as well as a broader set of conundrums about the sanctioned roles for women in public and political life. Similar concerns had accompanied the nomination of another Supreme Court nominee, Sonia Sotomayor, the previous year, ratcheting up and focalizing around statements the nominee had made about the judiciary value of the life experience of a "wise Latina woman."[56] The scrutiny of Kagan and Sotomayor represents a related if inverse case to the earlier refashioning of First Lady Michelle Obama, who quelled fears about her potentially unruly black femininity (symbolized in responses of consternation to a famous fist bump with her husband on the campaign trail) by declaring that she aspired only to be "mom in chief" and is also consistent with the tensions at work in the political personas of other female figures such as former Speaker of the House (now Minority Leader) Nancy Pelosi.[57]

The high media profile of conservative women, most obviously Sarah Palin, is also highly suggestive of the new character of public femininity in the culture of recession. Her neoliberal presentation of self is astutely deconstructed by Laurie Ouellette, who writes, "More than any political figure to date, Palin translates the traditional voter-politician relationship into the logic of fandom and branding."[58] Palin's lucrative circulation as an author and public speaker in recent years underlines the continuing success of a contradictory process whereby exceptional women gain cultural prominence and economic advantage via their charismatic advocacy of limiting women's working and reproductive lives more generally.[59] The vehement debates about Palin's invocations of feminism have received ample media coverage, with commentators like Rebecca Traister arguing that many on the left don't love feminism enough to fight for it.[60]

It seems clear that the global recession is ushering in new representational protocols that extend and sometimes recalibrate the cultural logics of postfeminism. The writers in this book work to explore these trends, identifying points of continuity and of rupture. In current popular culture, one site of such innovation is the high-profile and recurrent figure of the midlife woman who is "moving on" after the demise of a relationship and romantic or domestic disenchantment. From Sandra Bullock (whose husband was exposed as a serial adulterer the week after she won an Oscar) to Alicia Florrick, the female protagonist of the CBS hit series *The Good Wife*, recessionary popular culture is seemingly compelled by the figure of the woman who is regrouping. Far from arguing that such developments are wholly new, we contend that they are best understood as distinctive inflections on established tropes, efforts to suit evidently changed social and economic circumstances. For instance, where postfeminism has tended to trade heavily in fantasies of atemporal femininity, the high-profile emergence of the cougar in recessionary popular culture speaks to deep ambivalence about the material and sexual prerogatives of the midlife woman and her potential to rupture the stability of generational norms and coupling protocols. Centralized in such texts as the television series *Cougar Town* and films like *The Rebound* (2009), the underlying threat epitomized by this figure is illustrated by striking censorship activities. A May 14, 2010, article in the *New York Times* reported that Google had restricted ads for older woman–younger man dating sites out of a concern that such sites were not "family-friendly" while retaining ads for older man–younger woman sites.[61] In chapter 1, Suzanne Leonard considers recession media's ambivalent presentation of financially stable midlife women in hit television series and franchises like *The Good Wife* and *The Real Housewives* and films like *I Don't Know How She Does It* (2011). Pamela Thoma explores the films *Julie & Julia* (2009) and *Eat Pray Love* (2010) in terms of their presentation of entrepreneurial self-work and the domestic as a suitable site of female labor (chapter 4). Analyzing fashion blogs and vlogs, Elizabeth Nathanson develops these themes with respect to the increasingly blurred categories of consumption and production (chapter 5). As her chapter suggests, global recession has upped the ante on what Kathleen M. Kuehn aptly terms "hope labor," helping to proliferate the culture of internship and in general normalizing "un- or under-compensated work carried out in the present—often for experience or exposure—in the hopes that future employment opportunities may follow."[62] Recessionary "hope labor" is not inevitably female (as the repairing of *Wedding Crashers* [2005] stars Owen Wilson and Vince Vaughn in *The Internship* [2013] might attest) but it may well be disproportionately so.

Conclusion

Stuart Hall has observed that "in a culture where neo-liberal ideas represent a widely circulating current, the free, ubiquitous and all-encompassing character of 'wealth' is a dominant theme." [63] In this context, we suggest that myriad forms of recent popular culture strive to preserve verisimilitude in their representations of economic inequalities while doggedly refraining from systemic critique. An outcome of this is a proliferation of recuperative, capital-friendly narratives that call on the working class to deal privately rather than publicly with economic exigencies. It might be argued that those narratives that most forcefully address the notion of a crisis in capitalism shift the scene historically—witness the popularity of AMC's 1960s advertising agency drama *Mad Men*, whose articulation of past gender and racial inequalities speaks to the contemporary era. When the series' cast gathered to ring the opening bell at the New York Stock Exchange on March 21, 2012, an appearance nominally justified by the publicity imperatives of the series' fifth season, the moment resonated as a larger and highly complex act of cross-promotion.

Attentive to the effacing of certain kinds of recessionary experiences, this book insists upon the necessity of reading the market as a site of politics. At its heart it is based on an awareness that the recession has heightened a range of inequalities, not least among them inequalities of class, nation, and region. In light of the general neoliberal redistribution of wealth and power upward and insecurity downward (precisely manifested in such phenomena as the collapse of job security, attacks on organized labor and positioning of military spending and low taxation for the wealthy as sacred cows) we would do well to further our understanding of the ways that public consent is secured for developments that are so clearly not in the public interest.

Under the auspices of a postfeminist cultural regime that overarches the late twentieth and early twenty-first centuries, gender equality has been alternately celebrated and decried (despite abundant evidence it has yet to be achieved), female "choice" relentlessly hyped and gender norms vigorously reessentialized. Considering the ways that the postfeminist cultural ideation of the boom is being adapted for the postboom period, this book examines a postfeminist neoliberal culture in which we are cued to undertake routine physical and emotional work on the self while cultivating imperviousness to the decline of social health, democratic institutions, and meaningful manifestations of citizenship. Propitiously timed for a moment in which recovery rhetoric threatens to quell the economic and social analyses spurred by the global financial system's unraveling, the essays here proceed on the basis that "recovery must be understood as a project on the part of financial and political elites to reestablish and fortify an economic and social order that was on the brink of collapse and discredit."[64] Postfeminist culture has tended to suppress and stigmatize women's activism, an activism that is all the more necessary given the antipathy of twenty-first-century financial (and financialized) culture to femininity as a potential site and source of resistance.[65] Adept at epiphanizing complex decisions about the prospects and possibilities for women in their working and personal lives, postfeminist culture has tended to pay lip service to female individualism while undercutting it. Under new conditions of financial exigency, women now face enhanced pressure to manage their own (and often their family's) economic survival without threatening patriarchal norms. The essays here consider the ways in which recession has sometimes sustained and sometimes contested the abbreviated "choice" continuums of postfeminism. The efforts made to map recessionary media culture are inevitably provisional but they offer one means of coming to grips with the complexities, paradoxes, and problems that mark early twenty-first-century life in the West.

Notes

1. In a piece titled "Working Women Almost Certainly Caused the Credit Crunch," that ran in the *Irish Times* on February 2, 2009, Newton Emerson attempted a satire, suggesting that the recession could be alleviated if women left their jobs. "Women," wrote Emerson, "were the driving force behind the greed, consumerism and materialism of the Celtic Tiger years and it was female employment that funded their estrogen-crazed acquisitiveness." The piece caused a furor when many online readers did not pick up on its satirical tone and responded seriously and in agreement with the suggestions laid out by Emerson.

2. Tudor, "Twenty-First Century Neoliberal Man," 59.

3. Giroux, "Neoliberalism and the Death of the Social State," 592.

4. Gilmore, *Golden Gulag*.

5. Indeed, a critic like Sasha Abramsky in exploring the affective culture of the recession has argued that a "rage culture" has been installed at the heart of American politics. For Abramsky, "the rage culture has matured to the point where it is coming to be a dark, and perhaps even a dominant part of America's identity" ("Look Ahead in Anger," 87).

6. Ferguson and Marso, "Introduction," 7.

7. On the emergence of this term, see Singer, "A Label for a Pleather Economy." Singer defines a recessionista as "the personification of recession chic," a discursive invention of publicists, retailers, and consumers, and notes the proliferation of the term's usage on websites like Jezebel.com and style.com. This term is worked with more extensively by Elizabeth Nathanson in chapter 5.

8. In the ever more convergent postfeminist media landscape, it was not surprising

that Harvey's book was (rather awkwardly) adapted into chick flick form in the 2012 release *Think Like a Man*.

9. She goes on: "Attributions of happiness might be how social norms and ideals become affective, as if relative proximity to those norms and ideals creates happiness." Ahmed, *The Promise of Happiness*, 11.

10. Smith, "Bling Was a Bubble," 274.

11. Catherine Bennett satirizes wealthy and fashionable individuals' short-lived commitment to thrift rhetoric in her "Go On. Buy Yourself an It Bag."

12. See Negra, *What a Girl Wants?*; and Hollows, "Can I Go Home Yet?"

13. This unthreatening incarnation of female commercial activity registers as a failed figure in the summer 2011 hit *Bridesmaids* and as an aspirational ideal in the sitcom *2 Broke Girls*, which chronicles the efforts of a pair of waitresses (one a working-class striver, the other the daughter of a discredited Bernard Madoff–style tycoon found to have been running a Ponzi scheme) to raise money to open a cupcake bakery.

14. This may be in opposition to the gendering of other virtual gaming realms, where harassment of women players is widespread. See O'Leary, "In Virtual Play, Sex Harassment Is All Too Real."

15. Emily Yochim and Julie Wilson argue that media production of this kind is increasingly figured as an extension of mothering in "Mommy Media."

16. See Dow, "The Traffic in Men and the Fatal Attraction of Postfeminist Masculinity"; Hamad, "'My Wife Calls Him My Boyfriend'"; Hamad, "Dad TV"; and Marshall, "Bromance and the Boys of *Boston Legal*." For further reading note Alilunas, "Male Masculinity as the Celebration of Failure"; and Weber, "Puerile Pillars of the Frat Pack."

17. Farrell, *Berserk Style in American Culture*, 97.

18. Carroll also notes the existence of a number of female-centered novels of downward mobility and relocation in recession. Although beyond the scope of his essay (or this book) to examine, the phenomenal success of Gillian Flynn's 2012 *Gone Girl* (in production as a film), in which a couple's experience of job loss unravels postfeminist gender performativity, stands as a further rich example of the popular print fiction of the recession.

19. In her essay (chapter 4), Pamela Thoma too cites ads that depend on an invitation to male consumers to "man up."

20. Peck, "How a New Jobless Era Will Transform America," emphasis added.

21. Bose and Lyons, *Cultural Critique and the Global Corporation*, 2.

22. Hayward, "The Economic Crisis and After," 288.

23. See Martin, *The Financialization of Everyday Life*. In a more recent publication, *An Empire of Indifference*, Martin distinguishes between a privileged class marked by its ability to take risks with capital and an underclass deemed to be perpetually at risk.

24. Harris, "Back to the Workhouse."

25. See Bobo, *Wage Theft in America*. These developments have emerged even as white-collar professional overwork has been thoroughly normalized and facilitated by new technologies once touted as labor saving.

26. A film like *Side Effects* (2013) is indicative of a broader need to ideologically control the links between gender and the economic behaviors that led to the recession. In

it, the release from prison of a male banker after serving a sentence for insider trading tellingly serves only as a pretext for the unspooling of a complex narrative of female conspiracy and deception.

27. Advocates of "corporate personhood" hold that corporations possess the same rights entitlements as individuals. A Supreme Court decision in January 2010 ruled that corporations hold free speech rights that should enable them to make political donations without restraint, thus effectively ensuring a high degree of corporate influence in U.S. political elections.

28. Ho, *Liquidated*, 3.

29. See Roberts, "The Five Hottest Money Honeys to Break the News about Economic Catastrophe." "Money honey" emerged in tandem with this shift as a term of reference for attractive female financial news reporters. Situated as a sanctioned exceptional visitor to the male domain of finance, Bartiromo built her reputation through frequent reporting from the floor of the New York Stock Exchange, where she was invariably the only woman in view.

30. The inability of the political left to generate a potent media vocabulary of buzzwords and stock stories to explain the social and economic changes brought on by recession has led to a situation where terms with a rightist political provenance have entered widespread usage.

31. DeCarvalho, "Hannah and Her Entitled Sisters," 367.

32. In some ways the film itself acknowledges this unease in its geographical shift away from New York in the final section. And of course using female-oriented texts as a target for critique is hardly a new phenomenon.

33. See Traube, *Dreaming Identities*.

34. For one such analysis of *Fight Club*, see Giroux and Szeman, "Ikea Boy Fights Back."

35. Giroux, "Neoliberalism and the Death of the Social State," 592–93.

36. We analyze the corporate melodrama in "Neoliberal Frames and Genres of Inequality."

37. That Sarah Robertson is played by Demi Moore allows the evocation of the star's 1990s roles as an aggressively ambitious figure, notably in *Disclosure* (1994), a film that certainly falls within the ambit of corporate melodrama.

38. In "The Comfort Women of the Digital Industries," Lisa Nakamura argues that the film depicts Asian women as "idle hands in the digital industry, valued and included only for their sexual labor as hypersexualized exotic sirens."

39. Williams, "Melodrama Revised," 58.

40. Similar dynamics organize *The Five-Year Engagement* (2012), in which Jason Segel's protagonist is comically emasculated when he follows his fiancée to Wisconsin for the sake of her career, but order is restored when he returns to San Francisco and opens a taco truck. Suzanne Leonard makes mention of this film in her essay (chapter 1).

41. Publicized as a sort of companion film to *The Social Network* but in many ways far more interesting is *Catfish* (2010), in which social media site Facebook serves as a channel for an unlikely and initially deceptive relationship between a privileged young New York man and a dissatisfied midlife woman in Michigan. The film's emphasis on

Facebook's potential (through "misuse") for encounters with gender, class, and regional difference marks a significant contrast to *The Social Network*, where women function largely as sex objects, marauding hysterics, and threatening sources of rejection, and indeed the creation of Facebook itself is represented as sourced in misogynistic assessments of female sexual value.

42. For one such critique see Walters, "Why Is There So Much Movie Violence against Women?" In 2012 William Friedkin's equally violent *Killer Joe* experienced a largely similar reception.

43. In different ways, independent films *Teeth* (2007) and *Jennifer's Body* (2009) also suggest the place of an imagery of (grotesque) female power in the horror film.

44. In the U.S. there has been a tendency to inscribe the recession as a singular 2008 event now located in the past, a characterization we (and many other commentators) would not accept.

45. McCarthy, "Reality Television," 17.

46. Silva, *Coming Up Short*, 17, 18.

47. The striking exception here is *Bridesmaids* (2011), whose central figure, Annie, has lost her cupcake bakery business as the film opens and who is experiencing downward mobility and depression.

48. Rosin, *The End of Men*, 3.

49. In a remarkable twist on "end of men" discourse, the *New York Times* reported on March 20, 2013, the results of an MIT study that linked male economic decline to the impact of being raised in a single-parent (almost always a single mother) household. See Appelbaum, "As Men Lose Economic Ground." The article prompted a *Times* Motherlode column the same day by K. J. Dell'Antonia, "Single Parents: Unsupported, and Feeling the Blame," questioning the broad excoriation of single parents in regard to social problems.

50. Freeland, *Plutocrats*, 85.

51. Some cable news "infotainment" coverage misreads or oversimplifies academic research to arrive at the conclusion that the recession's impacts are more severe for men. See, for instance, "Recession Harder on Men Than Women."

52. Hartman, "Women, the Recession and the Stimulus Package," 43.

53. Stratton, "Women Will Bear Brunt of Budget Cuts." For another of many such accounts see Gentleman, "Women's Groups Struggle Amid Funding Cuts," which chronicles the defunding of the U.K. Resource Centre for Women in Science, Engineering and Technology and the Women's National Commission.

54. Gentleman, "Women's Refuge Chief Returns OBE in Protest over Cuts."

55. Lynch, "Women, Class and Gender." Another scholar working in and on the Irish context, Paula Gilligan, notes that one-third of working women in Ireland are employed in the public service in "Flexicurity/Insecurity."

56. In her essay (chapter 2), Isabel Molina-Guzmán reads the Sotomayor controversy in relation to the recession-era success of the sitcom *Modern Family*, noting the series' reliance on the comedic recuperation of Latina motherhood via Sofia Vergara's Gloria Delgado-Pritchett.

57. For an analysis of the way in which Pelosi balances "male" claims to political

power with reassuring invocations of traditional femininity, see Dabbous and Ladley, "A Spine of Steel and a Heart of Gold."

58. Ouellette, "Branding the Right," 190.

59. Media debates over Palin's attempts to lay claim to feminism point to the entrenched nature of postfeminist assumptions that the high-profile professional and economic success of individual women is a sign not only of feminism's success but that women are free to excel should they choose to do so. See, for example, Douthat, "No Mystique about Feminism."

60. See Traister, "Sarah Palin's Grab for Feminism." This political context arguably helped to make Amy Poehler's dedicated civil servant Leslie Knope in the NBC sitcom *Parks and Recreation* a cherished feminist heroine for some viewers.

61. See Kershaw, "Google Tells Sites for 'Cougars' to Go Prowl Elsewhere."

62. Kuehn, "Home/Work or Hope Labor?"

63. Hall, "The Neo-liberal Revolution," 722.

64. Hayward, "The Economic Crisis and After," 286.

65. This theme was spoofed in a satirical *New York Times* piece by Michael Lewis that takes the form of a fictional memo to Wall Street CEOs from their Washington lobbyist. The lobbyist of the piece advises, "We do not have a problem with the American people, we have a problem with American women" and notes the vigorous oversight efforts and attempts at regulatory reform made by Elizabeth Warren, Mary Schapiro, and Senator Blanche Lincoln (Lewis, "Shorting Reform").

ONE *SUZANNE LEONARD*

Escaping the Recession?
THE NEW VITALITY OF THE WOMAN WORKER

In February 2011, a plucky American five-year-old became an overnight You-Tube sensation with her adamant, direct address declaration, "I don't want to marry somebody if I don't have a job first. . . . I don't care if I marry you. I don't care if I marry another man. I care if I do something that's special."[1] In emphatic terms, the unnamed speaker designates her job rather than her relational prospects as her chance to do something special, a mind-set also reflected in demographic research over the last forty years, which finds marriage to be of diminished significance in the eyes of multiple constituencies of Americans. As with other videos that feature precocious young white girls parroting feminist logics, this one stars a small child voicing a very adult observation.[2] Yet, despite her young age, the speaker is also perfectly in sync with a postfeminist moment wherein securing work—and particularly the lucrative and self-actualizing kind—has begun to supplant marriage as the aspirational event of mediatized female lives.

Feminism has long supported the prospect of female labor as a route to financial empowerment while at the same time drawing attention to structural obstacles that thwart economic achievement, such as the wage gap, lack of adequate day care support and family-friendly work policies, and women's concentration in low-paying service industries.[3] Such histories are largely papered over in the little girl's monologue, however, for her stated devotion to her career more obviously confirms an ideological and economic dynamic that Angela McRobbie identified in 2009 as the "visibility of the well-educated working girl" around whom terms like "capacity, success, attainment, enjoyment, entitlement, social mobility, and participation" swirl.[4] Girls' claims to citizenship rest on these presumed attributes, and McRobbie observes that "the ability to earn a living is also the single most important feature of the social and cultural changes of which young women find themselves to be the privileged subjects."[5] The successful girl exists, in turn, as proof that even during one of the worst economic crises of recent history, postfeminist thought regimes continue to emphasize and inculcate notions of equality and choice, messages that resonate particularly with those who enjoy race and class privilege, evidenced in this case by the speaker's whiteness, the upper-middle-class milieu she apparently inhabits, and the fact that the video was allegedly posted and edited by her eleven-year-old sister, a singer-songwriter.

More than a mere affirmation of hegemonic notions of postfeminist femininity, this video establishes a commensurability between discourses of gender, labor, and marriage, an equation that has been particularly salient in organizing life cycle temporalities in a recession economy. The blithe association this video makes between women, work, and upward mobility, and its seeming disinterest in anything men have to offer in that respect, resonates with a predominant emphasis on females triumphing in a recessionary moment more aptly described as one in which the majority of Americans are suffering. The false assumption that assertiveness equals ascendance, and that career success represents an option available to women at all points in the life cycle likewise reflects a common discursive positioning of women as impervious to a financial crisis that has nevertheless devastated men. Such thought paradigms paradoxically position women's professional aspirations as taken for granted, and yet at the same time legible only in light of their relational prospects with men or male partners. In this essay, I untangle these various recessionary discourses, highlighting how myths of male potency are fractured and disrupted by narratives of economically independent women. Such regimes latently emphasize not only the differing prospects of employment and marriage for the sexes, but also establish hierarchies based on what it means to be employable and marriageable, categorizations that are inevitably raced and classed. As I identify, increasing polarization between men and women in the professional and marital economies refracts through contemporary recessionary rhetorics and foments multiple social divisions.

Masculinity in Crisis—Again

From its inception, the post-2007 economic crisis has been understood in gendered terms. While the crisis undeniably brought issues of financial instability and hence class to the forefront of the collective consciousness in ways that they had not been for quite some time, the perception that the recession affected males and females differently, and to different degrees, quickly gained prominence. The crisis featured a collision of events originating with the subprime mortgage crisis and housing market collapse, catastrophes that led in turn to the sudden bankruptcy of a number of Wall Street investment banks. These failures precipitated multiple government bailouts (AIG, Ford, and Chrysler), and ricochet effects were felt in the global economy (particularly apparent in the European debt crisis). This downfall was vertiginous, and in many ways incomprehensible, a confusion stemming from the fact that average citizens are largely bereft of a theoretical framework through which to understand the workings of financial capital. Like the concepts and practices they describe, lexical terms like "speculation," "securities," "credit-default swaps," and "derivatives" are untethered from any sort of concrete material reality.[6] To combat such abstractions, media outlets increasingly humanized the crisis, recounting numbers of job losses, vigilantly monitoring unemployment statistics, and reporting on average citizens whose homes had been foreclosed upon. In such scenarios, if the market collapse was precipitated by forces often too nebulous to visualize, the effects of it were all too easy to behold. In particular, mapping the recession onto actual job and home losses helped to order an otherwise unintelligible set of events, and thanks to the fact that one of the first conspicuous signs of the financial meltdown occurred in the male-dominated housing industry, the observation that the recession disproportionately disadvantaged male workers quickly became a structuring narrative.

If the housing boom in the United States was long taken (erroneously so, we now know) as an indicator of widespread national prosperity, one of the first signs that economies were amiss was the bust. New home and condominium construction in the United States ground to a halt around 2008–9, and hence so too did the mostly male-staffed jobs associated with this industry.[7] The Bureau of Labor Statistics reports that residential construction created and accounted for nearly 3 million jobs that would not have existed otherwise, an observation that bespeaks one way in which the workings of global capital trade in hallucinatory effects, mirages of affluence that dispersed once the bubble burst. These losses in the construction industry were conflated, in turn, in the cultural imaginary with the decline in manufacturing—the other sector most visibly associated with contemporary masculinities—and focalized through the sharply diminishing stature of the automobile industry. The evisceration of manufacturing has been occurring in the postindustrial United States since at least the 1970s, with its pummeling taken up explicitly by documentaries such as Michael Moore's *Roger and Me* (1989) and Susan Faludi's book *Stiffed: The Betrayal of the American Man* (1999), wherein she linked a crisis in masculinity to the decline in American manufacturing. Recession-era anxiety nevertheless provided an opening for renewed attention to this downward spiral. A March 2012 report from the Information Technology and Innovation Foundation observes that from 2000 to 2010, 33.1 percent of U.S. manufacturing jobs were lost. Though these numbers are devastating, it is perhaps important to note that manufacturing today represents about 11 percent of all jobs, but nearly one-third of the jobs lost during the recession, a reality that underscores the slightly disingenuous quality of the strong emphasis placed on manufacturing in recent cultural narratives.[8]

Afforded new legitimacy and exigency during the recession, nostalgic notions of both construction and manufacturing can be found in cultural products such as *The Company Men* (2010), which, though ostensibly concerned with redundancy and corporate downsizing, includes an elegiac sequence set in a now-vacated shipyard where an aging white male (Tommy Lee Jones) laments the fact that nothing gets made anymore. As if to further underscore the targeted losses that the recession economy has precipitated in men, in this film, the now-unemployed corporate worker's reembodiment occurs via carpentry, so that the act of fixing up houses serves as a nod to construction job losses in the wider economy, and provides a fairly transparent vehicle by which to remake his embattled masculinity, attenuated by the corporate and hence nonembodied labor market in which he had previously been participating.

The twinning of the construction and manufacturing industries in the cultural imagination fueled the perception that the recession hit men harder than women, as evidenced by the straightforward title of a March 2009 *New York Times* article by Floyd Norris, "In This Recession, More Men Are Losing Jobs." Stories about the "he-cession" or "man-cession" routinely compare male and female job losses and almost invariably invoke the specter of both the manufacturing and construction industries when they seek to explain the disproportionate effects of the recession on men. To name one of many representative examples, in her 2010 essay in the *Atlantic*, "The End of Men," Hanna Rosin writes, "In the wreckage of the Great Recession . . . three quarters of the 8 million jobs lost were lost by men. The worst hit industries were overwhelmingly male and deeply identified with macho: construction, manufac-

FIGURE 1.1. Liza Mundy's prediction that women would be the new breadwinners, at the helm of both familial and professional arrangements, garnered national media attention during the spring of 2012.

turing, high finance."[9] Such perceptions have been abetted by popular culture representations that extrapolate from these observations to suggest that all men are being hit harder by the recession, and impose the attendant fear that as a result of declines in traditionally masculine industries, men will have to accept more feminizing jobs—"He-Cession Has More Men Looking at Once 'Female' Jobs" claimed the *Baltimore Sun* in 2009, a story that was repeated in May 2012 in a *New York Times* article, "More Men Enter Fields Dominated by Women."[10]

Relatedly, because the financial downfall has been narrated predominantly though the lens of the heterosexual family, losses in the employment sphere are assumed to alter men's position in the familial sphere as well, an observation that structures Liza Mundy's widely publicized *The Richer Sex: How the New Majority of Female Breadwinners Is Transforming Sex, Love and Family* (2012). Her book, which predicted that in the future more families will be supported by women than by men, garnered a *Time* cover story featuring a female figure made of cash (figure 1.1). According to Mundy, this new order in which women outpace men financially will necessitate a different set of calculations on the domestic front; she predicts that "for the first time, men will start thinking of marriage as a bet on the economic potential of a spouse, exactly as women have done for generations."[11] While Mundy is rather cheerful about this prospect, Diane Negra and Yvonne Tasker note the preponderance of recession images that mournfully suggest that men are being left out, or left behind, as their female partners surge ahead. Reading a visual image wherein a man is left at home, cleaning and holding a baby, while his female partner goes to work, Negra and Tasker observe that "the usurped male breadwinner serves as a handy visual reference point."[12]

The wrapping together in this way of the economic and the domestic, and particularly the perception that men's professional woes concomitantly cripple them in the private sphere, has provided a structuring narrative of the recession, informing, for instance, the creation and release of a bevy of man-centric sitcoms in the 2011–12 network season such as *How to Be a Gentleman*, *Last Man Standing*, *Man Up!*, and *Work It*. As their almost cloned titles attest, all used fears of emasculation to pander to recession-era anxieties.[13] Perhaps the most egregious of these was ABC's *Work It*; as the network explained, "With unemployment an ongoing issue and women now outnumbering men in the workforce, the new comedy series *Work It* follows two alpha males who realize that the only way to beat the current 'mancession' and land a job in pharmaceutical sales is to pass themselves off as women."[14] Thanks to widespread disinterest in the show's regressive gender stereotyping and protests from LGBT groups who objected to its ignorance of transgender issues, *Work It* lasted for only two episodes.[15] (*How to Be a Gentleman* and *Man Up!* eventually succumbed to cancellation as well.) These shows' collective sense that men's professional futures turn on their ability to function in a women's world has, however, lingered, as has a tendency to reify retrograde models of masculinity in order to proclaim their embattled status. This observation underpins *Last Man Standing*, an ABC sitcom starring Tim Allen as Mike, a married father of three daughters and marketing manager of Outdoor Man, a sporting goods store, where he mentors a cookie-baking, romantic-comedy-loving, younger male employee. With a wink to his previous role as the "tool man," and a secure family breadwinner in the sitcom *Home Improvement* (1991–99), the series depicts Mike as repeatedly at sea in a world infused with newly feminine values, such as when his boss's daughter, a Wharton graduate, offers a presentation about how Outdoor Man should consider tapping into what she views as a burgeoning market: young women. The show gently pokes fun at Mike's attempts to navigate the new girl order, but nevertheless reinforces the idea that new masculinities and empowered femininities both collude to nudge out traditional forms of manhood.

By so overtly framing female gains as occurring in relation to male losses, the recession also offered a convenient opportunity to recirculate and revalidate misogynist tropes about how feminist ideals have hurt boys and men, attitudes that have held sway in conservative circles for some time. Christina Hoff Sommers's *The War against Boys: How Misguided Feminism Is Harming Our Young Men* (2001) represented an origin text with respect to such attitudes in the postfeminist era, serving as the first in a long line of reports that promulgate hand-wringing over the diminishing status of boys. The focus on proliferating rates of autism, an affliction that tends to affect more boys than girls, is but one discursive site that has contributed to the cultural perception of declining boys and flourishing girls. Related is the virtual cottage industry of alarmist accounts that proclaim boys to be losing ground on the educational front, as indicated by book titles such as *The Minds of Boys: Saving Our Sons from Falling Behind in School and Life* (2005); *Boys Adrift: The Five Factors Driving the Growing Epidemic of Unmotivated Boys and Underachieving Young Men* (2007); *The Trouble with Boys: A Surprising Report Card on Our Sons, Their Problems at School, and What Parents and Educators Must Do* (2008); *Why Boys Fail: Saving Our Sons from an Educational System That's Leaving Them Behind* (2010); and *The Demise of Guys: Why Boys Are Struggling and What We Can Do about It* (2012). These books ostensibly share a corrective sensibility, asking that we pay attention to boys because the spotlight has been turned away from them, and provide an implicit rejoinder to educators and parents who centralized girl students in previous eras. In a section titled "Rethinking Ophelia," the author of *The Trouble with Boys* writes, "In the 1990s the struggles of girls were so vividly documented and widely reported that in the minds of most people, girls remain a vulnerable and disadvantaged group."[16] In histrionic tones, this series of texts enjoins readers to wake up to the fact that a focus on girls hogs attention from the real problem: boys.

To be sure, the worry over boys preceded recessionary realities. Yet, recession-era anxieties have opened up space for a spate of like-minded accounts that figure boys and men as significantly disadvantaged, reports that predict the uneducated, unfocused boy's metamorphosis into the unmotivated and unemployable man.[17] Accounts that laud women's new professional prowess reliably begin with a set of educational statistics, namely that there are three women for every two men graduating from college.[18] Women also earn more PhDs, according to numbers released from the Council of Graduate Schools, though they lag behind men in obtaining degrees in either the hard sciences or engineering.[19] Because education patterns correlate in the popular imagination with more (and better) jobs, proclamations regarding female educational achievement segue into the observation that women have fared better professionally than men during the recession, a conclusion often buttressed by the statement that the job categories projected to grow in the next decade are those in which women tend to work. Hanna Rosin's "The End of Men" uses such data to make sweeping claims about the future, and Rosin wonders, "What if the economics of the new era are better suited to women?"[20] Such a question largely ignores the fact that the fastest-growing jobs are concentrated mostly in low-paying service industries, such as home health assistance, food and beverage service, child care, and retail.[21]

Rosin supports her supposition that the new economy provides better options for women by listing the affective traits it is likely to value, including "social intelligence, open communication, and the ability to sit still and focus."[22] Her claim that these abilities are more often associated with female skill sets presents a striking example of how gender essentialization has tended to circulate in recessionary discourse. Reihan Salam's article "The Death of Macho" (written in mid-2009, during the heart of the crisis) similarly postulated that because "aggressive, risk taking behavior" proved destructive in the financial markets, hypercompetitive masculine behaviors will be newly unwelcome in postrecession economies.[23] According to this gendered brand of conventional wisdom, if male aggression caused the problem, female compliance and malleability will remedy it. The view that a kinder, gentler phase of female-centeredness will emerge from fatigue with traditional masculinities has been popularized by business school professors — who often double as pundits in such reports — many of whom foresee new business models centered on feminized practices of "empathetic leadership." While these are admirable aims perhaps, the idea that the character and caliber of corporate work will fundamentally change as a result of recession-era gender politics feels more like a diversion meant to eclipse the fact that corporate malfeasance likely had a greater hand in precipitating the financial meltdown than did adherence to traditional gender roles.

Reports that celebrate an enlightened, postrecessionary era characterized by female economic strength also tend to overvalue the statistic that more than 40 percent of American women already serve as their family's breadwinners. As Rosalind Barnett and Caryl Rivers clarify, this watermark stands only if one counts women who outearn their working husbands by "as little as a dollar a day" as well as "single mothers who are sole providers."[24] Proclamations of women's new financial vitality also cling to the rather paltry statistic that women now comprise a whopping 51.4 percent of managerial jobs. To this way of thinking, the mythological businesswoman deserves far more attention than does the service worker, whose gendered domination in this sector has been solid for some time, and who is compensated for this domination by an average yearly salary of $14,792. Even then, however, the typical male service worker still ekes out more, ticking in at $21,104.[25] This bifurcation of the professional and working classes unquestionably works in concert with broad shifts in the overall economy, particularly the widening gap between rich and poor.[26] More surprising, perhaps, is the way that popular conceptions of gendered labor patterns collapse these two widely disparate economies, that of the service sector and that of the corporate one, and only in the name of the latter do notions such as the "death of macho," "the end of men," or the "new majority of female breadwinners" have any purchase.

Pulling these different narratives apart, in fact, invites wholly different conclusions about the state of the woman worker in a recession economy, a thought pattern distinctly traceable to the postfeminist notion that the financial health of the female workforce in total can be gauged based on the career trajectories of upwardly mobile, highly educated women. This bias rather parodically revealed itself in *Time*'s online September 1, 2010, story, brashly headlined, "Workplace Salaries: At Last, Women on Top." The article begins with supposedly game-changing news: "In 147 out of 150 of the biggest cities in the US, the median full-time salaries of young women are 8% higher than those of the guys in their peer group."[27] The real story reveals itself in the passage that follows, a clarification the author understates as a "slightly deflating caveat." As she writes, the "reverse gender gap applies only to *unmarried, childless women under 30 who live in cities*" (emphasis mine). Thanks to their high levels of disposable income, women in this demographic are likely the only kind who matter to the market research firm that conducted this study. (Such calculations similarly underpin the majority of postfeminist media, whose products are created for—and about—this same demographic.) Such a case study points to how postfeminist logics have not only inflected but provided the organizing principles for economic reports.

Turn one's attention to low-wage employees, working mothers, and aging women, on the other hand, and a whole different set of calibrations emerges. Instead of reveling in their newfound recession power, women are more vulnerable to austerity measures that roll back public spending. As a *New York Times* piece by Katrin Bennhold titled "Recession Seen Taking Toll on Gender Equality" explains, because women are more apt than men to be public sector employees, single parents, or retirees, and hence to rely on public funding in some form, they are also more likely to be hurt by economic cuts. Likewise, though trend stories tout the equalizing effects of having more men toil in traditionally female occupations, even men working in so-called pink-collar jobs earn more than their female counterparts and are more likely than women to move into supervisory positions in these jobs, a concept sociologists have termed the "glass elevator." My aim in rehearsing such inequities is not to pit men against women yet again, but rather to critique the relentless reduction of workers to their gendered identities as an explanatory framework for recession-era economies. I do, however, find prevailing narratives about women's resiliency to be specious, and dangerously so, particularly insofar as they mobilize resentment toward women at large.

Such currents of animosity are evident even in accounts that proclaim support for this supposed female dominance. Rosin, for example, visits a men's support group where working-class men voice vitriol at women like their former wives, who have decent-paying jobs but demand child support from former husbands who are on food stamps. Rosin tacitly endorses such views, observing that "the modern economy is becoming a place where women hold the cards."[28] Salam arrives at a similarly frightening point, arguing that economic power in places where domestic oppression remains portends a scary future for both sexes; he spends considerable time discussing the economic situation in Russia, where, in concert with a Putin-era romanticization of homemakers, Russian men have tremendously high levels of incarceration, alcoholism, and unemployment. While many women do have jobs, they are also "forced to accept skyrocketing levels of sexual exploitation at work and massive hypocrisy at home."[29] Forecasting a future of entrenched sexism, Salam predicts, "The axis of global conflict in this century will not be warring ideologies or competing geopolitics, or clashing civilizations. It won't be race or ethnicity. It will be gender."[30] If a man's role as the head of the nuclear family serves as the only structure standing between him and some sort of primal atavism, if and when women outperform men, such commentaries warn, aggression will be unleashed.

The futures predicted by these pieces cycle us back, finally, to the five-year-old who refuses to marry until she has "a job first," for at the heart of many of these lifestyle stories focused on women's new economic vitality lies the worry that job losses and gains will have a boomerang effect on both sexes' marital prospects. Such concern, not surprisingly, is both raced and classed in nature for, as I will illustrate, a primary preoccupation in such conversations is what will happen to upwardly mobile white women who cannot find partners to keep pace with their supposed aspirations. Such marital anxieties are likewise manifest in the two fictionalized types I subsequently discuss, figures axiomatically defined by their lack or possession of "maturity": the slacker male, trapped in a perpetual adolescence, and the professionally competent female who is an always already adult.

The End of Marriage? Slacker Men and the Husband Shortage

The conclusion that young men who cannot get jobs have neither the incentive nor the means to marry is one that many trend watchers reach with consternation. This perception accords with real data that have found declining numbers of marriages, particularly among the working poor; according to a 2010 study released by the Pew Center, a new marriage gap in the United States is increasingly aligned with a growing income gap. As the study concluded, "Marriage, while declining among all groups, remains the norm for adults with a college education and good income but is now markedly less prevalent among those on the lower rungs of the socio-economic ladder."[31] Such research tellingly reveals the existence of a "marriage differential," split along the fault lines of class, a growing divide notably exacerbated by recession economies. As the Associated Press detailed in a story by Hope Yen titled "Recession Rips at U.S. Marriages," in 2009 marriages fell to a record low of 52 percent, a dip sociologists linked to the fact that young people are "choosing to delay marriage as they struggle to find work and resist making long term commitments." As a result of such trends, in turn, traditional configurations such as the heterosexual nuclear family are becoming ever rarer.[32]

At the same time, richer and more educated people are those most likely to marry and also to stay married. As Bradley Wilcox, director of the National Marriage Project at the University of Virginia and author of a report titled "When Marriage Disappears: The Retreat from Marriage in Middle America," writes, "The roots of this growing marriage divide are economic (the post-industrial economy favors the college educated), cultural (less educated Americans are abandoning a marriage mindset even as college-educated Americans take up this mindset) and legal (less educated Americans seem particularly gun shy about marrying in a world where no fault divorce is the law of the land)."[33] Moreover, when race intersects with class and education, we see the deep historical entrenchment of such patterns. The lack of education and jobs for black men has, for instance, long contributed to their lower marital prospects. This reality only looks to be exacerbated by the recession, and the unemployment rate among black men aged twenty or older stands at around 17 percent. Such observations remind us of the classist and racist history of the marital institution, its ties to wealth accumulation and consolidation, and the ways in which marriage refracts through and reifies class hierarchies. Given that marriage remains a categorization so directly tied to social mobility, one might imagine it playing a germane role in discussions about how the current economic crisis is contributing to further wealth polarization.[34] Yet a very different story is currently being told in popular culture, one that reassures American audiences that men remain single not because of larger structural forces that delimit class mobility, but because they refuse to grow up.

The language of maturity and futurity associated with marriage has long been one of its covert selling points; as the queer theorist and gay marriage critic Michael Warner reminds us, "Marriage marks out the narrative of life. Adults who marry are not necessarily more mature than adults who do not; often the reverse is true. Yet, marriage is deeply embedded in the cultural consciousness as a sign of maturity attained."[35] This understanding is, in fact, central to a number of accounts which charge that twenty-somethings in the twenty-first century are less likely to marry precisely because they are not inclined to mature, a contention that organizes Kay Hymowitz's *Manning Up: How the Rise of Women Has Turned Men into Boys* (2011). Basing her argument on the growing prevalence of "preadulthood," Hymowitz observes that this phase has "helped to throw in doubt the very meaning of marriage" and laments that "preadults don't know what is supposed to come next. They are not sure what the gender scripts are, if any. . . . Marriage and parenthood come in many forms or can be skipped altogether."[36] One might, of course, read such temporal shifts as opening up the possibility of reimagining normative life stages. Such changes could then be ascertained as offering an antiteleological approach to the life cycle, wherein marriage and reproduction are no longer its centerpieces.[37]

Hymowitz clearly sees this period of delayed adolescence hurting both men and women, yet she reserves the bulk of her criticism for the "man-children" who feature prominently in her title and book cover. Accordingly, she blames self-infantilization rather than, say, a severely depressed job market for high school and college-age graduates alike, to explain the fact that the man-child "has no life script, no special reason to grow up."[38] In contrast, she writes, "women are reaching their twenties with more achievements, more education, more property, and arguably, more ambition than their male counterparts."[39] Such observations pointedly echo recessionary discourses that predict bright economic futures for women and dismal ones for men, and illustrate again the influence of popular culture products on perceptions of actual demographics. Additionally, by attributing a decline in marriage rates to individual failings rather than structural obstacles, Hymowitz reveals herself as willfully ignorant of the economic realities that may stall or foreclose participation in the marital institution.

Though Hymowitz believes herself to be diagnosing real-life psychological and sociological patterns, the gender profiles that inform her argument in fact mimic a recognizable cinematic stereotype that the film critic David Denby termed the "slacker-striver" dyad in 2007. Writing about this then-new trend in romantic comedies, Denby observed that the slovenly slacker "hardly breaks a sweat, and sometimes he does nothing at all" whereas the female striver "wants to get to the next stage of life."[40] As a narrative trope, the slacker defines himself by being everything the female striver is not, and

Denby identified his presence in a series of films including *Failure to Launch* (2006), *You, Me, and Dupree* (2006), and *Knocked Up* (2007), all of which imagine men who need to be corralled into the structures and formations desirable to capitalist markets, namely jobs, marriages, and homes. Though these films predate the recession, they have provided convenient vocabularies for recession-era categorizations that slot men and women into opposing teams, thus buttressing popular perceptions that men are struggling financially and emotionally, while ambitious women are (impatiently) showing them up.

Within the slacker-striver genre, the terms of female success and male incompetence were already well established, a commonplace that makes it a particularly fitting narrative form for a recessionary culture that increasingly believes the same. According to such a framework, lackadaisical men must be disciplined into recognizing the implicit rewards of hard work and normative familial commitments, notions that women, with their college degrees and professional careers, have already embraced.[41] Depictions of slacker masculinity posit a slacker who willfully embraces sloth and unproductivity—sitting around in his underwear, playing video games, hanging out with his friends, and participating in what Brenda Weber calls "fraternity-type puerile humor."[42] According to such formulations, the slacker could choose to behave otherwise and is thereby capable of reform. This belief accords with the slacker-striver genre's larger neoliberal investment in the power of self-governance, whereby men are urged to "take responsibility" for themselves, to quote Laurie Ouellette's now well-known formulation. According to this neoliberal worldview, the slacker could easily be a committed and responsible companion to the striver, if only he allowed himself to be.

Self-actualization for the slacker involves what Diane Negra, in "Where the Boys Are," calls "taking up his proper place in the domestic order." Hence, a prevailing ethos of the striver-slacker genre is a tension between transience and permanence, a struggle manifested in the slacker's desire to avoid or delay domestication. Because he remains cowed by the prospects of finding a relationship, getting married, or having a baby, the slacker's living and reproductive arrangements all tend to emphasize fleeting pleasures and impermanent connections, a condition literalized by the title of *Jeff, Who Lives at Home* (2012) (figure 1.2).[43] Slacker men also frequently act out the desire to escape from domestic imperatives, embarking on provisional rebellions that take the form of liminal areas of temporary indulgence, such as the bachelor party, the road trip, or the break from marriage. Because these adventures take place predominantly in the absence of women, slacker films share with bromances an affinity for male-only spaces, and participate in what Judith Halberstam calls "queer time" or a mode that emerges "once one leaves the temporal frames of

FIGURE 1.2. A desultory, unemployed man-child who typifies the "slacker male," Jeff (Jason Segel) lives in his mother's basement, smokes pot, and is repeatedly sidetracked from performing a minor home repair, the one favor his hard-working mother asks of him for her birthday in *Jeff, Who Lives at Home* (2012).

bourgeois reproduction and family, longevity, risk/safety, and inheritance."[44] While Halberstam intended her term to apply to queer counterpublics, her description of this group as one that lives "outside the logic of capital accumulation" also resonates with the slacker, in that he too is a figure who refuses the normative logics of reproductive time. What Halberstam finds liberating about this conception of time and future, however, is precisely what the genre itself finds distressing, namely, the slacker's deliberate rejection of a futurity based on familial models of normalcy.

The need to discipline the slacker is necessitated by the threat his lack of productivity poses to the capitalist order, and the responsibility for reform is displaced onto the striver, who does the work of mothering the slacker back into toeing the correct professional line. As Denby ruefully notes, "the slacker-striver genre reduces the role of women to vehicles. Their only real function is to make the men grow up."[45] Films featuring the slacker thereby share with recessionary reports the belief that men are neither ambitious nor directed enough to claim for themselves the sort of purposeful futures that strivers are achieving. At the same time, as if tapping into the hostility that roils beneath the surface of discussions that claim female dominance as the new status quo, cultural products display similar frustrations. Pointedly rejecting the futures proffered by their more successful female counterparts, slackers' rebellions are often made in the name of sticking it to the entitled women who enforce these untenable roles. In *Hall Pass* (2011), for instance, Fred (Jason Sudeikis) convinces a reluctant Rick (Owen Wilson) to use the weeklong pass from marriage that his wife has granted on the grounds that Rick deserves it because his wife's dreams are consistently given priority. Casting their wives as the gloating winners in a game in which they perennially lose, Fred asks, "Doesn't it ever bother you that all of our wives' dreams come true and ours don't?"

Posited thus, slacker films voice real hostilities toward women framed as enforcing normative commitments, women who ask men to accept responsibilities for which they feel ill equipped and in which they often have little interest. (One might speculate as well that the gross-out humor, primitive pastimes, and the relishing of incivility so prevalent in the slacker film is a way of deliberately resisting the civilizing function of the sort of commitment these women want and implicitly deserve.) Framed in terms of the recession, we might ask: to what extent are these portrayals merely turning the nightmare reality of joblessness into a bromance fantasy, hence rationalizing and attaching a sense of agency to a situation that offers so little? A generous reading of the slacker film might see it as acknowledging a brutal economic truth, namely that it is illogical to push young people toward narratives of maturity and futurity if the economic underpinnings that support these models have thoroughly eroded. Instead, however, a different narrative has emerged, one beholden to discourses of familial normalcy. Predicated on the necessity of teaching men the value of normative commitments, such narratives bestow maturity via marriage and family.

Though the tug of war between rejecting and accepting reproductive time and normative commitments is apparent across multiple texts and sites, it can be examined in its full collectivity through the star image of Jason Bateman, whose roles over the years 2007–12 bespeak how recessionary times have narrowed the imaginative landscape rather than expanded it. Bateman might seem like an odd choice for this discussion, for in many ways he is an antislacker, a position instantiated by his portrayal of the beleaguered straight man and responsible father on the satiric *Arrested Development* (2003–6). Here, his level head and sense of centeredness stood in direct contrast to the rest of his indulgent, idiosyncratic, wealthy family, associating him with a veneer of responsibility. This straight-man persona in turn informs his portrayal of the unfeeling corporate professional prepared to labor in the cutthroat business of firing people in *Up in the Air* (2009). Such roles are, however, integral to Bateman's positioning in a predictable narrative arc wherein he flirts with slacker ethics, but nevertheless ultimately attends to bottom-line exigencies. Dangling a promise of pleasurable irresponsibility that is never meant to be fully realized, such texts allow Bateman to nearly cheat on his wife when he momentarily gets to embody the life and body of his irresponsible, womanizing best friend in *The Change-Up* (2011); plot to kill his sadistic boss in *Horrible Bosses* (2011); and consider leaving his marriage when infertility problems threaten to derail it in *Couples Retreat* (2009).[46] With the exception of the independent film *Juno* (2009), in which Bateman's Mark Loring, skittish at the prospect of impending fatherhood, flees his sterile suburban home and child-obsessed wife, the Bateman character always does the right thing, realizing, predictably, that his true desires accord with sanctioned roles. He acts, for example, as a surrogate father to his best friend's seven-year-old son in *The Switch* (2010) before finding out that he is the boy's biological father, and hence destined to couple with the boy's mother, the woman with whom he has long been in love. Similar conclusions are offered in *The Change-Up* wherein the slacker character, played by Ryan Reynolds, learns to follow through with his commitments, lessons the hard-working family man played by Bateman has already absorbed. Bateman needs instruction on perhaps the only topic that American film sanctions the slacker to teach: how to have fun, a realization inevitably inculcated via pastimes that invoke adolescence, such as going rollerblading, driving a go-cart, and visiting the batting cage, all of which Bateman does prior to realizing how much he misses his wife and children.[47]

In such expert ideological machinations, though it may initially look like the family serves as the male's punishment, it is, in fact, decisively presented as his reward. With their initial polymorphous inclinations neutered and subdued, confirmed bachelors and wannabe wayward husbands capitulate to convention, learning, predictably, either how good they will have it when they marry, or, if they are married, how good they have had it all along. American cinema has, of course, long shamed and guilted men into recognizing that true happiness lies in heterosexual monogamy and procreation, with the 1987 *Fatal Attraction* being perhaps the zenith of such efforts.[48] This project of teaching men responsibility has nevertheless taken on new exigency in the recession era, in part because such portrayals also rehearse an attendant conversation circulating in female popular culture, which laments the loss of marriageable men for ambitious women who want husbands. Leaving no question as to who is to blame for this shortage, the November 2011 *Atlantic* cover proclaimed "What, Me Marry?" featuring the author, Kate Bolick, a well-dressed thirty-something woman visibly perturbed by the sentiments

FIGURE 1.3. Privileged women are represented as rethinking marriage, with a recession-inspired man shortage shifting their prospects and options.

superimposed on her image: "In today's economy, men are falling apart" (figure 1.3). In the article that follows, "All the Single Ladies," Bolick notes that "American women as a whole have never been confronted with such a radically shrinking pool of what are traditionally considered to be 'marriageable' men—those who are better educated and earn more than they do. So women are now contending with what we might call the new scarcity."[49] Bolick's observation accords with statistics which find that recession economies are taking a toll on marital futures, and yet simultaneously reminds us of how classed such discourses of marital scarcity are, assuming as they do a sizable population of educated, upwardly mobile, heterosexual women for whom there are few suitable prospects. Apprehended in this light, a romantic resolution whereby the slacker is seduced into domesticity can be understood to alleviate the anxiety that the marriage drought produces in the female imaginary, providing at least a fantasy answer to Kay Hymowitz's plaintive inquiry, "Where have all the good men gone?"[50]

Single women looking for a good man are surely not new to popular culture representation; as Anthea Taylor writes, "the most visible single woman in postfeminist media culture is she who proves her profound wish to be otherwise."[51] Yet, while prerecession postfeminist regimes were intent to show women who could find suitable mates, if they appropriately scaled back their ambition, recessionary representation is apparently newly aware that single women may remain that way due to a shortage of eligible men. To illustrate how extreme this quest could get—or better perhaps, how hyperbolic the discourse around finding a suitable man in recession times has gotten— Liza Mundy foresees that women will "take to the skies. High earning young women who remain determined to marry men who make as much or more than they do will . . . use their earnings to travel far and wide, flying from big cities to other big cities, keeping the travel industry afloat and turning the country—and the world—into one big marriage market." [52] Those without such financial resources may nevertheless find themselves, to use Mundy's metaphor, unable to soar.

As these discourses illustrate, popular culture remains most concerned about what diminishing marital prospects will mean for the affluent middle-class women that postfeminist culture privileges, and "All the Single Ladies" (to its credit) actually admits as much, noting that women of color and other disadvantaged groups within the American economy have long been contending with losses of marriageable men.[53] As the law professor Ralph Richard Banks writes in *Is Marriage for White People?* (2011), a man shortage has plagued not only working-class but all African American women, and he observes that "black women more frequently marry less-educated and lower earning men than any other group of women in our nation." [54] The implication that professional women who desire couplehood should therefore marry down inflects popular culture products geared to black women, particularly those in Tyler Perry's oeuvre such as *Why Did I Get Married?* (2007) and *Daddy's Little Girls* (2007). As Banks notes, Perry's works carry the message that "professional black women should abandon their highfalutin ways and go for the guy driving the bus or repairing the car." [55] In a prescient move, Banks predicts that "if the fortunes of white men and women diverge as they have among blacks . . . professional white women may confront the same challenges that professional black women do today." [56] The hand-wringing currently occurring over the status of marriage in the recession economy has therefore much to do with the perception that the marital calculations demanded of women of color as well as lower-status women are, thanks to all men's declining statures, soon to be the lot of white professional-class women as well. Identifying changes in marital economies that have been pervasive in everything but affluent communities for quite some time, recession trend pieces reveal the implicit racism and classism which fueled the idea that prior to the recession, no such man shortage existed. What the recession has done, perhaps, is to make manifest for white professionals what America's working classes have always known, namely the difficulty of maintaining breadwinner models premised on traditional gender roles while occupying unstable economic locations.[57]

One resolution to this dilemma comes in the form of a recessionary emphasis on the sorts of pairings that Banks identifies in the black community: the coupling of competent women with downshifted men. The un- or underemployed man whose accomplishments take a back seat to those of his female counterpart features, for instance, in *The Five-Year Engagement* (2012), wherein Tom (Jason Segel) gives up a prestigious job as a chef in a high-end San Francisco restaurant in order to follow his fiancé Violet (Emily Blunt) to Michigan, where she begins a protracted postdoctoral program. Tom flails in the Midwestern setting to spectacularly pathetic effect: after taking a job in a glorified fast-food restaurant, he hyperbolically fortifies his masculinity via hunting and bumbling attempts at philandering and clearly loses Violet's respect, before the two eventually reconcile. The film's underlying genre status as a romantic comedy likewise underscores that regardless of the lead couple's unequal professional statures, the maintenance of their union remains a priority.

Within such a zeitgeist, cultural products have resorted to employing creative tactics to keep the downshifted male appropriately coupled, such as by celebrating his role as a parent. These portrayals suggest that in traditional heterosexual arrangements, it is increasingly the male partner who has more time for caretaking, as in the N BC comedy *Up All Night* (2011–12), which premised its first-season storyline on the marital and professional negotiations of a high-powered working mom (Christina Applegate) who labors under an unforgiving female boss (Maya Rudolph) while her husband (Will Arnett) acts as a stay-at-home dad. Perhaps in an attempt to further piggyback on this new emphasis on fatherhood, the network premiered *Guys with Kids* in the fall of 2012, a sitcom that centers on three dads who strive to make fatherhood fun. The film *What to Expect When You're Expecting* (2012) similarly focuses on male parenting, and features a park-bound "dude's group," where fathers meet to discuss child raising. Such arrangements are, as these examples suggest, often quite lovingly depicted, and the effort to paint them as functional rather than cause for concern spurred the marriage historian Stephanie Coontz to pen "The M.R.S. and the Ph.D." in 2012, wherein she claimed that educated women who marry down tend to partner with men who define success in less materialistic ways and do more housework.[58] The gesture to recuperate men coupled with high-powered women as channeling excess energy into parenting or housekeeping nevertheless appears indebted to the idea that these men cannot be so easily relied on as workers.

Women without Men

Popular culture has, no doubt, worked hard to propose these alternate configurations in order to compensate for supposed imbalances between men and women. Yet, as the cultural imagination increasingly focuses on the economic troubles of downtrodden men, and in turn the diminishing marital prospects of upwardly mobile women, it may also leave high-status women with little to do but myopically focus on their own earning capacity.[59] Women who broker power in worlds where men are either absent or insignificant can, in fact, be located in a number of Hollywood's most-hyped women's films of recent years, including *Mamma Mia* (2008), *Sex and the City 2* (2010), *Eat Pray Love* (2010), *I Don't Know How She Does It* (2011), *Bridesmaids* (2011), and *Bachelorette* (2012), all of which send women on female-centered odysseys in which men figure little.[60] If bromances offer fantasy worlds without women, the inverse is often equally true of women's films, which script worlds without men. Though relational prospects and problems with men are part of these films' narrative fabric, finding the psychic space for self-actualization tends to register as the women's foremost concern. Likewise, with the exception of *Bridesmaids*, in which the central female character, Annie (Kristen Wiig), loses her bakery business as a result of the economic downturn, the recession tends not to factor in female representational culture, an observation that films and critics alike have used to frame the women featured in these texts as self-indulgent. Attacks were particularly vitriolic against *Sex and the City 2*, wherein the four friends who comprise the series' main cast luxuriate in the opulence of an expense-paid trip to Dubai. For many, viewing the film's orgy of overconsumption in light of the recession economy threw into rather disgusting relief the race and class privilege of the characters, elements that were barely suppressed in the popular television show and first movie. The film's egregiously out-of-step tone and ethos concomitantly rendered it an easy target for woman blaming, allowing for the cathexis of frustration that, though momentarily gratifying, would perhaps be more productively directed at structural corruption in corporate and political sectors.

I Don't Know How She Does It, also starring Sarah Jessica Parker, evidenced a similarly blithe ignorance of recessionary anxieties. Based on Allison Pearson's 2002 book of the same name about an overtaxed working mother, Kate Reddy envelops herself in the sort of economic cushions (nannies, mommy wars) that fell away for many women years ago—if, of course, they even enjoyed them at all. The film betrays its datedness through a tired focus on a harried Kate's attempt to achieve work-life balance, as she frantically attends to her professional and personal commitments offering profuse apologies at home and at work. Through its sidelining of Kate's milquetoast and under-employed husband (Greg Kinnear), and a limp possibility of a workplace affair with an otherwise rather neutered Pierce Brosnan, the film did, however, comply with other recession-era portrayals that centralize women as the figures on whom the financial future of the family rests. Crucially as well, unlike in the book version, Kate does not retreat in the film's conclusion, but rather keeps her job, a nod perhaps to the necessity of maintaining employment when one has married down.

As these examples show, women routinely serve as symbols of financial vitality in media representations that relatedly script male insignificance. Female-centered television dramas such as *Weeds* (2005–12), *Damages* (2007–12), *The Good Wife* (2009–), *Nurse Jackie* (2009–), and *The Killing* (2011–13) all, for instance, figure women as a family's primary breadwinner and suggest that women are capable of laboring to meet financial pressures, often to compensate for men who, through death, incarceration, divorce, or unemployment, are unable to shoulder their own or their family's economic burdens. The notion that women can not only regroup but also thrive in the face of male absence and financial ruin has become a convenient and compelling narrative paradigm, evident, for instance, in a *Damages* season three storyline centered on a Bernie Madoff–esque ponzi scheme. The ever-shrewd Patty Hewes (Glenn Close) presides over the ferreting out of the disgraced banker's vast hidden fortune, and, in addition to witnessing the demise of the banker and the incarceration of his son, the show foregrounds another male casualty via the murder of Patty's longtime associate Tom Shayes (Tate Donovan). This plotline simultaneously and tellingly rectifies Patty's estrangement from her younger protégée, Ellen (Rose Byrne), whom she has been grooming as the symbolic heir to her immensely successful law firm, thus establishing female solidarity in the wake of multiple male deaths.[61]

The CBS drama *The Good Wife* provides another excellent example of how recession-era gender imbalances script male ineffectuality as female opportunity. In the initial episodes, Alicia Florrick (Julianna Margulies), the aggrieved spouse of a philandering and possibly corrupt politician, returns to work as a lawyer after a thirteen-year hiatus, while her husband, the former state's attorney, sits in jail. The show multiply overdetermines its investment in the specter of a working woman keeping both the economy and the family afloat—not only does Alicia retain her job when myriad others are fired, and while the firm investigates numerous other cost-saving measures the economic downturn necessitates, she also garners plum assignments, competing offers from other firms, and even a significant raise. Though the show has featured plenty of successful men throughout its tenure, the idea that men have become increasingly tangential to female-centered economies was nevertheless made salient during a season three storyline featuring the disciplining of law partner (and Alicia's sometime lover) Will Gardner (Josh Charles). Faced with a six-month suspension for embezzlement, Will's presence in the law firm becomes increasingly spectral, and partner Diane Lockhart (Christine Baranski) takes the reins in his absence. While the men in subordinate positions behave like wolves circling the henhouse, Diane rules from within, keeping a level head in the face of the men's increasingly childish and ineffectual power maneuvers. Notably, Alicia secures from Diane a significant promotion during this time, a bump that coincides perfectly with a period of male meltdown.

While the aforementioned examples singularly register the privileging of female-centered economies in the face of recession culture, the widespread nature of this emergence is more holistically evidenced by the Bravo network, a channel that cultivates female prowess not merely as a narrative script but as a brand identity. Organizing its programming around ambitious and often exorbitantly rich professional women, Bravo headliners include *Millionaire Matchmaker*, *The Rachel Zoe Project*, *Tabatha's Salon Takeover*, *Kathy Griffin: My Life on the D List*, and the ever-spawning *Real Housewives* franchise, including the spin-offs *Bethenny Ever After*, *Tamra's OC Wedding*, and *I Dream of Nene: The Wedding*. As this list indicates, the network relies on the professionalization of labor roles that were once explicitly associated with domestic realms, such as matchmaker, stylist, fashion designer, and chef, turning them from underappreciated service occupations into forms of monetized celebrity. The network's *Real Housewives* franchise also professionalizes and commodifies wifedom—perhaps the ur-service job—and appearing on the show now stands predominantly as a career maker for the women who star in it. Since the *Real Housewives of Orange County* began in 2006 as a companion piece to ABC's *Desperate Housewives*, the series has gotten increasingly blatant about its lack of interest in marriage as any sort of organizing trope. The fact that many of these wives have neither a marriage nor a husband speaks again to marriage's increasing decentralization in the realm of female media culture.

Relatedly, though in prerecession times the men who populate the various shows under the *Real Housewives* umbrella were instrumentalized mainly for the money they could lavish on their wives and girlfriends, since the recession began they have increasingly become an afterthought. Associated with a number of high-profile insolvencies involving evictions, mortgage defaults, and foreclosures, the men have tended to figure more as burdens than sugar daddies.[62] Meanwhile, the housewives launch makeup, skin care, and clothing lines, and hawk handbags, nutritional supplements, and diet and cooking books, using their housewife designation to associate their brand identities with feminized pursuits. This trajectory was exemplified by Bethenny Frankel, the enterprising natural foods chef who initially appeared on the reality food competition *The Apprentice: Martha Stewart* prior to her casting in *The Real Housewives of New York*. A whirlwind romance, unplanned pregnancy, and quickie marriage subsequently garnered her two spinoffs—*Bethenny Getting Married* and *Bethenny Ever After*—in which to foment her celebrity brand, and Frankel presently manages a multiplatformed media empire featuring cookbooks, diet, exercise and lifestyle advice, shapewear, and food products, most famously the Skinnygirl Margarita, a drink brand she sold to Jim Beam in 2011 for over $100 million. As evidence of this success, Frankel appeared on the cover of *Forbes* in June 2011, the main personality featured in an article devoted to "the rise of Hollywood's entrepreneurial elite" and her talk show, *Bethenny*, was picked up for national syndication the following year.[63] In late 2012, however, Frankel announced her separation and impending divorce from husband Jason Hoppy, a parting scripted in the press as occurring in part because his level of ambition did not match hers.

As these examples illustrate, the *Housewives* franchise repeatedly frames women and not men as the new face of professional competence, and its affinity for showcasing lopsided gender organizations can also be discerned in the coupling of *The Real Housewives of Orange County*'s Gretchen Rossi and Slade Smiley. Featured as the materialistically minded boyfriend of housewife Jo De La Rosa in season one, Smiley subsequently lost a high-profile job in real estate and has been roundly criticized for dodging child support in conjunction with a son from a previous relationship. Since he began dating Rossi in 2009, Smiley has remained unemployed and debt ridden, and he routinely acts as Rossi's assistant during publicity appearances and events related to her makeup and handbag business. Season seven, which aired in 2012, repeatedly thematized his ineffectuality, showcasing a pursuit of an impractical labor scheme as he tried to launch a career as a stand-up comedian, and his attempt to buy Rossi an imitation engagement ring because he could not afford a real stone. Meanwhile, Rossi steadfastly asserted to the camera, to friends, and to him that she refused to marry or consider starting a family until he organized his financial life. As she says in a monologue in the episode "Scream Therapy," "I could easily pay his child support and make all the bullshit that's out there about him go away, but it's like a parent who continues to enable a child to do something that you don't want them to do." This infantilizing discourse, and the fact that Rossi is willing to delay marriage until Smiley grows up again perfectly follows a recessionary script; as Harriet Fraad argues in "The Great Recession and Gender Marriage Transformation," "Women have responded to men's financial incapacity. . . . Women now increasingly refuse to marry the men who cannot provide for them."[64] Taken as a representative trope, Rossi and Smiley's pairing suggests that the contrast between male and female economies gets ever starker, as men occupy increasingly dependent or spectral positions in the lives of the women with whom they are associated. Such abject positions for each gender, and the wretched divide between them, was also poignantly and rather tragically literalized when, in August 2011, Russell Armstrong, the estranged husband of Beverly Hills housewife Taylor Armstrong, committed suicide. Rumored to have been facing impending economic ruin, Armstrong was also apparently cognizant that in the upcoming season of the show he would be accused of physically abusing his wife.

As this rather bleak incident portends, a future in which men have no future and are outpaced by women who thrive on money and power, will in turn encourage toxic levels of resentment toward women in the name of an elusive plea for fairness. Recession narratives of this kind mobilize resentment in the name of righting gender imbalance and yet have proven increasingly compelling to an American culture seeking to understand how the bottom could have fallen out quite so precipitously. If women are scripted as undeterred by the meltdown (at best) and indulgent, self-centered, or cruel (at worst), the division between the sexes is sure to widen, with misogyny emerging as a means by which to right the perceived wrongs directed at men. Organized through a mutually interdependent vocabulary of work, marriage, and gender, recessionary discourses have tended to encourage hostility between the sexes by creating the mythology that in a new economic order, motivation and opportunity are both unequally apportioned in favor of women. If prevailing narratives continue to centralize and lament male deficiencies and vulnerabilities, it will become commonplace, in turn, to punish women who are too selfish or self-absorbed to notice men's pain. This eventuality has troubling implications for both sexes; though recession discourses routinely and relentlessly proclaim women winners within these new frameworks, to anyone invested in equitable and compassionate economies, such a vision hardly looks like winning at all.

Notes

1. AnnaGraceMusic, "Five Year Old Needs a Job before Getting Married," YouTube, February 22, 2011, www.youtube.com/watch?v=orbMHLDY1pA.

2. For an evidently middle-class girl discussing the gender bias evident in the toy industry, see dbarry1917, "Riley on Marketing," YouTube, May 6, 2011, www.youtube.com/watch?v=-CU04oHqbas.

3. Books that detail such inequalities include Edin and Lein, *Making Ends Meet*; Hays, *Flat Broke with Children*; and Brush, *Poverty, Battered Women and Work in U.S. Public Policy*.

4. McRobbie, *The Aftermath of Feminism*, 72, 57.

5. McRobbie, *The Aftermath of Feminism*, 72.

6. The film *Inside Job* (2010) ambitiously attempts to connect these dots, offering a sobering perspective on how those working in the investment industry—as well as those charged with its oversight—were both often spectacularly corrupt.

7. What appeared to be a ready supply of jobs involving manual labor prior to this crisis, however, may have been a blip rather than a sustainable state of affairs, if one accepts that the housing "bubble actually represented an economic policy that disguised the declining prospects of blue-collar men" (Salam, "The Death of Macho," 68).

8. Historicizing the long hemorrhaging of this industry, the *Fiscal Times* reports that manufacturing jobs constituted 20 percent of private-sector payrolls in 1990, 15 percent in 2000, and just over 10 percent in April 2011. See Cooper, "Where Have All the High Paying Jobs Gone?"

9. Rosin, "The End of Men," 60. Rosin's rather specious—yet widely read—article was two years later adapted into a book titled *The End of Men: And the Rise of Women*.

10. Hancock, "He-Cession Has More Men Looking at Once 'Female' Jobs"; Dewan and Gebeloff, "More Men Enter Fields Dominated by Women."

11. Mundy, *The Richer Sex*, 15.

12. Negra and Tasker, "Neoliberal Frames and Genres of Inequality," 345.

13. According to Rosin in "Primetime's Looming Male Identity Crisis," her previous article, "The End of Men," was repeatedly referenced by producers as they planned this palette of new shows.

14. West, "ABC 2012 Midseason Premiere."

15. Protests against *Work It* were organized by groups including the Gay and Lesbian Alliance against Defamation and the Human Rights Campaign. Feminist groups were not, however, publicly represented as involved in this groundswell, which speaks perhaps to their diminishing cultural profile.

16. Tyre, *The Trouble with Boys*, 8.

17. Relying on similar cultural understandings of stagnating boys, the NBC sitcom *1600 Penn* nevertheless frames affable goofball and "first son" Skip Gilchrist (Josh Gad) as a cult hero who lends his brand of naive goodwill to the personal and professional goings-on inside the White House. The show thus uses humor to neutralize the threat that might otherwise have been posed by Skip's position as a twenty-something, unemployed college dropout.

18. The newness of this statistic is debatable; according to a 2010 story in the *Chronicle of Higher Education*, men have composed 42–44 percent of college students fairly consistently since the mid-1990s. The article also mentions that for black and Hispanic men, the numbers are significantly lower, a fact that is generally neglected in news stories about the recession and yet far more alarming.

19. See de Vise, "More Women Than Men Got PhDs Last Year."

20. Rosin, "The End of Men," 60.

21. Labeling women as the "engine" for the new economy, an NBC *Nightly News* segment that aired in March 2011 as a part of an "America at the Crossroads" series like-

wise celebrated female dominance in the "fastest growing" professions. Yet, with the exception of nursing, all were unskilled, service work positions. Service labor was not, however, the occupation of either of the women most predominantly featured in the segment: an advertising executive and the president of Kimpton hotels, a luxury hotel chain.

22. Rosin, "The End of Men," 60.

23. Salam, "The Death of Macho," 66.

24. Barnett and Rivers, "Don't Call Women the Richer Sex!"

25. See Tavernise, "Gains Made in Equality of Incomes in Downturn."

26. On the toll these disparities are taking, see Bartels, *Unequal Democracy*; and Noah, *The Great Divergence*.

27. Luscombe, "Workplace Salaries."

28. Rosin, "The End of Men," 60.

29. Salam, "The Death of Macho," 69.

30. Salam, "The Death of Macho," 70.

31. "The Decline of Marriage and the Rise of New Families," i.

32. According to Census Bureau figures collected in 2010, married couples make up only about 48 percent of all households. Likewise, married couples living with one or more children—what would in popular parlance be called the nuclear family—now account for only about a fifth of all living arrangements.

33. Wilcox, "When Marriage Disappears."

34. Unfortunately, even reports that do take these statistics seriously tend to pathologize Americans who do not marry or do so multiple times. The underlying point of Andrew Cherlin's *The Marriage-Go-Round*, for instance, is that shifting family structures hurt children.

35. Warner, *The Trouble with Normal*, 136.

36. Hymowitz, *Manning Up*, 10, 9.

37. These new flexibilities have already made room in representational culture for previously underrepresented groups whose life trajectories do not correspond to conventional timelines, for instance, the much-sensationalized female midlife "cougar." It has also resulted in the visibility (though not normalization) of what were previously stigmatized familial categories, including teen mothers; lesbian, gay, and transgender parents; polygamous marriages; and hyperprocreative families.

38. Hymowitz, *Manning Up*, 135.

39. Hymowitz, *Manning Up*, 58.

40. Denby, "A Fine Romance," 59.

41. Men's active resistance to such norms organizes Comedy Central's ironically titled *Workaholics* (2010–), which focuses on a group of three twenty-something white males who engage in what are often scatological pranks designed to buck their stifling marketing jobs and humorless female boss.

42. Weber, "Puerile Pillars of the Frat Pack," 70.

43. The film stars hulking man-child Jason Segel, gaining traction from his previous work in *Knocked Up* (2007), *I Love You, Man* (2009), and *The Muppets* (2011). For an even

more extreme infantilization plot that anthropomorphizes the theme of arrested development, see *Ted* (2012), in which a young boy's beloved teddy bear comes to life and shadows the now thirty-five-year-old man.

44. Halberstam, *In a Queer Time and Place*, 6.

45. Denby, "A Fine Romance," 59.

46. During a conversation in which the three male leads consider quitting jobs that leave them beholden to unethical bosses and practices, *Horrible Bosses* announces itself as mindful of recession economies, yet uses an offensive homophobic joke to emphasize worker entrapment. Drinking at a bar, the group encounters an acquaintance who went to Yale, worked at (the now bankrupt) Lehman Brothers, and is presently so destitute that he offers to give blow jobs in the bathroom to earn extra cash.

47. Further reinforcing his status as the American everyman, Bateman also appears in, and served as an executive producer for, Morgan Spurlock's *Mansome* (2012), a documentary on male grooming rituals.

48. See Leonard, *Fatal Attraction*.

49. Bolick, "All the Single Ladies," 122. Lori Gottlieb's 2010 *Marry Him: The Case for Settling for Mr. Good Enough* premises itself on a similar scarcity model, though Gottlieb's advice that women marry before it is too late is not explicitly linked to recession-era economies.

50. Hymowitz, *Manning Up*, 3.

51. Taylor, *Single Women in Popular Culture*, 15.

52. Mundy, *The Richer Sex*, 16.

53. See particularly Edin and Kefalas, *Promises I Can Keep*.

54. Banks, *Is Marriage for White People?*, 92.

55. Banks, *Is Marriage for White People?*, 90.

56. Banks, *Is Marriage for White People?*, 48.

57. In fact, for dual-earner families in the lowest socioeconomic brackets, the income differentials between husbands and wives rarely comply with traditional gender hierarchies. According to Barnett and Rivers, in families who occupy the bottom twentieth percentile, wives routinely make more money than their husbands.

58. Coontz's singular focus on celebrating educated professional women once again confirms, however, popular culture's tendency to typify this figure as representative of all women.

59. This dynamic played out in rather toxic terms in the TLC series *Jon and Kate Plus 8* cum *Kate Plus 8*, which scripted a family's disintegration as the result, in part, of a husband's slacker ethic and his controlling, shrewish wife's bid for celebrity and money.

60. This absence of men was literalized in the anticipated but commercially unsuccessful remake of *The Women* (2008), which, like the Cukor original, featured a cast composed completely of women.

61. The novel *Silver Girl* (2011) by Elin Hilderbrand similarly feminizes the Madoff scandal as a tale of female comeback. In this thinly veiled portrayal, Madoff's exiled wife finds healing and redemption through a retreat to Nantucket and the rekindling of a lost female friendship.

62. Financial troubles are also rumored to be the cause of a number of the franchise's divorces. To date, there are fourteen divorces and counting, and there is talk of a marriage curse associated with the series.

63. The article is Casserly, "The New Celebrity Money Makers." The quote is from the front cover.

64. Fraad, "The Great Recession and Gender Marriage Transformation," 131.

TWO *ISABEL MOLINA-GUZMÁN*

"Latina Wisdom" in "Postrace" Recession Media

On September 2009, one month after the politically contested swearing-in of Puerto Rican Sonia Sotomayor to the U.S. Supreme Court, millions of audiences welcomed into their homes another "wise Latina," Gloria Pritchett (Sofía Vergara) on the ABC sitcom *Modern Family* (2009–present). Premiering to international critical acclaim and ratings success at a time of declining traditional television viewership, *Modern Family* would become a top three new program, top twenty-five program overall, and a top ten program in the most coveted eighteen–forty-nine-year-old rating category.[1] By the end of its 2010–11 season, *Modern Family* would be renewed for a third season, be sold into syndication, and become the most popular situation comedy on U.S. television, beating out CBS's *Two and a Half Men* and *Big Bang Theory*. In 2013 it won its third Screen Actors Guild award for best comedic cast in a television program.

What is most interesting about the series, however, is the way it features an undocumented Latina character in the midst of a backlash toward Latina/o immigration, elides the effects of the Great Recession, and ignores ongoing cultural and economic anxieties related to the United States' slow economic recovery. In this essay, I engage *Modern Family*'s Gloria to think through how the show navigates what Cameron McCarthy and Warren Dimitriadis have named the "white discourse of resentment," defined as the xenophobic public discourses produced by economic and cultural distress. Specifically, *Modern Family*'s characters and storylines, particularly those surrounding Gloria, are compelling precisely because as a recession-era text it nurtures the wounds of white resentment by calling forth gendered ethnoracial stereotypes of Latinidad, supressing the effects of the recession and producing instead a romantic image of white upward mobility and heteronormative domesticity.[2]

In particular, the positioning of Gloria in Modern Family suggests something of the ways that gender and racial inequality come to be naturalized at a time when the effects of the global recession in the United States are being felt most by ethnoracial minority women and children. According to the Pew Research Hispanic Center, by 2010 the Latina/o poverty rate hit 26.6 percent, the highest since 1993 and up by 5.1 percent since the global recession began in 2007. Latina/o childhood poverty in 2010 stood at 35 percent, with the poverty rate of Latina/o children of immigrant parents setting a record at 40.2 percent.[3] Among other things, Modern Family's erasure of recessionary effects illustrates Anikó Imre's argument that "fictional media forms have been particularly effective at rationalizing the logic of inequality that propels neoliberal economies" (chapter 10, this volume).

Public policy discussions, such as debates over social welfare policies and the federal government's role in helping those most in economic need, illustrate how the discourse of white resentment requires that difference (sexual, ethnic, racial, or linguistic) be culturally disciplined to maintain the naturalness of economic hierarchies. Thus, the storylines and character development surrounding Gloria implicitly reinforce post–Cold War–era notions of Latina femininity and motherhood and traditionally gendered economic domestic arrangements. Modern Family tells the story of an "American family" safe from the economic recession and the social and cultural changes that moved women from the private sphere of the home to the public sphere of the workplace. Its discourse of white resentment reaffirms the traditional ideology of U.S. liberalism that posits the United States as a "colorblind" society, affording those with the skills and desire the ability to move to the top of the democratic marketplace regardless of the economic environment and their gender or ethnoracial identities. Modern Family's narrative and characters rest on the assumption that women no longer need or desire professional or economic success but rather choose to define themselves through marriage and motherhood. Indeed, Gloria's claim to happiness on the show is dependent on her success at heterosexual marriage and motherhood.

As was evident in 2012 U.S. presidential campaign rhetoric, adherence to meritocratic liberal ideology has only intensified since the uneven and slow U.S. recovery from the Great Recession, resulting in fictional narratives that normalize white resentment by reinforcing that ethnicity, race, and gender are no longer relevant to public or economic policy. Privileging middle-class whiteness and patriarchal authority and ignoring recessionary effects on income inequality and ethnoracial minority communities, *Modern Family* reinforces neoliberal postrace discourses and leaves white resentment uncritiqued. Jennifer Esposito proposes that with regard to contemporary U.S. network television programming, the ideology of liberalism has been rearticulated and "recently redefined by the media as 'postracial' (meaning that we have moved beyond race and that race no longer structures our thinking or our actions)."[4] Filmed in a thirty-minute mockumentary style, *Modern Family* focuses on the interconnected lives of the extended Pritchett clan and its patriarch Jay, played by the iconic Ed O'Neill of FOX's *Married with Children*. The Pritchett family is modern in its demographic: Jay is married to a much younger immigrant-Colombian wife Gloria, with a stepson Manny (Rico Rodriguez); his son-in-law Phil Dunphy (Ty Burrell) and daughter Claire (Julie Bowen) function as a more traditional family, while his son Mitchell (Jesse Ferguson) is married to gay partner Cameron (Eric Stonestreet) and cofather to Lily (Aubrey Anderson-Emmons), their adopted Vietnamese daughter.

Clearly bidding for cultural timeliness, *Modern Family* delinks a romanticized domestic sphere from national and global economic crises through its dependence on a conservative depiction of domestic femininity and masculine economic power that belies persistent economic and cultural inequalities that define contemporary U.S. life. That said, in a conservative postrace and postfeminist recessionary context defined by economic, class, racial, and gender resentment, it is also critical to explore the potentially transformative narratives of popular texts such as *Modern Family*. At a time when U.S. Latina/o citizenship is under political contestation across the country, Latina/o economic labor is under increased militarization and surveillance, and the poverty of Latina/o children and women is greater than ever before, analyzing how a portrayal of Latina identity in a prominent television program may disrupt discourses of resentment is central to a broader analysis of the cultural and political implications of recession-era media narratives.

In the introduction, Diane Negra and Yvonne Tasker document how many of the essays in this book illustrate a collective symbolic environment that redirects cultural attention away from the structural realities and effects of the Great Recession through depictions of failed masculinity and financially empowered femininity. For example, Suzanne Leonard documents how popular media during the Great Recession perpetuate narratives of men as "disproportionally disadvantaged" and in crisis (chapter 1). In her analysis, she shows how the downfall of the heterosexual family is consistently connected to the economic failure of the patriarch and the financial excess of unmarried womanhood. However, *Modern Family* resists such recession-era popular narratives through its romantic recuperation of the male breadwinner, feminine housewife, and traditional domestic arrangements. By doing so, *Modern Family* inverts the recessionary tropes identified by Leonard that position women as symbols of financial stability and men as feminized and domestically insignificant. In this way, the series contributes to what Negra and Tasker term "magical thinking around issues of economic security and mobility," with the commodification of domestic Latina femininity and motherhood becoming central to the cultural reimagining of whiteness (see introduction). This chapter analyzes how *Modern Family* overlooks recessionary wealth redistribution and social inequality by favoring a return to nostalgic familial and gender arrangements.

The U.S. Cultural Context: Racializing and Gendering the Great Recession

Sonia Sotomayor (figure 2.1) joined the Supreme Court in the midst of high unemployment, declining property values, increasing foreclosures, growing income disparity, and unprecedented federal debt.[5] Her nomination (the first ever Latina/U.S.-born Puerto Rican) elicited a conservative backlash, with conservative news commentators claiming she represented everything from "hardcore racism" to a "threat" to white male privilege.[6] Fueling the response to Sotomayor's nomination was one line in a speech she gave to a mostly U.S. Latina/o audience, which was published in a specialized Chicano-based law journal in 2002, *Berkeley La Raza Journal of Law*: "I would hope that a wise Latina woman with the richness of her experiences would more often than not reach a better conclusion than a white male who hasn't lived that life."[7] Although economists have identified June 2009 as the beginning of the U.S. recovery, Sotomayor's nomination exacerbated the narrative of white male disenfranchisement prevalent during the Great Recession.

Sotomayor's advocacy of Latina/o educational attainment and political empowerment and her claims to a privileged "wisdom" produced a complicated moment. Her nomination and the publicity surrounding her Horatio Alger story as the daughter of poor Puerto Rican immigrants challenged postfeminist discourses enabled by the economic boom and bolstered the discourse of male anger and white resentment that defines the contemporary recessionary era (see introduction). Sotomayor consciously built a high-status public career as a progressive practitioner of the law particularly concerned with social, political, and economic inequality. The media's framing of her nomination as historically monumental served as a stark reminder that indeed ethnoracial women minorities in the United States have not achieved equality. Moreover, it drew attention to the contested status of Latinas/os in a

FIGURE 2.1. Sonia Sotomayor, then a nominee to the Supreme Court, pictured with Barack Obama and Joe Biden in 2009. Senator Lindsey Graham (R, SC) led the charge against Sotomayor by characterizing her judicial temperament as that of a "hot bench" (official White House photo by Pete Souza).

recessionary period that bore witness to virulent anti-immigration legislation at federal, state, and local levels of government.

Leo Chavez historically documents how U.S. backlash against Latinas/os and Latina/o immigration correlates with moments of economic anxiety such as the Great Depression, the post–World War II recession and the most recent Great Recession. Indeed, it is not coincidental that a heated domestic debate over U.S. immigration policy occurred against the backdrop of national debates over domestic deficits and the role of federal funding for the social welfare state during a time of fiscal crisis. Not surprisingly, Latinas/os and Latina/o immigration continue to be primary targets of the resentments produced by the economic uncertainty of the U.S. recession. For example, hate crimes against Latinos have increased disproportionately to those against other groups during the past decade.[8] The result is a political and cultural atmosphere defined by hostility toward Latina/o immigrants, women, mothers, and their children. While the Pew Research Center documents that public opinion identifying undocumented immigration as a critical political issue has fallen since 2007, anti-immigration laws at the local and state level have spiked, culminating in the 2012 U.S. Supreme Court decision severely limiting Arizona's Senate Bill 1070, heralded as the most restrictive anti-immigration law in the country.

Thus, running alongside headlines about Sotomayor's historical nomination were newsmagazine articles on the effects of high unemployment on white men, what has been referred to as the "mancession," such as a Georgia Labor Department report titled "Georgia Men Hit Hardest by Recession December 2007–May 2009."[9] Laying out the analysis more explicitly, a July 2009 USA Today article suggested the following:

> White men over 55 had a record 6.5% unemployment rate in the second quarter, far above the previous post-Depression high of 5.4% in 1983. The jobless rate for older black men was higher—10.5%—but more than a percentage point below its 1983 peak.
>
> The most remarkable change is in the unemployment rate for black women: 12.2%, far below the historic peak of 20% in 1983. Hispanic unemployment is about 6 percentage points below historic highs, too.
>
> In other words, this recession has shrunk the racial gap in unemployment, largely because white men are doing so much worse than usual.[10]

Although overall white male unemployment estimated at about 5 percent is far below the national unemployment rate and nearly half the unemployment rate for ethnoracial minorities, it is the continuing perceived effect of the recession on white men that draws the most attention and fuels much of the conservative angst about ethnicity, race, and gender in the Obama era.[11]

At the time of Modern Family's premiere, news articles and news blogs about the impact of unemployment on traditional notions of white masculinity contrasted sharply with the Horatio Alger story of Sotomayor's Puerto Rican working-class roots and spectacular professional achievements. A putatively postracial climate opened a space for conservative legal commentators to engage Sotomayor's gender and racialized ethnicity in critiquing her judicial competence. For example, one conservative legal scholar commented to the New York Times, "She thinks that judges should dictate policy and that one's sex, race and ethnicity ought to affect the decisions one renders from the bench." And conservative pundits Newt Gingrich and Rush Limbaugh took the rhetoric one step further: "Mr. Gingrich, echoing the conservative commentator Rush Limbaugh, said on his blog that such a statement [Sotomayor's "Latina wisdom" remarks] would be construed as racism if it came from a white man. 'A white man racist nominee would be forced to withdraw,' he wrote. 'A Latina woman racist should also withdraw.'"[12] Such comments are illustrative of the discourse of white resentment prevalent in mainstream U.S. media since the Great Recession. In the postfeminist and postrace era where gender and racial equality is presumed to have been achieved, Sotomayor's desire to foreground and privilege her gender, Latina identity, and life experiences as important to her jurisprudence and commitment to social justice was read by political conservatives as a sign of reverse discrimination toward white men precisely during a moment of economic crisis and limited employment opportunities.

In nominating Sonia Sotomayor to the Supreme Court, Obama sought to privilege identity and biography, specifically Sotomayor's rise from her working-class immigrant youth in the Puerto Rican Bronx to her achievement of the American Dream as a nominee to the highest court in the United States. Politically, he also sought to maintain the liberal weight of the court, balance the Supreme Court's gender makeup, diversify its ethnic composition, and make history by providing high-level judicial representation for the United States' largest ethnoracial minority group. It was exactly his attempt to foreground Sotomayor's gender, ethnicity, and class in a supposedly postrace era that raised the ire of an increasingly racialized conservative U.S. movement.

In a moment of economic crisis, the publicly decontexualized foregrounding of Sotomayor's "wise Latina" comment in a community empowerment speech exemplifies U.S. political and cultural tensions over changing gender roles, shifting ethnoracial demographics, and attacks on affirmative action and other equal opportunity policies.[13] Indeed, the Supreme Court Sotomayor joined in 2009 has been characterized as one of the most conservative courts in history, consistently handing down key procorporation decisions lessening financial regulations, most notably the 2010 *Citizens United v. Federal Elections Commission* decision that provided corporations and corporate donors involved in political campaigns with First Amendment constitutional protection. Justice Sotomayor was part of the dissenting minority in that decision, and she is expected to play a significant role in Supreme Court cases currently under review.

It is within the recessionary context of the conservative reception of Sotomayor's nomination and appointment that a situation comedy featuring a Latina living with a white U.S. family must be read. As I argue elsewhere, representations of Latinas within mainstream media serve the ideological interest of a neoliberal state that economically benefits from the feminization of labor and transnational migration even as it erases that labor from popular fictional narratives.[14] Unlike the many Latina immigrants that work in the domestic service industry, Latinas in the popular media function as glamorous and commodifiable racially ambiguous and hypersexualized ethnic women. In particular, Gloria/Vergara can be commodified internationally because within global discourses about race and blackness, she is phenotypically marked as white.[15] Vergara's exotic ethnic whiteness combined with her hyperfeminine sexuality makes her more globally marketable by tapping into audiences who may identify with or occupy a multiplicity of identities—white, brown, ethnic, Latina, Colombian, immigrant, woman, mother, and so on. Her whiteness and exoticism also make her more commodifiable to nonethnic white audiences.

Contextualizing the Production and Reception of *Modern Family*

In the global neoliberal era, the white discourse of resentment is often uncritically circulated through the cultural sphere and most efficaciously produced through the interconnected gendering and racialization of Latinas/os and Latina/o immigrant bodies.[16] Lucila Vargas's study of mainstream news practices and coverage of Latinas/os illustrates that Latinos are sexualized, feminized, and racialized through the gendered verbal, visual, and narrative language of mainstream news media.[17] The gendering of Latinidad presupposes that femininity and masculinity are interconnected with class, sexuality, race, and ethnicity in a system of social signification. Mainstream media discourses of Latinas are often gendered as feminine through language about their assumed fertility, sexuality, domesticity, and subservience, among other characteristics. Gendering is interconnected with racialization as both work to create a media discourse of Latinidad as racially other, outside of both blackness and whiteness. Together, gendering and racialization produce media discourses that racialize the feminine other.

Myra Mendible writes that the gendering and racialization of Latina bodies has been central to U.S. discourses about the nation.[18] For instance, during World War II the Hollywood film industry played a pivotal role in soothing cultural and economic relations between the United States and Latin America through the production of movies supportive of Franklin D. Roosevelt's Good Neighbor Policy. By using popular Latin American actors, scholars suggest the "Good Neighbor movies" played a key financial role in U.S. colonialism and imperialism. In particular, movies produced during this era allowed Hollywood to successfully expand into Latin America during a time when European movie markets were not viable.[19] Additionally, at a moment when the United States needed military allies, introducing audiences to exotic, desirable, and safely consumable Latin American bodies and spaces became politically exigent. Good Neighbor cinema gave rise to such superstars as Carmen Miranda, Dolores del Río, and Lupé Vélez and helped establish still-dominant narrative tropes defining Latina characters such as the spitfire, the dark lady, and the señorita.

Contemporary storytelling about Latinas is equally informative about U.S. economic recession-era anxieties and influenced by this representational history. As Latino media scholars document, Latinas in the media perform a commodifiable racialized and hypersexualized femininity that reinforces whiteness and potentially disrupts white victimhood.[20] Avery Gordon and Christopher Newfield identified the backlash against civil rights in the economic recession of the 1980s as central to the postrace moment: "The backlash against civil rights achieved the greatest gains not by celebrating white racial consciousness but by officially restricting the relevance of race. It did not defend white racism but claimed that racism had passed from the scene."[21] Thus, much like postfeminist media that suggest sexism is no longer relevant to culture and policy, postrace media leave white racism critically unquestioned and conceive racial equity as unnecessary. In a postrace media context, ethnoracial difference and multiculturalism are still regulated and managed in the interests of capitalism, often through their cultural commodification. The commodification of Latino identity in postrace contemporary television programming is one such example of how ethnoracial difference remains a political and economic threat and a desirable economic and cultural commodity, a commodity that must be carefully regulated and normalized.

I read Vergara's performance of Gloria as a recession-era contemporary Latina spitfire designed to allay the anxieties of white resentment. Gloria narratively recuperates a nostalgic construction of white masculinity that draws attention away from Latina/o immigration and the effects of the recession on inequality. Simultaneously, Vergara's complex representation of Latina motherhood provides a moment of ethnoracial visibility and a narrative rupture by introducing viewers to a safe and romanticized image of "illegal immigrant motherhood" that contrasts with news images of Latina motherhood as social problem. Vergara's take on the spitfire in conjunction with her own biography presents the potential for producing a transformative representation of Latina motherhood that destabilizes the increasing hostility toward immigrants and ethnoracial minorities experienced during the recession era.

"Wise" Gloria as the Contemporary Latina Spitfire

The performances of Latina spitfire characters beginning with Lupé Vélez and Dolores Del Río's Good Neighbor films in the 1940s often focused on the comedy of errors created by intercultural miscommunication and the comedic tensions inherent in the romantic relationship between the Latina star and her white U.S. paramour. (The term was actually coined for Vélez's portrayals in a cycle of Mexican spitfire movies.)[22] Also referred to as the female clown, the ideological role of the spitfire archetype was to make foreign Latin America less threatening through humor while celebrating the potential for intercultural exchange and heterosexual romance.[23]

Vergara's Gloria combines stereotypical physicality and traditional linguis-

FIGURE 2.2. In *Modern Family*'s series premiere, Gloria (Sofía Vergara) displays the kind of brightly colored, tight-fitting, and cleavage-exposing dress that would become typical of her costuming.

tic delivery to update the Latina spitfire as safely consumable during a heightened moment of social and political hostility toward Latinas/os (figure 2.2). Whereas the Good Neighbor spitfire was meant to ease foreign relations in a time of war, Vergara's spitfire needs to manage her difference in a time of white conservative anger and backlash toward Latina/o immigration. Thus, Gloria performs a familiar ideological role as the spitfire in *Modern Family*. Her incarnation of forever-foreign difference, celebration of traditional motherhood, hypersexualized body, and self-deprecating humor constructs Vergara's character as consumable by a broad range of audiences. As a contemporary Latina spitfire she is ultimately coded as ethnically safe through her ability to serve as an intercultural bridge and comedic foil to her white upper-middle-class second husband and his family. Gloria's character hides the inequality that surrounds immigrant women and their children.

By cultivating an authentic connection between her sitcom character and her own celebrity biography, Vergara further contributes to an erasure of the experiences of Latina/o immigration. Like Gloria, Vergara divorced at an early age and emigrated with her young son from Colombia to the United States. Vergara has stated in interviews that she brings her experiences as a mother and a Colombian Latina to her television role. In an interview with *Redbook*, Vergara was asked, "There was a hilarious scene in the first season when you're at your TV son Manny's soccer game, hollering at the other parents. How much of you is in that portrayal?" Vergara responded, "A lot. Every time I get a script, I think, how would my mother or my aunt do it? And that's Gloria."[24] The character is made more authentic and presumably less racially offensive because she is seemingly grounded in the real experiences of Colombian women even though the real experiences of Colombian women look little like those of Gloria.

Vergara self-consciously acknowledges in media interviews that her performance of Gloria is equally informed by the representational legacy of the Latina spitfire.[25] She uses her Colombian identity and exaggerates her curvaceous physicality to produce moments of safe postracial humor. The physical performance of Latinidad through dominant tropes — "spicy" sexuality, curvy body, dark hair and eyes — is thus central to Vergara's spitfire depiction. Discussing her decision to change her hair color to appear more stereotypically Latina, Vergara recounts a stock story in countless media outlets:

> "But when I started acting, I would go to auditions and they didn't know where to put me because I was voluptuous and had the accent — but I had blonde hair," reports OK magazine.
>
> Changing her hair color made a world of difference in her career.
>
> The industry's response was, "'Oh, she's the hot Latin girl.' I loved it," Vergara said, reports OK Magazine.[26]

Fast-talking Gloria is often depicted wearing colorful leopard prints, low-cut shirts, and tight-fitting pants and dresses.[27] Throughout most episodes, Gloria/Vergara's large breasts and curvaceous body are on display and central to the visual spectacle. For example, her breasts actually had their own scene in the episode "Fizbo" (November 25, 2009) when Gloria decides to jump in a bouncy tent and her breasts become the center of attention, much to her husband Jay's chagrin.

Equally as important to the spitfire archetype as stereotypical physical signifiers of Latinidad is the comedic use of language. Gloria is prone to emotional outbursts delivered loudly in Spanish, a standard marker of the Latina spitfire, and is the least sexually reserved of the romantic partners on the show. Jay, the family patriarch, tiptoes around Gloria's potential emotional outbursts and generally capitulates to her demands presumably because of his romantic and sexual desire for her. Through language Gloria is further marked as different, exotic, forever an outsider. For instance, introducing herself in the series pilot (September 23, 2009), Gloria remarks in strongly accented English,

> Gloria: We're very different. Jay's from the city, he has big business. I come from a small village — very poor, but very, very beautiful. It's the number one village in all Colombia for all the . . . what's the word?

Jay: Murders.

Gloria: Yes, the murders.

Both the heavily accented "Jes" and the allusion to coming from the murder capital of Colombia reinforce Gloria's racial difference from her husband's whiteness and presumably from the program's English-speaking audiences. As Vergara emphasized in her interview on *Inside the Actors Studio* (June 9, 2011), her markedly pronounced accent on the show is key to her performance of the character. In combination with grammatical errors, mistakes in vocabulary, linguistic misunderstandings, and deadpan mockumentary delivery, it further emphasizes her foreignness and difference. The accent situates the character outside normative whiteness and positions her as a socially acceptable source of racial humor. Through the caricaturing of her Latinidad, U.S. socioeconomic racial hierarchies are maintained during a period of anxiety about the cultural influence of Latinas/os and economic scapegoating of Latina/o immigration.

Modern Family's Nostalgic Recuperation of White Male Empowerment

Indeed, the ethnoracial humor surrounding Gloria is key to her appeal to a broad audience by providing visibility (albeit stereotypical) to Latinas/os, now the largest ethnoracial minority audience in the United States, and making her safely consumable to audiences potentially resentful of Latina/o empowerment and success. Illustrating this dual appeal is the episode "The Incident" (October 14, 2009). After Jay's ex-wife Deedee (Shelley Long) convinces Jay and Gloria to invite her to their wedding, she drunkenly refers to Gloria as "Charo," the iconic 1970s spitfire, at the reception: "To the bride and the groom, my ex, thirty-five years we were together. Seriously, I knew they were perfect for each other when I saw his wallet and her boobs." Deedee's dialogue states what perhaps some series audience members are thinking. By implying that money and sex fuel the marriage, the humor underlying the dialogue assumes that there can be no other logical reason for the intercultural coupling. The dialogue and narratives surrounding Gloria often engage in an ironic type of comedic racial microaggression, in other words, subtle forms of racism that potentially demean or marginalize ethnoracial minorities through subtle implication.[28]

Indeed, much of the racial humor on *Modern Family* exemplifies an ironic type of comedic racial microaggression. In the episode "Run for Your Wife" (October 29, 2009), the narrative foregrounds and makes fun of Gloria's cultural desire to dress Manny in traditional Colombian garb. When Jay pulls Manny from class because of the outfit, Gloria's deadpan response is, "In Colombia, when we got pulled out of class, it was, you know, to identify a body." Together, these types of comedic moments humorously reinforce the racial foreignness of Latinidad and the privileged position of whiteness, especially during a moment of growing unease with Latina/o immigration in the United States.

Together the dialogue and character development in *Modern Family* commodify Gloria/Vergara as sexually desirable yet always foreign to the family and the nation. By turning her difference into a source of racial humor, she stabilizes white masculinity and heterosexuality. She is regularly disciplined as an outsider to whiteness and this makes *Modern Family* ideologically safe to consume during a moment of heightened racial and economic anxiety in the United States. Gloria's physicality, sexuality, and language consistently reinforce her difference from the other characters. At the same time, Vergara's contemporary performance of the Latin spitfire makes Gloria familiar and nonthreatening. Lupé Vélez, Dolores del Río, Carmen Miranda, Charo, Rosie Perez, Salma Hayek — U.S. audiences have been watching characters like Vergara's Gloria since the 1940s.

In stark contrast to news coverage of Sotomayor, *Modern Family*'s commodification of Gloria/Vergara depoliticizes the symbolic labor of Latina visibility within the cultural sphere during a period of heightened white male economic resentment and nativist backlash against Latin American immigration. Situated within a neo-Marxist framework, the process of cultural commodification makes invisible the exploitative social and labor relations that produce the commodity.[29] Applying Marx to discussions of communication, Vince Mosco argues that the value of media commodities in the global marketplace must then be understood in terms of the ideological needs and desires the commodity fulfills as well as its ability to maximize profits.[30] In the case of Latinidad, much like the phenomenon that surrounds the commodification of black culture, it is the authentic production of an exotic but desirable difference that fulfills ideological and economic demands.[31]

Sometimes the humor surrounding Gloria's character satirically critiques racism. Other times it undercuts the transformative potential of Latina visibility. Gloria's financial dependence on her second much-older husband to maintain her upper-middle-class lifestyle and access to the American Dream positions her as a "good minority" and nonthreatening foreigner. By placing a Latina immigrant in an economically subservient role in a heteronormative white middle-class home, *Modern Family* humorously reframes discourses of white male disempowerment by satirizing ethnic and female enfranchisement. Gloria, like the other housewives and partners in *Modern Family*, does not seek to compete economically with other men or women for work outside the home. Her character privileges the nostalgic heteronormative life and values of familial domesticity, particularly her traditional desire to be a nurturing mother and wife. Despite representations of Gloria's unique Colombian traditions and social relationships with gays and lesbians, the narratives of the show always conclude by recuperating the normative and nostalgic values of whiteness and U.S. heterosexual family life.

The upper-middle-class comfort surrounding Gloria cultivates magical thinking about the status of Latinas/os during the recession era and eases potential audience discomfort with the intergenerational, interethnic marriage, while eliding the social and economic challenges that characterize Latina motherhood and immigrant life in the United States. Given that Colombians make up only 1.9 percent of the U.S. Latina/o population, with 64.9 percent of Latina/o immigrants of Mexican origin, the decision to cast a Colombian woman in the role shifts representational attention from the journalistic focus on Mexicans and Mexican immigration in the U.S. news—the Latina/o ethnic group that has borne the brunt of anti-immigration sentiments.[32] Because the population of Colombians in the United States is relatively small, potential Latina/o audience backlash against the program's racial microaggression is minimized. At the same time, Gloria's Colombian, as opposed to Mexican, identity enhances her exoticism. Finally, the affluence in which Gloria and her son live makes it possible for U.S. audiences to ignore the circumstances facing some immigrant Latina mothers and their children. One of the continuing effects of the Great Recession is that Latina/o household wealth has declined. Additionally, the overall rates of unemployment for women have increased while men's have declined since the slow economic recovery began in 2010.[33] Not surprisingly, Latina-headed households have correlated strongly with increased childhood poverty during this period.[34] Additionally, according to the Pew Hispanic Center, 67 percent of poor Latina/o children live with an immigrant parent.[35] Thus, Gloria's marriage into upper-middle-class whiteness contributes to a symbolic environment where audiences do not have to think about the dire conditions facing more than 6.1 million Latina/o children and families.

According to the U.S. Census, those mothers who stay at home tend to be younger, Latina, and immigrant, living with a preschool child and less likely to hold a high school diploma—the very profile of Gloria Pritchett and the very profile of Latino families living in poverty. Ironically, Gloria, who lacks a college education, who came to the United States as an undocumented immigrant and who raised her son as a working-class single mother, is most realistic in terms of recession-era U.S. demographics even while the character is deployed in the service of maintaining a nostalgic return to white middle-class normativity.[36] U.S. Census figures in 2011 reported that just 5 million U.S. women out of more than 97 million over the age of eighteen (23 percent of the population of married women) were stay-at-home mothers.[37] Compared to the 44 percent of married women who stayed at home in 1969, this is a sharp and significant drop underscoring the extent to which stay-at-home mothers are now a minority and further enhancing the magical thinking of *Modern Family*.[38] The demographic shift in U.S. family life is attributed to the increase of white women college graduates, the decision by educated white women to delay or forgo marriage and childbirth, and the contemporary economic demands of dual-income households with children.[39]

Although most U.S. women are not married and do not stay at home with their children, the domestic partners on *Modern Family* do. I raise these demographic statistics not to critique the realism or factuality of an entertainment show, but to illustrate the program's ideological message. Part of the charm of *Modern Family* is that its racial and gender elements are not that modern at all. Its women/mothers remain financially dependent on their husbands at a time when few traditional heterosexual families can afford to rely on one income. Furthermore, it romanticizes Latina motherhood during a moment when Latina mothers and children are structurally facing poverty in greater historical numbers. *Modern Family* nostalgically returns to a bygone era when white men were the financial providers of the middle-class family. In doing so, the program allows its racial and gender/sexual transgressions, which consist of a gay married couple, a May–December romance, and an unruly Latina spitfire, to remain unthreatening to white masculinity even as popular discourses reinforce the claim that white masculinity is under threat.

While Jay, Phil, and Mitchell are the financial providers and paternal nurturers of their children, Cameron, Gloria, and Claire privilege feminine and maternal wisdom and safely rule the private domain of family life. For example, the relationship between Claire and Phil is defined by her level headedness and Phil's constant desire to break or change the domestic rules. Comedy in Phil and Claire's relationship is based on the unexpected, sometimes beneficial, consequences of Phil's zany actions and Claire's maternal redress. Similarly, Gloria and Jay's relationship is often characterized by Jay's desire to be a better father and husband and Gloria's innately wise tutelage. For instance, in the episode "Fifteen Percent" (January 20, 2010), Gloria convinces Jay that he must illustrate to Mitchell his comfort with gay sexuality by reaching out to a friend his son mischievously convinces Jay is gay. Although the friend turns out not to be gay, Jay's attempt to heed Gloria's council is indicative of her good influence and Jay's desire to be a better father. Gloria can deploy her Latina wisdom in an unthreatening way as long as she also maintains and reinforces the privileged status of whiteness and white masculinity.

While the gender relationships at play in the storylines do at times challenge the balance of power in the heterosexual marriages—ornery Jay capitulates to Gloria's desires; level-headed Claire must come to Phil's rescue—the normative patriarchal order is always reaffirmed. Regardless of the modern issues raised in the episodes—new technology as a family distraction, gay transcultural adoption, ex-spouses crashing family events—the normative structure of the family is reinforced. For instance, although a gay family is depicted, the couple rarely engages in displays of physical affection and the program's episodes usually foreground the domestic conventionality of the gay marriage between Mitchell and Cameron. In the second season, the lack of physical contact between the couple actually became the theme of "The Kiss" (September 29, 2010) when Gloria and Jay's children blame him for never displaying affection. Jay resists taking responsibility for Mitchell's problem, yet the episode concludes with Jay's closing voice-over reflection on wanting to be a better father as the program shows him sneaking into his stepson's bedroom to give him a goodnight kiss. Even though Jay, the patriarch, may have to modify his behavior and engage in intercultural compromises, *Modern Family*'s episodes usually close with a sympathetic celebration of the normative values of the Pritchett's extended family. For example, the Christmas episode "Undeck the Halls" (December 9, 2009), in which tensions arise between Manny, Gloria, and Jay over which cultural traditions will be celebrated, concludes with images of the extended family celebrating Christmas as Jay's voice-over reflects: "Sometimes the best memories are the most untraditional. This is the year the word 'tradition' got a lot bigger."

Given the show's nostalgic reification of white masculine authority and normative family life, Vergara's spitfire character and the postracial imagining of her ethnic identity become significant elements for understanding the constraints surrounding Latina representations in an era of heightened resentments. A fused Gloria/Vergara persona is consumable because of the efficacious gendering and racialization of Latina immigrant bodies in mainstream culture.[40] Gloria as a highly feminine, sexual, domestic, middle-class, and financially dependent Latina cannot meaningfully destabilize the dominant anti-Latino immigration discourse. She is thus both racialized and gendered as the feminized, foreign, but desirable ethnoracial other. Her gender and ethnic difference simultaneously foregrounds the normative whiteness of the extended family and is assimilated within the overall narrative as not completely dissimilar to the other characters. After all, they might celebrate Christmas in Colombia by playing practical jokes on family members, but the important lesson is that they still celebrate Christmas at home with their extended families. Gloria remains the source of postracial humor grounded in microaggressions and it is that humor that reinforces the centrality of whiteness.

Gloria's Wisdom as Symbolic Rupture in *Modern Family*

One primary site of rupture between stereotypical media narratives of Latinidad and Vergara's depiction of the spitfire is founded on *Modern Family*'s negotiations of Gloria's undocumented immigrant past and her maternal devotion to her son. Throughout the series Gloria's past is evoked as a significant marker of her difference and a complex source of comedy. Gloria/Vergara's beauty, sexuality, class position, and maternal demeanor protect the character and the actress from the virulent anti-immigrant Latino rhetoric that surrounded Sotomayor's nomination and recession-era debates over the role of the federal government in the social safety net. The racial microaggressions that define the comedic treatment of Gloria's undocumented immigrant past function as a safe source of humor for audiences who might be critical of Latino immigration. For instance, speaking to his stepson Manny about his biological father on the episode "The Bicycle Thief" (September 30, 2009), Jay makes the following comparison: "The only way he's like Superman is that they both landed in this country illegally." Foregrounding the association of illegal immigration with Latin American illegality makes the political situation of citizenship for Latino immigrants a socially acceptable source of racialized humor, a comedic racial microaggression.

Nevertheless, the comedic invocation of Gloria's undocumented status and Colombian identity smartly critique Eurocentric anti-immigrant discourse by drawing attention to the complexities of citizenship and usage of the word "alien." For some audiences, Jay's comment serves as a subtle reminder of the irrational anti-immigration fervor that has swept across the United States since the global recession began. For other audiences, Gloria and the humor that surrounds her is a subtle reminder of the estimated 11 million undocumented Latinos under attack by anti-immigration laws in Georgia, Arizona, and Indiana, among other states.[41] Much like other mockumentary programs such as *The Office*, *Modern Family* draws upon ethnicity, race, and anti-immigrant discourse in ambiguous ways that can be read as either a racist microaggression or a critique depending on viewer positionality.

Other ethnic women on *Modern Family* are written through a similar comedic strategy. For instance, Mitchell and Cameron's assimilated Vietnamese pediatrician becomes a foil for poking fun at the couple's desire to be ethnically sensitive for the sake of their adopted Vietnamese daughter. When ethnicity is explicitly invoked, it is often in a passing reference to domestic help such as maids and gardeners. Such references potentially work to rupture the show's dominant discourse of nostalgic whiteness. In "Up All Night" (January 6, 2010), Phil and Claire's son Luke finally admits that he was the one who broke the coffee table that resulted in "Esperanza's getting fired and getting deported." His parents' practice of hiring undocumented domestic labor and their guilty response to Luke's confession is visible yet never verbally articulated. The silent dismissal of the ways in which their white middle-class family benefits from such labor signals the inequitable power dynamics that increasingly define U.S. racial and economic life and differentially benefit white middle-class families. For the most part, Asian and Latino ethnicities are part of the comedic background evoked primarily to naturalize the whiteness and white privilege of *Modern Family*'s characters.

Nevertheless, the caricaturing of Gloria's ethnicity and its racialized linkage to immigration are always in the background threatening to disrupt the discourse of white privilege by calling out its racism. From the first season, three episodes in particular demonstrate this type of discursive rupture: "The Incident," "Not in My House" (January 13, 2010), and "Starry Night" (March 24, 2010) explicitly challenge the white privilege of the family and call attention to the implicit prejudice that often underlies the racialized humor on *Modern Family*. In this final section, I focus on Gloria's Latina wisdom and the program's potential challenge to dominant discourses of nostalgic whiteness in the recession era of white resentment.

Cameron and Mitchell often position themselves as the more racially enlightened and socially just of the series' couples. And they are also the couple most explicitly forced to confront their white privilege and stereotypical assumptions about ethnicity and race. In "Not in My House" and "Starry Night," their racial sensitivity or insensitivity becomes the source of humor. "Not in My House" finds Cameron and Mitchell conflicted about how to respond to their extremely emotionally upset gardener, who does not speak English and is crying uncontrollably in their home. In an effort at kindness and a social rebuke to his partner, Cameron attempts to ask the gardener in broken Spanish if he would like to have a glass of water: "I just asked him if he wanted to have a glass of water and sit down for a minute like any kind person would." What Cameron actually says in Spanish is, "Would you like to make water and have our bed?" After realizing that Cameron has failed to communicate effectively in Spanish, Mitchell decides to call upon Gloria.

Always the wise and loving mother, Gloria is often called into family situations to resolve them. In this case, she uses her Spanish to figure out that the gardener was supposed to be married that day, and she helps the man, whose name the audience never learns, to reconcile with his fiancé and her family. After Gloria's intervention, Cameron and Mitchell invite him to hold his wedding at their home. During the wedding, Mitchell bitterly remarks to his father, "Because of him [Cameron], I have a house full of Latinos." To which Jay responds, "Welcome to my world." The assumption underlying both statements is that there is something inappropriate or distasteful in sharing a domestic space with Latinos, even the ones you marry. While Jay the patriarch never pretends to be racially enlightened—indeed, his nickname for his Vietnamese granddaughter Lily is "fortune cookie"—the gay couple's position as more racially educated is called into question, and it is the prejudice of the sexual minorities on the show, not the heterosexual white male, that is highlighted. Mitchell's whiteness and privileged class status is critiqued through his flawed interaction with his domestic help and his response to his home being "invaded" by Latinos.

Cameron, who presents himself as more racially sensitive than his partner, is similarly challenged in "Starry Night." After inadvertently racially offending Gloria at a family party, Cameron, who is unsure how Gloria feels about gay people, decides to make peace with her by inviting her to spend a night out with him. Their plans to eat at an exclusive restaurant are foiled and Gloria convinces Cameron to go to her favorite restaurant in a working-class Colombian neighborhood of Los Angeles. While there, Gloria reminisces about her days as an economically struggling, divorced, single mother and attempts to make her son-in-law feel comfortable. Cameron, who is trying hard not to offend Gloria, is clearly anxious about being in a space so foreign and unfamiliar to him. When they walk out to Cameron's vandalized car, he freaks out when Gloria starts yelling and threatening the person who committed the crime. They bond over their evening together, with Gloria confessing how much she misses spending time with gay men and Cameron realizing how little he really knows about the complexity of Gloria's life history.

That the critique of whiteness and white racism have to occur through the bodies and lives of white gay men is as interesting as the role Gloria performs as the peacemaker, the domestic nurturer, the truly wise one. For instance, in "Starry Night" Gloria pushes Jay to be a more accepting and nurturing father to his biological children and stepson. And she ends up being more complex and socially enlightened than Cameron. While Cameron is uncomfortable in Gloria's working-class Colombian neighborhood and is not confident about how to relate to her, she seamlessly moves between the white middle-class world she currently inhabits and the working-class immigrant space she once lived in. In the end, not only is Gloria accepting of gay men, she confesses she prefers the less sexually complicated friendship they provide. Through her actions, she teaches Jay to be comfortable with a less traditional definition of white masculinity and Cameron to question his stereotypical assumptions about Latinos.

Though Gloria is an archetypical Latina spitfire character, she is also a nuanced representation of Latinidad. As the unconditionally loving mother, she deviates from the traditional spitfire. Moreover, as an undocumented Colombian immigrant who leaves an emotionally abusive marriage to stake out a better life for her son, her character's life experiences provide comedic grist to critique the racial and class privilege of the white characters. Whatever disasters or conflicts the other couples are coping with, Gloria's interjections allude to far more serious incidents from her past, such as the comment about being pulled out of class to identify dead bodies. The gay couple is not as racially conscious as they assume themselves to be, but ethnic working-class Gloria is sexually progressive. Claire privileges her authority as the professional mother, but it is often Gloria who pragmatically solves the current family dilemma through her commonsense ethnic wisdom. Her nostalgic memories of a more difficult past provide nuance to Vergara's depiction of Gloria. Vergara's representation of the spitfire reminds audiences that Latino lives are compelling and multidimensional. Her performance thus opens up a space of unprecedented visibility and the potential for representational dignity during a moment of economic angst, racial backlash, and affirmation of the liberal ideology of a postrace neoliberal state.

Conclusion

Gloria's life experiences make her wise, but her wisdom must always be mitigated. Because her character functions as the racial straight woman to the white characters, the symbolic power of Gloria's character is inevitably contained. Consequently, *Modern Family* both reaffirms and ruptures contemporary narratives of feminine Latinidad in the global recession era in significant and telling ways. Latina bodies are narratively safe when they perform the role of domestic nurturers stabilizing the heteronormative family unit and soothing the sexual and economic needs of white heterosexual masculinity. As the editors of this volume argue, global recession-era media narratives consistently rearticulate traditional conceptualizations of both femininity and masculinity. At its best, *Modern Family* provides a sympathetic narrative of single-motherhood poverty and the economic and social vulnerability of women immigrants. At its worst, the series engages in a "gendered rhetoric of power, success, family and community membership" (see introduction) that produces racial humor grounded in microaggressions and romanticizes the economic and cultural role of Latinas as domestic nurturers. Situating ethno-racial minority women in the middle-class home, *Modern Family* humorously reframes discourses of white male disempowerment while containing female enfranchisement. Thus, the series becomes a significant text for understanding media management of ethnic femininity in the era of discursive resentment; its efficacious circulation through the interconnected gendering and racialization of Latina immigrant bodies offers one mode of response to the tensions and pressures that subtend economic austerity.[42]

My analysis suggests that Gloria's comedic function and commodifiability is grounded in the historical tradition of the Latin American spitfire. Unlike Sonia Sotomayor, Gloria/Vergara is consumable and socially acceptable because of her hypersexualized, always foreign, at times cartoonish performance of gendered ethnic identity. Yet any Latina visibility in the context of broader cultural invisibility presents opportunities to create ruptures in the dominant discourse about gender and ethnicity. Vergara's nuanced performance of the Latina spitfire, of a former undocumented single mother, produces such a potentially transformative moment.

Notes

1. For up-to-date ratings information, see "TV by the Numbers," Zap2it, http://tvbythenumbers.zap2it.com, retrieved June 13, 2011.

2. McCarthy and Dimitriadis, "Govermentality and the Sociology of Education."

3. For more information, see Kochhar, "The Demographics of the Jobs Recovery."

4. Esposito, "What Does Race Have to Do with *Ugly Betty*?," 521.

5. I use the terms Latina, Latino, and Latina/o to refer to the general population of Mexican, Latin American, and Spanish Caribbean people living in the United States. My use of the label acknowledges that each ethnic or national group has a unique and specific set of historical experiences and contemporary trajectories and at the same time recognizes the shared experiences of racialized prejudice, class oppression, and linguistic discrimination. I refer to characters, actors, and news figures with ethnic-specific labels such as Puerto Rican, Mexican, Chicana/o, and Euro-Spanish when it is particular to the analysis. While I recognize the great diversity within each category, non-Latina/o populations in the United States are referenced through racial labels such as black and white or ethnic labels such as Asian, African, and Italian.

6. For examples of conservative blog coverage of the nomination, see Matrix, "Obama Appoints a Stone Cold Racist to US Supreme Court"; and Weigel, "Sotomayor, Enemy of the White Male."

7. Sotomayor, "A Latina Judge's Voice."

8. National Institute of Justice, "Research Briefing."

9. Georgia Department of Labor, "Georgia Men Hit Hardest by Recession."

10. Cauchon, "Tough Times for Older Male Workers."

11. For U.S. unemployment statistics, see U.S. Department of Labor statistics retrieved from Bureau of Labor Statistics, "Labor Force Statistics from the Current Population Survey," http://data.bls.gov/timeseries/LNS14000000, April 10, 2012.

12. Baker and Zeleny, "Obama Chooses Hispanic Judge for Supreme Court Seat." Stolberg, "Sotomayor's Opponents and Allies Prepare Strategies."

13. For a discussion of race during the Obama presidency, see Wanzer, "Barack Obama, the Tea Party, and the Threat of Race."

14. Molina-Guzmán, *Dangerous Curves.*

15. Clark and Thomas, *Globalization and Race.*

16. Molina-Guzmán "Gendering Latinidad in the Elián News Discourse about Cuban Women"; Vargas, "Genderizing Latino News."

17. Vargas, "Genderizing Latino News."

18. Mendible, "Introduction."

19. Mendible, "Introduction"; López, "Are All Latins from Manhattan?"

20. See Aparicio, "Jennifer as Selena"; Báez, "Speaking of Jennifer Lopez"; Beltrán, *Latina/o Stars in U.S. Eyes*; Cepeda, *Musical ImagiNation*; Fregoso, *MeXicana Encounters*; Habell-Pallán, *Loca Motion*; Habell-Pallán and Romero, eds., *Latino/a Popular Culture*; Molina-Guzmán, "Mediating Frida"; Molina-Guzmán and Valdivia, "Brain, Brow or Bootie"; Negrón-Muntaner, *Boricua Pop*; Valdivia, *Latina/o Communication Studies Today*; Molina-Guzmán, *Dangerous Curves.*

21. Gordon and Newfield, "Introduction," 3.

22. Ramirez Berg, *Latino Images in Film.*

23. Ramirez Berg, *Latino Images in Film.*

24. Dunn, "Sofia Vergara Spills All."

25. Dunn, "Sofia Vergara Spills All."

26. "Ellen to Sofia Vergara."

27. It is a physical typecasting also resonant with working-class femininity and perhaps a nod to Peggy Bundy's (Katey Sagal) performance of motherhood in the 1990s recession-era *Married with Children*, the series that starred *Modern Family's* Ed O'Neill.

28. Sue et al., "Racial Microaggressions in Everyday Life."

29. Marx, *Das Kapital*, 320–31.

30. Mosco, *The Political Economy of Communication.*

31. Molina-Guzmán, "Salma Hayek's Celebrity Activism."

32. Mothel and Patten, "Hispanics of Colombian Origin in the United States, 2010."

33. Kochar, "A Recovery No Better Than the Recession."

34. Lopez and Velasco, "The Toll of the Great Recession."

35. Lopez and Velasco, "The Toll of the Great Recession."

36. See United States Census Bureau, "Mother's Day."

37. For statistical information regarding mothers and the prevalence of stay-at-home mothers, see United States Census Bureau, "Mother's Day"; Krieder and Elliot, "Historical Changes in Stay-at-Home Mothers."

38. See Krieder and Elliot, "Historical Changes in Stay-at-Home Mothers."

39. See Krieder and Elliot, "Historical Changes in Stay-at-Home Mothers."

40. Molina-Guzmán, "Gendering Latinidad in the Elián News Discourse about Cuban Women"; Vargas, "Genderizing Latino News."

41. Passel, Cohn, and Gonzaléz-Barrera, "Net Migration from Mexico Falls to Zero."

42. Molina-Guzmán, "Gendering Latinidad in the Elián News Discourse about Cuban Women"; Vargas, "Genderizing Latino News."

THREE   SARAH BANET-WEISER

"We Are All Workers"

ECONOMIC CRISIS, MASCULINITY, AND THE AMERICAN WORKING CLASS

Folk and rock icon Bruce Springsteen has spent much of his career writing about Americans' struggles with economic justice. His blue-collar aesthetic has resonated with a large swath of American culture, with signature songs such as "Born in the U.S.A." and "Nebraska" critiquing and questioning the politics of class in the United States. Amid the global economic crisis, he created the album *Wrecking Ball*, which, with its inclusion of songs such as "Death to Our Hometown" ("They destroyed our families' factories and they took our homes. . . . The vultures picked our bones") is unmistakably dedicated to documenting the ravages of contemporary global capitalism and corporate greed.[1] When asked about the anger that seems to emanate from this album, Springsteen replied, "I think our politics come out of psychology. And psychology of course comes out of your formative years. I grew up in a house where my mother was the primary breadwinner, and my father struggled to find work. I saw that that was deeply painful, and created a crisis of masculinity, let's say. And that was something that was unreparable. Lack of work creates a loss of self. Work creates an enormous sense of self."[2]

Taking Springsteen's comments about the connections between work, labor, and a crisis of masculinity as a starting point, in this essay I look to contemporary advertising's use of the theme of work to explore the gendering of the current recession. Work, as Springsteen points out, powerfully signals the deep connections and interrelations between national identity and masculine identity; indeed, according to one reviewer, Springsteen's *Wrecking Ball* "is a melodic indictment of the recessionary moment, of income disparity, emasculated workers, and what [Springsteen] calls 'the distance between the American reality and the American dream.'"[3] Work is not only the (material and symbolic) center of the current global economic crisis, and concomitant rapidly accelerating unemployment rates, home loan foreclosures, and more general deindustrialization and declining value of real wages; it also centers the figuring of traditional American male identity as the primary breadwinner in an imagined heteronormative family (indeed, the fact that Springsteen's father was not the breadwinner is ostensibly the cause of his personal masculinity crisis). In this way, Springsteen uses narratives about masculinity and work as analytic prisms through which to understand his own history and to problematize other identities (including corporate identity).

Of course, a rock album is only one mode of response to or expression of the economic recession and its wide-ranging impacts. The effects of what has unfolded as global economic crisis have been vast and varied: the collapse of the U.S. subprime mortgage market and the reversal of the housing boom in other industrialized economies has had a ripple effect in other nations, and the failure of the national economies of Spain and Greece (to name just two) has had resounding effects on the European Union and global trade. Because capitalism circulates in culture in varied ways, there are different responses to the current global economic crisis, including economic, national, and cultural responses. Springsteen's album is one form of cultural response; another (in the United States and elsewhere) has been to stage the crisis as a kind of "media event."[4] As Daniel Dayan and Elihu Katz have argued, media events are those historic events that are broadcast through the media as they are happening, as a kind of world ritual, what they call "high holidays of mass communication."[5] The ongoing global economic crisis takes shape as a media event in a variety of ways: through staged debates on television, pundits arguing over the causes of the crisis, and hysterical "shock jocks" on talk radio placing blame on liberal politics, among others.[6] Here, I do not attempt to explain the varied causes of the global economic crisis, or to forecast its lasting effects. Indeed, it is impossible to predict long-term effects, for the responses by different nation-states to the global crisis have been so varied, and because the crisis is yet unfolding in many places around the globe, with most nations still in the process of responding, restructuring, and politically reorganizing. The shape of the consequences of the global recession remains unclear. What is more clear is that the economic crisis and its aftermaths demonstrate the social economist Viviana Zelizer's important point that economic exchange is organized by cultural meanings.[7]

However, contemporary culture also comes at this dynamic from the opposite direction: cultural meanings are organized by economic exchange. The culture of the economy, and the economy of culture, have generated a variety of impulses and reactions to the Great Recession of the early twenty-first century: there have been financial responses in the form of government bailouts; subversive challenges to capitalism in terms of alternative economies; ideological proclamations about what capitalism is and should be; recuperative answers that privilege a new, leaner, global market; and yet another kind of an (ongoing) masculinity crisis in terms of American workers.[8] Here, I am interested in how the cultural and gendered meanings of the economic crisis are organized by the economic practice of advertising. In particular, I am interested in how advertising works to brand the crisis as an inevitable obstacle in the progressive march of capitalism, one that individuals, especially men, are asked to overcome in order to fulfill their obligation to both morality and the nation. While I take a somewhat narrow approach, analyzing one specific corporate ad campaign, the branding strategies employed by this campaign rely on a broader crisis trope, one that encapsulates culture beyond crisis but is still enmeshed in the ongoing impact of recession by using a recuperative, capital-friendly narrative to mobilize and authorize American working-class men to deal with the crisis individually, rather than call a flawed capitalist structure into question. Rhetorics of hope, meritocracy, and new frontiers are used to frame the ads in this campaign and thus maintain a narrative of American liberal masculine exceptionalism as well as a neoliberal mandate for individuals to "take care of themselves."[9]

More specifically, the ads I analyze position America as broken by the global economic crisis. Yet this same malfunction is also framed by these ads as a unique, and perhaps even destined, experience of Americanness; through powerful visual and textual narratives, the ads conceive U.S. corporate culture as offering the means for individuals, especially men, to rescue the broken nation.[10] This is, of course, a very different sort of broken America than the one Springsteen references—and the ways in which the United States can be symbolically fixed in these advertisements are also different from the solutions Springsteen recommends. Unlike the scathing indictment of corporate America found in Springsteen's lyrics, the broken America referenced by advertising is one that can only be fixed by a reinvestment in consumer capitalism. Indeed, the cases I examine offer particularly clear examples of the ways in which corporate brands may attempt to reconcile their contradictory positions through the reconfiguration of classic American tropes with a contemporary neoliberal, masculine twist.

Contemporary Brand Culture and Advertising

Contemporary brand culture is not a consequence of the current global economic crisis. To the contrary, branding and brand strategies have influenced liberal and post-Fordist capitalism for decades. As a key component of branding, advertising also has a central role in establishing a narrative, as well as a relationship between corporate culture and consumers, that assists individuals in interpreting the world economic crisis through a national frame. Clearly, advertising consists of more than discrete media artifacts, and is more than simply an economic tool for selling products.[11] Advertising is a social and cultural system; it is part of what Raymond Williams defined as a "structure of feeling," an ethos of intangible qualities that resonate in different ways with distinct communities.[12] As a social and cultural system, advertising and branding help to create this intangible ethos that resonates in affective, emotional ways for a variety of citizens. But branding is also part of what Ruth Wilson Gilmore calls an "infrastructure of feeling," a broader, more diffused environment that undergirds, legitimates, and authorizes capitalist circuits of economic and cultural exchange.[13]

As I have argued elsewhere, branding became a specifically cultural phenomenon in the United States in the 1980s.[14] During that time, corporations and businesses began to concentrate less on manufacturing and more on the marketing of goods; labor began to be outsourced from the United States in significant numbers; and branding began to take on a heightened economic significance and cultural value, as Naomi Klein has argued.[15] Within advanced capitalism, brand strategies and management are situated not merely as economic principles or good business, but as the affective stuff of culture. Thus, within neoliberal capitalism, those realms of culture and society once considered outside the official economy are harnessed, reshaped, and made legible in economic—and cultural—terms.[16] One result of neoliberal practices has been the reimagining of not just economic transactions and resources, but also practices and institutions such as social relations, individual relations, emotion, social action, and culture itself. Among other things, neoliberalism, like liberalism, privileges a free-market ideology and focuses on the individual at the expense of social and public services.

Rather than inserting brands into existing culture, then, contemporary brand managers seek to build culture around brands through emotive, affective relationships. Within brand culture, consumers produce identity, community, emotional attachments, affective practices, and relationships; brand culture within neoliberal capitalism provides an infrastructure for this kind of social and political behavior. For marketers in the contemporary United

States, building a brand is about building an affective, authentic relationship with a consumer, one based on a set of memories, emotions, personal narratives, and expectations. Given the affective involvement in branding, when some of the biggest brands failed in the global economic collapse, it is not surprising that eventually an effort to rebrand, and thus rebuild, corporate culture would take place.

Thus, while U.S. press accounts breathlessly proclaimed the death of capitalism in the wake of 2008, I analyze an American advertising campaign as a method of unpacking the ways in which some U.S. companies did not, in fact, celebrate the death of capitalism in the least.[17] Rather, advertising can be put to work to brand the crisis in such a way as to obscure some of the lasting ravages of capitalist power on individual and collective subjectivities. The campaign I examine, the Levi Strauss clothing company's *Go Forth* advertisements from 2010–11, operates in a strong affective register, establishing a relationship between consumers and corporations as a media assemblage, a cohering force, in the chaos and uncertainty that accompany global economic crisis.[18] Specifically, this campaign works to brand the economic crisis as a moment of individual opportunity, because authorizing capitalist circuits of exchange is critical in moments of capitalist failure. The campaign, that is, does not address the broader issues that caused an economic recession in the first place. Rather, through lush, creative visuals and stirring soundtracks, the themes of the campaign abstractly focus on hard work, persistence, national identity, recuperation, and masculinity through a series of ads that emphasize rebuilding and revitalizing cities, individualism, and what Levi's calls "real workers." These themes are represented in a nostalgic focus on Rust Belt cities in the United States, some of the hardest-hit locales of the global economic crisis, and position the masculine subject in this landscape as a recuperative hero, an entrepreneurial subject who can liberate capitalism from its crisis.[19]

Historically, advertising has had a crucial role in nation-building, through its reassuring messages to citizens that consumption not only should be a habit but is more profoundly a national duty.[20] In the contemporary moment, advertising continues to create narratives that work to validate and confirm the nation and national identity. But in the aftermath of the global economic crisis, advertising, as well as other strategies such as corporate public relations and marketing campaigns, go a step further and brand the crisis for consumers. Indeed, the efforts of contemporary U.S. corporations to brand the crisis as an opportunity for American workers renders the global economic crisis culturally consumable. To do this effectively, Levi's focuses its campaign on a masculinist, nostalgic discourse of the authenticity of the self-made man.

The Levi's campaign thus narratively accounts for the Great Recession in abstract terms, placing no specific blame on any one entity, but rather centralizing a normative masculine subject in a generalized narrative of recession. The ads I examine offer a narrative of how the nation and particularly its masculine citizens need to overcome crisis. The Great Recession has witnessed ongoing shifts in the legitimacy of the liberal welfare state, as well as the coincident turn in attitudes toward social and redistributive programs hitherto managed and administered by the state, which raises troubling questions about the merits and meaning of the nation-state, globalization, and the consumer-citizen in the current era.[21] One space that authorizes a specific role for the consumer-citizen as a nation builder is advertising; as a space of affect, of sentiment, of feeling, advertising provides reassurance in the face of troubling questions.

Among other things, some of those troubling questions involve the failure of brands. For many Americans, the failure of the Big Three automobile manufacturers (Chrysler, General Motors, and Ford) and banks such as Lehman Brothers and Goldman Sachs represented not simply the financial failure of companies but, more diffusely, the failure of brands with which individuals trusted their lives and their livelihoods (and indeed, the failure of these brands is ongoing, as five years after their collapse, they still have not regained the trust of investors and citizens, although they have been slowly rebuilding). For brands, then, as with banks, the job becomes how to rebuild trust. This means, in part, imagining a powerful narrative to salvage the brand's constitutive story. It also means positioning the individual as a shifted central character in the story of the brand. Rather than calling attention to larger infrastructural failures that contributed to the global economic crisis (such as mortgage fraud, corporate greed, and so on), contemporary efforts to brand the crisis frame it as an opportunity for—indeed, a moral obligation of—the individual worker to address.[22] Importantly, the maintenance of bank brands is deeply interrelated with a particular representation of American masculinity, where individual financial success and economic prowess have historically been crucial in terms of maintaining identity.

Representations of hegemonic masculinity, found in popular, political, and cultural forms, are deeply imbricated in economic and financial discourse. The normative idea of a man as breadwinner in a family is only one manifestation of this interrelation; the manly blue-collar worker is often also invoked as an authentic expression of American national identity. Consider, for example, the iconic masculine representation associated with Marlboro cigarettes, the Marlboro Man. As Marita Sturken and Lisa Cartwright have remarked, Marlboro advertisements featuring the Marlboro Man "connote rugged individualism and life on the American frontier, when men were 'real'" men. The Marlboro Man embodies a romantic ideal of freedom that stands in contrast to the more confined lives of most everyday working people."[23] It is no surprise, then, that the resurgence in bank branding in the twenty-first century is connected to an ongoing maintenance of representations of hegemonic masculinity. In the contemporary moment, recentering the individual masculine citizen's role in the nation via a brand narrative is one way to reassert cultural control over an otherwise destabilizing crisis.

The ready legibility and familiarity of tropes of hegemonic masculinity in ads offers a certainty to the brand narrative, therefore guaranteeing the brand story. That is, because advertising is the language of an increasingly normative and pervasive culture of consumption, ads are a particularly rich and central vehicle through which to create and maintain brand narratives about both the economy and masculinity.[24] As Michael Schudson has said about the role of advertising in the United States, advertising is "capitalism's way of saying 'I love you' to itself."[25] But when capitalism has failed, and the world is in economic crisis, how is this love regained, reimagined, rethought?

As a way to address such questions, here I look at specific strategies that have worked to rebrand corporate culture, and have in turn worked to brand the crisis itself. Rather than examining the hegemonic behemoths that were so visibly at the center of the crisis, such as the banks, the International Monetary Fund, and so on, I look at one U.S. space that was hit hard by the financial crisis: the Rust Belt industrial towns in the northeastern United States. Using nostalgic, jingoistic representations and rhetoric, the Levi's clothing brand has launched new campaigns that feature the Rust Belt industrial town and brand the crisis as a space of possibility for these towns — the possibility for a new frontier, represented by Levi's.

To argue that branding attempts to create relationships with consumers is not in turn to insist that advertising, as a component of branding, works to persuade individuals to buy particular products. The Levi's campaign, for instance, is not striking for its success in selling more jeans. Rather, it is effective for the ways in which it establishes an affective relationship with consumers, one that brands the economic crisis as a problem, indeed, an inevitable consequence, of entrepreneurial individualism. Not merely an economic strategy of capitalism, brands such as Levi's establish an emotional relationship with consumers, where individuals feel safe, secure, relevant, and authentic, and seek to build generalized communities rather than immediate commercial returns. In this way, the exceptional longevity of the Levi's brand makes sense and shores up ideologies about American exceptionalism and individualism.

As not just economic tools, but also cultural statements within broader brand culture, advertising cultivates relationships between consumers and brands through the use of resonant tropes and ideologies such as individual empowerment and masculine entrepreneurialism. Advertising has, of course, long relied upon affective rhetoric and a focus on the masculine individual, as evidenced by the aforementioned Marlboro campaign. To take an even starker example, in 1984 the Ronald Reagan presidential committee produced a political ad called "Morning in America." The ad opens to a mélange of images featuring Americans (all white males) going to work: a barge in the Hudson river, a man getting out of a taxi, a farmer on a tractor, a young boy riding his bike on his newspaper route. A calm, soothing male voice begins:

> It's morning again in America. Today more men and women will go to work than ever before in our country's history. With interest rates at about half the record highs of 1980, nearly 2,000 families today will buy new homes, more than at any time in the past four years. This afternoon 6,500 young men and women will be married, and with inflation at less than half of what it was just four years ago, they can look forward with confidence to the future. It's morning again in America, and under the leadership of President Reagan, our country is prouder and stronger and better. Why would we ever want to return to where we were less than four short years ago?[26]

"Morning in America" relies upon patriotic tropes and a utopian tone to convey its product, Ronald Reagan. There are certainly similarities in more current advertising campaigns, but there are also important differences within brand culture in terms of the citizen consumer.[27] While American exceptionalism has long been a trope in advertising, as evidenced by "Morning in America," in the current moment the role of the individual consumer-citizen is more prominent.[28] In contemporary brand culture, advertising offers a promise, one that can be fulfilled in the relationship between branding and consumer-citizens. That is, there is a cultural shift away from the individual consumer-citizen and toward the relationship between brands and consumers. The promise of ads, then, is accessible only through the intimate relationship between the brand and the consumer-citizen. But in the middle of the Great Recession, what is the promise that is offered? How can advertising and branding infuse an affective relationship into an economic crisis and rebrand it as an opportunity for affective recuperation? Moreover, how can advertising and branding assuage not only an economic crisis, but also a crisis in masculinity, one that emerges from the dismantling of a historical masculine subject as the primary breadwinner in American households?

Masculinity, Advertising, and the Nation

Before I move to my analysis of the Levi's ads, it is necessary to explore the context of masculine representation that informs these ads. Historical American mythologies of rugged individualism, stoicism, and persistence have shaped the symbolic construction of the male blue-collar worker as the quintessential American man, the self-made individual who perseveres under hardship, who sees every crisis as an opportunity. In both nationalist and masculinist discourse, this rugged, authentic working man is often juxtaposed with the effete, feminized, anxiety-ridden businessman. This juxtaposition is a moral one, where the businessman is cast as an individual driven by money and personal gain, in contrast to the working man, motivated by a Protestant work ethic and authenticity. This juxtaposition is expressed in a variety of forms; for instance, in the mid-twentieth century, U.S. state programs were created to beef up Americans emasculated by indoor work and not enough physical activity. In a 1960 *Sports Illustrated* article titled "The Soft American," then-president John F. Kennedy stated that by 1970, "the man who works with his hands will be almost extinct" and also claimed that "the physical vigor of our citizens is one of America's most precious resources. If we waste and neglect this resource, if we allow it to dwindle and grow soft then we will destroy much of our ability to meet the great and vital challenges which confront our people. We will be unable to realize our full potential as a nation."[29] These state programs were largely directed to white men employed in corporate jobs and in the military, and were situated alongside cultural portrayals (in film, television, and politics) of ethnic men and immigrants as tireless (and thus exploitable) workhorses.[30] There are also countless examples of American literature documenting the struggles of men to find purpose in the world of business (Fitzgerald, Steinbeck, and Whitman to name but a few of the canonical authors who produced work in this mode).[31] These cultural examples center a nostalgic, idealized construction of the white blue-collar worker and his authentic place in the American landscape as a hard, dedicated laborer; as Kennedy wrote, the "softness" of American men "can help to strip and destroy the vitality of a nation."[32] This idealization of the working man also centers and celebrates a specific kind of whiteness, one that is (ostensibly) repeatedly under attack from racial others. As George Lipsitz has detailed, the "possessive investment in whiteness" persists in institutionalized racism, and is a key element in the trope of the working man and his "real" laboring practices.[33] Despite the fact that U.S.-based industry has been in rapid decline since the 1970s, and the divide between the wealthy and the poor continues to grow, the white working-class man continues to have symbolic power as the heart of America (and indeed, Springsteen's music is often a reminder of the disconnect between the symbolic power of this figure and the actual material reality of the working class in the United States).

Maintaining masculinity as the symbolic heart of American national identity involves, not surprisingly, the devaluation of women. Indeed, as in most historical crises of masculinity, women and their accomplishments are often found to be blameworthy (we need only look to postwar American culture, when women in the workforce were conceptualized as sources for the crisis in masculinity experienced by returning soldiers; or to the Moynihan report of 1965, when Senator Daniel Moynihan blamed African American women in the workforce for a crisis in black masculinity; or to the economic recession in the 1980s when then-president Reagan blamed the recession on increasing numbers of women in the workplace, suggesting that they had displaced men).[34] In the first decades of the twenty-first century, it has been suggested that the economic environment that emerges from global financial collapse is "better suited for women." Reporter Hanna Rosin, for instance, argues that evidence for this claim is all around us: "It can be found, most immediately, in the wreckage of the Great Recession, in which three-quarters of the 8 million jobs lost were lost by men. The worst-hit industries were overwhelmingly male and deeply identified with macho: construction, manufacturing, high finance. Some of these jobs will come back, but the overall pattern of dislocation is neither temporary nor random. The recession merely revealed—and accelerated—a profound economic shift that has been going on for at least 30 years, and in some respects even longer."[35] Rosin continues by stating, "The working class, which has long defined our notions of masculinity, is slowly turning into a matriarchy, with men increasingly absent from the home and women making all the decisions."[36]

Of course, the idea that women are "making all the decisions" and somehow occupying positions of power is conceptualized here as explicitly at the expense of men, as if it is a zero-sum game.[37] And, for all Rosin's statistics about the good economic shape of American women, there is, of course, copious evidence that women continue to be discriminated against economically (the continuing gap between men's and women's wages for the same job may be an old-fashioned complaint, but it is justified with depressing persistence). That said, Rosin's point about a contemporary crisis in masculinity that is directly linked to the economy is in many ways well taken. Working-class men are losing ground, but the emphasis on women's putative gains is a feint that helps conceal the structural economic forces that are more determinative of their position. In other words, the idea that the working class is "slowly turning into a matriarchy" works to signal a crisis because the rugged, self-made man of the working class has been the symbolic heart of hegemonic masculinity for decades, if not centuries. Such crises in masculinity cause anxiety not only for individuals but also about the future of a nation. Since hegemonic masculinity invokes the working man, the threat to this discursive formation not only jeopardizes the centrality of the masculine figure in nationalist rhetoric (the fear of the soft American), but is also construed as a threat for the future prosperity of a nation. So the deployment of a masculine figure around the anxiety over the working class "turning into a matriarchy" serves in part to assuage this anxiety and deliver a more certain future. In light of such crises, it is no wonder that the key to recovery for the U.S. economy is so often figured as the working-class man. In this regard, we need only recall the way in which the Republican candidates for the U.S. presidency in 2008 repeatedly used the figure of "Joe the Plumber" as a metaphor for the working class, and a vital element in economic recovery.[38]

Advertising has been culturally effective in providing a sort of resolution to the ongoing crisis in masculinity. Ads for liquor, sports, and cars have historically targeted men as their audience, where the focus of the ads has moved from specific details about products to a more general branding strategy about a hegemonic masculine lifestyle. As Michael Messner and Jeffrey Montez de Oca point out, alcohol ads that brand products for men "paint a series of images that evoke feelings, moods, and ways of being" that resonate with hegemonic masculinity.[39] As Ella Shohat and Robert Stam have argued, in much popular cultural representation, there is an "inferential ethnic presence," where ethnicity is represented in media without always referencing an actual character.[40] Advertisements often have an "inferential gendered presence," or what Carol Cohn has theorized as the symbolic system of gender, where the representational context of the ad signals the masculine or the feminine.[41] For the Levi's ads I examine here, the inferential gendered presence is masculine (which is not to say that female actors are not present in the ads, but the undergirding ethos is a masculinist one, highlighting values of individualism, stoicism, and resilience). For Levi's, rebuilding the nation after economic crisis is, quite simply, a man's job. The long history of associating nation building with masculinity (despite crucial interventions by feminists to recuperate this history as one that centrally involved women) has particular purchase in rebuilding a nation after economic crisis—a project that has historically involved "masculine institutions, masculine processes and masculine activities."[42] These masculine activities are organized around a conventional and hegemonic set of normative values, such as competitiveness, adventurousness, stoicism, willpower, independence, honor, authenticity, and persistence—all of which are central to the narrative logic of the

Levi's ads. Additionally, the perceived masculinity of these values and the actions invoked by them are mutually sustaining. These values are only normative, in other words, insofar as they are accessed by and benefit men.

I now turn to the Levi's 2010–11 advertising and branding campaign as a way to demonstrate how, and in what ways, the Great Recession of the twenty-first century has been branded. As the examples I consider here illustrate, advertising and branding narratives offer a promise that seemingly is available only because of the economic crisis, an opportunity to rebuild, a rewriting of a historical American mythology of individual entrepreneurship, rugged labor and work ethic, the open frontier, and the recentering of the blue-collar man as recuperative hero.

Levi's: *Go Forth*

In a 2012 self-description of their brand and their recent campaign, *Go Forth*, Levi's clothing company stated:

> For over a century, men and women have done amazing things in their Levi's® jeans. They have built countries, tunneled into the earth for fuel and treasure, fought for ideals, changed perceptions, and expressed themselves through film, art, music, and literature.
>
> The Levi's® brand embodies a pioneering spirit that is always driven to innovate. Levi's® jeans have been worn by presidents and ranchers, Americans and Russians, doctors and outlaws, kings and coal miners. They are a common thread with a common promise: to provide quality clothing in which to Go Forth.[43]

While this press release purposely includes the word "women," it is abundantly clear that Levi's has been a company that primarily produces clothing for men (after all, how many female kings have there been? Or U.S. presidents?). In fact, the current campaign separates into a general one and another designed especially for women, which trades on conventional stereotypes about the objectified female body. A billboard in the Levi's campaign directed at women, *Love Your Body*, for example, features the backsides of three women (remarkably similar in [small] size), and the tagline: "Hotness comes in all shapes and sizes." "Hotness," a powerful and ubiquitous postfeminist advertising trope, relies upon assessments of women's bodies and perceived sex appeal.[44] Levi's focus on women's hotness is a fundamentally different marketing message than the *Go Forth* campaign's emphasis on individualism, loyalty, and the highlighting of men at work. The Levi's ads that target women make it clear that women should identify primarily with their bodies and how hot they are (or can be if they wear the right pair of jeans).

The Go Forth campaign, again, does not signify hotness and is rather constructed within an inferential gendered presence that signifies masculinity, notably through the $55 million multimedia ad campaign in 2010 that featured the struggling steel mill town of Braddock, Pennsylvania. The press release for the Braddock ads, titled "Ready to Work: Portraits of Braddock," was part of the larger campaign, and began: "Amid today's widespread need for revitalization and recovery, a new generation of 'real workers' has emerged, those who see challenges around them and are inspired to drive positive, meaningful change. This fall, with the introduction of Go Forth 'Ready to Work,' the Levi's® brand will empower and inspire workers everywhere through Levi's® crafted product and stories of the new American Worker."[45] The Levi's Braddock ads featured eleven short video episodes (posted on YouTube and various social media sites), created in conjunction with the Independent Film Channel and the Sundance Film Festival, and showcased a community rebuilding a city ravaged in recent decades of economic recession, home foreclosures, and plummeting employment. The ads featured people at work, in homes, in industry and farming, and tapped into the trope of the authentic American, default white and male, long a staple of both narrative and documentary films, while also aligning the Levi's videos with a tradition of media activism. Not surprisingly, while the global economic crisis of the twenty-first century is referenced through vague recognitions that the United States needs "widespread revitalization and recovery," the actual reasons for the crisis, the collapse of capitalist practices in banking and trade, go unmentioned; rather, the individual authentic worker is the one responsible for, and indeed the most capable of, bringing about the country's recovery. (The campaign even states, with clichés that would make Horatio Alger proud, that Braddock is a town of real workers who—with Levi's help—are "rolling up their sleeves to make real change happen.") A small town with a current population of just over two thousand, Braddock has a storied history in industry, as Andrew Carnegie built one of the first steel mills in America there, establishing it as a central industrial town. Yet the collapse of the U.S. steel industry in the 1970s and 1980s (and the global economic recession of that era) saw the virtual disintegration of Braddock as well, which has lost 90 percent of its population in the past century, and current statistics show that 35 percent of the remaining population lives below the national poverty line.[46]

The eleven video episodes feature individuals who "tell the story of Braddock" through their efforts, funded by Levi's, to revitalize the town through enterprises including a new community center and the development of an urban farm. The efforts of the mayor of Braddock, John Fetterman, to enlist the help of what Levi's calls "modern pioneers"—artists, musicians, craftsmen—to rebuild the town are also showcased.[47] Through the sponsorship and direction of the videos, Levi's becomes a kind of town patron, with the town's infrastructure being rebuilt in the vision of the Levi's brand (a company town in a new sense of the concept). The videos are moving, offering a clichéd but effective pastiche of dilapidated buildings, hollowed-out schools, and boarded-up businesses, all set to stirring soundtracks.[48] As the viewer moves through the eleven episodes, the town is slowly built up through the efforts of these pioneers, who become central citizens in the Levi's brand community.

The videos and the ancillary print and billboard ads that are part of the broader *Go Forth* campaign were created by the ad firm Wieden + Kennedy. The campaign, according to Levi's, is targeted toward Americans who are living through the "jobless recovery" of the global economic crisis (though Braddock had been in recession for years before 2008), and uses actual Braddock citizens as models. Fetterman is the face of the campaign, and has been adamant that the Levi's partnership constitutes an opportunity to rebuild his town rather than exploitation. In an interview, he said, "If someone wants to give me $100 million, I'll kiss their ass and call it ice cream. . . . It's not about kissing anyone's ring—it's about folks in the business community that are enjoying a high level of success looking at communities that are struggling."[49] Indeed, the branded efforts of companies like Levi's are often positioned by economically struggling towns as not only the best, but the only, way to fund the creation and refurbishment of public spaces. Braddock, in this way, makes the case for branded, privatized communities. These branded communities are positioned as the best environment for the ideal masculine subject, the self-made, individualist, entrepreneurial man. As Fetterman continued, "I think that this kind of private philanthropy—I'd like to see it continue. . . . It really does deliver benefit in a way that government assistance and foundation assistance can't."[50] Fetterman articulates here how fault for the recession is shifted away from capitalism and the withdrawing of public funding, and directs attention instead to the opportunities these gaps create for corporations.

Other ads in Levi's larger, more conventional campaign, *Go Forth*, put a similarly nostalgic and optimistic spin on the decline of the blue-collar laborer and industry in the United States, and clearly attempt to address American anxiety in recession. The ads, "We Are All Workers," capitalize on a historical rhetoric of American pioneers using generalized images, and were created by the same ad firm, Wieden + Kennedy. While it is implied that the images were shot in Braddock, the visuality of the ads clearly resonates with many small towns in the United States; they conjure generally recognizable

FIGURE 3.1. This shot from the Levi's ad "We Are All Workers" depicts a dilapidated industry town, hard hit by economic recession, ready to be revitalized and reborn with the help of corporate sponsors such as Levi's.

Rust Belt towns, complete with images of industrial landscapes and people hard at work, together with heteronormative families, revitalizing the city. The ads depict images of heartbreak and depression alongside more nostalgic images of a "simpler" time. One ad, for instance, opens with a man and a dog standing in front of a campfire in a vast field as a freight train rushes by (reminiscent of the isolation and stoicism of the Marlboro Man); followed by panning shots of abandoned buildings framed by the rising sun; old, broken cars and toys under fallen trees; and then a small child jumping into bed with his sleeping father. Instrumental music—horns and strings—plays as a child's voice begins the narration: "We were taught how the pioneers went into the West. They opened their eyes and made up what things could be. A long time ago, things got broken here. People got sad and left." [51]

The ad then depicts the town beginning to move and wake up: people performing everyday routines, moving around, going to work (figure 3.1). The music picks up momentum, and the child continues: "Maybe the world breaks on purpose, so we can have work to do. People think there aren't frontiers anymore; they can't see how frontiers are all around us." The music stops abruptly, and the tagline appears on the screen: "*Go Forth. Levi's.*" The ad is emotionally powerful, the images lush and arresting. The dramatic music juxtaposes with the deliberate and innocent voice of the child to create an affective montage that reinforces struggle, labor, and an American mythology of the frontier. As with other frontiers conquered by the United States (expressed historically ranging from Native American genocide to nineteenth-century colonialism, Manifest Destiny and westward expansion, the space race with the Soviet Union, and the Iraq War, to name but a few), the rhetoric of this ad emphasizes American destiny and inevitability as well as the moral value of work: "Maybe the world breaks on purpose, so we can have work to do." The stunning abstraction of the ad's rhetoric—"things got broken here"—corresponds with an ahistorical neoliberal conceit that economic crises present opportunities for individual entrepreneurs (historically male) to imagine, create, and conquer a seemingly endless field of new frontiers and bring about economic progress. The visual and auditory elements of the ad capitalize on, and resonate with, a larger project of rebranding the 2008 global economic crisis. This branding effort, represented in the Levi's ads but also found within corporate public relations, media representations, and nationalist marketing, reimagines the global economic crisis as one that was inevitable—but not because of the downward spiral of corporate greed or misuse of funds, but because this is what Americans do: they fix things. Orchestrating this resolution, the ad insists, is a uniquely American destiny.

The focus on Braddock, and the "real workers" in the "We Are All Workers" ads, is in part a strategic response to an earlier series of ads in the Levi's Go Forth campaign.[52] Two ads, "O Pioneers!" and "America," also created by Wieden + Kennedy, are more abstract than the "We Are All Workers" ad in their juxtaposition of images: quick shots of individuals, almost all young adults, of various races and ethnicities, in a range of situations. Both ads use the poetry of Walt Whitman as voice-over content. The "America" ad opens with a black-and-white shot of a broken neon sign depicting the word "America," sinking in a pool of water (figure 3.2). This is followed by a mélange of images, shot with independent film aesthetics, including quick shots, handheld camera work, and no real discernible narrative linking the images together. The striking opening image of a broken America is juxtaposed with shooting fireworks, a subway ride, telephone poles in a stark landscape, and an American flag fluttering in a breeze. The voice-over is a recording of Walt Whitman's poem "America," presumably by Whitman himself, recorded in 1890, scratchy and nostalgic:

America
Centre of equal daughters, equal sons
All alike endear'd, grown, ungrown, young or old
Strong, ample, fair, enduring, capable, rich
Perennial with the earth, with freedom, law, and love.[53]

FIGURE 3.2. The broken America sign, half-submerged in a pool of water, opens the Levi's "America" ad, accompanied by a voice-over of Walt Whitman's poem "America." The end of the ad depicts the sign triumphantly above water, restored to its natural destiny.

The ad ends dramatically, with the neon sign "America" restored, hovering above the waterline, gloriously lit up. The Levi's tagline, "Go Forth," sketched on a blanket held by young people, fades to black.

The other ad in the Whitman series, "O Pioneers!," is similarly melancholy and nostalgic. It opens with a young white woman raising her hand in the air in imitation of a statue, a white man running alone through a field, young people of various ethnicities embracing (dressed in Levi's jeans, of course), standing in abandoned buildings, and driving. There is no coherent visual narrative, but the images are held together by the recorded reading of a portion of Whitman's 1865 "Pioneers! O Pioneers!":

Come, my tan-faced children,
Follow well in order, get your weapons ready;
Have you your pistols? Have you your sharp edged axes?
Pioneers! O Pioneers!

For we cannot tarry here,
We must march my darlings, we must bear the brunt of danger,
We, the youthful sinewy races, all the rest on us depend,
Pioneers! O Pioneers!

O you youths, western youths,
So impatient, full of action, full of manly pride and friendship

Plain I see you, western youths, see you tramping with the foremost,
Pioneers! O Pioneers!

We debouch upon a newer, mightier world, varied world,
Fresh and strong the world we seize,
Pioneers! O Pioneers![54]

The ad stitches Whitman's odes to Western expansion and the stark images of industrial ravages after economic collapse together as a coherent narrative, through the use of a quintessential American poet to sell a quintessential American brand to quintessential American men "full of manly pride." In so doing, the ad clearly marks the Levi's campaign as a deliberate attempt to brand the crisis as a nostalgic narrative of hope and capital-friendly opportunity, rather than a crisis that calls into question the very structure of capitalism and corporate legitimacy. As the reporter Seth Stevenson points out, the ad "acts as a galvanizing call to generational action: Times may be tough, but we've been here before, and America's youth will not be broken."[55] Calling on an explicit nostalgia and casting the current global economic crisis as part of a cyclical dynamic, Levi's relies on the continuing currency of American liberal exceptionalism—we have been here before; we overcame crisis then; we can do it again—as a way to brand the current crisis as one in a series that Americans have overcome and through which they have proven their strength. Indeed, Levi's positions the contemporary crisis as a sort of evidence of American destiny to overcome and flourish; after all, as Whitman reminds us, "We debouch upon a newer, mightier world, varied world / Fresh and strong the world we seize."[56] The ad thus emphasizes the ideology that overcoming crisis is a uniquely American duty, a sort of citizenship rite of passage: in this way, rebuilding and overcoming is like a nationalist allegiance, proving rightful national citizenship (a sentiment also expressed on bumper stickers across the United States that claim "Freedom is not free," and in conservative politicians' oft-repeated refrain that freedom is not passed on to Americans; every generation has to fight for it). Seizing this world, however, in the twenty-first century, means branding nationalism and the crisis as a deeply interrelated, inevitable dynamic: Americans are, Whitman tells us, "perennial with the Earth, with freedom, law, and love."

The Whitman Levi's ads make a liberal, intended use of historical references and images that are meant to provoke nostalgia, but one that is haunting and dire, rather than idealistic. The Whitman ads also directly aim to resonate with fear through the use of what might be termed apocalyptic aesthetics, heavily relying upon a kind of postindustrial wasteland crisis chic as a visual trope that runs through the ads. There is an element of danger in the visual and poetic narratives of these ads that is juxtaposed with an implicit call for courageous adventure. The ads, rather than reassuring us, capitalize on unknowns and anxieties. In "America," the broken America sign sets a war-zone tone for the rest of the ad via burned-out buildings, somber faces, and haunting cinematography. The ads do not celebrate national exceptionalism in the customary way of American ads, but rather seek to explicitly harness the fear and anxiety generated by global economic crisis in order to rescue viewers from the crisis—or, perhaps more accurately, to encourage viewers, as consumer-citizens, to rescue themselves.

In other words, the Whitman ads do not work conventionally to rebuild trust in capitalism. But the fear aesthetics that frame these ads perform important cultural work: they entreat the American audience (and Levi's) to rescue themselves, yet again; this time as optimistic pioneers and courageous adventurers. In these ads, corporate culture and capitalist exploits become part of the natural, rough, even dangerous landscape that sets the stage for the story of American courage to retell—indeed, rebrand—itself. The ads reinforce a naturalization of the dangers of unregulated neoliberal corporate capitalism by positioning the individual entrepreneur as the central character in the brand narrative.

Maintaining the Brand: Emotional Capitalism, Masculine Entrepreneurs, and Contradiction

I do not mean to diminish the possible rewards the collaboration of Levi's with the impoverished town of Braddock could bring forth. However, I do want to point out how the Levi's ads offer telling illustrations of how what Eva Illouz calls "emotional capitalism" works to build brand cultures through multiple spaces (such as conventional advertising in print and television, YouTube, blogs, DIY production, consumer-generated content, and so on).[57] While I examine specific ads in this chapter, I suggest that the logic framing these ads exceeds a mere attempt to resuscitate failing industries in an economic crisis, but rather is characteristic of broader neoliberal practices, which seek to expand market logic and strategies beyond simply vaunting a particular product.[58] The entrepreneurialism, pioneering spirit, and hegemonic masculinity the ads encourage do not simply normalize the uncertainty and unpredictability of capitalism; they also speak to a neoliberal expansion of markets. Indeed, the ads naturalize the current economic crisis as a dangerous, if inevitable, moment of unregulated capitalism, one that centers the individual man as a responsible savior, a recuperative hero, even as the role of the state or nation in the crisis is abdicated.

The way the Levi's *Go Forth* campaign ad brands a specific city, company, and product, however, is only part of the larger branding process; these ad campaigns also work as part of the infrastructure of feeling that brands the crisis more globally as an opportunity for the American working class to buy into an alternative, capital-friendly narrative, and secure America's superior place in the world. The maintenance of the narrative of American liberal exceptionalism is positioned not only side by side with a neoliberal mandate for individuals to take care of themselves but, relatedly, alongside state actions to radically reduce support for the unemployed and other vulnerable constituencies.

While the global economic crisis is referenced in the ads through vague recognitions that the United States needs "widespread revitalization and recovery" or, more ridiculously, that something "got broken here," the actual reasons for the crisis—the collapse in banking and trade brought on by neoliberal practices, the disintegration of the U.S. automobile industry, the global reach and ripple effect of economic devastation—are never even acknowledged; rather, the individual authentic, courageous, and optimistic worker is the one who is responsible for bringing about change.[59] Indeed, within these ad campaigns, the worker or laborer is deeply associated with the brand itself, as well as being positioned as the central character in the larger narrative that brands the crisis. Rather than calling attention to systemic failure in the global banking industry, or the effects of generations living on credit, or the subprime mortgage crisis, these ads call our attention to the lone, rugged masculine entrepreneur; the individualist laborer who is nostalgically created and positioned as the only way out of what got broken, the mess that was somehow, and abstractly, "made" so that Americans can come along and "fix things."

The male worker is thus positioned in these campaigns as (in part) a symbol for a nation under threat. Indeed, the Go Forth campaign even vaguely references the Communist Party slogan with its tagline "We Are All Workers," but without any of the party's reference to and reliance on communal work. The "We" of "We Are All Workers" is a community of individual workers, each free in a free market, called upon to go forth and work, with the backdrop of economic crisis that will encourage these workers to be leaner and ever more vigilant, within capitalism. With help from Levi's, Braddock is transformed into a town of "real workers" who are "rolling up their sleeves to make real change happen."[60]

Part of the affective narrative of global neoliberalism is precisely this focus on the individual as opposed to the state. The ads take a particular position on the nation in the midst of a global crisis, and embedded within that position is a specific representation of hegemonic masculinity, one that affirms the cultural and moral value of the working man. Rather than gesturing toward a vague global community that needs to unite in response to global economic collapse, Levi's positions the nation as under threat—from outside and from within. This is, however, an ambiguous threat, as opposed to placing accountability on concrete identifiable actors and structures.[61]

As is increasingly common in contemporary brand culture, the Levi's ad campaign challenges the historical reliance of advertising on a product's efficiency and unique qualities in a competitive market. Rather, these ads utilize the language of the brand, what Celia Lury calls the "logos" of the brand, which is maintained by a personal, individual narrative, one that revolves around lifestyle, identity, and individual empowerment.[62] In this sense, the ads are about much more than a discrete product or thing, a pair of Levi's jeans. As Lury points out, "To assume that the brand is a single thing would be to mistake the multiple and sometimes divergent layers of activity that have gone into producing the brand. . . . [These activities] have multiple histories, are internally divided, in tension with each other, and may even be contradictory or opposed."[63] Thus, while it is important to point out the contradictions in the ads—Levi's utilizes a nationalist rhetoric to sell American products and shamelessly exploits the disintegrating Rust Belt industrial towns to do so—I am also arguing that it is precisely this kind of disconnect or contradiction that makes the ad campaigns so successful in an emotional or affective register, and what makes them effective as mechanisms to brand the current global economic crisis. These contradictions are the primary mechanisms of the brand's affective language.[64] The contemporary global economic crisis presents an extreme case for advertisers to mobilize fear and anxiety as a dominant trope, and because the crisis has so drastically affected consumption practices, it is a trope that is unavoidable for marketers to address.

The Levi's ads rely upon a strategy of using selective history to brand the current crisis. The title of an article detailing the campaign in the trade magazine *Adweek* frames this strategy sardonically and succinctly: "Walt Whitman Is Reborn. To Sell Jeans."[65] As Doug Sweeny, the vice president of Levi's brand marketing, more earnestly notes, "The idea of . . . putting people back to work is clearly top of mind [culturally]."[66] Although the Levi's campaign focuses on the economically depressed Rust Belt town of Braddock, its rhetorical focus is not on the town specifically. Rather, the ads focus on a general ideology of American heritage and the destiny of the blue-collar working-class man as a means to symbolize the opportunity presented by the economic crisis. In so doing, the Levi's campaign obscures material realities—such as ethnic diversity, the ravages of Manifest Destiny, and the fact that many Americans actually do want to "go forth" and work but no jobs are available. This obfuscation was pointedly referred to on a Levi's billboard in New York featuring an ad in the *Go Forth* series. The billboard depicted a young white girl running through fields with the text, "This country was not built by men in suits." Someone unofficially responded to this claim, writing below it, "It was built by slaves." The obvious strategy of the billboard—to appeal to hard-working, blue-collar workers, not corporate "suits" or overpaid, effete executives—backfired at least in this case because of the way the campaign renders certain historical narratives invisible while privileging the ideology of the frontier.

The Levi's advertising campaigns function not only to rebuild the brand of individual struggling corporations but, more generally, to brand the current global economic crisis itself. As I have discussed, that crisis has come to represent many things, one of which is the failure of brands. The job for struggling corporations in the aftermath of the crisis is not only to attempt to incentivize purchases by consumers. It has become, more importantly, about how to restore trust in brands, the market, and, indeed, in neoliberal capitalism itself. What better way for the United States to reestablish trust for consumers than to position the crisis as a brand: a brand about America, about consumer-citizens, about working men, about the inevitable triumph of capitalism? Within contemporary brand culture, branders and marketers invest in establishing an authentic, affective relationship between products and consumers. In the current environment of global economic crisis, the most important product in this relationship is capitalism itself.

Notes

Part of this chapter is from an earlier essay, "Branding the Crisis," in *Aftermath: The Cultures of the Economic Crisis*, ed. Manuel Castells, João Caraça, and Gustavo Cardoso (London: Oxford University Press, 2012), as well as from *Authentic™: The Politics of Ambivalence in a Brand Culture* (New York: New York University Press, 2012). I'd also like to thank Evan Brody and Inna Arzumanova for their helpful feedback on this version.

1. As David Remnick points out in a July 30, 2012, *New Yorker* piece on Bruce Springsteen, on *Wrecking Ball*, Springsteen draws on "Irish Rebel songs, Dust Bowl ballads, Civil War tunes, and chain gang chants." Remnick, "We Are Alive."

2. Bruce Springsteen, promotional video on *Wrecking Ball*; see also Remnick, "We Are Alive."

3. Remnick, "We Are Alive."

4. Dayan and Katz, *Media Events*.

5. Dayan and Katz, *Media Events*, 6.

6. Smith, "We Have Armageddon!"

7. Zelizer, *Economic Lives*.

8. For more on this, see Castells, Caraça, and Cardoso, *Aftermath*.

9. For a discussion of "taking care of the self," see Foucault, *The Birth of Biopolitics*. In-

deed, another song on Springsteen's *Wrecking Ball*, "We Take Care of Our Own," seems to specifically recognize the disingenuousness of the rhetoric of "taking care of ourselves."

10. The role that many men play in the current economic recession has led some to characterize it also as a "mancession." For more on this, see the introduction to this volume.

11. See Ewen, *Captains of Consciousness*; Schudson, *Advertising, the Uneasy Persuasion*; Williams, *Dream Worlds*; Lears, *No Place of Grace*; Goldman and Papson, *Sign Wars*; Sturken and Cartwright, *Practices of Looking*.

12. Williams, *The Long Revolution*.

13. Gilmore, *Golden Gulag*.

14. Banet-Weiser, *Authentic™*.

15. Klein, *No Logo*.

16. Duggan, *The Twilight of Equality?*; Harvey, *A Brief History of Neoliberalism*. See also Banet-Weiser, *Authentic™*.

17. Foster, "No End to Capitalism." See also Mukherjee and Banet-Weiser, *Commodity Activism*.

18. For more on media assemblage, see Ong, *Neoliberalism as Exception*.

19. The Levi's Go Forth campaign is but one example found in advertising that represents and invokes the "mancession," or the connection between economic recession and crises in masculinity. Others include the Chrysler "Imported from Detroit" ads that star hip-hop musician Eminem as a comeback kid for a comeback city, the economically devastated Detroit; and the now iconic "Old Spice guy" ads, which ironically refer to effeminate men as a way to validate the manly man who uses manly deodorant.

20. For more on the role of advertising in nation building, see Sturken and Cartwright, *Practices of Looking*.

21. See Duggan, *The Twilight of Equality?*; Harvey, *A Brief History of Neoliberalism*; Castells, *Communication Power*; Brown, *Politics out of History*; Mukherjee and Banet-Weiser, *Commodity Activism*.

22. For more on individual consumption habits after and during crisis, see Sturken, *Tourists of History*.

23. Sturken and Cartwright, *Practices of Looking*, 29.

24. Banet-Weiser, *Authentic™*.

25. Schudson, *Advertising, the Uneasy Persuasion*, 232.

26. "Prouder, Better, Stronger," Official U.S. Presidential Campaign Advertisement for the Republican Party of the United States of America, 1984.

27. An example of the kind of similarity I have in mind (and of the cultural memory of "Morning in America") could be found during the 2012 Superbowl when Chrysler aired an ad, "Halftime in America," featuring the actor-director Clint Eastwood. His voiceover says, among other things, "It's halftime in America . . . people are out of work and they're hurting. And they're all wondering what they're going to do to make a comeback." The ad ends with a sober Eastwood looking at the camera, saying, "This country can't be knocked out with one punch. We'll get right back up again and

when we do the world is going to hear the roar of our engines." Chrysler, "Halftime in America," airdate February 5, 2012.

28. See the discussion of advertising in Sturken and Cartwright, *Practices of Looking*. See also Dávila, *Latinos, Inc.*

29. Kennedy, "The Soft American." This article came after President Eisenhower had instituted a federal mandate on national fitness, the President's Council on Youth and Fitness, in 1956. For earlier efforts to harden and remasculinize American men, see the efforts of Charles Atlas and his successful ad campaign that helped establish the "ninety-seven-pound weakling" as the nemesis of American men.

30. See, among others, Lipsitz, *Time Passages*; Peiss, *Cheap Amusements*; Ross, *Working-Class Hollywood*.

31. For example, Whitman's *Leaves of Grass* (1855), Fitzgerald's *The Great Gatsby* (1925), and Steinbeck's *The Grapes of Wrath* (1939).

32. Kennedy, "The Soft American."

33. Lipsitz, *The Possessive Investment in Whiteness*.

34. For more on the scapegoating of women during the Reagan years, see Suzanne Leonard, *Fatal Attraction*; and Jeffords, *Hard Bodies*.

35. Rosin, "The End of Men." See also Rosin, "Who Wears the Pants in this Economy?"

36. Rosin, "The End of Men."

37. See the introduction to this volume for a more extensive discussion of this kind of zero-sum game.

38. The McCain-Palin Republican presidential campaign repeatedly invoked "Joe the Plumber" in rallies and speeches. Joe the Plumber is an actual man named Samuel Wurzelbacher, who became famous when he asked Barack Obama a question about small business taxes; Obama's answer, "When you spread the wealth around, it is good for everybody," was seized by Republicans as evidence of a socialist program. McCain then brought "Joe" to rallies and events as a metaphor for the average working American. "Joe the Plumber" resonated so well with voters that in 2012, he actually ran for office himself.

39. Messner and Montez de Oca, "The Male Consumer as Loser," 1880.

40. Shohat and Stam, *Unthinking Eurocentrism*, 223.

41. Cohn, "War, Wimps and Women."

42. Nagel, "Masculinity and Nationalism," 243; see also Connell, *Masculinities*.

43. Levi's *Go Forth* press release.

44. For more on hotness as a postfeminist trope, see McRobbie, "Notes on Post-feminism and Popular Culture"; Levy, *Female Chauvinist Pigs*; Tasker and Negra, *Interrogating Postfeminism*; and Gill, "Postfeminist Media Culture," 147–66, among others.

45. Levi Strauss and Co., "Levi's Proclaims 'We Are All Workers' with Launch of Latest Go Forth Marketing Campaign" [press release], June 24, 2010, www.levistrauss.com/news/press-releases/levis-proclaims-we-are-all-workers-launch-latest-go-forth-marketing-campaign.

46. Streitfeld, "Rock Bottom for Decades, but Showing Signs of Life." For town statistics, see the table "Profile of General Population and Housing Characteris-

tics: 2010," U.S. Census Bureau, factfinder2.census.gov/faces/tableservices/jsf/pages/productview.xhtml?pid=DEC_10_DP_DPDP1&prodType=table.

47. Halpern, "Mayor of Rust." Indeed, Fetterman is an excellent representative of the performances of working-class masculinity I discuss in this essay. His Ivy League education (he is a Harvard graduate) is belied by his personal appearance: he is six feet eight inches tall and often described as looking like a professional wrestler with a shaved head, goatee, and a tattoo that reads: "I will make you hurt." For more on Fetterman, see Manning, "I Will Make You Hurt."

48. This trend of "ruin porn" or "poverty porn" is seen not only in videos of Braddock but also in media productions of other struggling U.S. cities, such as Detroit, Michigan.

49. NPR, "Levi's Gives Struggling Town Cinderella Treatment."

50. NPR, "Levi's Gives Struggling Town Cinderella Treatment."

51. It is beyond the scope of this essay to discuss how children (and the innocence and purity they invoke) are used to mediate and narrate global catastrophe. As I have argued previously in "Elian Gonzalez and 'The Purpose of America,'" this trope of childish innocence was used in the Elian Gonzalez national citizenship case in the United States, as well as in more current films such as *Slumdog Millionaire* (2008) and *Beasts of the Southern Wild* (2012).

52. As the reporter Matthew Newton puts it in "Levi's Attempts to Salvage 'Go Forth' Campaign with Sincerity":

The first time around, Levi's attempted to channel gritty realism by simulating it. Now, by going on-location to Braddock—a Rust Belt town that's lost 90% of its population since the American steel industry dried up—Levi's will attempt to capture gritty realism in action. As the site of Andrew Carnegie's first steel mill, Braddock once embodied the spirit of the American worker, which makes the town a receptive home to the words of a poet like Walt Whitman. But that spirit of an unswerving American work ethic has long since been replaced by vacant storefronts and burned-out homes, contentious small town politics and a sense of abandonment. . . . It's obvious Levi's is hoping this move will lend a sense of sincerity to its beleaguered ad campaign. Which, who knows, it very well may. After all, it's a nice gesture—whether PR-motivated or not—for Levi's to invest a million dollars over two years in Braddock.

53. Whitman, "America."

54. Whitman, "Pioneers! O Pioneers."

55. Stevenson, "Levi's Commercials, Now Starring Walt Whitman."

56. Whitman, "Pioneers! O Pioneers."

57. Illouz, *Cold Intimacies*.

58. See Illouz, *Cold Intimacies*; and Littler, *Radical Consumption*.

59. For more on the branding of the authentic, see Banet-Weiser, *Authentic™*.

60. The Levi's focus on "real" workers not only juxtaposes blue-collar workers with the greedy corporate world, it also gestures toward other forms of labor that have been (symbolically and materially) deemed illegitimate or not real, in particular, the un-

documented worker who is at the center of U.S. debates on immigration reform and immigrant rights.

61. Indeed, this threat is all the more ambiguous given the fact that in 2002, the Levi's corporation shut down domestic production and moved most of its manufacturing outside the United States.

62. Lury, *Brands*.

63. Lury, *Brands*, 14.

64. The use of cultural contradictions in advertising certainly did not begin with the global economic crisis. Advertising has long succeeded in co-opting counterculture aesthetics, reformulating an aesthetics of resistance into something marketable, thus dissipating any fear or anxiety about what might be the consequences of resistance. See Frank, *The Conquest of Cool*; Klein, *No Logo*; Heath and Potter, *Nation of Rebels*.

65. Kiefaber, "Walt Whitman Is Reborn."

66. Kiefaber, "Walt Whitman Is Reborn."

FOUR   *PAMELA THOMA*

What Julia Knew

DOMESTIC LABOR IN THE RECESSION-ERA CHICK FLICK

In the Food Network's slogan "Way More Than Cooking," "Way More" refers to the ancillary website and an array of food-related programming offered to more than 96 million households in the United States, the United Kingdom, and Asia.[1] "Way More" is also suggestive with respect to popular culinary narratives in general, whether on the small or the large screen, in new or old media, through visual or print texts. For if the Food Network has taught viewers anything in twenty years, it is that culinary narratives—even those with the primary goal of providing cooking instruction—are always about more than cooking. Julia Child knew this fact long before 1993 when the Food Network emerged and filled several of its original six hours with reruns of her show *The French Chef* (1963–73), and her insight helped her succeed as author and memoirist, as well as cooking show celebrity. As Dana Polan has pointed out, in a period of major change Child offered Americans "lessons in a whole way of living and being and doing."[2] She was, he writes, "key to the cultivation of modern American lifestyle and leisure in the latter part of the twentieth century," bringing the world of international cuisine to American taste cultures and tying "kitchen work" to consumption, defined not only as pragmatic necessity but as pleasure, enjoyment, and reinvention.[3] Simultaneously, Child carefully bracketed reality by banishing the larger contexts of 1950s and 1960s geopolitical nuclear threats and social upheaval from her culinary discourse, crafting an optimistic "tale of comfort."[4]

Nora Ephron's 2009 film *Julie & Julia* celebrates Child's cultural production and influence, reproducing her comfort narrative by depicting the nonthreatening and circumscribed space of a conventionally feminized domestic sphere and dramatizing the rewards of discerning consumption, both of food and of less perishable commodities. Although this culinary narrative similarly attempts to banish its larger context, declining to explicitly acknowledge the mass under- and unemployment, insecure working structures, and low wages of the Great Recession, the film is fundamentally a tale about work, not only the work of cooking, but also the work of professional writing. More specifically, *Julie & Julia* emphasizes the importance of the makeover for female workers, underlining the continuing cultural significance—and adaptability—of this trope.

This chapter recognizes *Julie & Julia* and Ryan Murphy's 2010 film *Eat Pray Love* as recession-era chick flicks, arguing that these films respond to the context of the economic downturn through a reinscription of entrepreneurial labor in feminine terms of domestic activity. In situating appropriately feminine female labor in the home, they update an earlier cycle of postfeminist films that had registered deep anxiety about women in the workplace. If postfeminist popular culture seems most visible in its engagements with neoliberal consumerism, I here highlight labor as one of its primary concerns. In these films leisure and labor, consumption and production are repeatedly blurred, reassuring audiences of the femininity of female workers and in the process disavowing the economic adversity experienced by many women amid the recession. In response to Anne-Marie Slaughter's 2012 article bemoaning the impossibility of elite professional women achieving work-life balance ("Why Women Still Can't Have It All"), Ellen Bravo suggests a different question, one to do with the majority of U.S. women who are not contemplating leaving high-status jobs for the sake of normative family life and motherhood. Rather, they are "worried about losing it all—their jobs, their children's health, their families' financial stability."[5]

While undoubtedly a response to a context of economic hardship, anxiety about the precarious financial health of women is not a question that explicitly interests the recessionary chick flick. Maintaining the fantasy of a decorous withdrawal from wage labor, the recession-era chick flick centralizes women who possess the resources for weathering economic turmoil, valorizes even more work for women by associating it with leisure, and ultimately rationalizes long hours for low or no wages for women through the revival of a gender division of domestic labor. Inflected by the recessionary context of financial instability, with the rapid conversion of more and more occupations into precarious labor and the accelerated dismantling or privatization of public supports, *Julie & Julia* and *Eat Pray Love* suggest both historical continuities and ideological shifts within postfeminism.[6] They achieve this relocation of public to domestic femininity through an emphasis on women's self-work and through the trope of writing as both a creative activity and a safe and lucrative form of employment.

To harness the comfort of culinary narrative and to rewrite the chick flick for the recession era, *Julie & Julia* and *Eat Pray Love* mobilize the conventions of the female biopic, a reliable formula preoccupied with reinvention.[7] Showcasing celebrity nonfiction writers Julia Child (Meryl Streep) and Julie Powell (Amy Adams) in *Julie & Julia*, and Elizabeth Gilbert (Julia Roberts) in *Eat Pray Love*, the films achieved a commercial success that underscored the continued potency of these themes for the contemporary chick flick.[8] The memoir successfully adapted for an era defined by recession was actually crafted in a prerecessionary context: Julia Child's *My Life in France* (2006), Julie Powell's *Julie and Julia: 365 Days, 524 Recipes, 1 Tiny Apartment Kitchen: How One Girl Risked Her Marriage, Her Job, and Her Sanity to Master the Art of Living* (2005), and Elizabeth Gilbert's *Eat, Pray, Love: One Woman's Search for Everything across Italy, India and Indonesia* (2006). Child's memoir recounts the period in France when she wrote *Mastering the Art of French Cooking* (1961) with Simone Beck and Louisette Bertholle; Powell's book details her blog project on Salon.com that chronicled how she cooked her way through Child's famous cookbook; and Gilbert's volume describes a year of culinary travel in which she recorded her recovery from depression. These best-selling memoirs have been variously described as "foodie romance," "confessional memoir," "culinary adventure," "gastronomic travelogue," or "priv-lit."[9] All three make use of culinary narrative, and they are all also recognizable variations of chick lit. As such, both *Julie & Julia* and *Eat Pray Love* are firmly situated within postfeminist popular culture. Both films feature heroines who are also professional writers, a role that neatly encapsulates tropes of female agency, commercial success, and creativity and that frequently appears within postfeminist media forms.

The first part of this essay explores links between *Julie & Julia*, *Eat Pray Love*, and the memoirs they adapt, paying specific attention to the subjective dimensions of the larger arena of postfeminist popular culture, especially chick lit and the televisual makeover narrative. I suggest that these recession-era chick flicks attempt to distance themselves from the consumerist patterns typically found in postfeminist culture. I also connect them to earlier chick flicks that registered increased demands for female labor under neoliberalism only to easily resolve concerns and anxieties surrounding women's participation in the workplace. The resolution of workplace strife in prerecession postfeminist popular culture customarily involved "downshifting" a female protagonist's work ethic, another trope that reads quite differently in the context of the downturn.[10] The second section describes the ways in which recession-inflected narratives feature self-transformations or makeovers inspired by destabilized or dissatisfying market employment and by the entrepreneurial potential of certain forms of labor, particularly writing, that may be allied and closely associated with gendered domestic labor.[11] The third section of the essay explores the construction of writing as a socially approved form of entrepreneurial labor for women in popular culture, in large part because it facilitates the working woman's makeover; self-making renders the female worker compatible with a postfeminist model of feminine subjectivity that accommodates traditionalist forms of gendered domestic labor and thus purportedly relieves a social crisis in masculinity and a financial crisis in the social order. Reconstituting triumphant narratives of white, middle-class American women in recession-era postfeminist popular culture, *Julie & Julia* and *Eat Pray Love* are clearly about work but continue to symbolically evade the conditions of marketplace labor for a broad spectrum of women, disguising the systemic transfer of risk from unregulated corporate industry to female worker-subject; calls for sacrifice and belabored self-improvement further blur the lines between paid marketplace labor and unpaid reproductive or domestic labor and communicate that women should take still more responsibility for a neoliberal economic order that relies upon deepening social cleavage and financial instability.[12]

Chick Flick and Chick Lit Makeovers

As recession-era chick flicks and as adaptations of prerecession chick lit, *Julie & Julia* and *Eat Pray Love* are part of an expansive and dynamic postfeminist popular culture tied to audiences in the United States, the United Kingdom, and well beyond. To briefly review, about a decade after "postfeminism" first appeared as a term in mainstream U.S. news media, postfeminist popular culture exploded in the 1990s.[13] This marked the moment when expectations and fears over change brought about by feminism and other political movements mounted and met the hegemony of neoliberal market fundamentalism. Not only chick flicks, chick lit, primetime TV dramas, advertisements, music, and women's magazines, but late twentieth-century consumer culture at large began to aggressively address a female subject and target female consumers to an unprecedented degree.[14] Feminist scholars and media critics have focused on the consumerist patterns of behavior that permeate postfeminist cultural texts, critiquing the ways in which they align with neoliberal ideology to present a model of feminine subjectivity that replaces the political subject with an empowered consumer—most often but not exclusively white, middle-class, and heterosexual—whose marketplace choices are nonetheless constrained within a ruggedly individualizing discourse.[15] Yvonne Tasker and Diane Negra observe that affluence is assumed in this gendered version of neoliberal consumer citizenship, which incorporates feminism in selective ways that often overlap with post–civil rights, postracial, and postmodern discourses.[16] Blithely disregarding structural inequalities and social differences, postfeminist popular culture typically constructs access to social belonging or citizenship as a simple matter of individual consumer choice that is universally available.

Like the postfeminist chick flick, chick lit is most commonly understood as a dramatic remodeling of popular romance that creates narrative space for a limited recognition of changes in contemporary social life. While it has been described as a humorous genre of fiction that "features single women in their twenties and thirties 'navigating their generation's challenges of balancing demanding careers with personal relationships,'" much nonfiction has been written, marketed, and read as chick lit, as for example in the growing category of "mommy lit," or in the specific examples of Candace Bushnell's *Sex and the City* and Helen Fielding's *Bridget Jones's Diary*, both considered chick lit urtexts and whose joint origins lie in precedent newspaper columns.[17] Even with explicitly fictional texts, a deep investment in realism, direct address of the reader, first-person narration, the frequent use of the diary form, and the inclusion of "documents" such as e-mail messages and letters encourage the reading of texts as autobiographical, factual, authentic narratives about contemporary life.[18] Equally important for this discussion, and despite the established role of wage labor in the genre and in subgenres such as "nanny lit," and "assistant lit," chick lit is most often read for its focus on consumption.[19] In short and more accurately, chick lit recombines the fantasies of romance and consumer culture with the realities of the workaday world of women's lives.

For some critics, chick lit is the signature cultural manifestation of the ideology of postfeminism because consumer culture provides the context for the heroine, is often fully detailed in its pages, and is just as often featured prominently in the codified iconography of book covers, depicting fashionable high heels, designer power bags, and other must-have feminizing accessories. Some books are actually sponsored by commercial interests that appear in the text, similar to the embedded advertising of reality TV.[20] Debates about the cultural work performed by chick lit circulate around either its celebration of the successes of middle-class women who are defined by their commitment to commodity fetishism, or its parodic chronicling of the unfulfilled promises of both capitalism and heteropatriarchal romance. That is, chick lit is held either to promote contemporary neoliberal capitalism or to provide compensatory, vicarious pleasures in relation to it.[21] For both positions, and as Tania Modleski observes, "to the extent that there exists a gap between the relatively privileged life of . . . chick-lit protagonists and life as the majority of women live it (shopping for Payless shoes, not Manolo Blahnik's), there is room for a feminist politics to insert itself."[22] Feminist critique regularly takes chick lit to task for depictions of women as upscale or aspiring high-end consumers, lamenting a partial or metonymic representational politics because it relies upon retrograde gender stereotypes of women as superficial, reproduces racial and class hierarchies, and aggressively contains women's political agency.

Commentary on Powell's and Gilbert's chick lit memoirs is no exception, typically questioning their idealization of economic privilege and luxury consumption via gourmet cuisine in *Julie and Julia* and international culinary tourism in *Eat, Pray, Love*. Of *Julie and Julia*, for example, Anita Mannur writes that "the politics of Powell's culinary leanings" operates "within a matrix of nostalgia for an imagined whiteness, one that is also constructed around privilege and cultural capital" and communicated through the culinary narrative.[23] Observing that Powell is "decidedly frustrated" with living in multiethnic Queens, where she has difficulty buying the European foodstuffs needed for the recipes in *Mastering the Art of French Cooking*, Mannur suggests that the text reestablishes dominant ideologies of social class, race, and gender.[24] Powell's frustration with Queens and her fascination with Child's life exhibit obvious racial and class anxiety, and in many ways this echoes the postfeminist fixation on heterosexual white women and the neoliberal preoccupation with wealth.

Similarly, but also taking issue with consumption as the key to empowering transformations, Joshunda Sanders and Diana Barnes-Brown scathingly rename Gilbert's book "Wealthy, Whiny, White," in a 2010 *Bitch* magazine article titled "Eat, Pray, Spend." They categorize it and Powell's memoir in the genre of "priv-lit," which they describe as a wide variety of media forms that have created a "destructive cacophony of insecurity, spending, and false wellness."[25] As a developing subset of the self-help industry that aggressively plies female consumers with the promise of "the new, enlightened American Dream," priv-lit media texts sell what is deemed an "acceptable splurge" in the recession era, since its goal "is one of spiritual, existential, or philosophical enlightenment contingent upon women's hard work, commitment and patience," but most importantly a significant financial "investment."[26] Priv-lit's pitch relies, Sanders and Barnes-Brown write, upon deeply problematic assumptions about women's relationship to money, especially the assumption that they have it, but also that they should "spend extravagantly," make sacrifices, even risk it all, "in order to fit ill-defined notions of what it is to be 'whole.'"[27] Texts interpellate or position women as inherently flawed and needing guides for improvement throughout their lives but particularly in a moment of economic crisis; finally, "those who don't invest in addressing those flaws are ultimately doomed to making themselves, if not others, miserable."[28]

According to this account, priv-lit texts are stories about self-making that involve upscale consumption. As such they echo the makeover formula that primarily targets women and has become pervasive on reality TV in the past decade. Brenda Weber identifies a number of stages for the TV makeover formula: an initial shaming of the pre-made-over subject; surveillance by audiences and experts; pledges from the subjects to put themselves in the hands of authorities; the actual work of the transformation (sometimes with teaching moments included for the benefit of the subject and the audience); the shock and awe of reveals; and the euphoria of the new and improved or "after" subject who satisfies experts.[29] More precisely, Sanders and Barnes-Brown's analysis of priv-lit echoes those of scholars such as Laurie Ouellette who position reality TV within the larger category of self-help media, a broader phenomenon that is conceptualized as "a cultural manifestation of neoliberalism." Echoing a Foucauldian understanding of modern discipline, power, and governance, Sanders and Barnes-Brown consider popular media texts about transformation as templates for and "technologies of" citizenship.[30] In this view, media texts tacitly instruct the citizen-subject in neoliberal ideologies and practices, which place full responsibility on the individual and keep her coming back to the marketplace to make additional purchases to secure socially sanctioned feminine belonging in the neoliberal state.

Reality TV is understood as a key site of the makeover, and essays in this collection by Hannah Hamad and Anikó Imre (chapters 9 and 10) speak to recessionary inflections in the makeover canon. At the same time, scholars have outlined deep historical roots and medium-specific versions of the makeover narrative, identifying variations in film, television, the novel, and women's magazines, albeit without clear consensus about differences. Weber draws a distinction between the reality TV makeover and the fictional makeover narratives of film, the novel, and dramatic television. Whereas film and novel makeovers are typically used in the service of "a narrative larger than the scope of the transformation itself," and television characters "learn that though a makeover is nice, they were really just fine in their Before states," in reality TV the makeover motif functions as its own genre and transformation is assumed to be a positive end in and of itself because it displays self-making.[31] Ferriss describes makeover films in much the same way Weber describes makeover fictional television, classifying them as a chick flick subgenre that fuses the external and the internal. Makeover chick flick narratives conclude, as per Ferriss, that the makeover is "ultimately unnecessary since the protagonist never really needed to change physically, but only to recognize—and be recognized for—her true worth."[32] The necessity of the makeover is, as I show, expanding in postfeminist cultural texts.

The distinction between the fictional and the nonfictional makeover acknowledges the importance of fantasy to specific cultural forms, especially the novel and narrative film. I suggest that the chick lit makeover text operates as a kind of bridge between the fictional and nonfictional makeover, particularly given the genre's commitment to managing the challenges of everyday life. Beyond the formal use of realism in the genre and the slippage in reading between fictional and nonfictional chick lit, material patterns of consumption ally chick lit with cultural forms such as television that are marked by regularity. These include marketing to and purchase by female commuters as "the archetypal woman's read for their journeys to and from work" and purchase patterns of several novels a month.[33] This bridging function has made chick lit readily available for revision and remediation, with migrations and collisions that have transported it to television, as in HBO's *Sex and the City*, and to film, as indicated especially in the adaptation of fictionalized biographies and autobiographies, such as *The Devil Wears Prada* (2006) and *The Nanny Diaries* (2007). Finally, adaptation of chick lit to the biopic, which is itself a hybrid and fictionalized form of biography, recombines fantasy and realism for further variation of the makeover narrative that confounds strict medium formulation.

As the chick flick versions of Powell's and Gilbert's memoirs suggest, recession-era popular media that address female audiences expand the makeover ethos, elaborating variations across forms to couple the reinvention of the individual female subject with the recovery of social health. Women, it is suggested, should sacrifice themselves to adapt to new social demands and willingly take responsibility for revitalizing a nation in a moment of economic crisis. In part this is achieved through the naturalization of consumption as an indispensable element in individual psychic well-being, familial relations, and a peaceful social order, in the process obfuscating the materiality of consumption.

In some respects, the film versions of *Julie and Julia* and *Eat, Pray, Love* attempt to disavow the postfeminist consumer ideology so evident in the memoirs they adapt. Ephron's *Julie & Julia* seems particularly aware of a U.S. audience with diminished capacity for consumption. While Powell uses the details of specific recipes (boeuf Bourguignon and roast lamb marinade au Laurier, for example) and shopping for pricey ingredients to structure her memoir, the film reduces the frequent mention of costly ingredients. Ephron also develops a scene from the book in which a friend comes up with the idea for a PayPal feature to help finance the Julie/Julia Project blog. A recognition of expensive tastes but limited means builds from a humorously choreographed "Lobster Killer" scene that shows Julie wrestling with crustaceans as the soundtrack blares the Talking Heads song "Psycho Killer," referencing the psychic maneuvers and various physical labors such meals require. Still, as this rather grisly scene demonstrates, avoiding Julie's purchase of expensive foodie ingredients and equipment entails a comedic evasion of contemporary conditions.

More importantly, Julia Child functions in the film both as an "idol of production," the biopic's visionary woman who made the world a better place, and an "idol of consumption," who actually displaces consumption to a certain degree.[34] As an idol of consumption, Child is an entertainer-celebrity who is herself a consumer product and whose conspicuous consumption of a gastronomic lifestyle the spectator vicariously enjoys. The film locates Child's conspicuous consumption in an earlier era, so spectators of Julie & Julia and Julie the protagonist (a stand-in for the spectator) may enjoy consumption from a temporal remove. This framing also structures scenes in which Julie watches rerun episodes of The French Chef and the 1978 Saturday Night Live episode in which Dan Aykroyd parodies Child's unflappable determination to make French cooking appear fun and nonthreatening. In addition to relieving possible feelings of guilt about the pleasures of conspicuous consumption in audiences contending with austerity, placing Child in a different time (and place) may simultaneously suggest the abundance of what has been lost in the recession. Tellingly, such historical distance also mediates and forecloses the only suggestion of female solidarity in the film, which is that between Julie and Julia; as I discuss in the next section, Julie's contemporaries are interested only in individual success.

Murphy's Eat Pray Love attempts to obscure its consumer ideology by framing Liz's year of culinary travel as a spiritual quest and placing it in explicit opposition to her more mundane enterprises and the worldly desire to "have it all." When the film opens, Liz is in Bali visiting a medicine man for a magazine article she is writing. The interview turns into a reading of Liz's future, and the man describes a journey in which Liz will divorce, lose all of her money, get her money back, and remarry. For spiritual guidance, he gives her a drawing, which he says depicts her looking through her heart instead of her head as a way to stay grounded. Although the first several scenes show Liz performing her job as a New York City–based professional writer, and her voice-over reminds the audience of the best-selling memoir she wrote about her travels, the medicine man's prescription suggests that the work of the mind Liz performs in her occupation as a writer is, similar to money or wealth, a material and transitory impediment to her spiritual happiness and self-fulfillment. Unlike the memoir, moreover, the film does not explicitly acknowledge that Liz is financing her culinary travel/spiritual quest through an advance contract and salary to write a book about it. In this way, Eat Pray Love presents Liz's culinary tourism as a spiritual quest, obscuring her primary role as a consumer. It also sidelines the labor of writing the culinary travel/spiritual quest narrative and its conversion by Liz into a best-selling commodity—a memoir that adapts the makeover formula.

While avoiding any mention of tourism, Liz nevertheless expresses her reasons for undertaking such travel in terms of a desire for general cultural consumption and the literal consumption of food: "I want to go someplace where I can marvel at something: language, gelato, spaghetti, something!" Cousin to such food adventuring television series as Anthony Bourdain: No Reservations (2005–2012) and Andrew Zimmern's Bizarre Foods (2006–), Eat Pray Love is part of "the capitalist version of the popular global landscape" that revises older colonial and anthropological narrative enterprises or "travel reports" which were used for the construction and consumption of the Other in the quest for Western self-discovery.[35] R. Diyah Larasati characterizes Liz as "the white American writer" whose travels to Asia and consumption of exotica produce the neoliberal consumer subject-citizen. According to Larasati, Liz "feeds off a mesmerizing Indian religion and encounters an Indonesian medicine man to fill the blank smudge of loneliness. Being present in the 'Orient' of the global South allows her to transcend and reconfigure identity based on her choice."[36]

If recessionary contexts heighten the fantasy of transcending material concerns through a spiritual journey, the depiction of this process in Murphy's Eat Pray Love is nevertheless not very convincing, and the film has been far more susceptible to a critique of postfeminist consumer ideology than Ephron's Julie & Julia. Ruth Williams describes Liz's extravagantly precious quest as "spiritual tourism," detailing how her path is strewn with the detritus of over four hundred product tie-ins, most of which the Home Shopping Network marketed after the film's premiere.[37] These include such items as meditation wrap bracelets from Dogeared Jewels and Gifts, black tea blended by Republic of Tea with ingredients from Italy, India, and Indonesia, and a line of food and cooking equipment created by model-turned-celebrity cookbook author Padma Lakshmi. The Eat Pray Love branding machine has few peers, at least among films for adults, and it even produced a crash course in enlightenment at the Royal Palms Resort and Spa in Phoenix where guests might squeeze gourmet food, yoga, and meditation into a twenty-four-hour stay. Such experiential substitutes or aftermarkets may take the place of more serious spiritual journeys, but they are also surely extensions of the film's Indochic, the contemporary neo-orientalist interest in consuming cultural artifacts and practices of the East, such as henna, yoga, and saris, that showcase sophisticated and expensive travel experiences and/or the cultural capital of the neoliberal global cosmopolitan.[38]

Recognizing the ways in which both *Julie & Julia* and *Eat Pray Love* centralize economic privilege and luxury consumption, despite recessionary culture's efforts to mute the prerecession extravagances of the Powell and Gilbert memoirs, confirms their participation in the postfeminist cultural production of the female neoliberal consumer subject. But when ruthless wealth stratification is a thoroughly accepted aspect of market fundamentalism, critical identification of consumption by affluent white women as a retrograde reification of dominant ideology is not sufficient, even if texts are soundly discredited both for excluding or othering women of color and for insidiously undermining the social and financial health of working-class women far less able to afford costly transformations. A full-fledged analysis must also be attentive to neoliberalism's increased demands for labor and to the production of the female working subject, especially in a recession both requiring more work from women and producing anxieties about women's share of the workforce, which underwrite every iteration of "the mancession." The pedagogy of the makeover narrative is at least as concerned with schooling women in work as it is with instructing them to consume. The self-making labor of transformation is prodigious indeed, and it relies on women's paid work. Furthermore, its centralization of a privileged female figure depends on the effacement of many other women laboring to perform the services purchased for and purportedly crucial to self-improvement and happiness.

As Angela McRobbie's summary of the new sexual contract makes clear, consumption is predicated on paid labor, which is the key component of what she deems "new femininities" or neoliberal modes of feminine citizenship that urge young women "to make good use of the opportunity to work, to gain qualifications, to control fertility, and to earn enough money to participate in consumer culture."[39] Moreover, Micki McGee observes in her study of makeover culture that "changes in the nature of the labor market have made efforts at self-making and self-invention increasingly urgent"; she frames the contemporary preoccupation with the self in the United States as manifest in self-help culture through the notion of the "belabored self," a phenomenon in which workers, and especially female workers clustered at the low end of the wage scale, are asked to continually work on themselves in efforts to remain employable.[40] Certainly, in the United States, where work values go largely unquestioned, "wage labor constitutes an important site of interpellation into a range of subjectivities," generating "not just income and capital, but disciplined individuals, governable subjects, worthy citizens, and responsible family members."[41] "Work plays," as Kathi Weeks reminds us, "a significant role in both the production and reproduction of gendered identities and hierarchies," particularly in gendered labor or "women's work" in which "doing femininity is part of doing the job."[42] Rather than diminishing, the segregation of occupations by gender has been stagnant or, in some lines of work, increasing, and the recession has exacerbated this pattern.[43] Indeed, the subjective dimensions of work have become even more influential as the importance of work in organizing social life has been magnified within neoliberal capitalism. In concert with consumption, work produces the neoliberal female subject.

As women in the United States have been further drawn into waged work for economic reasons, as well as by the desire for autonomy and to participate in a variety of activities, paid labor for all has become naturalized as a moral imperative, coming to dominate our social and political imaginaries as well as our time and energies.[44] In this context, Weeks argues, "enforcing work, as the other side of defending property rights, is a key function of the state, and a particular preoccupation of the postwelfare, neoliberal state."[45] The enforcement of work for women in the United States is perhaps most identifiable in "welfare reform" or the Personal Responsibility and Work Reconciliation Act of 1996, in which work requirements dubbed "workfare" were instituted for poor women who receive public assistance. From this perspective, the increased labor demands evident in the recession, in which workers are asked to do more and more—picking up the duties of laid-off colleagues, taking on a second job to compensate for the lost wages of a laid-off spouse, and declining earned vacation time, holidays, or sick leave as "shared sacrifice"—are not only part of downturn austerity measures but also part of a more fundamental restructuring in the neoliberal enforcement of work. Such demands operate in combination with the reduction of public programs that increase caring and domestic labor in the family, unpaid work that largely falls to women.

I am not seeking to lament the loss of privilege for white, middle-class American women who, once able to avoid overwork or "dirty work," are now compelled to labor in these ways. Rather, I wish to foreground how *Julie & Julia* and *Eat Pray Love* deceptively celebrate the female working subject who undertakes a costly self-transformation, willingly reforming her marketplace labor in ways that increase it and also reanimate normative gender identity and power relations for unpaid labor. Thus these scenarios are both fantasies of economic achievement in a recessionary context and instructional texts that educate women as to the flexibility associated with contemporary working lives. Both heroines seek better work and find it by embracing the unwaged labor associated with bourgeois domesticity that is coded as leisure or "spontaneous expressions of women's nature," namely cooking and the production of emotional intimacy.[46] Instead of securing wages for domestic labor through revaluation, they discover ways of accommodating it, which actually expands the category of women's work. In the context of neoliberalism and especially the pressure that recessionary mass under- and unemployment are putting on wages and workloads, we must be wary of calls for more labor.[47] Weeks asserts that feminists "should focus on the demands not simply or exclusively for more work and better work, but also for less work; we should focus not only on revaluing feminized forms of unwaged labor but also challenge the sanctification of such work that can accompany or be enabled by these efforts."[48]

As I have noted, *Julie & Julia* and *Eat Pray Love* are linked to a previous generation of postfeminist popular cultural texts that register the gendering of labor in far less celebratory terms. For these biopics, recession-era Hollywood draws on the postfeminist archetype of the conflicted working woman and revives psychological retreatism in narratives that rearticulate career ambition to bourgeois domesticity and a traditionalist gender division of labor.[49] Further, the racialized gender division of labor is nearly invisible in these films, which is in keeping with the postfeminist disregard for social inequities and hierarchies among women that would otherwise reveal social constraints on individual choice.[50] In contrast to the ways in which risk is masculinized in recession-themed popular films featuring beset corporate executives and transnational businessmen (such as *The Company Men* [2010] or *Margin Call* [2011]), *Julie & Julia* and *Eat Pray Love* discount and rationalize the disproportionately feminized distribution of sacrifice, risk, and flexibilization to low-wage workers.[51]

So while *Julie & Julia* and *Eat Pray Love* celebrate professionally successful women, they simultaneously reproduce many of the habits of 1990s and early 2000s postfeminist chick flicks that registered profound social ambivalence about women's increased participation in the U.S. labor force by presenting corrective narratives about working women's "miswanting." As Diane Negra observes, dramas such as *Picture Perfect* (1997), *Two Weeks Notice* (2002), *How to Lose a Guy in Ten Days* (2003), and *Just Like Heaven* (2005) feature a heroine who "realizes [that] her professional aspirations are misplaced."[52] Indeed, prerecession chick flicks most often resolved problems, tensions, and anxieties about working life fantastically through windfalls, creative manipulations, or more simply through diminishing a female protagonist's career ambitions.[53] Negra identifies this pattern as the postfeminist "master narrative of retreatism," which shepherds women out of the workplace, at times literally relocating the urban female professional to an idealized hometown.[54] At other times, the retreat is more of a psychological adjustment, as narratives feature female heroines who remain in the workforce but no longer pin their identities to careers.

Instead of displacing the importance of work in female subjectivity, recession-era chick flicks such as Julie & Julia and Eat Pray Love resolve conflicts and ambivalence about work through self-transformations. The filmic narratives initially suggest that the heroines will reject the dream of "doing it all" (a variant of "having it all"); yet female ambition remains intact and is even reinforced, reflecting recessionary culture's intensification of the makeover ethos. Rather than narrowly focusing on career, or off-loading domestic labor to working-class women, however, the white, middle-class women in these films perform marketplace labor and domestic labor, as well as the crucial neoliberal work of entrepreneurialism and self-care.[55]

Crisis, Self-Transformation, and Domesticity

Remaining true to the time frame of the books they adapt, Julie & Julia and Eat Pray Love do not explicitly reference the recession but present other destabilizing crises that allegorize it and function as the backstories or occasions that trigger recognition of unsatisfying work and the need for self-transformation by the protagonists. In fact, while crises are catalysts, femininity is largely dissociated from crisis per se, so the mediation of recession in these films is ideologically bound, consistent with the pattern of current media imagery that focuses attention on "the middle-aged, middle-class white guy as the sign, symptom and victim of recession."[56] Even as Julie & Julia and Eat Pray Love celebrate the work of successful female American writers, the labor that is valorized is comforting. The gendering of labor is thus presented as a kind of antidote or palliative to crisis, even as female labor is disavowed as a form of labor at all.

Julie & Julia's first full scene follows Julie on her way to work, the frame widening to expose an altered post-9/11 skyline; we see her head toward the Court Square station to take the subway from Queens to Manhattan, exiting at Ground Zero, and surrounded by makeshift public memorials, armed military guards, and firemen. Julie is then seen installed in a cubicle with a headset, as she spends her day containing the psychic aftermath of 9/11 for the Lower Manhattan Development Corporation (LMDC), answering hotline calls from survivors and family members of victims who want to object to the plans for the memorial or simply talk to a sympathetic government representative. To her first caller, who relates that her son died in the second tower, Julie can only apologize, and when a second caller who doesn't like the plan for the official memorial asks directly, "Do you have any power?" she must answer, "No." A third accuses her of being "a heartless, bureaucratic goon" and ridicules her for being a cubicle worker, and the fourth cries about her husband's fiberglass-filled lungs, reducing Julie to tears. On the commute home that night, Julie buys chocolate because, "after a day when nothing is sure, and I mean nothing, you can come home and absolutely know that if you add egg yolks to chocolate, sugar, and milk it will get thick. It's such a comfort." A day in the life of Julie Powell at the LMDC makes plain what many women know all too well: service work is not only precarious and low paid, but also demeaning and emotionally draining, standing in stark contrast to the socially valued labor of male-dominated occupations such as finance, firefighting, and soldiering.

Early scenes in *Eat Pray Love* highlight a decidedly more personal identity crisis, involving both professional and marital disillusionment, which spurs Liz to self-transformation. Though a successful writer, Liz nevertheless battles depression, and opening scenes show her bored or embarrassed by the superficiality of her career and unhappy in her marriage. Liz's agent, Dahlia Shiraz (Viola Davis), unmistakably positioned as the "Black Best Friend" (BBF), offers sage advice in response to her distress and Liz quickly recognizes that she is not committed to her marriage.[57] When Liz and her husband Stephen (Billy Crudup) formally meet to discuss the terms of their divorce, he flatly refuses her offer to "take it all, take everything." Liz confesses that she wants out of her marriage not because she has a patriarchal husband who demands an exclusively caregiving wife; rather, she is disappointed in Stephen's lack of ambition. Liz expresses longing for a traditionalist gender division of labor, which the film suggests is not actually available because her wage labor has overtaken more conventional power relations and rendered the male breadwinner–female homemaker model irrelevant. While she decisively ends the marriage, Liz's professional quandary entails a more tortured departure, and indeed she never truly leaves work behind.

In symbolic ways, recession-era chick flicks register social anxieties about how women in the workforce may disrupt customary status relations between white, middle-class femininity and hegemonic masculinity. As I have suggested, these long-standing anxieties have found their most direct expression in the crisis rhetorics of "the mancession" and "the end of men." In Hanna Rosin's controversial 2010 article, "The End of Men," the characterization of male manufacturing workers as redundant labor reduces to a panicked "role reversal" in all areas of social life or at least to a distressing "economic and cultural power shift from men to women," with men replaced by female workers in the economy, intimate relationships and marriage, and the post-industrial family.

Both films thus begin by depicting crises that are connected to the workplace and the retreat of alienated working women, decidedly middle class and white, from public occupations. Heroines then take up more private enterprises in which they try their hands at life writing in food writing formats, the gustatory travel memoir in the case of Gilbert and the culinary Internet memoir or cooking blog in the case of Powell. Even the portrayal of patrician Julia Child, who was financially dependent on her husband to complete *Mastering the Art of French Cooking*, presents the icon as searching for more personally satisfying and meaningful work in a departure from her earlier career as a secretary for the U.S. Office of Strategic Services. While audiences know that these privileged heroines will achieve inordinate commercial success, the films take care to establish their ambivalence about the workplace, the management of career ambition, and processes of self-transformation. Work, here the professional and entrepreneurial act of writing, is the vehicle by which these heroines seek happiness.

While the makeovers in these films are fundamentally psychological retreats that move heroines closer to reassuring domesticity, the films emphasize their transformational journeys, spatializing them via physical movement, relocations, and the governing metaphor of travel as development. *Julie & Julia* weaves the two "true stories" (as the promotional material termed it) of the memoirs it fictionalizes, drawing together Child's multiyear project writing her influential cookbook while living in Europe and Powell's yearlong effort to become a writer and leave behind her low-paid cubicle job and eventually the city for a house in the country and happiness. "Government employee by day, renegade foodie by night," Julie's commute home from work each day is a reminder of the shift she is trying to make by blogging about recipes from Child's classic cookbook that she tests and serves to her husband and friends. The film's title sequence provides alternating shots of physical relocation to newly established domiciles: one of the Childs picking up their car in Le Havre after arriving in France for Paul's new post, and the second of Amy and Eric moving from Brooklyn to a 900-square-foot Queens loft above a pizzeria.

Similarly, *Eat Pray Love* portrays the story of a writer, albeit one already established, whose yearlong global tour is a search for a new sense of home or feeling of belonging through which she hopes to rekindle her emotional passion and restore a satisfying spiritual life to achieve that ever-elusive work-life balance. The Gilbert narrative initially seems far less heteronormative than that constructed around Powell, since Liz acknowledges an ambivalence about the bourgeois married life, complete with house in the suburbs, that she had "fully participated in creating but could no longer see herself in." In some ways, the film promises a rebellious move toward independence and a more bohemian, scaled-back career for its protagonist. But that all changes by the conclusion, after Liz learns how to be alone, meets suave Brazilian love interest Filipe (Javier Bardem), and overcomes her fear of commitment on the island of Bali. Narrative closure comes just as Liz's efforts to find a new spiritual home take on a material expression in an ambitious fund-raising endeavor, accomplished through an e-mail letter writing campaign, to build an impoverished Balinese mother her own house. The suggestion seems to be that Liz has relocated the domestic ability to care about others and can now appropriately labor in the service of affective bonds. With these films, a predominantly female, recession-ravaged audience watches white, middle-class American women who do not abstain from paid work but who willingly relocate it to a new home where they successfully revise and realign with domestic labor or women's work, conventionally defined as the creation of emotional or affective comfort.[58]

Even if physical relocations are in many ways narrative conceits, the spaces in which Julie and Liz rearticulate ambition with normative femininity are appropriated. A new work site is created via the self-renewing, entrepreneurial writing projects the heroines undertake, but the characters also literally inhabit new spaces. Julie moves to the gentrifying immigrant neighborhood of Long Island City, in the outer borough of Queens in which all sorts of new cultural enterprises such as Silvercup Studios (production facility of high-profile postfeminist media, including *Julie & Julia* itself, *Sex and the City*, and *30 Rock*) have replaced former factories. Liz more obviously appropriates space via her cosmopolitan tour. As the Indonesian scholar Larasati comments, Liz's search for a different domestic space "is done by conquering, owning, and reproducing some of my cultural imaginary as her discovery. *It means translating herself into the familiar and myself into the unfamiliar.*"[59] This is especially apparent to Larasati when Liz takes over the menial, daily work of local women and cleans the ashram as a way to achieve transcendence. Liz's writing project "relegates the 'other' women in India and Indonesia to the position of marginal characters" in their own homes.[60] By relocating the professional American woman and recoding her in a space that she defines through reclaiming domestic labor, *Julie & Julia* and *Eat Pray Love* deploy the makeover to contain anxieties, including not only those long-standing concerns about the place of white middle-class femininity in relation to hegemonic masculinity but also recession-inflected anxieties about the place of Americans in the world and the status of the United States in the global economy.

Writing for Makeover and Crisis Management

The previous section emphasized that Julie & Julia and Eat Pray Love are recession-inflected chick flicks, comfort narratives that adopt the makeover formula to perform the affective work of culinary discourses that manage cultural anxieties, particularly about women in the workplace. This section explores the contention that the entrepreneurial labor of writing is a sanctioned form of work because it aids the self-making considered crucial for the appropriately feminized postfeminist female worker who willingly accommodates a gendered division of domestic labor. Julie & Julia and Eat Pray Love thus add "writer" to the short list of marketplace occupations in postfeminist popular culture considered "expressive of women's essential femininity," a list that also includes nanny, flight attendant, and female sex worker, all low-wage, female-dominated service occupations with high degrees of insecurity.[61] If popular culture once commonly equated "women's work and sexual display or performance" to reflect as well as to assuage audience anxiety about working women, as Yvonne Tasker observed, it is today far more concerned with feminizing working women.[62] Certainly, we should understand this shift in terms of a femininity that signifies comfort in binary relation to a white masculinity defined by crisis, as noted earlier. The trope of masculinity in crisis is a familiar one and its amplification in recession-era culture comes as no surprise. A related cultural pattern is evident in the intensification of the makeover ethos and the adaptation of the makeover formula in feminizing narratives across media forms.

A corollary explanation for the feminization of the working woman in popular culture is the strengthening role for popular media as neoliberal technologies of citizenship in the production of self-governing subjects who properly consume and labor. Specifically, representations tacitly tutor women in the gendering of labor or the various kinds of work society expects from them in a labor market deeply segregated both horizontally by occupation and vertically within occupations. It also prepares them for a gender division of domestic labor that still requires women to do most of the caring work and emotional labor in families and intimate relationships. To be sure, the role of professional writer demands more cultural capital than other occupations frequently endorsed in postfeminism, and it is less obviously a feminized category, associated as it is with white-collar work. But as McRobbie has pointed out, creative workers in the neoliberal "talent-led economy" often toil in their own homes, operate casually and flexibly as part-time and contingent workers, and frequently work without benefits as subcontractors or freelancers, relieving capital of the overhead of a physical office space and health care costs.[63] According to the feminist economists Drucilla Barker and Susan Feiner, economic restructuring in the neoliberal era may well entail a conversion of all labor to "the conditions of female labor . . . where the global economy promises jobs that are more insecure, more flexible, and even more poorly paid."[64] Recession accelerates this process such that the expanded list of acceptable occupations for women (as featured within popular cultural forms such as the chick flick) registers pervasive white-collar job insecurity.[65]

The kinds of writing that typically function as expressive of women's essential femininity in postfeminist culture are not the aestheticized, literary forms associated with the masculinized figure of writer as artist. More often than not, that sort of writer is either an elite figure ensconced in a literary culture understood to operate outside of and unconcerned with commercial culture, or positioned as someone who suffers nobly for the rewards of participating in high culture. In postfeminist popular culture, by contrast, it is devocationalized commercial forms of writing that are sanctioned for women. As aspiring blogger, journalist, or popular author, the female writer participates willingly in an expanding global media industry, effectively modeling an abiding interest in the production and consumption of the texts in which her work appears.

The protagonist as striving professional writer of some description is actually ubiquitous in postfeminist culture; the trope is particularly well established in chick lit, which features heroines employed in media outlets such as women's magazines, newspapers, TV stations, or bookstores.[66] Writerly occupations with commercial potential are nearly as common in chick flicks, not only adaptations of chick lit such as *The Devil Wears Prada* and *Confessions of a Shopaholic* (2009), but also such films as *You've Got Mail* (1998), *How to Lose a Guy in Ten Days*, *The Ugly Truth* (2009), and *The Proposal* (2009). Finally, television is definitely in on the act with NBC's Liz Lemon in *30 Rock* (2006–13) and HBO's series *Girls* (2012–), whose protagonist, Hannah Horvath, is an aspiring memoirist contending with downturn conditions and played by the show's creator and much-celebrated media "auteur," Lena Dunham.[67]

In postfeminist culture, it is now often the case that professional or commercial writing enables the self-work that is increasingly required in the neoliberal global economy's labor market. Certainly, the gourmet cooking and global travel written about in *Julie & Julia* and *Eat Pray Love* are activities significantly premised on (or at least associated with) affluence. Sanders and Barnes-Brown identify such practices as necessary to those recessionary makeover narratives that promote consumption as a route to emotional health. Moreover, in *Julie & Julia* and *Eat Pray Love* writing is represented as an appropriate form of entrepreneurial labor because it simultaneously monitors, reflects on, and expresses the heroines' unambiguous and authentic femininity. As a recurrent trope of female endeavor, writing facilitates the overt display of self-work via the extensive use of a first-person mode. Moreover, the expressive occupations of these protagonists provide a pretext for both autobiographical statements and a broadly confessional mode. Such a mode tends to operate via a set formula: shaming of the flawed female subject, coupled with surveillance by audiences; her subsequent commitment to a makeover (with aid provided by wise friends or lifestyling experts); and the presentation of a significantly changed heroine.

Along with *Julie & Julia*'s opening scene of Julie's cubicle job, an early scene of lunch with friends (figure 4.1), which Julie dreads and refers to as the "ritual Cobb salad lunch," highlights Julie's demeaning and precarious employment while underlining the vacuity of her more successful peers. A subsequent scene introduces the possibility of commercial writing as a viable profession; not only is writing aspirational but its creativity is clearly contrasted to the implicitly superficial labors of her executive friends. When two of them begin complaining at lunch about their assistants, Julie identifies with the challenge of pleasing bosses who make unrealistic demands. She flippantly tells her friends the solution: "Just fire your assistant and be your own assistant." Underscoring her own vulnerability, Julie's idea is dismissed by her friends, who assume that she does not understand the efficient operation of the marketplace. Similarly, the scene signifies that Julie does not possess the requisite expertise for professional marketplace success when one friend completes a transaction over her mobile phone for a $190 million "parcel," and Julie asks what the term means. After explaining, the high-powered friends ask about Julie's job at the LMDC, but before she has a chance to respond, they both speak for her to characterize it as "so sad" and "painful." The scene ends with incoming calls and Julie reprimanded for snacking on a breadstick while the others use their mobile devices. The Cobb salad lunch with friends is a ritual not so much because it is a regular meeting but because it ritually shames Julie for not having enough ambition or not gaining the qualifications needed for professional success in the labor market, which obviously requires, the scene suggests, a knowledge of high-level business practices as well as a command of new technology. The scene conveys the judgment that Julie is "the author of [her] own misfortune," as Nikolas Rose describes the primary ideological precept of neoliberal governance that places full responsibility for failure or success on the individual and disavows any structural need for market regulation.[68]

FIGURE 4.1. The ritual Cobb salad lunch in *Julie & Julia* confirms the need for Julie's makeover.

At the same time, this scene represents Julie's friends as workaholics or "career bitches" who have lost their ability to maintain genuine connections or relationships with people, as signified by their devotion to cell phones and PalmPilots, their imperious attitudes toward the low-paid feminized labor of pink-collar occupations, and their insensitive celebration of "tearing down high rises," which only Julie recognizes will surely displace more people in Manhattan soon after 9/11. In short, the highly successful friends have lost their femininity, especially their ability to nurture relationships. Both the shaming of Julie for her cubicle job and the disdain for career success set the stage for Julie's subsequent makeover; her blog promises to be a reassuringly domestic and authentically feminine self-improvement project. Whenever her dedication to it threatens to also render Julie a "bitch," she apologizes to Eric. In addition, the Julie/Julia Project blog garners a reading public or "bleaders," so the film portrays how the blog allows Julie to publicly express and display her aspirational neoliberal values in the makeover process. When a subject writes a chronicle of her makeover process and its semiotic inscription of gender normativity, the act endorses and becomes part of the makeover process.

The scene immediately following the Cobb salad lunch represents the ways in which commercial writing may incorporate the surveillance as well as the shaming mechanisms of the postfeminist makeover. At the lunch, Julie's journalist friend Annabelle Smith, who writes for *New York*, asks Julie if she can interview her about their generation turning thirty. When the story appears in print and its headline is plastered all over bus stops, she learns that she has been used as an example of failure. After memorizing it, Julie recites her career trajectory as described in Annabelle's article, which is titled "Portrait of a Lost Generation" and which reports that Julie has not kept pace with expectations, whether those of her friends or the neoliberal economy, so Julie then commits to the Julie/Julia Project blog. In these scenes, commercial writing functions as a shaming and surveillance medium and also furthers makeover objectives. Being a writer is presented as an appropriate and potentially lucrative alternative to the all-consuming professions that will leave women emotionally disconnected from others and only interested in individual career success.

While Julie must cautiously, and without compromising her femininity, work up her ambition in the face of job dissatisfaction and precarious employment, Liz seems to fall more closely in line with the prerecessionary model of downshifting ambition. *Eat Pray Love* portrays Liz's success as a wedge in her marriage and the cause of her self-alienation. As the primary breadwinner and supporting a bourgeois lifestyle that she no longer knows how to perform, Liz feels as if she is faking it. After the divorce, Stephen is quickly replaced with a rebound lover in the form of New Age actor David Piccolo (James Franco), who, like Stephen, has unclear goals. Unhappy with how her career ambition seems to always eclipse or even displace men, Liz reassesses her priorities. She embarks on her quest, all the while chronicling a search for her authentic feminine self. As Weber observes, "the makeover as social practice does not teach individuals how to cultivate the self but how to locate it." [69] But, instead of locating a self who rejects the coupledom that she has been faking, the film suggests that Liz relocates an authentic or essential femininity that privileges relationships with people, conventional power relations, and the emotional labor they entail. As part of this process, Liz eats with and cooks an American Thanksgiving meal for friends in Italy, prays with fellow worshipers at an ashram in India, and reflects on life's wonders with spiritual soul mates in Indonesia. Although the film obscures that Liz writes a memoir of her yearlong journey, she is a perfect example of the pattern in postfeminist popular culture in which commercial writing becomes the entrepreneurial labor of choice for heroines precisely because it allows for the expression of feelings and a working out of anxieties about laboring, paid and unpaid, on behalf of the self and others. Additionally, writing enacts a makeover process, one that ultimately confirms a psychological essentialism rationalizing a gendered division of labor that females are urged (or compelled) to resign themselves to under current economic conditions. [70]

Julie & Julia and Eat Pray Love suggest that authentic women willingly take

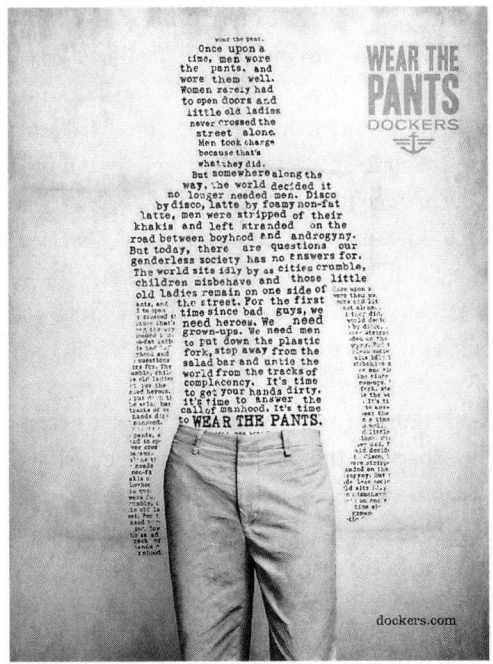

FIGURE 4.2. The Dockers "man-ifesto" advertisement reanimates gendered labor while inviting men to consume.

responsibility for rebalancing an economic system in crisis, adapting to a social order that can no longer afford entirely separate spheres of labor for the privileged, and certainly not the luxury of regulated equality for the majority. The message of women's essential psychological difference from men as a rationale for gendered labor now appears across the media landscape, from the many websites — such as She Writes and BlogHer — that offer commercial services (and some free advice) to assist women in becoming professional writers and bloggers with the flexibility to work at home, to the 2009 Dockers "man-ifesto" (figure 4.2) that urges men, "get your hands dirty," and "wear the pants" in the family. In such recessionary calls to work, both women and men are exhorted to labor in conventionally gendered ways, but demands are qualified, with women performing entrepreneurial labor in the domestic sphere and men focusing on fashion and consumption in manly trades.

The print text that expressly claims authentic gender identity in the Dockers advertisement gives shape to the male figure, literally representing the (fashionable) male subject. Interestingly, the text that shapes the male subject is not a first-person expression of the masculine self who desires work or even an invitation to men to express themselves, but rather a description of desirable male behavior coupled with an invitation to consume. A recession context seems to require, by contrast, far more explicit and public statements about self-transformation specifically from women, with exhortations at every turn to "express yourself," such as in the February 2012 issue of *O, The Oprah Magazine*. The issue's chalk art cover promises advice for "26 ways to share your story with the world" and the results of a mini memoir project, modeled after SMITH *Magazine*'s Six-Word Memoirs contest. While calls "seeking the fullest expression of Self" are not new or specific to the recession, as Negra has observed, the Oprah universe, including Oprah's Book Club and *O, The Oprah Magazine*, is a system "that glorifies individual self-making but is studiously inattentive to any context of social and/or economic inequality."[71] Such inattention actually raises questions, as it does for *Julie & Julia* and *Eat Pray Love*, about the focus on forms of self-expression that are sanctioned as entrepreneurial labor in postfeminist popular culture and touted in a distressed economy as a way for young women, especially those with strong media skills, to "create your own job."[72] To what extent are such exhortations for self-expression part of the neoliberal enforcement of work? Certainly, they can be connected to self-making. But we should note their links to low or even unpaid work, since so much of this type of cultural work operates as free labor performed by amateur media producers for commercial concerns, as in blogs that rate commodities, Pinterest boards on which members curate (or advertise) for retailers in "virtual hope chests" that function as mail order catalogs, or even on reality TV, where cast members fill the creative gap that once would have been filled by screenwriters.[73] While I do not intend to participate in the denigration of women's writing, reduce the Oprah Winfrey phenomenon to neoliberal complicity, or belittle the skills and rewards of designing a blog or other creative expression on social media, it is worth interrogating how popular memoir writing, culinary and otherwise, is connected to the seemingly limitless demands for women's flexible labor in the marketplace and at home.

Conclusion

As depicted in the two recession-era films I discuss, yearlong writing projects most explicitly about domestic labor disclose the long-term work that must be devoted to the self to be successful in the neoliberal job market. The privileged status of American heroines Julie and Liz also conveys that work on the feminine self and a commitment to constant improvement require substantial resources. In this sense, the heroines in *Julie & Julia* and *Eat Pray Love* are less portraits of exceptional, individual celebrities than they are subjects turned experts and ideal models of the neoliberal female self who works mightily to meet the mandates for market employment, all the while accommodating a traditionalist gender division of labor in the domestic sphere. These films rely on meritocratic myths, largely glossing over the privileges and opportunities that create success since they suggest that Julie, Liz, and perhaps even Julia triumph spectacularly because they are paragons of the flexible female worker who learns how to navigate the volatile conditions of neoliberalism and retain authentic femininity.

I close by returning to this chapter's title: "What Julia Knew." In 1948 Julia Child, newlywed and newly arrived in Paris after several years in China, undertook what we might now call an extreme makeover, from low-level government worker to culinary student at Le Cordon Bleu. She did not need to work for wages, and she was not interested in "having it all," but she was privileged and had the cultural and financial capital to "do something." Child decided to direct her self-making efforts toward an activity with entrepreneurial potential and one appropriate to her gender: writing a cookbook. Possessing the racial and social class privileges of normative gender identity with which she could transform herself into an unassailable celebrity chef, perhaps America's most beloved, Child used culinary discourse to create feelings of comfort and safety in a period of intense change and ideological contestation. This was a period in which Americans were urged to extend the work of government surveillance, be on the watch for foreign threats, and report anything suspicious. Julia and Paul, who had also worked for the U.S. government in China during the war years, were prime targets for charges of communism, homosexuality, and even national treason, and Paul was investigated, as the film recounts. While many women may not identify with Child, perhaps because she relied too much on her white, heterosexual, and bourgeois privilege, or because she hails from an earlier era in which choices were circumscribed by conditions that purportedly do not exist today, surveillance is something contemporary women have in common with Child.[74] Now, however, surveillance is even more deeply embedded in U.S. society, especially through the work on the self that neoliberalism has consolidated in new ways in the recession. Despite the more sophisticated media technologies of our day, and the postfeminist and postracial claims that any woman can achieve success if she simply makes authentically feminine and wise marketplace choices, the constraints of a neoliberal society characterized by crisis seem akin in some ways to Child's era, with women exhorted to self-governance as a means to locate acceptable forms of entrepreneurial labor.

Notes

1. See Food Network, "About Foodnetwork.com," http://www.foodnetwork.com /about-us/about-foodnetworkcom/index.html, for its self-description.

2. Polan, *Julia Child's "The French Chef,"* 3.

3. Polan, *Julia Child's "The French Chef,"* 3, 11.

4. Polan, Julia Child's "The French Chef," 237. According to Polan, managing anxieties about changing social conditions while also helping to realign Americans in a changing world "fraught with global tensions" were major accomplishments of Child's *Mastering the Art of French Cooking*, particularly when she translated its pedagogy to television through *The French Chef* (78).

5. Bravo, "'Having It All?'" See Slaughter, "Why Women Still Can't Have It All."

6. According to Christopher Petrella, "Precarious labor . . . refers to forms of work typically marked by temporary contracts, limited or no social benefits and statutory guarantees, high degrees of job insecurity, low job tenure, sub-standard wages, and high risks of occupational injury and disease. From a workers' perspective, precarious employment is unpredictable and ultimately subject to the caprice of the 1%. Further, such forms of labor transfer social risks from employers (and the state) to individual workers and their families — to those who can least absorb them." Petrella, "Recovery for the 1%, Recession for the Rest."

7. For a generic description of the biopic, see Bingham, *Whose Lives Are They Anyway?*, 26. For an extensive discussion, see book two, "A Woman's Life Is Never Done: Female Biopics."

8. According to the Internet Movie Database, *Julie & Julia* grossed nearly $120 million worldwide, while *Eat Pray Love* earned almost $200 million. The memoirs were also spectacularly successful, aided by cross media synergies and marketing, especially in the case of Gilbert's memoir, which spent two hundred weeks on the *New York Times* paperback nonfiction bestseller list and earned Viking Penguin at least $15 million. For a discussion of Viking Penguin's marketing of *Eat, Pray, Love*, see Williams, "Eat, Pray, Love."

9. For a discussion of Julie Powell's memoir as "foodie romance," see Van Slooten, "A Marriage Made in the Kitchen." For a discussion of confessional memoir, see Day, "True Confessions in New Women's Lit." In *Julia Child's "The French Chef,"* Polan reads *My Life in France* as a story about a transformation, one that "replays the recurrent trope of the American visitor to France who has a special meal that, in a veritable epiphany, is a life-transforming lesson in culinary purity and intensity of taste" (5).

10. Negra, *What a Girl Wants?*, 5–7. On "downshifting" and the rise of the Food Network, see Collins, *Watching What We Eat*, particularly her final chapter, 232–52.

11. Several texts that have been marketed as "recession lit" feature narratives of redemptive austerity, including *The Penny Pinchers Club* by Sarah Strohmeyer.

12. For a brief commentary on the distribution of risk, see Folbre, "Economix."

13. McRobbie, *The Aftermath of Feminism*, 31.

14. Negra, *What a Girl Wants?*, 5.

15. See Gamble, "Postfeminism."

16. Tasker and Negra, *Interrogating Postfeminism*, 2–8.

17. The definition is Heather Cabot's, cited in Ferriss and Young, *Chick Lit*, 3.

18. Ferriss and Young discuss this slippage in their introduction, describing how Fielding felt compelled to announce that she was not Bridget Jones (*Chick Lit*, 4).

19. For a discussion of how labor and employment are represented in chick lit, see Hale, "Long Suffering Professional Females." For a more recent discussion, see Har-

zewski, *Chick Lit and Postfeminism*. Rosalind Gill and Elena Herdieckerhoff observe that chick lit heroines are characteristically committed to the idea of a career, while often employed in the "dead end" service sector, and "portrayed as dissatisfied and struggling in their jobs." Gill and Herdieckerhoff, "Rewriting the Romance," 495.

20. For a discussion of embedded advertising in reality TV, see Pozner, *Reality Bites Back*, 273–99.

21. For a representative discussion of this tension in Sophie Kinsella's *Shopaholic* book series, see Scanlon, "Making Shopping Safe for the Rest of Us." Offering a complex assessment, Caroline Smith argues that chick lit dialogues with other neoliberal cultural forms that address women, responding specifically to popular advice manuals to problematize their ideology of "consume and achieve" and to offer alternative instruction in helping female readers become discerning consumers. Smith, *Cosmopolitan Culture and Consumerism in Chick Lit*, 6. Jim Collins has suggested popular "post-literary" chick lit novels function as guides for self-improvement and connoisseurship, and for negotiating new "transactions between cultural and financial capital." Collins, *Bring on the Books for Everybody*, 189. See also Harzewski, who contends that chick lit combines "popular romance with the satiric elements of the novel of manners." Harzewski, *Chick Lit and Postfeminism*, 4.

22. Modleski, *Loving with a Vengeance*, xxvii.

23. Mannur, "Eat, Dwell, Orient," 12.

24. Mannur, "Eat, Dwell, Orient," 9.

25. Sanders and Barnes-Brown, "Eat, Pray, Spend," 30.

26. Sanders and Barnes-Brown, "Eat, Pray, Spend," 30.

27. Sanders and Barnes-Brown, "Eat, Pray, Spend," 31.

28. Sanders and Barnes-Brown, "Eat, Pray, Spend," 31.

29. Weber, *Makeover TV*, 31.

30. Ouellette, "'Take Responsibility for Yourself,'" 226.

31. Weber, *Makeover TV*, 19.

32. Ferriss, "Fashioning Femininity in the Makeover Chick Flick," 44.

33. For discussion of consumption of chick lit, see Gill and Herdieckerhoff, "Rewriting the Romance," 488.

34. See Bingham's discussion of Lowenthal's idol of consumption and idol of production in *Whose Lives Are They Anyway?*, 4–6. See also the influential use of the paradigm by Dyer, *Stars*.

35. Larasati, "Eat, Pray, Love, Mimic," 91.

36. Larasati, "Eat, Pray, Love, Mimic," 91.

37. Williams, "Eat, Pray, Love," 1–3.

38. Huggan, *The Postcolonial Exotic*, 67.

39. McRobbie, *The Aftermath of Feminism*, 54.

40. McGee, *Self-Help, Inc.*, 16. See p. 12 for description of the term "belabored self."

41. Weeks, *The Problem with Work*, 8. Weeks defines traditional work values as those that preach the moral worth and dignity of waged work and privilege such work as the essential source of individual growth, self-fulfillment, social recognition, and status (11).

42. Weeks, *The Problem with Work*, 10.

43. For discussion of trends in occupational segregation in the United States, see Ariane Hegewisch et al., "Separate and Not Equal?"

44. Weeks, *The Problem with Work*, 36.

45. Weeks, *The Problem with Work*, 7.

46. Weeks, *The Problem with Work*, 24.

47. Weeks, *The Problem with Work*, 12.

48. Weeks, *The Problem with Work*, 13.

49. Negra, *What a Girl Wants?*, 87.

50. As Evelyn Nakano Glenn influentially established some time ago, the gender division of labor is always racialized. Glenn, "From Servitude to Service Work."

51. Boushey, "Jobs Returning, Slowly."

52. Negra, "Structural Integrity, Historical Reversion, and the Post 9/11 Chick Flick," 53.

53. Negra, *What a Girl Wants?*, 7.

54. Negra, *What a Girl Wants?*, 5.

55. Wendy Brown defines "self-care" as the ability to provide for one's own needs and service one's own ambitions. Brown, *Edgework*, 6–7.

56. Negra and Tasker, "Neoliberal Frames and Genres of Inequality," 5.

57. "Black Best Friend" or BBF was coined by Stewart, "Black Women."

58. Diane Negra discusses romantic comedies that similarly "privatize" female work in "Structural Integrity, Historical Reversion, and the Post 9/11 Chick Flick," 54.

59. Larasati, "Eat, Pray, Love, Mimic," 92, emphasis in original.

60. Larasati, "Eat, Pray, Love, Mimic," 93.

61. Negra, *What a Girl Wants?*, 87.

62. Tasker, *Working Girls*, 4.

63. Quoted in Hendershot, "Belabored Reality," 246.

64. Barker and Feiner, *Liberating Economics*, 111.

65. Negra observes that the trend has been repressed in postfeminist representations in *What a Girl Wants?*, 91.

66. Ferriss and Young begin their volume with the point that the heroine as professional writer is a generic convention (*Chick Lit*, 1). Bushnell's *Sex and the City* (1997) tops the list, but other best-selling titles are Amy Sohn's *Run Catch Kiss* (1999), Jennifer Weiner's *Good in Bed* (2002), Kathryn Stockett's *The Help* (2009), and even Lynn Harris's parodic *Death by Chick Lit* (2007). Not only for protagonists, but for the chick lit genre itself, writing is a self-consciously entrepreneurial endeavor; an extremely robust publishing phenomenon, chick lit has reinvented popular women's fiction through a seemingly endless hybridization of subgenres, frequent remediation with other cultural forms that target female audiences, and a clear path of migration to other media such as television and film. For a suggestive discussion of remediation in HBO's *Sex and the City*, see Arthurs, "*Sex and the City* and Consumer Culture," 83–98.

67. Episode 4, "Hannah's Diary," speaks to the narrative function of the protagonist as writer in postfeminist popular culture. *Girls* has been described by Rory Carroll as "a *Sex and the City* for Recession-era America." Carroll, "Is HBO's New Hit Show a Sex and the City for Recession-Era America?"

68. Rose, "Governing 'Advanced' Liberal Democracies," 59.

69. Weber, *Makeover TV*, 6.

70. See Jane Gerhard for discussion of psychological essentialism. Gerhard, "*Sex and the City.*"

71. Negra, *What a Girl Wants?*, 143.

72. Buchheit, "Three Ways the Rich and Powerful Have Cheated Young Americans."

73. For a discussion of how "pinners" perform postfeminism, see Smith, "Pinning Postfeminism." For a brief discussion of "social marketing" on Pinterest, see Oler, "Pinned Down."

74. For a discussion of generational disidentification in feminism, see Brunsdon, "Feminism, Postfeminism, Martha, Martha, and Nigella."

FIVE *ELIZABETH NATHANSON*

Dressed for Economic Distress

BLOGGING AND THE "NEW" PLEASURES OF FASHION

In fall 2011 a TV commercial for the discount designer clothing store T.J.Maxx featuring the fashion blogger Lindsey Calla aired in the United States. As creator of the website Saucy Glossie, Calla is one of a number of young women who have found fame by using blogs to depict themselves modeling everyday outfits. As she proclaims on her blog, the goal of such online work is to model "style on a real girl budget!"[1] The ad re-creates what we are encouraged to imagine is Calla's daily life as a fashion blogger; it depicts the slender, white brunette twenty-something frolicking on Manhattan rooftops, posing for photographs as if she were a professional model, typing in a coffee shop on her sleek laptop, and desirously browsing handbags in her local T.J.Maxx. With a cheery and upbeat attitude, Calla explains how she sees herself as the "voice of real girls" and finds fashion personally inspiring. The demands of daily fashion blogging require that she shop frequently and the affordability of T.J.Maxx satisfies such requirements. Through an apparently confident articulation of self, Calla promotes both her own brand and T.J.Maxx when she declares, "I post for fashionistas, but I'm a Maxxonista."

In a performance of shopping savvy, Calla is presented as deftly navigating the options put forth by consumer culture, displaying the results in a public sphere of urban and virtual environments. Depictions of this young woman happily sorting through racks of clothing recreates a common trope in postfeminist popular culture through which women articulate a liberated sense of self by expressing consumer choices. As this commercial implies, however, new stresses are attached to the fantasy of shopping as a straightforward route to happiness. In the wake of the Wall Street crash in 2008, the press reported a significant decline in consumer spending; for example, the Consumer Confidence Index fell from 76.4 to 25.0 between February 2008 and February 2009.[2] In such a context, a "real girl" like Calla must be a canny bargain hunter who makes T.J.Maxx work for her.

Calla does not casually see an item in the pages of a magazine and then easily purchase it in a department store; instead, she labors for her fashion by plowing through the racks in her local T.J.Maxx to find an item that appeals to both her sense of style and her wallet. The commercial offers an image of postfeminist femininity as defined by an efficient and frugal combination of production and consumption; shopping may represent a pleasurable activity, but it also requires some work in the context of anxieties about consumer spending. This commercial presents Calla, and the "real girls" she represents, as knowledgeable, efficient, and economical consumers who navigate consumer and virtual environments while upholding hegemonic definitions of femininity as objectified, managed, and scrutinized.

This commercial also demonstrates the profitability of the "recessionista" as a new media celebrity identity category. Calla, along with a range of other fashion bloggers and vloggers, have found both fame and paid labor by mobilizing new media resources to appeal to readers and consumers. Calla explains on her site how she launched her fashion blog in 2009 after working at magazines like *Seventeen* and for brands like Prada and L'Oreal. As tastemakers and style promoters, bloggers like Calla can turn blogging into a career, "command[ing] four- and five-figure fees from brands" just for featuring items on their blogs.[3] This essay argues that such entrepreneurial online success must be considered in light of the recessionary context, and by extension, the construction of the recessionista figure. Popular culture representations of women like Calla demonstrate how a new taste culture can form in the space between postfeminist discourse and economic exigency. Blogs produced by fashion-forward "everyday girls" celebrate the potential for the individual to become a successful entrepreneur through online work in consumer culture, offering a means to reconcile postfeminist identities with recessionary anxieties by transforming shopping into a kind of pleasurable work. In figure 5.1 Calla is shown typing on a sleek laptop in a coffee shop, typifying a recessionary postfeminist identity informed by a logic of consumption as production.

The recessionista taste culture centralizes the importance of personal style and the role of the tastemaker, both of which link stylish consumption to the public production of the self and future prosperity. Through analysis of fash-

FIGURE 5.1. As a fashion blogger, Lindsey Calla represents shopping at T.J.Maxx as enjoyable entrepreneurial work.

ion blogs produced by "real girls" like Calla and YouTube video blogs (vlogs) produced by makeup entrepreneurs Michelle Phan and Lauren Luke, I argue here that recessionary postfeminist femininity comprises an identity informed by a logic of consumption as production. Such a conflation of consumption and production is a component of user-generated convergence culture more generally. For example, Jean Burgess argues that "the democratization of technologies discourse from the 'grassroots' converges persistently with emerging neoliberal business and economic models under which consumers (or 'users'), particularly of technology, are considered to possess and exercise more creativity and agency than before, combined with a surge in both the participation in and power of voluntary work and 'productive' leisure."[4] While this fusion of consumption with production is part of a larger phenomenon in both online and postfeminist popular culture, economic exigency has shaped these trends into the figure of the recessionista. This essay explores how this logic of consumption as production takes two forms. First, creating outfits literally becomes a form of work for everyday young women for whom fashion blogging may become a career. Second, these new media texts present fashion as a productive source of semiotic pleasures that when deployed correctly reveal a sense of self. Here, the postfeminist language of choice is recast as versatility and creativity. New media resources like blogs employ an autobiographical rhetoric to illustrate the fantasy of self-determination and future prosperity through fashion. These online resources reify neoliberal and postfeminist logics that articulate the primacy of individual consumer spending and the pleasures found in consumer identities and objectified femininity.

They do this through capitalizing on the efficiency, immediate gratification, and productivity promised by digital resources, and by mobilizing a fantasy of self-determination promised by online work. Such self-oriented entrepreneurial rhetoric implicitly promises to guide recessionistas through online media into a future of plenty.

The Functional and Fanciful Recessionista

The term "recessionista" started to appear in the popular press around 2008 and was coined by the economist Larry Kudlow, who used it to refer to someone who anticipated the coming recession.[5] It was quickly transformed into a word used by the fashion industry to identify and target an audience it regarded as rightfully fearful about spending in such an economically unstable climate.[6] In publications ranging from the *Times* of London to *Vogue* to the *New York Times*, the recessionista and the related figure of the "frugalista" came to define a careful shopper who does not abandon consumer culture altogether in light of the global recession;[7] instead, a recessionista is a resourceful consumer for whom "frugality and fashion aren't mutually exclusive," someone willing to expend time and energy to discover the most affordable items.[8] The term "frugalista" resonated to such an extent with the economic crisis of 2008 that it made the short list for the Word of the Year in the *New Oxford American Dictionary*.[9] Not surprisingly, given the long-standing association between femininity and shopping, women dominate popular discourse about recessionistas and frugalistas. As Sarah McAbbe argues, this fiscally reformed style maven is gendered feminine, such that *Cosmo* and *Vogue* evaluate women on their rigorous bargain-hunting skills while *Esquire* and *Maxim* praise men for their "pragmatism."[10]

The recessionista fits squarely within postfeminist discourse by representing appearance as a source of liberation and power for modern femininity. The representation of the empowering potential of consumer culture is a notable manifestation of postfeminist media culture that strives to render feminist politics unnecessary because now women have it all. For example, popular film and television programs like *The Devil Wears Prada* (2006) and *Sex and the City* (on HBO 1998–2004, in films 2008 and 2010) depict women expressing their power and independence by embracing fashion and then effortlessly teetering around in $800 shoes.[11] Michelle Lazar argues that this notion of entitled femininity presumes that women have earned the ability to amuse themselves through shopping: "This identity gets discursively represented in terms of self-indulgence and pampering, as well as through related notions of pleasuring the self and enjoying an exclusive space of consumption."[12] The problems and contradictions of such an identity in these depictions abound;[13]

in particular, professional success is marked through conspicuous consumption, and while women may be more economically free now than they were in the past, that freedom is constrained by the demand to present one's self as appropriately "feminine" and objectified.[14] As Diane Negra argues, "Popular culture insistently asserts that if women can productively manage home, time, work, and their commodity choices, they will be rewarded with a more authentic, intact, and achieved self."[15] Feminine freedom and a discovery of the feminine "self" is predicated on careful self-management and self-scrutiny that upholds traditional feminine values such as feminine beauty, girlishness, and heteronormative desire, as well as the hegemony of whiteness. Women like those subjected to the critical gaze of "experts" on programs like *What Not to Wear* (TLC 2003–present), illustrate how punishing postfeminist consumer freedom can be.[16] Women may have made gains that permit more access to public world careers, but those successes are limited by rigid value systems that continue to sexualize and objectify women's bodies.

In the recessionary context, the postfeminist power of shopping is somewhat restrained as women are represented working harder to maintain consumer identities. As I have suggested, the recessionista archetype functions to hold in place a new taste culture through which women display and ally their real-world concerns through careful deployment of consumer choice. Accompanying the terms "frugalista" and "recessionista" is an increased concern in the popular press about what defines style in the context of the economic downturn. For some, "recession chic" means clipping coupons, shopping at discount stores, and recycling items in one's closet.[17] When buying new items, the recessionista wants both investment pieces and splurge items. On the one hand, items that seem both timeless and versatile are described as appealing to budget-savvy consumers.[18] The stress on garments like the perennial little black dress promises a big return on investment; consumers will presumably wear such an item more than once and can mix and match it with other items to create new outfits.[19] These articles of clothing promise consumers stability in fiscally unstable times as these more functional clothes have the temporal fortitude to outlast both the whims of the fashion industry and the financial crisis. Such items also seem more appropriate to the economic climate; as Hope Greenberg, fashion director of *Lucky Magazine*, said in 2008, "There's a mood: It doesn't feel right to show things that are overly opulent or steeped in luxury, in light of everything going on in the world."[20] Conspicuous consumption accommodates a modesty that respects the economic times; through the rhetoric of functionality and versatility, frugality is transformed into a new taste culture that distinguishes between responsible and irresponsible citizens. This taste culture is implicitly temporary, however, for its proper deployment promises to help women cope in the frugal present while also impelling them toward a prosperous future.

On the other hand, the fashion industry claims consumers are also seeking items that serve a consolatory or fanciful function in uncertain times. As Teresa Wiltz of the *Washington Post* explained in 2008, "life shouldn't be confined to just the basics. Everyone's life—and wardrobe—benefits from a little sartorial sunshine. Perhaps you find it in the guise of an artfully crafted bag . . . A marvelous pair of boots. An amazing pair of earrings . . . A to-die-for cocktail dress."[21] While an investment piece might be smart, a splurge piece is fun; desirable items in this context are not only those that are timeless but also "statement" pieces that promise escape from harsh realities. In 2010, Saks Fifth Avenue fashion director Colleen Sherin said, "'Women are not necessarily looking for basics. . . . They're looking for wow pieces, something that inspires more of an emotional reaction."[22] Luxury brands and stores like Neiman Marcus promote the notion of emotionally driven purchasing, and the power of individual pieces of clothing to raise the mood of financially strapped consumers. Indeed, some even argue that to compensate for having a depressed bank account, consumers look to fashion to literally raise them up; in 2010 the *New York Times* reported that there is evidence to support the claim that economic recessions result in even higher high heels.[23] These items are marketed as defying practicality and offering emotional pleasures that escape the restraints of fiscal realities.

Such descriptions of recessionista style may appeal to a range of consumers, both those who can afford luxury goods and those who cannot. Furthermore, recessionista fashion promises consumers a way to inhabit the functional needs of the contemporary moment without relinquishing the fanciful expectations of postfeminist identities that promise happiness through consumer culture. Recessionista pleasures speak to the needs of both the present and the future by representing clothing and personal style as something a woman uses to create a narrative about herself for both the present moment of economic anxiety and for a future of consumer extravagance. The items a consumer purchases are not as key to the production of the postfeminist self as the ways in which they are used; the little black dress becomes meaningful because it is worn in a variety of contexts and with different accessories and thus the user produces a variety of different looks. The splurge handbag is meaningful because the shopper uses it to produce therapeutic enjoyment, releasing her from present concerns, and enabling her to carve her identity in and through style. Immediate gratification in consumer purchases may not come easily when purse strings are tight, but if a recessionista works hard using her skills of consumer choice, she can liberate herself from present anxieties, reclaim an image of successful femininity, and look forward to a future of consumer extravagance.

The Everyday Recessionista Blog

New media formats have become increasingly helpful to the commercial fashion industry in the recessionary context as it works to attract potential consumers at various price points. The Internet appears to provide consumers more autonomy and participatory power while simultaneously offering more ways for media industries to generate profit as the medium collapses traditional distinctions between consumption and production, user and producer.[24] Although luxury retailers previously resisted using the Internet to make fashion more accessible, in the wake of the recession brands like Marc Jacobs and Donna Karan moved online for the first time in an attempt to reach consumers.[25] The language of new media's authenticity, immediacy, and interactivity serves this recessionista moment well, as new media formats invest shopping with a feeling of participation that constitutes fashion as a site of productive consumption. Similarly, fashion blogs produced by everyday women are drawing audiences away from traditional fashion magazines. With digital access one can read these blogs for free, but they also speak to the larger concerns of the contemporary moment by rendering fashion more approachable and thus seemingly less frivolous and more useful. In the words of one reader, blogs are "more authentic and eclectic than the fashion magazines . . . more obtainable for me."[26] Online interactivity and the overarching speed of web-based communications appeal to readers seeking not only fantasy but also a sense of functionality from their clothing. The press claims that bloggers are "democratizing the coverage of style" and influencing the rhythms of the fashion industry; bloggers post immediate updates about fashion shows, thus scooping magazines that must contend with the delays inherent to print media.[27]

Fashion blogs hail a cost-conscious audience invested in rendering the fantasy world of the catwalk accessible. These blogs turn shopping into a regulated task, and bloggers position themselves as shopping assistants who efficiently and economically aid readers in conforming postfeminist demands for fashion to a moment of economic exigency. In 2008, Mary Hall founded the blog The Recessionista, going on to trademark the terms "The Recessionista" and "The Chic Recessionista" in 2008.[28] The idealized reader of Hall's blog is gendered female; her blog mostly features women's clothing and in interviews she frequently refers to her readers as "women."[29] With the tagline "surviving the downturn in style," Hall's blog expresses confidence that the economic recession is temporary and that fashion can help ease economic stresses. She claims to bring deals to desiring readers, teaching them how to use online resources to maintain a particular lifestyle and see a future beyond the downturn. On a daily basis, Hall steers readers through the Internet, referring them to shopping sites offering deals and promotions. She provides links to sales being held online and at brick-and-mortar stores, thus extending the bargain-hunting reach of readers at home. In this way, the blog promises to ease the transition from carefree postfeminist spending to a moment when consumer choice is at least nominally constrained by economic anxieties. Hall's blog illustrates how a recessionista must labor to maintain her postfeminist identity by mining online resources. By instructing readers how to work efficiently to maintain a fashionable identity, this site underscores the class specificity of ideal femininity; economic anxieties make maintaining a well-dressed upper-middle-class postfeminist self a challenge.

While The Recessionista circulates daily bargain opportunities, other blogs like Lindsey Calla's represent fashion as a daily performance, presenting it as a pleasure that augments everyday life. Popular fashion blogs like The Coveted, eat.sleep.wear, Lucy Laucht, and Cupcakes and Cashmere, sites that I refer to as "everyday girl" blogs, are written by young women who document their daily outfits with photographs of themselves and text describing what they wore and on what occasion. Unlike The Recessionista, these fashion blogs are not explicitly devoted to shopping and sales, but the pleasures of consumption are implicitly integrated into their representations of postfeminist femininity. They use an autobiographical format, representing the contemporary woman as merging the pleasures of postfeminist choice with a language of work. While this identity appears as if it were authentic to and controlled by the girl, it is ultimately never actually free from the work it does for postfeminist, neoliberal capitalist culture.

The presentation of self on everyday girl fashion blogs forms part of larger sociohistorical trends that predate the recession but which appear with particular vehemence in this moment of economic exigency. Sarah Banet-Weiser argues how in the twenty-first century authentic spaces like selfhood and creativity have been increasingly subject to branding. Such brands collapse traditional distinctions between producer and consumer, authenticity and consumer culture, and privilege the individual entrepreneur who is a seemingly empowered citizen in the consumer marketplace.[30] Self-branding has particular relevance to postfeminist femininity as well as online culture as both are shaped by the rhetoric of choice and autonomy. As Banet-Weiser argues, "The ideals shaping the discursive and ideological space of the Internet—freedom, equality, innovation, entrepreneurship—are the same discourses that provide the logic for girls' self-branding, a practice that situates girls ever more securely into the norms and values of hegemonic gendered consumer culture, as they also reshape definitions of a new interactive femininity."[31] Online spaces, like fashion blogs, offer a platform for the production of an individual brand that promises to help an everyday girl realize a sense of self. In a recessionary context, young women are encouraged to define themselves through working within economic restraints that encourage heightened attention to creative approaches to consumer culture. The recessionista cultivates a self-brand through blogs that present stylish, entrepreneurial ingenuity that promises to transform frugality into abundance.

These everyday girl blogs illustrate how recessionary postfeminist identities are informed by a logic that depicts fashion as not merely pleasurable but also as generating an enterprising identity. On the one hand, bloggers turn sartorial pleasures into literal economic labors. Some fashion bloggers have been asked to produce their own fashion lines for popular clothing companies like Urban Outfitters.[32] By 2009, fashion blogs were making great strides in readership while magazines like *Vogue* and *Glamour* were being forced to make cutbacks due to loss of advertising revenue. Bloggers have displaced magazine staff members at fashion shows, and some, like Lindsey Calla, have agents and are able to garner more than just free merchandise, receiving thousands of dollars in compensation for including specific items in their blogs.[33] As an article in *Women's Wear Daily* explained, bloggers can charge between $5,000 and $50,000 for featuring items on their sites, appearing at store openings or hosting events for brands.[34] By 2012, the fashion industry openly embraced the usefulness of the seemingly casual spontaneity and attendant authenticity invoked by such bloggers; as the *New York Times* reported, "the marketing clout of fashion bloggers can equal or surpass that of a red carpet ingénue."[35] In some ways, these blogs undermine traditional modes of production by demanding that the industry keep pace with them, rather than the other way around. In this respect, fashion bloggers have impacted the temporality of fashion.[36] While each season brings revised styles determined by the fashion industry, these bloggers pressure the industry to increase the pace at which they move styles from the runway to the department stores.[37]

These professional successes are significant in a context of mass unemployment because these blogs stage the democratic potential of new media sites to provide a field for self-creation and material gains; some young women have literally fashioned careers for themselves out of their blogs. These endeavors are supported by such organizations as the Independent Fashion Bloggers (IFB) association, started in 2007 by Jennine of The Coveted to help fellow bloggers "build a better blog."[38] The IFB features articles ranging from how to take self-portraits, to advice on attracting readers, to suggestions on turning blogs into money-making ventures, thus providing resources to support entrepreneurial aspirations. The line between fostering entrepreneurialism and enabling exploitation is unstable, however, and online resources are not free from power relations at the level of either production or consumption.[39] Many bloggers receive little or no compensation for promoting items and brands on their blogs.[40] While the IFB features numerous articles advising bloggers how to monetize their blogs through niche marketing and PR, many articles also acknowledge that featuring brands without receiving compensation can be beneficial, especially for new bloggers trying to build a profile.[41] Ultimately, these blogs need an audience, and while blogging promises to be a career replete with the pleasures of self-determination, entrepreneurial success is predicated on marketing personal style, which fundamentally always also serves the interests of the fashion industry by producing future consumers.

The careers these blogging women self-fashion perpetuate fantasies about the pleasures of autonomous choice and consumer freedoms as the everyday girl fashion blogs represent not only how clothing can produce a career but also an individual sense of self. Like a fashion magazine, they primarily feature photographs, often including a spread of one outfit with multiple shots of the same scene from a variety of angles. The spread is given a title and a blurb about the outfit and circumstances in which it was worn. The present-tense language differentiates these blogs from traditional magazines and represents fashion and self as seamlessly integrated through autobiographical language. In text the bloggers describe what they were doing on the day on which they wore the outfit and how they selected the clothes that would be appropriate for that activity. For example, in an entry on eat.sleep.wear, blogger Kim writes, "This past Sunday was a super fun day for me. I got a chance to meet up with my dear friend Jenni . . . we chatted over brunch outside in Old City . . . It was humid out yesterday but the loose skirt and tight lace top were perfect for walking around."[42] Through such vernacular language these blogs cultivate a sense of intimacy; the reader is positioned as confidant or friendly listener, thus seemingly moving away from elite sartorial authorities like *Vogue*.[43] This autobiographical language leads these blogs to sound like diaries and present the blogger's reflections on her everyday experiences as they unfold. The depiction of the quotidian reifies the notion that readers are learning of the actual emotional experiences of the blogger in real time. For example, in a post about yellow jeans, Jeannie (The Coveted) explained, "yellow is one of the colors I can surround myself in and feel happy with."[44]

On these blogs, clothing, context, and emotion blend together, and the blogger presents herself as in control of all through the autobiographical mode of representation.

The autobiographical language used on these websites constructs a sense of "authenticity" by demonstrating how the individual self is articulated through clothing and text. For example, Lucy Laucht explains, "My namesake blog is the story of my life in New York and a document of my personal style."[45] Her life and style are collapsible concepts, easily integrated through her presumably unfettered deployment of new media technologies, and the blogs promise a free space for self-determination and expression. The bloggers write the text, put together the outfits, and then model them. In essence, these bloggers "do it all," and thus fit with both postfeminist representations of femininity and neoliberal discourses of the entrepreneurial self; they reap the benefits of second-wave feminism, free to pursue successes in public and private worlds. While these blogs narrate and market an image of femininity that presumably represents the real girl in her own terms, she is nonetheless always marketing an image of herself as a body for displaying clothing.[46]

Photographs are a major focus of many of everyday girl blogs, and here bloggers present themselves as if they are fully in control of their own image. One key way they articulate a sense of control and power is through the settings of images, which are almost invariably in urban public space. The women model their outfits while posing on cobblestone streets, in city parks, and while strolling through shopping districts. This urban environment proves a vital background for these images, recalling iconic depictions of girls striking out on their own and conquering the urban jungle that have long defined popular culture depictions of feminist femininity. From the 1920s flaneuse to Mary Tyler Moore to Carrie Bradshaw, the city promises to be the ground on which young women discover their independence.[47] On the streets of New York, Philadelphia, London, or Los Angeles, these young bloggers are presumably free to discover a sense of self that is liberated from the restraints of domestic or traditional femininity. They are not only representing themselves as in control of their image but as in control of their performance of independence in their constructions of both self and style.

Fashion blog authors represent not merely how a young woman finds herself, but moreover how she creates herself through clothing and self-fashioning. We see this, for example, on blogs that offer an "about me" section in which the blogger customarily declares her love for fashion and describes her attempts to unite her lifestyle choices with her (aspired) career path. Many of these bloggers have come to fashion blogging through magazine publishing; for example, Emily from Cupcakes and Cashmere describes her career path as first working at *Teen Vogue* and *Domino* magazines and blogging on the side: "I started my blog as a way to document the things I loved and over time was able to turn it into my career."[48] Independent financial success is painted here as a by-product of personal passion and innate creativity that can be packaged and sold to others for profit. This language of the lucrative potential of individual creativity resonates in a recessionary context in which individual entrepreneurial aspirations are imagined to be a solution to economic woes. For example, in a 2009 editorial published in *USA Today*, Amy Wilkinson argued, "Our prosperity depends on innovative thinking. Instead of bailing out behemoths that are 'too big to fail,' we must remember that mom-and-pop businesses, garage start-ups and small ventures are the reason we succeed."[49] Fashion blogger statements about lifestyle and career blend postfeminist and entrepreneurial discourses and fit in this recessionary context by marketing fashionable lifestyle choices as individual business practices, in effect marketing the so-called personal deployment of choice for pay.

In declaring passions for creativity and aesthetics, everyday girl blogs blend labor and leisure, production and consumption through the rhetoric of personal style. Like the blog, style is created out of a range of materials that together promise to create a coherent story of the blogger's self through lifestyle choices. Such a discourse fits into a wider field in which fashion and feminism are bound through an array of media outlets and reproduce associations of femininity with physical display. For example, Elizabeth Groeneveld argues that *Bust* magazine's "fashion spread is symptomatic of a larger set of trends within third-wave feminist praxis, which include both the reclamation of feminism as stylish and sexy and the representation of feminist politics as a set of individual lifestyle choices."[50] Similarly, these blogs celebrate individual flair both to appeal to readers and to define the blogger's online identity. These identities are articulated through the presumably creative combination of clothing items through a particular kind of labor called styling. The bloggers create outfits using items ranging from mainstream brands like J.Crew to high-end designers like Opening Ceremony and Prada. By combining high and low, these bloggers represent fashion as an open field not restricted to luxury items. The combination of elite and mainstream products suits the recessionista moment, and such combinations of taste cultures renders the fanciful functional through appropriation and combination.

Everyday girl bloggers follow in the successful footsteps of figures like Rachel Zoe (the celebrity stylist and reality TV star) who have made a career out of assembling outfits. Dressing is celebrated as a form of bricolage in which the more unique the pairing, the more ideal the style, and the more successful articulation of authentic selfhood. The labor of self-fashioning is presented through a pedagogical discourse that presents everyday styles as inspiration to at-home readers and styling as something anyone can do. The bloggers perform their expertise as stylists in the text below the series of photographs illustrating their fashion choices. Kim of eat.sleep.wear writes, "Never underestimate the power of a bold blouse. Paired with these purple jeans it was the pop of color I was looking for." [51] Or Natalie of Natalie Off Duty describes the versatility of her new "maxi" dress: "It's a [sic] super light-weight material flows beautifully at my feet. This is something I could easily take from day to night. For the casual afternoon on my rooftop, I dressed it down with a stunning pair of red ballet flats." [52] Such postings illustrate that happiness is predicated on creative selections, arrangements, and re-sourcefulness. This rhetoric speaks to how the recessionista embraces versatile clothing. Furthermore, everyday girl blogs demonstrate how postfeminist taste is defined through the public presentation of choice; freed from the obligations of brand loyalty, these blogs show how successful modern femininity involves making productive and creative choices that help communicate individuality to the public eye and contain the promise of a satisfying future full of opportunity.

Everyday girl blogs transform fashion into a form of labor that promises to be an economic investment in a long-term public presentation of self. For example, on The Coveted, Jennine chronicles her search for the perfect white blouse: "For the longest time I've wanted a beautiful classic white button down blouse. . . . After experimenting with cheaper silk blouses, I realized that adding up all the cheap silk blouses I almost loved ended up being more expensive than the one I really loved . . . so I took the plunge and got the Equipment Signature Blouse in bright white." [53] Jennine reflects a cost consciousness that appeals to the recessionary context, while also valuing the future usefulness of a classic that will prove functional for years. Here, readers see how they need not relinquish extravagant purchases in the recessionary context and that a splurge can be reconfigured as a smart investment in a fashionable future filled with the creative pleasures of mixing and matching different items in order to perform one's autonomy.

Everyday girl blogs thus construct a temporality positioned between the present tense of economic frugality and hopefulness for a future replete with endless outfits that shore up confident, successful femininity. While the blogs promise to work for real girls, they ultimately work for consumer culture, undermining the liberating potential promised through styling. These blogs transform readers into potential consumers, for many clothing items are tagged with a hyperlink to connect the reader directly to the website where she too can purchase that item. These hyperlinks offer efficient and seamless connections between the virtual world of the blogger and that of the at-home consumer. The stress on unique styling further perpetuates this consumerist discourse of productive creativity in which individuality is dependent upon the public presentation of fashionable purchases; even if the reader of the blog buys the same items as the blogger, presumably she will not wear or style them the same way. This articulation of individuality in the service of consumer culture forms part of what Angela McRobbie terms "the new sexual contract," in which "the production of girlhood now comprises a constant stream of incitements and enticements to engage in a range of specified practices which are understood to be both progressive but also consummately and reassuringly feminine."[54] The stylish girl appears to be the agent of her own production, all the while producing a self who is ultimately defined by her appearance.

The moment of economic anxiety ignited by the global economic crisis could inspire consumers to disengage from the routines of consumer culture, to rewear items and interpret looks without purchasing new clothes; instead, these new media sites encourage readers to keep buying. While the Internet seems to promise free expression of self, it simultaneously allows for the efficient appropriation of autobiography by the online shopping and consumer product industries.[55] Everyday girl blogs appear to participate in what Lauren Berlant terms "cruel optimism," a condition "of maintaining an attachment to a significantly problematic object."[56] These blogs articulate hopefulness about a self-determined future obtained through consumer culture even while consumer culture objectifies female bodies. Through text and images that illustrate how new media sites and fashion can be used as modes of self-determination, these blogs demonstrate how an investment in the production of an online, fashionable self has the potential to turn into a more lucrative future. And yet this drive for control over self-presentation simultaneously reveals how femininity continues to be evaluated through an objectified gaze. While fashion could be praised for its liberating potential to expose identity construction, we must be wary of overly laudatory theories of fashion. For Llwellyn Negrin, such claims leave "unchallenged the reduction of self-identity to image which the advertising and fashion industries now endorse and promote."[57] As these new media sites illustrate, postfeminist identities remain constrained by the fashions that shape and cover female bodies. While these blogs offer the promise of a more creative, frugal, and democratic use of consumer culture, they ultimately perpetuate and reward the same standards that bind postfeminist femininity to restrictive and static hegemonic consumer identities.

Everyday Transformations and Makeup Vlogs

The fashion blogs produced by so-called everyday girls present fashion as a means to articulate the self and as an investment in future career successes. These sites illustrate how the recessionista dovetails with postfeminist notions about the liberating power of style through discourses of resourcefulness, ingenuity, and fantasy. Similarly, YouTube has proven to be a platform for representing the productive potential of consumer culture for postfeminist femininity; as Banet-Weiser argues, "for YouTube, and for an increasing number of social network sites, self-expression is a business."[58] Michelle Phan and Lauren Luke's makeup application tutorials for YouTube have turned these everyday women into new media celebrities. Like the everyday girl fashion bloggers, Phan and Luke present their stylish choices online and turn fashion into a type of labor that generates entrepreneurial success as well as contributing to the production of the self. By demonstrating how to create a range of makeup looks, they perform their expertise for the masses, promising to democratize glamour and style by teaching others, while simultaneously establishing strict standards for appropriate femininity. Their vlogs foreground the recessionista as a gendered figure as well as one marked by race and class privilege. While Luke and Phan are presumably free to choose both their style and by extension a profitable and productive identity in a postfeminist context, their star status is dependent upon ever-changing and ever-malleable looks that work to control their identities as women of color and of the working class.

Luke and Phan started producing YouTube videos around the same time and are described in press profiles in terms that praise their entrepreneurial aspirations. They are presented as self-made professional heroines who persevered over adversity by mobilizing their innate creativity and ambition. Phan, a Vietnamese American, grew up in Los Angeles and by age sixteen was writing blogs about makeup and style, starting to create video tutorials for her friends and readers in 2007. In 2009 she quit her day job as a waitress in a sushi restaurant to focus on producing YouTube video tutorials.[59] Today, Phan is a YouTube partner and through her YouTube success has been made a Lancôme spokeswoman and official makeup artist.[60] Following a similar rags-to-riches story, Luke is described as having a modest upbringing as the child of divorced parents and the victim of school bullying. A single mother at age sixteen, she worked a variety of "dead-end jobs" before finally quitting her job as a taxi operator at twenty-eight to sell makeup on eBay. To advertise the makeup, Luke took pictures of herself wearing her products, and, encouraged by the response she received asking for different tips, she began making You-

Tube videos on July 22, 2007. She now has her own cosmetics line that is sold by Sephora and a Nintendo DS Game, Supermodel Makeover.[61] By 2009 Luke had received over 50 million views on her YouTube channel and was watched by over 250,000 subscribers in over seventy countries.[62] Phan has the distinction of being "the most subscribed woman on YouTube, with more than 1.5 million followers . . . whose beauty tutorial videos have been viewed more than 445 million times."[63] Both Luke and Phan are part of YouTube's "partnership program," in which they receive a portion of ad revenue generated by their channels.[64]

Phan and Luke are typically represented as self-sufficient innovators who through a combination of resolve and creativity turned a personal interest in makeup into a business. The celebrity status of the pair apparently did not come easy, and the press describes how their humble beginnings bolstered their distinctive fame. For example, Phan was reportedly rejected for a job at the Lancôme makeup counter but once her vlog proved popular she was hired as a spokesperson for the company.[65] By overcoming adversity through determination, they appear as examples of the relatable, successful everywoman type familiar within lifestyle culture. Their celebrity status is also contingent on a context in which media genres like the makeover flourish, as Brenda Weber argues: "appearance in the twenty-first century functions as an indicator of professional competence and ability. . . . Such appearance-based citizenship is critical for business success."[66] Like the everyday girl bloggers, these vloggers use their appearance to do it all: they apply makeup, produce videos, and create makeup products, using consumer culture (in the form of makeup) to turn themselves into entrepreneurial success stories. As "average" women they demonstrate how makeup, and by extension fashion, can be productive for all women by satisfying a fantasy of self-transformation through the creative deployment of consumer products.

The makeup tutorials that Phan and Luke upload to YouTube share certain formal qualities that help to present makeup transformations as feasible and low budget. They both depict one look per tutorial, and at least initially both Luke and Phan's videos appeared to be filmed on one camera, in a long take. The women appear in close-up and do their own makeup, describing in direct address what they are doing and why they are doing it, as they apply foundation, eye shadow, mascara, and lipstick. Unlike the everyday girl blogs that cast fashion in an urban landscape, these tutorials are frequently set in a domestic space such as a bedroom or bathroom. Luke and Phan speak directly to their viewers, and Luke's appeal is especially personal since she addresses her viewers as friends. For example, in a 2012 tutorial she confesses to feeling better about herself when she is thinner and expresses her desire to jump-start her diet by attending a "boot camp." [67] She creates space for inspiring spectatorial confidence and identification through this performance of authenticity in much the same way as the everyday girl bloggers use images and text to create autobiographical narratives. While both Luke and Phan employ an intimate address, Phan's videos have always had more complex production qualities; for example, incorporating title screens to introduce each section of the tutorial, often using music on the soundtrack, and occasionally employing editing to elide lengthy parts of the process. While her earliest videos seemed to be shot at home, as her career evolves tutorials are often shot on location in parks, on rooftops, or in front of video screens. This shift from domestic to public sphere marks a movement away from autobiographical vlogger to company spokesperson and career professional.

The formal similarities between Phan's and Luke's videos are matched with a shared construction of femininity through representing makeup as a functional, easy tool for self-transformation. Phan and Luke apply makeup in real time, moving closer to the camera lens when an extreme close-up is necessary to show more detail, and moving away from the camera to offer a sense of perspective on the whole face. Their videos thus replicate the experience of applying makeup in one's bathroom mirror, conveying an immediacy that constructs a sense of authenticity. For example, in a video from 2009, some dirt falls out of the corner of Luke's eye while she is applying eye shadow. She exclaims, "Sorry you had to witness that. . . . I do apologize, but it happens and if we pretended it didn't we would think we were all freaks when it did happen so you get to see it all here." [68] Luke presents herself as relatable and real, a woman who is self-aware. This presentation would seem to appeal to an audience of viewers who may similarly be struggling with the stresses of a public performance of confident, constructed femininity.

Such depictions of intimacy and approachability appear to empower viewers through lessons on the creation of femininity while these videos also depend upon rehabilitating one's face to conform to particular standards. Phan and Luke interpret for viewers how tools like eye shadow, concealer, and lip gloss can be used to transform a woman's face. While such acts of interpretation could signify creativity and uniqueness, the looks they create depict beauty in conventional hegemonic terms that bolster postfeminist definitions of femininity and a consumer product industry dependent upon such definitions. For example, Phan has been quoted as saying that she is "empowering women with lipstick and stilettos." [69] These tutorials both depict femininity as an image over which individual women have control and assume that this control involves women subjecting themselves to the desiring gaze of others. Beauty products are inextricably linked to happy and successful femininity, and the presentation of a distinctly feminine self is presented here as a source of strength. Such a subject position is indicative of a larger trend in postfeminist culture that represents women as "self-policing," a discourse that Rosalind Gill finds particularly insidious: "It can be argued that this represents a higher or deeper form of exploitation than objectification—one in which the objectifying male gaze is internalized to form a new disciplinary regime."[70] This ambivalent subject position is articulated by the depiction of Luke's and Phan's gaze. Both women move between looking directly into the camera and then just off screen as they presumably apply their makeup in an off-screen mirror; thus they both catch our gaze and subject themselves to it. These videos demonstrate that while women may possess the tools for constructing their own identities, the image they create has changed little: Phan and Luke present empowered femininity as to-be-looked-at. Entrepreneurialism transforms into exploitation when women labor in order to become the object of desiring gazes.

While Phan and Luke's tutorials presumably offer women tools with which to construct their self-image, the assumption is that viewers at home will follow the detailed steps they illustrate. Their step-by-step narration presents the process from start to finish, showing how makeup looks require layering an assortment of products. This layering is similar to the bloggers' styling in that it involves multiple brands and items. But the YouTube format facilitates mimicking a kind of work that is distinctly uncreative; through controls that allow the viewer to pause, rewind, and rewatch the video tutorial, she can strive to re-create the look produced onscreen. The perils of not following these steps are steep; on her "Smokey Eyes" tutorial from 2007, Phan explained the importance of proper application of eyeliner: if applied correctly, the wearer would look "sexy and youthful" but if applied incorrectly, she would look "old and sad."[71] The postfeminist ideal of girly femininity is articulated here, as well as in the many tutorials Phan produces that teach viewers to re-create the look of Disney characters like Snow White. As Diane Negra has argued, the marketing of princess paraphernalia to adults is "another way of reinforcing the centrality and value of youth to femininity."[72] Phan's looks foreground the postfeminist ideal of choice while illustrating how feminine power is always filtered through traditional codes of feminine appearance.

Luke's and Phan's tutorials include everyday fanciful looks and in this way appeal to the recessionista definition of fashion. They embody the entrepreneurial spirit of creativity increasingly familiar within postfeminist femininity; their faces are the palettes on which they have formed their careers, and through which they promise viewers confidence and happiness. They prioritize the functionality of makeup to render looks that appeal to viewers seeking to play with self-presentation. Many of their tutorials focus on "everyday looks" like Phan's "Everyday Chic School Look" or Luke's "Quick and Easy Everyday Makeup for Teens." Here, Phan and Luke present makeup as integrated into and integral to everyday life. They also represent how the pleasure of play with makeup and self-representation speaks of a desire to escape from everyday realities. This fantasy of escape is especially apparent in tutorials inspired by celebrities—both Phan and Luke feature tutorials that re-create the style of celebrities like Angelina Jolie and Kelly Clarkson.[73] These videos illustrate the pleasures of replicating the looks of popular and well-known celebrities and the potential of aspiration through emulation. Their constant transformation may prove profitable for these celebrities, but their success, and by extension their viewers', is always predicated on traditional associations of femininity and beauty. As Angela McRobbie writes, "The successful young woman must now get herself endlessly and repetitively done up, so as to mask her rivalry with men in the world of work."[74] Like the everyday girl bloggers who are always depicted modeling outfits, Phan and Luke are constantly putting on makeup, a performance of feminine style that promises individual success but actually contains the threat of truly liberated femininity, a threat that may be even more keenly felt in a recessionary context.

While these two YouTube stars promote the role of postfeminist creativity, Phan and Luke cannot be separated from the classed and raced discourses that define them, as well as broader postfeminist and postrace contexts. As Ralina Joseph argues, notions of postrace and postfeminism are inextricable: "discourses of post-race are undeniably gendered, and discourses of postfeminism are undeniably raced."[75] And, while we might assume that new media bring new freedoms to groups of citizens otherwise denied access to the means of production, such as women and people of color, this access is always constrained by gendered and raced discourses. Lisa Nakamura characterizes the Internet as bound by relations of power that are circulated and produced throughout digital visual culture. While it may seem to offer a free space for color blindness and counterhegemonic user autonomy, it is actually "an intensely active, productive space of visual signification where these differences are intensified, modulated, reiterated, and challenged by former objects of interactivity, whose subjectivity is expressed by their negotiations of the shifting terrain of identity."[76] In a historic recession, YouTube may offer a channel for entrepreneurial success, but that success is predicated on adherence to conventional norms of gender, race, and class.

YouTube user-generated makeup tutorials tap into fantasies about the Internet as a space free from gendered and racialized power structures. Both Phan and Luke present makeup as transformational and applicable for women

FIGURE 5.2. Michelle Phan and Lancôme promise that red lipstick will work for all women (Phan, "Perfect Red Lips").

regardless of race or class, and thus represent makeup as a democratic tool for all citizens. For example, in a video produced in conjunction with Lancôme, Phan instructs women how to choose the right red lipstick. She, along with two other women, one white and one African American, demonstrate how a cool or a warm skin tone can dictate the right kind of red lipstick. While these women may choose a different color red, they all ultimately find a red that suits them, and situate themselves within the choices offered by consumer culture.[77] This tutorial underscores how women at home can make consumer culture work for their individual identities, but only within the prescribed sameness offered by the popular culture marketplace. While this tutorial apparently presents women with the right to choose their red lipstick, the definition of correct color choice is highly determined by the authoritative voice of Phan and by extension Lancôme. Figure 5.2 illustrates Phan's ability to facilitate fantasies of the Internet as a space free from gendered and racialized power structures.

While these YouTube videos are carefully situated within the postfeminist, postracial context, and thus presume women are empowered to choose their gendered identity free of racist and sexist discourse, they simultaneously assert the primacy of objectification as central to feminine identities. Indeed, Phan's and Luke's marked identities as Asian American and working-class respectively render them vulnerable to objectification even through narratives of transformation. For example, in her video about re-creating the look from the Disney film *Mulan*, Phan explains how we live in an age in which all skin colors and variations of beauty are appreciated, even while she spackles her face with white, geisha-like makeup. In this tutorial, she explains how she has never had surgery on her eyes to make them appear more "Western" but that "the cool thing about makeup is that you can create almost any eye shape."[78] She demonstrates that her identity is not entirely determined by biology but can be endlessly tweaked and altered through the proper application of makeup. Phan offers contradictory praise for multiracial beauty while simultaneously illustrating the desirability of transforming her own look into one that re-creates Western beauty ideals of Caucasian femininity. These women present themselves as always able to be transformed and to meld into new identities and new roles through the application of makeup. In this way, they represent themselves as to-be-transformed, as blank slates ready and wanting to be turned into someone else. This rhetoric of transformation undermines the potency of these women's makeup-free faces. Moreover, the representation of transformation re-creates postracial logics that assume racial equality has been achieved while simultaneously denying persistent inequalities.

Conclusion

While fashion and makeup promise to work for women in the recessionary and postfeminist context, the fashionista blogs and makeup vlogs discussed here illustrate the pitfalls of such a fantasy. In their introduction to this volume, the editors allude to the heightened profile and prevalence of hope labor in the recession, a key context for these new media sources that promise a democratic and liberatory space for exploring the function of style and the uses to which it can be put. As function and fantasy merge in this hopeful, forward-looking space of consumption as production, such combinations remain bound to hegemonic power structures that subject women to scrutiny and obfuscate racist and classist discourse in the name of transformation and aspiration. These new media texts proclaim the power of the individual, and in this way speak to broader concerns of the neoliberal context. Other media forms such as reality TV also demonstrate the makeover's function as a tool for governmentality; as Laurie Ouellette and James Hay argue, such programs offer "demonstrations in civic virtues and good citizenship through self-fashioning."[79] Similarly, the genre of the new media makeover cultivates propriety and responsibility to the self and to consumer capitalism.

The promise of future prosperity through the transformation of shopping into work is especially resonant in the current recessionary context, an economic environment in which young women are doubly disadvantaged, seeking work in a difficult job market that privileges men.[80] While bloggers and vloggers manifest creative ways to generate an income, demonstrating a laudable entrepreneurial drive, my analysis of the recessionista prompts us to query what is sacrificed in this exchange. In particular, by cultivating consumer responsibility, these postfeminist new media celebrities take care of both themselves and, by implication, a nation dependent on consumer capitalism. Rather than retreating from consumer culture, the recessionista is seen to merely alter her free-spending ways, encouraging readers to craft a style that is both fiscally responsible and fashionable. Retaining a commitment to consumption and objectification, these blogs and vlogs prompt consideration of the ways women are figured as helping to repair the nation through postfeminist discourses of self-determination and consumer pleasure. Rosalind Gill underlines these connections at a broader level, writing, "It is clear that the autonomous, calculating, self-regulating subject of neoliberalism bears a strong resemblance to the active, freely choosing, self-reinventing subject of postfeminism."[81] Recognizing the mutually constitutive relationship between neoliberal governmentality and contemporary gender ideology furthers understanding of the ways femininity specifically bears the burden of both self- and national care in the contemporary context.

Notes

1. Calla, "FAQ — Saucy Glossie."
2. Marages, "I'm Not Buying Recession Chic."
3. Kurutz, "Fashion Bloggers, Posted and Represented."
4. Burgess, "Hearing Ordinary Voices," 202.
5. McAbbe, "He-Cession, She-Cession," 21.
6. Safire, "The Way We Live Now," 34.
7. Singer, "A Label for a Pleather Economy."
8. "Where to Find High Style at Penny-Pinching Prices."
9. The Word of the Year that beat "frugalistas" was "hypermiling," which refers to careful driving techniques with the goal of conserving gas. Clearly, both words illustrate the concerns faced by consumers in the economic crisis. Safire, "The Way We Live Now," 34.
10. McAbbe, "He-Cession, She-Cession," 22.
11. See, for example, Arthurs, "*Sex and the City* and Consumer Culture," 83–98; McRobbie, *The Aftermath of Feminism*; Diane Negra, *What a Girl Wants?*; Hilary Radner, *Neo-feminist Cinema*.
12. Lazar, "Entitled to Consume," 375.
13. As Diane Negra and Yvonne Tasker argue, "Postfeminism is . . . inherently contradictory, characterized by a double discourse that works to construct feminism as a phenomenon of the past, traces of which can be found (and sometimes even valued) in the present; postfeminism suggests that it is the very success of feminism that produces its irrelevance for contemporary culture." Tasker and Negra, "Introduction," 8.
14. For further explanation of the relationship between postfeminist femininity and

consumer culture, see, for example, McRobbie, *The Aftermath of Feminism*; Negra, *What a Girl Wants?*; Tasker and Negra, *Interrogating Postfeminism*; Radner, *Neo-feminist Cinema*; Hollows, *Feminism, Femininity and Popular Culture*; Lotz, "Postfeminist Television Criticism," 105–21.

15. Negra, *What a Girl Wants?*, 5.

16. Roberts, "The Fashion Police," 227–48.

17. Marages, "I'm Not Buying Recession Chic."

18. Blume, "High Styles for Low Times."

19. Miller, "Fashion Week's Runway Recession."

20. Blume, "High Styles for Low Times."

21. Wiltz, "Shopper."

22. Nichols, "Recession Creates New Trend in Fashion Shopping."

23. Rowlands and Berrie, "OP-ART."

24. For example, see Jenkins, *Convergence Culture*; Burgess and Green, *YouTube*.

25. As Amy Odell of *New York* magazine explained, "In recent years, fancy labels were wary of adding e-commerce to their websites because, even though they stand to profit off such a thing, it didn't seem like a very exclusive, fashion-y thing to do. . . . When the economy took a nosedive and department stores aggressively knocked down retail prices, seemingly devaluing the luxuriousness of very expensive apparel, the labels realized they would have to take back control." Odell, "The Recession Has Forced High-Fashion Companies to Use the Internet." See also Clifford, "High Fashion Relents to Web's Pull."

26. La Ferla, "The New Icons of Fashion."

27. Wilson, "Bloggers Crashed Fashion's Front Row."

28. Mary Hall, "The Recessionista," U.S. Trademark 77634948, December 17, 2008.

29. Pou, "'Recessionista' Talks about the Success of Recession-Friendly Blog."

30. Banet-Weiser, *Authentic*™, 48.

31. Banet-Weiser, *Authentic*™, 69.

32. Pfeiffer, "Young Bloggers Have Ear of Fashion Heavyweights."

33. Wilson, "Bloggers Crashed Fashion's Front Row"; Kurutz, "Fashion Bloggers, Posted and Represented."

34. Strugatz, "To Pay or Not to Pay."

35. La Ferla, "Who Am I Wearing?"

36. Style has long depended upon a discourse of the new, as Elizabeth Wilson argues: "Fashion is dress in which the key feature is rapid and continual changing of styles. Fashion, in a sense is change." Wilson, *Adorned in Dreams*, 3.

37. Wilson, "Bloggers Crashed Fashion's Front Row."

38. Independent Fashion Bloggers, "About," http://heartifb.com/about/.

39. In his essay on autobiographical photography, Ori Schwartz is similarly concerned about the unfettered embrace of online self-determination. Schwarz, "On Friendship, Boobs and the Logic of the Catalogue," 163–83.

40. Increasingly, however, brands are compensating bloggers for featuring items. Clifford, "Sites That Pay the Shopper for Being a Seller."

41. Jacob, "Blogger Compensation."

42. Pesch, "A Pretty Woman Moment."

43. Laurie McNeill equates blogging with diaries and demonstrates that the new media text appeals to readers through a confessionary language. McNeill, "Teaching an Old Genre New Tricks," 24–47.

44. Jacob, "Yellow Jeans for Work."

45. Lucy Laucht, "About," http://www.lucylaucht.com/about/.

46. These online declarations of a girl's self through autobiographical, consumerist language are increasingly widespread. In an insightful essay on young women's "hauler" videos, Sarah Banet-Weiser and Inna Arzumanova explore similar postfeminist declarations of selfhood through both autobiographical and confessional use of online media and consumer culture. They argue that hauler videos claim empowerment through language that brands a feminine self as an expert consumer and media-savvy producer who is simultaneously subject to neoliberal disciplinary regimes. Banet-Weiser and Arzumanova, "Creative Authorship."

47. See, for example, Friedberg, *Window Shopping*.

48. Schuman, "FAQ—Cupcakes and Cashmere."

49. Wilkinson, "Entrepreneurial Nation."

50. Groeneveld, "'Be a Feminist or Just Dress Like One,'" 179.

51. Pesch, "Bold + Bright."

52. Suarez, "Rooftop Breeze."

53. Jacob, "Perfect White Button Down Blouse."

54. McRobbie, *The Aftermath of Feminism*, 57.

55. Ori Schwartz argues that "we are witnessing a shift from photographing others for self-consumption to documentation of self for consumption by others, in a way that serves the interest of the internet and mobile communication industries that developed these platforms." Schwartz, "On Friendship, Boobs and the Logic of the Catalogue," 165.

56. Berlant, *Cruel Optimism*, 24.

57. Negrin, "The Self as Image," 100.

58. Banet-Weiser, *Authentic™*, 74.

59. Hayes, "Modern Makeover."

60. Muhlke, "Video Artist," 146.

61. Cunningham, "I Was Little Miss No Mates."

62. La Ferla, "An Everywoman as Beauty Queen."

63. "YouTube Stars."

64. Neate, "YouTube to Allow Its Users to Cash In."

65. Considine, "For Asian Stars, Many Web Fans."

66. Weber, *Makeover TV*.

67. Luke, "Kelly Clarkson Stronger Make Up Look."

68. Luke, "My Vintage Glams Make Up Tutorial."

69. Wong and Yip, "Guru Faces Global Appeal."

70. Gill, "Postfeminist Media Culture," 152.

71. Phan, "Seductive Smokey Eyes Tutorial."

72. Negra, *What a Girl Wants?*, 49.

73. Luke found initial fame through her Leona Lewis look in 2007, which to date has almost 4 million hits. Luke, "LEONA LEWIS Bleeding Love Inspired Make Up Look."

74. McRobbie, The Aftermath of Feminism, 67.

75. Joseph, "'Tyra Banks Is Fat,'" 240.

76. Nakamura, Digitizing Race, 34.

77. Phan, "Perfect Red Lips."

78. Phan, "Mulan Bride."

79. Ouellette and Hay, Better Living through Reality TV, 16.

80. Gans, "Hard Times Are Harder for Women."

81. Gill, "Postfeminist Media Culture," 164.

The (Re)possession of the American Home

NEGATIVE EQUITY, GENDER INEQUALITY, AND THE HOUSING CRISIS HORROR STORY

> In these troubled times, the continuing determination to turn *Paranormal Activity* into a blockbuster franchise is strangely reassuring.
>
> STUART HERITAGE, *"PARANORMAL ACTIVITY 3"*

In an ongoing cycle of cross-media production, the American home has fallen victim to violent takeovers by demons, spirits, and supernatural curses. This proliferation of popular narratives has prompted mainstream media to declare that the "paranormal is the new normal," interpreting this trend as an "escapist sign of the unsettled times."[1] This chapter argues that rather than pure escapism, the morbid fascination—of both industry and audiences—with the disruption, takeover, and abandonment of homes resonates with the reality of many recession-era households and particularly the gendered power relations therein. As Deborah Thorne highlights, during the current economic crisis the "gendered division of household labor [has] intensified among families who experience severe financial distress," with the burden of responsibility and emotional turmoil falling onto women.[2] Correspondingly, within these narratives it is women—in the face of disbelief, ineffectuality, even murderous desires on the parts of their male partners—who are forced to make the difficult decisions and take the necessary actions to reclaim the American home from malevolent forces. This obsession with the violent possession of the domestic realm has emerged at a time when the model of patriarchal authority focused upon the myth of home-owning democracy has brutally unraveled. These narratives not only draw attention to the gendered power relations and symbolic violence enacted within the American home, but also work to reveal the fragility of the wider economic system.

The recent cycle of domestic possession narratives includes *Foreclosure* (2012), in which an allegorical link between spiritual possession and the housing crisis is actualized in a narrative in which a ghost—the victim of a racist murder—returns to haunt the bankrupt inhabitants of a foreclosed home, and *Innkeepers* (2012)—promoted as a "ghost story for the minimum wage"—that shifts these themes to the haunting of a foreclosed hotel in its last few days of business.[3] While these titles suggest the continuing cultural resonance of the associations between horror and the housing market explored here, the main focus of this chapter is the phenomenally successful *Paranormal Activity* franchise (2009/2010/2011) and FX's popular TV series *An American Horror Story* (2011–).[4] Both serve as high-profile examples of the "paranormal turn in popular culture" evident in reality television and live "spirit medium" shows.[5] This recession-era interest in the occult—particularly its infiltration of the home in media spanning *Most Haunted* to *Paranormal Activity*—might be understood in relation to women's historical use of the occult as a medium to articulate anxieties and angst in times of depression and war.[6] However, this chapter does not suggest that these diverse texts represent a coherent counterhegemonic space for women to articulate or escape their recessionary anxieties and oppressions. Rather, it discusses the *Paranormal Activity* franchise and *American Horror Story*'s complex and contradictory dialogues with their brutal economic contexts. The repositioning of the home as a site of threat, instability, and disruption serves to expose the inequalities of recession-era households. However, the centering of housewives and mothers as the only defense against the (re)possession of the American home might ultimately act to reinforce the ideology of female domesticity.

The Home (Re)possession Cycle

In October 2010, *Variety* highlighted a cyclical shift in horror hits, with "supernatural fare" like the *Paranormal Activity* franchise and *The Haunting in Connecticut* (2009) "on the upswing after the reign" of torture porn and slasher remakes in the mid-2000s.[7] This paranormal (re)turn in popular culture can be compared to the similarly pervasive and popular cycle of possessed and haunted house narratives from the late 1970s to the mid-1980s. The *Poltergeist* (1982/1986/1988) and *Amityville Horror* (1979/1982/1983) franchises were also discussed by contemporary critics in relation to their recessionary subtexts of economic insecurity and downward mobility; for example, Stephen King suggested that "*The Amityville Horror*, beneath its ghost-story exterior, is really a financial demolition derby."[8] However, while these films were seen to reflect middle-class anxieties over "loss of homes and breaking up of families during an era of economic insecurity" and aggressive fiscal policy, Douglas Kellner suggests that "the project of the *Poltergeist* films is . . . ultimately to suture the spectator into desire for typical middle-class life after allowing experience of threats to it to be played out."[9] Despite the crisis played out across the *Poltergeist* films, a desire for restoration of the patriarchal household is ultimately granted. "Who," Kellner asks, "would want to watch a drama of a family losing job, home, and then being torn apart, an event which has become all too familiar during the past decade of permanent economic crisis?"[10] The answer to his question would seem to be post-2008 audiences.

Whether or not one accepts Kellner's argument about the hegemonic profamily agenda of these texts, his final observation allows a distinction to be drawn between the Reagan-era films he discusses and the current recession-era cycle explored here. In both the *Paranormal Activity* franchise and *American Horror Story*, for example, there is no reprieve for the American home, and neither, it could be argued, is the spectator primed to desire such a conclusion. In the earlier cycle the stability of the American home—and the patriarchal authority it stands for—is disrupted by paranormal threats external to these families and embedded in the home's histories. However, in *Paranormal Activity* and *American Horror Story*, repeated cycles of violence, trauma, and infidelity are embedded in the families' histories before the narratives begin. "Dispossession" of these haunted homes, in both senses, is not a possibility as it was in the 1980s films; thus, while the poster for *The Amityville* Horror warns "For God's Sake Get Out," there is no redemptive getting out for the horror-home owners of the post-2008 cycle.

The historically overlaid narrative structures of the most recent cycle evince the fatalistic repetition of violence embedded within the families' and homes' histories; the *Paranormal Activity* franchise works backward toward the family's original trauma through its ongoing prequel structure while *American Horror Story* employs overlaid flashbacks to blur past and present happenings within a haunted Los Angeles mansion. In the series, the Harmon family, the home's present occupiers, have relocated to what they later discover is the notorious "Murder House" in order to start a new life following husband and father Ben's (Dylan McDermott) adultery. However, the family's ongoing domestic problems are interrupted, and exacerbated, by the home's many ghosts, whose arrivals in the show's narrative trigger flashbacks to their shocking murders. Both strategies serve to reveal the destructive gender relations at the heart of these domestic arrangements; these escalating tensions and traumas serve to manifest, if not exacerbate, the paranormal violence within these deceptive dream homes. It is not so much that bad things happen to good families — as in the earlier cycle — but that bad faith is the structuring principle of the domestic arrangements these couples have resigned themselves to in order to have (what appears from the outside to be) the perfect home and family. It is the explosion (or implosion) of these internal tensions that serves to tear these families apart.[11]

Paranormal Activities

It is not surprising that horror iconography has been used to articulate Americans' experiences of economic crisis — as the plethora of intertextual references to classic and contemporary horror monsters in foreclosure fraud and housing crisis advice websites attests (figure 6.1) — but is surprising perhaps that the genre has been embraced by economists as containing its resolutions.[12] In an October 2011 editorial for the *Wall Street Journal*, the chief economist at the British Embassy in Washington suggested that "economic policymakers" should look to the *Paranormal Activity* franchise for "some broad, light-hearted yet serious lessons for trying to negotiate the best economic outcomes for their national economies and as a novel lens through which to understand the broad sweep of economic history." He suggests that, individually, these films favor "sensible, sober, long-term policies" and employ "imaginative forms of defence." Furthermore, through their ongoing sequelization, the films alert spectators to the expectations of evil returning and creating new challenges, thus encouraging them to be attuned to early signs of trouble. He explains, "In the first *Paranormal Activity* movie, the scariest part in the first half hour is when an open door moves an inch. Seemingly inconsequential at that moment, this small development of the plot represents a harbinger of more horrific things lurking around the corner. Economic policymakers should learn from this common error made by protagonists in horror flicks; they should be vigilant to the risks around them, paying proportionate heed and not waiting until cold-blooded terror is looking them in the eye before doing anything about it."[13] Ever the optimist, the economist here sees *Paranormal Activity* as highlighting the strategic solutions — rather than systematic failings — of the American economy, not just in its "determination" to turn a modest investment into a "blockbuster franchise," but in its call to remain attentive and vigilant in the face of overwhelming negative energy.[14]

 Paranormal Activity's delayed release allowed it to serve as a potent critique of boom-era norms as the realities of the recession were being felt. The film was produced in 2007 but rereleased to phenomenal success in 2009 backed by an innovative viral marketing campaign, backing up Annette Hill's claim

FIGURE 6.1. The 4closureFraud website appropriates the iconic "Here's Johnny" image from *The Shining* (1980) to illustrate the nefarious activities of banks and property contractors during the housing crisis.

that the "audience is the show" within contemporary mainstream paranormal culture.[15] Hill suggests that within spiritualist medium shows and televised live shows such as Living TV's *Most Haunted* (2002–2010), the active audience "co-performs and co-produces a cultural experience"; their willed commitment and embodiment of "experience" is the essence of such live events.[16] For Hill this is a symptom of skepticism rather than susceptibility to media representation of the paranormal, "a form of solipsism where experience, instinct and intuition are [the] basis for belief formation."[17] The film's now much-replicated "faux-found-footage" aesthetic (influenced in turn by similar sleeper hit *The Blair Witch Project* [1999]) requires attentive spectators to analyze the screen in order to experience for themselves—at least initially— its subtle paranormal activities. The trailer for *Paranormal Activity*'s 2009 re-release focuses upon the terrified responses of its test cinema audience— claimed as "amongst the first to *experience* the movie"—rather than footage from the film itself, replicating the film's night-vision aesthetic in order to blur the distinction between the perceived safe and unsafe spaces of auditorium and screen. It calls upon the spectator: "*experience* it for yourself" and if the film is "not playing in your city—demand it"; the trailer then directs us to the film's website where we can sign a petition to get the film released in our

FIGURE 6.2. The façade of Katie and Micah's happiness is shattered when the tensions underlying their unequal partnership materialize in violent *Paranormal Activity*.

locality. This innovative multimedia campaign centers audience participation and individual experience—these discourses were summarily central to the film's mostly positive reception.[18]

Highlighting Hill's idea that the "audience is the show," the *New York Times* reviewer asserts that "by far the most entertaining thing about the movie was the audience. . . . There was, above all, the sense of a communal, half-clandestine good time that is all too rare in an age of corporate entertainment."[19] It is significant that the audience's activity and communality are positioned outside the economic imperatives of Hollywood—a discourse that is inverted in later critiques of the franchise's manipulative exploitation of its formula. However, significantly for my purposes, the *New York Times* review highlights that the audience is equally invested in the more secular domestic clashes between the film's couple, Katie and Micah, which bifurcated rather than collectivized the audience (presumably on gendered lines). The review continues, "Their quarrels occasioned some interesting relationship advice from members of the audience. Half expressed the strong conviction that Micah should get as far away from that crazy shrew as possible, while the other half thought she should throw that idiot and his camera out of the house."[20] In *Paranormal Activity*, English graduate student Katie is subjected to demonic haunting, but it is her day trader boyfriend, Micah, who is responsible for the violent disruption of their household (figure 6.2). Self-serving, materialist, and unwaveringly rationalist, early in the film Micah mocks

Katie's fears and her attempts to address them, joking, "Is the psychic going to give me some stock tips while he's here?"

Feminist critiques of the economic crisis have highlighted the contributory role played by the masculine norms entrenched in capitalist institutions such as day trading. Annesley and Scheele suggest that "the male dominance and masculine macho culture in the finance sector holds reckless decision making and risk in higher regard than responsibility" and neglects the mutual independence between actors.[21] Qualitative analysis of the financial sector highlights fields such as investment banking and day trading as spaces marked by male dominance and the institutionalized masculinization of the market.[22] In these fields, hegemonic forms of masculinity are discursively constructed and reinforced both on the trading floor and in leisure, implicitly, through an essentialized equivalence between competence and physicality, and explicitly, through sexually aggressive language "at work and at play."[23]

Micah's stubborn and reckless assertion of this type of trading floor masculinity creates the negative energy upon which the demon feeds. Sidelining Katie's agency, he reinscribes her problems as his personal battle for the entitlements of patriarchal masculinity; he rages, "This is my house. You are my girlfriend. I'm gonna fuckin' solve this problem." While finally persuaded of the demon's existence, Micah continues to exploit their unequal financial partnership, mocking and summarily disregarding "Katie's rules" regarding the use of both Ouija board and camera, which she correctly asserts will antagonize the demon. As the continued point of contention, Micah's new camera stands as a potent symbol of Micah's financial and, perhaps resultant, sexual domination of Katie. Micah finally responds to Katie's repeated attempts to find out how much he spent on the camera by asserting his superior earning power; Katie wilts at his response, "About half of what I earned today." Correspondingly, Micah repeatedly attempts to trick Katie into having sex on camera even though she is traumatized by the ongoing paranormal activities in their home. By the later stages of the film, Micah's assertion of macho bravado—"No one comes in my house, fucks with my girlfriend and gets away with it"—has become ridiculous in the face of the overwhelming physical power of paranormal forces. Micah finally concedes to Katie that they should "get the fuck out of this house now" but she, either already possessed or simply resigned to their fate, thinks, "It will be better if we stay." In the film's shocking climax, the possessed Katie stages the final violent overthrow of Micah's patriarchal authority, using supernatural strength to launch his mangled body at the screen.

In other recent horror films it is precisely women's adoption of dispassionate, financially motivated decision making—and, as a result, their disavowal of an inherently feminine, caring relationship to the home—that forms the corrupting influence therein. For example, in *Drag Me to Hell* (2009), ambitious female loan officer Christine is cursed after she forecloses on an old woman's mortgage following pressure from her boss to prove that she is worthy of promotion. Specifically, she must prove that she is as ruthless as a male banking colleague with whom she is competing for a middle management position. Her choice to transgress her own moral code—and thus what is within the logic of the narrative her caring, feminine nature—by following the bank's unethical protocol engenders her spiritual and, ultimately, corporeal corruption. Christine is cursed not because of her choice to work in the masculine sphere of banking, but because of her decision to transgress the gendering of power relations within it. The middlebrow press explicitly discussed "recession-era movie" *Drag Me to Hell* in relation to the banking crisis.[24] Such references ranged from a flippant joke that director Sam Raimi should be "added to the Obama economic recovery team" to a utilization of the film as the basis for a serious discussion of recession ethics in the wider corporate world.[25] The financial context of these texts serves therefore to act simultaneously as critique and alibi for the patriarchal domination of the economic system in highlighting its corrupting role on an essentialized feminine nature as its ultimate and most unacceptable violence.

The failure of male authority is also central to *Paranormal Activity 2* (2010)—a prequel focusing upon Katie's sister Kristi's family—with Kristi's husband, Daniel, and Micah shown at the outset bonding through their mockery of their partners' paranormal beliefs, when they jump "straight to ghost" to explain their recent home "break-ins." However, halfway in, the film begins to point toward the financially motivated, matriarchal curse that has evinced the family's corruption. As Daniel's daughter Ali reveals, "It has been said that if a human makes a bargain with a demon for wealth, power or any other benefit they must forfeit their first born male." Her speculation that "Kristi's grandmother made a deal with demons so she could get rich" in the Depression-era context of the early 1930s is subsequently confirmed in *Paranormal Activity 3* (2011). Tracing the origins of the family's possession beyond Kristi and Katie's childhood in 1988 (when the film is set), it presents their grandmother as a member of a coven who has practiced witchcraft since the 1930s. The economic inequality of the household is reversed here, with impoverished video photographer Dennis trying to persuade his affluent partner, Julie, that her children are indeed being plagued by a demon called Toby. The grandmother expresses her disapproval of her daughter's choice of partner, deriding her for buying videos on her credit card for Dennis, who she wishes "was a bit more financially secure." Finally the grandmother expresses her ultimate disapproval of her daughter's choice of partner by having the demon Toby snap him in half. While the issue of financial (in)stability lingers uneasily throughout the franchise—perhaps nowhere more than in Katie and Micah's domestic compromises—it materializes as an explicit motivating force in the third film.

At a roundtable discussion on the *Paranormal Activity* franchise prior to the third film's release, Julia Leyda linked the "mobility and ethereality" of the demon to that of finance capital, specifically in the way in which debt follows families and individuals. Leyda continued, "Just as the demon demands payment of an ancestor's contract, the predatory mortgage allows an outsider to take away the very home and hearth (as generic and characterless as it is)."[26] The inescapability of debt remains central to *Paranormal Activity 3* but in "discover[ing] how the activity began"—as the film's poster provokes—we are arguably primed to read the grandmother's pernicious pursuit of financial stability for her family as the result of an individual rather than systematic failing. If *Paranormal Activity 4* traces the origins of the coven back to its Depression-era context of the 1930s, then it may reveal more socially embedded financial motivations, though as a cynical *Guardian* critic highlighted, "unless one of their number happened to be a particularly obsessive kinetoscope enthusiast, [the witches'] movements would be impossible to record."[27]

A mother's Faustian financial contract also evinces the corruption of family lineage in *The Box* (2009). In this supernatural morality tale, a mysterious man calls on the home of English teacher Norma (Cameron Diaz) to make her an offer of $1 million in exchange for pressing the button on "the box"; the catch is that a stranger will die as a result. Norma gives in to temptation despite her husband Arthur's reservations; her choice to press the button results in their son becoming blind and deaf. The only way to restore the boy's senses is for Norma to be willingly killed by her husband. This act restores the gendered dichotomy of female life giver and male life taker, thus reversing the erosion of the family/household and women's reproductive labor therein. Such reversals and their symbolic correction can be considered in light of recession-era concerns around women's reproductive labor, evinced in widespread reports regarding the destructive effect of the recession on declining birth rates, but also wider discursive feminizations of the corruption of the market.[28] *The Box*'s financially motivated Fall might seem extreme, but the film's hyperbolic device can nonetheless be linked to the wider gendering of financial crisis discourse in contemporary reporting, in which "financial man is never safe from [Lady Credit's] temptations and the internal desires and weaknesses she generates in him."[29]

Marieke De Goede highlights the extent to which the "gendered representation of financial crises as instances of madness, delusion, hysteria, and irrationality has had particular historical durability, which simultaneously constructs the sphere of financial normality or rationality."[30] The corporeal manifestation of woman's "pathology of the imagination"—and her resultant threat to the male rational order—has clear resonance with De Goede's discussions of financial reporting;[31] this includes the myth of the mancession reorienting the gender gap in unemployment and pay in women's favor.[32] Despite ongoing debates around whether the financial crisis might have been avoided through the presence of more women in key economic decision-making positions, texts such as *Drag Me to Hell* and *The Box* evince the violent rejection of women from this masculine realm. In these films the regendering of public and private finances serves to further corrupt rather than restore economic stability.[33]

American Horror Stories

The theme of maternal corruption is also central to the television series *American Horror Story*—produced by Ryan Murphy and Brad Falchuk of *Glee* and *Nip/Tuck* fame—but, like the first *Paranormal Activity*, this TV horror series is highly critical of the violent patriarchal underpinnings of the American home.[34] Like the first *Paranormal Activity* movie, *American Horror Story* was a surprise hit—at least for the trade press—topping the Nielsen ratings for cable drama shows in November 2011 alongside AMC's *The Walking Dead*. Significantly, *Variety* highlighted, the series "led all of its broadcast drama competition in adults 18–34"—TV's key and "harder to reach demographic"—and arguably the key demographic for the *Paranormal Activity* films.[35] In the series, Connie Britton plays Vivien, a "strong but wounded wife and mother," who agrees to relocate the family across the country following her miscarriage and her psychiatrist husband Ben's subsequent adultery.[36] Initially, Vivien plans to leave Ben after discovering him in bed with one of his students, Hayden, but Ben persuades her to try to fix their marriage by making a fresh start in Los Angeles, where he has found her dream house for a vastly reduced price (figure 6.3). He tells Vivien, "When I look at this place for the first time I feel like there's hope" to keep the family together. Vivien acquiesces to the temptation of happiness in this bargain-basement dream home; far from a steal, the property turns out to be the site of almost a century of ongoing torture, sexual violence, and murder—mostly enacted upon women—in which the spirits of the victims remain. Perhaps unsurprisingly, the house's history—in conjunction with the housing crisis—makes it impossible for the Harmons to resell the home for anywhere near the deceptive bargain price they paid. As the Machiavellian realtor Marcy explains to Vivien: "You might have to adjust your expectations: the housing market is dropping daily."

FIGURE 6.3. Ben persuades wife Vivien to stay in their disintegrating marriage through the temptation of her dream house in *American Horror Story*.

New York magazine's film critic, Julieanne Smolinski, interpreted the program's post–housing bubble context as predominantly an expedient plot device, suggesting, "You have to wonder what Ryan Murphy and Brad Falchuk would have done if we weren't in the midst of a historic real-estate slump. Otherwise, it might be harder to logically counter the typical horror-audience screams to *Just Leave the* GD *House Already*. Thank goodness for the real-estate bubble and Bernie Madoff and the stock market, which all get their due for keeping the Harmons in their hell home. I can only imagine if the show had taken place in 1997, in seller-friendly, bull-market halcyon times."[37] Smolinski condescendingly observes that *American Horror Story*'s tenuous "realism" is at least somewhat enhanced by the fortuitous context of the "real estate slump." However, what is most significant about the show's housing-crisis setting is not that these families have to remain in these horrific homes, but that their members have to remain within these families, despite the physical and psychological horror at the heart of their domestic arrangements. Despite their disintegrating marriage and their daughter's resultant self-harm and depression, the Harmons have to remain together in the home, because, as Ben suggests, "We are not broke. We have money, but it is tied up in this house." Even when they finally separate—after Vivien discovers that her husband has impregnated Hayden—Ben continues to come back to the house to see patients, against Vivien's wishes, because, as he asserts, "We need the money" and "we can't afford to rent an office." Vivien reluctantly acquiesces, albeit while expressing a desire to "bash [his face] in" when he is in the home.

Rolling Stone summarily interpreted the show as a "hate letter to the nuclear family," suggesting that "for Murphy, the real American horror story isn't how families break apart. It's how families stay together."[38] As the critic highlights here, the show's real terror emanates from the violent tensions at the heart of the family's enforced domestic arrangement. This would appear to resonate with the reality of many recession-era households, in which separated and divorced couples have been forced to stay together because they cannot sell or cannot afford to sell their homes. Citing the causes of escalating mortgage payments and negative equities, a divorce lawyer in *Lawyers Weekly* explains, "I am seeing this situation more and more often, and while it is the last thing these couples want to consider, sometimes there is financially no other option."[39] The *New York Times* highlighted this as an almost entirely new phenomenon, "rarely seen before outside Manhattan," resulting from the recent "boom-and-bust cycle." The article moves on to explain how power is transferred to the home itself, which becomes a "toxic asset" that entraps warring couples and escalates their conflicts further; as the president of the American Academy of Matrimonial Lawyers suggests, "We used to fight about who gets to keep the house—now we fight about who gets stuck with the dead cow."[40] Concurrent articles highlight reports from psychiatrists, social workers, and the courts reporting increased suicides, mental health problems—often preexisting but exposed by financial stresses—and domestic violence resulting from the pressures of unmanageable mortgage repayments, and subsequent defaults and foreclosures.[41] In Florida, one of the hardest-hit states, the clerk of Palm Beach's overrun courts highlights that "more unhappy cohabitation and more fighting over money means domestic violence is up."[42]

Within such a climate, it is understandable that media producers and critics would foreground impacting cycles of physical and psychological violence as the structuring principle of gendered family relations.[43] As in *Paranormal Activity*, psychiatrist Ben dominates Vivien and denies her subjectivity, though through the disciplinary technology of medical rather than economic discourse. Vehement rationalist Ben diagnoses her paranormal experiences variously as symptoms of depression, post-traumatic stress disorder, even mad cow disease, refusing to allow her to take their daughter and leave the house; her leaving is finally permitted, under his discursive terms, only when he has her committed to a mental institution. Ben's more subtle domination of Vivien is constantly blurred with previous tenants' domination of women, including Larry, who warns Ben that the house made him burn his family to death and that Ben will do the same; a series of unethical and deranged medical practitioners who secretly operated upon and murdered women in the home in the 1920s, 1930s, and 1940s (including the dentist murderer of the Blue Dahlia victim); and the "Rubber Man"—the S&M suit–clad ghost whom Vivien mistakes for her husband and who resultantly coimpregnates her with twins. The home's kindly, ghostly maid, Moira, explains to Vivien, "Since the beginning of time men have found excuses to lock women away. They make up diseases like hysteria. . . . Men are still inventing ways to drive women over the edge. Look at you and Mr. Harmon, cheating on you and leaving you here pregnant with twins alone to take care of your truant daughter. Any woman would lose her mind."

Moira's appraisal of Vivien's situation can be usefully compared with Deborah Thorne's qualitative study of indebted American households and the inequitable gendering of labor therein. As Thorne highlights, "even when wives pleaded for help, husbands often refused. The strain of the [new] financial chores left many wives battling severe emotional distress. In the most extreme cases, a few wished for death."[44] Vivien—at least until her death—experiences by far the greater emotional effects and obligations for maintaining the security of the home; these range from responsibility for reselling the home to protecting against the invasions of secular and supernatural threats. For example, when Ben goes on a secret trip to Boston to make sure ex-mistress Hayden has an abortion, Vivien and daughter Violet have to fight off a group of serial killer enthusiasts attempting to reenact a serial murder that happened in the home in the 1960s. Violet's depression and disillusionment—and her parents' subsequent fears for her future—also resonate with the series' recessionary context; psychological research into post-2008 parent-child relationships indicates that the pressures and anxieties of families' present financial problems and children's future opportunities increased self-reporting of anxiety and depression in both parents and older children, serving to exacerbate conflict and reduce closeness between the two groups.[45]

In *American Horror Story*, Violet commits suicide halfway through the series, though she is so shut off from the outside world that she does not realize she has been successful for a couple of episodes. The cause of Violet's suicide is underlying depression brought on by the unresolved and ongoing family tensions discussed above, but the trigger is Violet seeing the message "I love you" that has been written on her bedroom wall by the teenage ghost Tate. Tate is repeatedly doubled with Violet's father both through the Rubber Man suit and through Ben's comment, "I was kind of like you, Tate" before he was given the "amazing gift of [his] family." Violet therefore chooses to take her own life rather than repeat the familial cycle of domestic violence and abuse. This unromanticized relationship between Violet and Tate is therefore very different from the postfeminist phenomenon of "dating the dead" in the cross-media Twilight and True Blood franchises.[46] The narrative of American Horror Story appears to work against what Anthea Taylor describes as the rendering of a "masochistic relationship and an undead subjectivity for a teenage girl . . . as utopic sites" in the Twilight novels and films. However, the brooding character Tate has become an emo pinup for female teens, and the doomed Violet/Tate relationship (dubbed Viol/ate) has been endlessly extended in Tumblr blogs and fanfiction.[47]

Despite the allusions to the female Gothic and topical critiques of domestic power relations, American Horror Story could hardly be characterized as feminist in any straightforward manner. The series' extreme awareness of popularized academic discourse and genre conventions (particularly those of horror and film noir) more often serve as an alibi for its simultaneous objectification and monstrous representation of female characters; for example, the maid Moira is seen as a sexualized "pinup" and matronly "old crone" by male and female spectators (within the diegesis) respectively. While Ben (and other men) see Moira as a scantily clad femme fatale played by young actress Alexandra Breckenridge — Moira before her murder — Vivien (and other women) see her as grandmotherly Frances Conroy (of Six Feet Under) who has continued to age in ghost form. As Moira anticipates, Ben is tempted by her seductions, which are aimed at revealing him (and by extension men generally) as inherently unfaithful. The resultant objectification of the young Moira (and other female characters) thus serves both to satisfy the male gaze and to act as a critique of it;[48] however, the show also repeatedly fetishizes Dylan McDermott (Ben's) naked body even though his character is positioned as far from a figure of desire.[49]

American Horror Story equally references classic film noir as much as horror, particularly in its series of femme fatale roles, most notably Jessica Lange's character, Constance, the first season's only "survivor" in a central role, perhaps in part because she is the show's most interesting and complex character. This might well be linked to the evocation of noirish visual landscapes and themes in other quality TV dramas such as HBO's Boardwalk Empire (2010–) and Mildred Pierce (2011), and their wider connection to the nostalgic generic and gendered modes in TV texts spanning Mad Men (2007–) to Downton Abbey (2010–).[50] Constance fits the corrupted maternal principles discussed in relation to The Box, in her reproductive history of a series of physically and psychologically "flawed" children and desire to reproduce (or acquire) a "perfect" child for herself. It is significant that Constance (ex-inhabitant and constant uninvited visitor to the Harmons' home) is the only one who is able to navigate and exploit the Murder House's threats unscathed; this is in part because she is responsible—at least from the 1980s onward—for many of the home's ghosts, either directly (she murdered the maid Moira and her husband for having an affair; and her subsequent affair with Larry is the reason that his wife burns the family to death—rather than Larry as it is later revealed) or through her dead son Tate's ghost (he murdered the gay couple who lived there prior to the Harmons because they would not be having a child anymore, and impregnated Vivien with the "Antichrist" twin that kills her in childbirth and becomes Constance's perfect adopted son at the end of season one).[51] Her narrative trajectory and identity are thus entwined, even imprinted upon the house, suggesting the workings of a monstrous femme fatale ultimately pulling the strings.

Perhaps more nihilistic than feminist, *American Horror Story* provides the Harmon family with tranquillity and stability only in the annihilation of death, when instead of trying to pass on the Murder House to other unsuspecting families—as throughout the series—their bad example becomes a warning to other families to flee. In the season finale, realtor Marcy reinscribes the Harmons' experiences as a "tragically romantic love story" when quizzed on why the asking price is "so below market" even for an economic downturn, thus convincing the Ramos family to move in. However, in a sinister twist on the *Beetlejuice* (1988) premise, the Harmon family's ghosts haunt the home's new inhabitants, not to reclaim their idealized home from gauche secular intruders as in *Beetlejuice*, but rather to save the new family from replicating their own domestic horror. As Vivien's ghost gouges the guts out of Ben's ghost in front of the new inhabitants, she tells them, "You have no idea how long I've been wanting to do that." The family flees and the house goes on the market at an even further reduced price.

Ultimately, therefore, Ben gets his wish to keep the family together in the house for eternity. The opening of the season finale stages a macabre juxtaposition of Ben's speech persuading Vivien to "just come see the house"—a narrative of domestic bliss that seeing the brochure for the house triggered "like a movie in his mind"—and a montage of shots from the series, including Vivien's sexual violation (though by Ben, not the Rubber Man) and subsequent loss of bodily control (through her violent impregnation) and Violet's self-harm. Cutting to widower Ben in the empty house in the present, the opening scene of the season finale makes clear that husband and father Ben triggered the family's brutal fate.

The Daniel Craig vehicle *Dream House* (2011) initially promises a similarly "teasing variation on the haunted house movie" that highlights the patriarchal violence underlying the veneer of American home life.[52] At the start of the film, Will Attenton (Craig) leaves his high-powered editor's job in Manhattan to join his nuclear family in their new suburban dream home, where he will write his long-in-the-works first novel. The home soon comes under attack from secular, then seemingly supernatural, threats from which Will must protect his family. However, the film's midway point reveals that we have been experiencing not the haunting of Will's idealized family but his psychological delusions following his release from a mental institution, after being committed for murdering his wife and family five years previously. Following this revelation, the spectator sees the reality of the home's boarded-up, graffiti-strewn present of 2011 rather than the delusion of the 2006 dream house prior to the family's murder. Unlike *American Horror Story*, *Dream House* ultimately clears the widowed father of his guilt and ghostly visions—it is revealed that a neighbor had hired an incompetent hit man to murder his wife, but the hit man went into the wrong house—even affording him the financial redemption of a best-selling novel based upon his horrific experiences. However, in the central perceptual shift from Will's 2006 to 2011, the spectator is forced to witness the visceral housing crisis fallout experienced by a growing number of American families and neighborhoods.

WITH THE CYCLE OF housing crisis horror stories showing little sign of abating—whether on or off screen—the real *American Horror Story* home went on sale in January 2012 for \$4.5 million, highlighting the unabated, more likely exacerbated, disparity between the 99 percent and the 1 percent.[53] While popular horror like *Paranormal Activity* and *American Horror Story* materializes the structural violence and gendered inequalities underlying capitalist cycles of boom and recession, they still serve to stress white, middle-class families as the main victims of the current housing crisis. Likewise, within these nuclear families, it is the paranormal threat to women's "inherent" roles as life givers and protectors that is foregrounded as the ultimate horror of tough economic times. These texts do not finally call for a rethinking of the gendering of markets or homes, but rather enact a vigilant reinforcing of the parameters of both.

Notes

1. Elliott, "In TV Pilots, Paranormal Is the New Normal."

2. Thorne, "Extreme Financial Strain," 185.

3. In an attempt to build a topical viral buzz for *Foreclosure*, the film's website calls for visitors to "Submit Your Real-Life 'Foreclosure' Horror Stories and Win Stuff." www .ghostsdontmoveout.com/foreclosure/yourstory (accessed February 12, 2012).

4. Other texts that I would position within this cycle include Hollywood films such as *The Haunting in Connecticut* (2009), *The Last Exorcism* (2010), *Insidious* (2011), and *Dream House* (2011). However, the cycle could also be seen to have manifested in recent re-vampings of Hammer Horror in the U.K.—with the film *Woman in Black* (2012) and Helen Dunmore's novel *The Greatcoat* (2012) within its literary imprint—and linked to the popularity of vampire romances in film, TV, and popular fiction, particularly the *Twilight* and *True Blood* franchises, with their preoccupations with negotiating the nature of family and home.

5. Hill, *Paranormal Media*.

6. Snelson, "The Ghost in the Machine," 16–32.

7. Graser and Stewart, "Fright Plan for All Seasons," 11.

8. King, "Why We Crave Horror Movies," 237. See also Williams, "*Poltergeist* and Freddy's Nightmares," 225–37; Kellner, "*Poltergeist*, Gender and Class in the Age of Bush and Reagan," 127–39.

9. Kellner, "*Poltergeist*, Gender and Class in the Age of Bush and Reagan," 131, 139. Since the 1970s, horror scholarship has highlighted the genre's historical engagement with shifting political, economic, and social anxieties as well as its positioning of the family home as the primary institution of patriarchal aggression and repression in American society. These critics, I would argue, typically make an unproductive distinction between the progressive politics of the dysfunctional family horror films of the 1960s and 1970s (e.g., *Psycho* [1960] and *Texas Chainsaw Massacre* [1974]) and the reactionary Reagan-era horror homes overseen by patriarchal avengers such as Freddy Krueger and Michael Myers (see Wood, *Hollywood from Vietnam to Reagan*; Williams, "*Poltergeist* and Freddy's Nightmares").

10. Kellner, "*Poltergeist*, Gender and Class in the Age of Bush and Reagan," 138.

11. I am using "bad faith" in a de Beauvoirian sense here. See de Beauvoir, *Ethics of Ambiguity*.

12. For example, StopForeclosureFraud.com's logo superimposes the image of Frankenstein's monster over the map of America's most foreclosed states while 4closureFraud stamps "I'm from the bank" on Jack Nicholson's forehead in the famous "Here's Johnny" scene from *The Shining* (1980). 4closureFraud, "Jackbooted Thugs Break into Occupied Homes, Terrify Residents, Lawsuits Say," July 19, 2012, http://4closurefraud.org/2012/07/19/jackbooted-thugs-break-into-occupied-homes -terrify-residents-lawsuits-say/.

13. Matheson, "What Horror Movies Can Teach Economic Policy Makers."

14. Heritage, "*Paranormal Activity 3*."

15. Hill, *Paranormal Media*. This is not to suggest that Hill's scholarship was a reference point for the campaign. However, the films and their marketing—like *American Horror Story*—are very knowledgeable of horror history, generic conventions, and audience pleasures. It is worth noting that the *Paranormal Activity* rerelease was overseen by executive producer Steven Schneider, who went on to produce the other *Paranormal Activity* films as well as *Insidious* (2011) and *The Devil Inside* (2011). *Paranormal Activity* marked Schneider's career shift from horror scholar to horror producer; Schneider's books include *Horror Film and Psychoanalysis*.

16. Hill, *Paranormal Media*, 19.

17. Hill, *Paranormal Media*, 127.

18. Caetlin Benson-Allott suggests that *Paranormal Activity* and its sequels must be read in the context of the culture of illegal file sharing and the M PAA's resultant war on piracy. She maintains that the films' faux footage aesthetics—and, by extension, the viral marketing campaign discussed here—evokes the simultaneous excitement and horror of "pirate spectatorship." She concludes, however, that they ultimately serve a hegemonic function in teaching spectators that "sometimes watching the wrong thing can be deadly." Benson-Allott, *Killer Tapes*, 192.

19. Scott, "Ghostbusters on a Budget."

20. Scott, "Ghostbusters on a Budget."

21. Annesley and Scheele, "Gender, Capitalism and Economic Crisis," 336.

22. Connell, "Inside the Glass Tower," 8–24.

23. Levin, "Gender, Work, and Time," 249–81.

24. Brown, "Recession Era Movie."

25. Sharkey, "Drag Me to Hell"; Goodman, "Recession Ethics."

26. Leyda, Rombes, Shaviro, and Grisham, "Roundtable Discussion."

27. Heritage, "*Paranormal Activity 4* Is Haunted by the Sequel Problem."

28. Roberts, "Birth Rate Is Said to Fall as a Result of Recession." The economic crisis's corruption of motherhood is a theme explored in nonsupernatural horrors such as *Mother's Day* (2010), in which backlash veteran Rebecca De Mornay (*The Hand That Rocks the Cradle* [1992]) returns as the deranged "mother from hell" following the repossession of her house. However, as with the reception of *Drag Me to Hell*, *The Box*, and *The Haunting in Connecticut*, critics highlighted how the film raises questions regarding recession-era ethics; as *Variety* highlights, in *Mother's Day* the "perils of buying foreclosed properties are made painfully clear." Gant, "Mother's Day."

29. De Goede, *Virtue, Fortune and Faith*, 45.

30. De Goede, *Virtue, Fortune and Faith*, 39.

31. Foucault, *Madness and Civilisation*, 138.

32. Cook, "What Mancession?"; Mattioli, "Few Gender Differences in a Recession."

33. Vinnicombe et al., "The Female FTSE Board Report 2010"; Davies, "Women on Boards."

34. Lyons, "Miami Slice," 2–11. James Lyons highlights *Nip/Tuck*'s deployment of classic Gothic tropes through its male doppelgänger theme and symbolic "figuration of monstrosity and vampirism" (9). *American Horror Story* might be seen therefore to extend and literalize underlying themes in Falchuk's earlier productions, but also significantly flips the focus of this male doppelgänger struggle from the fraternal love triangle to a wife's horror at living with a potentially monstrous and internally conflicted husband.

35. Kissell, "Cable Dramas Win Key Demo," 41.

36. Hale, "They Said It Had Good Bones."

37. Smolinski, "*American Horror Story* Recap."

38. Sheffield, "*American Horror Story* Will Restore Your Faith in Ryan Murphy's Dark Side."

39. Heather Cooper quoted in Stephenson, "Breaking Up Is Even Harder to Do."

40. Leland, "In Housing Fall, Breaking Up Is Harder to Do."

41. Ehrenreich, "The Suicide Solution"; Turse, "The Body Count on Main Street"; Armour, "Foreclosures Take Toll on Mental Health."

42. Stapleton, "New Rules Aim for Smoother Defaults." On the eve of the 2012 Oscars ceremony, the *New York Times* reported that even the "dream factory" of "Tinseltown" was becoming a "ghost town," where "dark, vacant houses, emblazoned with the public notices taped in the windows like shameful scarlet A's, are holes in the hidden, fraying social fabric of Hollywood, where a vast majority belong not to the 1 percent but to the 99." De Vries, "Tinseltown, Ghost Town."

43. In the Halloween double episode, an opening flashback reveals that, like the Harmons, the warring gay couple living in the house before them were forced to stay together because, as Zachary Quinto's character Chad tells his cheating partner, "all of your money and mine is in this house we decided to flip but can't because the economy is in the shitter." The episode concludes with Chad's ghost coming to the realization, "I'm doomed for all of eternity to be trapped in an unhappy, adulterous relationship, working on this goddamn house."

44. Thorne, "Extreme Financial Strain," 185.

45. Stein et al., "Family Ties in Tough Times," 449–54.

46. See Hill, *Paranormal Media*, 48; Taylor, "The Urge towards Love Is an Urge towards (Un)death," 31–46. The *Twilight* saga and its "Twihard" fans have come under attack for a variety of sins including regressive gender politics; fetishizing the male body; fueling a feminized consumer culture; and transgressing the generic expectations of horror. While *Twilight* is certainly postfeminist in its stylistic and thematic concerns, a highly gendered cultural politics of taste is clearly at work in its denigration by male critics and the resultant reification of masculine horror tastes (see Bode, "Transitional Tastes," 707–19; Jancovich, "Critical Reception of the *Twilight* Saga").

47. Taylor, "The Urge towards Love Is an Urge towards (Un)death," 31. See for example tumblr, #violate, www.tumblr.com/tagged/violate.

48. Mulvey, "Visual Pleasure and Narrative Cinema," 6–18.

49. The extensive media dialogue around the sexualization of McDermott's body in the series serves to highlight its atypicality. See for example Nederdog, "*American Horror Story*'s Dylan McDermott on Nude Scenes"; Hilton, "Dylan McDermott Is Nekkid and Seksi in *American Horror Story*."

50. The global success of *Downton Abbey* in particular has been debated widely in relation to its recessionary context, potentially reflecting either a conservative political turn, a "response to tough times, or it may be that a full experience of culture and imagination embraces new and old, experimental and orderly, and that all worthwhile art contains both conservative and radical possibilities." Jones, "From Hockney to *Downton Abbey*."

51. In her presentation at Console-ing Passions International Conference on Television, Video, Audio, New Media and Feminism, 2012, Beth Pentney situated the mother blame in *American Horror Story* and *We Need to Talk about Kevin* (2011) in relation to wider obsessions with the consequences of bad mothering in postfeminist media

culture. Pentney suggested that, like bad mother Constance, Eva (Tilda Swinton) is held responsible and made to suffer for the actions of her mass murderer son Kevin. Pentney, "'We're Still Blaming Mothers.'"

52. Koeher, "Dream House," 29.

53. Glink, "*American Horror Story* Home for Sale."

SEVEN   *SINÉAD MOLONY*

House and Home

STRUCTURING ABSENCES IN POST–CELTIC TIGER DOCUMENTARY

The term "Celtic Tiger" describes the period of Irish history circa 1995–2007 in which proponents of free-market, neoliberal ideology contended that the Republic of Ireland (Ireland from here on) had been transformed from one of the poorest European countries to the fastest-growing Western economy. This boom exemplifies a tendency seen across several European nations involving an economy built on support for financial industries, inducements for the wealthy, and increasing levels of income inequality. Neoliberal government policies introduced during the 1980s and 1990s, such as low corporate tax rates of 12.5 percent, the development of the Irish Financial Services Centre (IFSC) as a "centre for a wide variety of *trans*-national financial activity," and "light-touch financial regulation," had reconfigured Ireland as a low-tax haven.[1] Given that—as Donagh Brennan argues—such economic policies form part of a system "by which very profitable corporations can avoid tax" not only in Ireland but "in other jurisdictions," it is unsurprising that at the peak of its economic boom, Ireland was heralded internationally as "the poster child of free-market globalization."[2]

Although living standards improved during the Celtic Tiger years, they did so in extremely unequal proportion, cementing age-old class divisions rather than alleviating them. Gerry Smyth notes that in comparison to the early 1990s, "by 2000, the income of the poorest 20% of the population rose by less than 1%; those of the middle income groups rose by 2–3%; and those in the top 30% rose by about 4%."[3] Prior to this economic boom, it was not unusual for Ireland to be described as a third world country: sixty years after independence, the former British colony had high unemployment and net emigration, and was an extremely conservative state dominated by Catholic Church doctrine.[4] From the 1950s onward, drawn-out and haphazard processes of urban renewal, decentralization, and relocation divided close-knit inner-city communities into poorly serviced estates in small towns like Ballyfermot, Tallaght, and Coolock on the outskirts of the city center. During the 1980s, inner-city Dublin suffered from extremely poor housing conditions, endemic unemployment—the 1981 census gives a rate of 24 percent unemployment in the inner city—and a population heavily dependent on social welfare.[5]

Dublin's working-class population was further damaged in the 1980s by a heroin epidemic that swept through the capital city. The problem particularly impacted the already besieged communities that remained in the inner city. Michael Punch cites an early study that "found that prevalence of heroin abuse among young people in the 15–24 age group in one north inner city community was 10% and as high as 12% in the 15–19 age group."[6] According to Aileen O'Gorman, while the 1983 Government Task Force on Drug Abuse acknowledged that "drug problems in Dublin were largely explicable in terms of the poverty and powerlessness of a small number of working class neighborhoods," proposals for "additional financial resources to tackle disadvantage" were omitted from the task force's published press releases, "which, in contrast, suggested that drug problems were randomly distributed in society and could be explained in terms of individual personalities and choices."[7] That the state's earliest response was to emphasize choice and lifestyle rather than inequality in the drug crisis is characteristic of a neoliberal agenda that is primarily concerned with the citizen as consumer and that imagines the state as an entrepreneurial entity rather than the protector of social justice.

The 1986 Urban Renewal Act provided a brief hope that the then–Fianna Fáil government would commit to tackling the inner-city drug crisis. The 1986 act, which Niamh Moore describes as "a pro-development rather than regulatory instrument," foresaw the development of the IFSC in Dublin's traditionally working-class Docklands.[8] The act was only passed in Parliament because then Taoiseach (Prime Minister) Charles Haughey made a deal with Independent TD (Minister of Parliament) Tony Gregory to invest IR£14 million on housing schemes for the north inner city: an "integrated plan for the social regeneration of Dublin's inner city, and more."[9] In an article remembering the thirtieth anniversary of the "Gregory Deal," Mick Rafferty—who was part of the negotiating team—suggests that Haughey also committed to tackling the heroin crisis. Rafferty says that, having been informed that Dublin's heroin problem wasn't a subculture of choice, but a deliberate attempt to create a drugs market based on addiction Haughey asked who should be targeted, and Gregory told him the name of the family who were the chief importers and distributors of heroin in the city, the Xs.

Haughey immediately rang then Garda commissioner Patrick McLaughlin. He told him of his concerns about the emerging drug problem, asked him to put resources into surveillance on the family we had mentioned, and put the issue on the agenda for their next meeting.[10]

However, only a couple of weeks following the deal, Haughey's government collapsed and with it, the promise of social regeneration. Although the superseding Fine Gael–Labour coalition implemented the economic policies of the prior government, the social protections that had been promised in return for the development of the Docklands were largely neglected. Rafferty regrets that "the whole docklands were . . . developed as a financial hub with profit as the god, and bankers and speculators as its ardent high priests."[11] Rather than being developed to address social need, private profit was the ultimate beneficiary of the 1986 Urban Renewal Act and the IFSC project became the epicenter of Irish neoliberal policy.

The negligence of the state response to the 1980s heroin epidemic is evidenced by the fact that thirty years later, Dublin's drug treatment centers are currently "faced with a third generation of users."[12] With this in mind, it is no longer useful to talk about the Irish heroin epidemic; rather, we need to think about drug addiction as an endemic factor of contemporary Irish society, a scene of "capitalist structural subordination and governmentality" that illustrates the "dispersed management of the biological threat posed by certain populations to the reproduction of the normatively framed general good life of a society."[13] Under a neoliberal regime that fetishizes consumption, choice, and agency, but also contradictorily "produces a hypervigilance about control and deservingness," the very ordinariness of drug and drink addiction in Ireland is an example of how the pressure and labor of everyday living is negotiated through practices of self-interruption that result in the slow attrition of life itself, particularly for the increasingly poor populations of contemporary austerity regimes.[14] For Lauren Berlant, "the phrase *slow death* refers to the physical wearing out of a population and the deterioration of people in that population that is very nearly a defining condition of their experience and historical existence."[15]

In what follows, I draw on Berlant's discussion of slow death as a way of examining how the ordinary and everyday attrition of life is represented (or evaded) in the contemporary age of austerity.[16] In particular, I want to explore the gendered dimensions of austerity, drawing attention to disparities between the trope of the family home as the ultimate signifier of the moral middle-class good life, and embodied experiences of domestic space as the scene of slow death. I am particularly interested in how intersecting discourses of gender and class have shaped representations of the Irish home as symbolic of the recessionary nation. Dominated by an unquestioned middle-class gaze, Irish documentary presents the working-class female body as a site of national shame and disruption that troubles ordinary heteronormative domesticity. As the case of documentary shows, in Ireland's recession culture those who do not abide by middle-class gender norms are pathologized as other and framed outside the national collective.

Neoliberalism and the Gendered Discourse of Irish Nationalism

The gendered discourse of Irish nationalism offers a commonsense conceptual apparatus for the advancement of neoliberal ideology. In turn, the neoliberal fetishization of individual agency facilitates the exclusionary trajectories of nationalism. Thus, for example, politicians' branding of the nation as "Team Ireland," "the Green Jersey," and "Ireland Inc." works to naturalize a Darwinian narrative of survival of the fittest or richest and to justify successive Irish governments' extraordinary collaboration in international financialization.

Distinctly gendered stereotypes of the Irish nation as rebellious and anti-authoritarian pervaded the myth of the Celtic Tiger; as Terrence McDonough and Tony Dundon argue, "the (de)regulatory approach can be traced to a peculiarly Irish anti-authoritarian populism with an ideological neoliberal tenor."[17] Proponents of the neoliberal agenda, such as former finance minister Charlie McCreevey, decry the social state as stultifying masculine virility: "Don't try to protect everyone from every possible accident. . . . And leave industry with the space to breathe and investors with the freedom to learn from their mistakes. . . . Many of us in this room are from the generation that had the luck to grow up before governments got working and lawyers got rich on regulating our lives. We were part of the 'unregulated generation'—the generation that has produced some of the best risk-takers, problem-solvers and inventors."[18] McCreevey's use of the collective pronoun "we" hints at the cohort of politicians, bankers, and developers who are recognized as largely profiting from the neoliberal turn in Ireland. Irish media presented an elite class of businessmen, bankers, property developers, and politicians as the canny, ballsy progenitors of an impossible economic boom. For example, at the 2005 Irish Times Property Awards, Seán Fitzpatrick, then chairman of Anglo Irish Bank, described the Celtic Tiger as a result of potent masculine virility: "We had ideas and . . . balls . . . as we worked the scene and maximised the moment the world watched in astonishment."[19] As a central trope of celebratory Celtic Tiger discourse, this figure of virile entrepreneurial masculinity functions as an ideal neoliberal body around which all other modes of living must adjust. Accordingly, working-class areas of inner-city Dublin saw the development of high-rise office blocks, gated apartment buildings, and luxury shopping malls; in the process, the descriptor "regeneration" justified the private profit of the risk-taking Celtic Tiger man as opposed to the social needs of impoverished communities. Ultimately, the inflection of neoliberal state policy with nationalist discourse justified the ever-increasing class stratification of Irish society as in the national interest.

Following decades of disinvestment, the Celtic Tiger years saw Irish land prices escalate, and the development of high-end property for commercial and residential use resulted in the further displacement of local Dublin communities. According to McDonough and Dundon, "economic expansion eventually created a bottleneck in housing and commercial property."[20] This in turn resulted in a property bubble in which "a disproportionate amount of both economic activity and employment depended on construction."[21] Meanwhile, the remarkable "national preference for private home ownership" (discussed in more detail shortly) was exploited by the triarchy of bankers, developers, and politicians as well as the mainstream media, promoting home ownership as a necessary condition of successful citizenship.[22]

Faced with the necessity of improving inner-city social housing, the policy of Public Private Partnership initiated in Ireland in the late 1990s took "entrepreneurial governance to its limits."[23] While local banks were "tapping . . . international capital flows to finance both the development of Irish property and the private purchase of this property once completed," the partnership model offered the state a way to "reconstruct rundown estates at zero cost. The private sector partner would redevelop the whole site, providing an agreed number of social housing units and amenities in return for the development rights on the rest of the site."[24] Michael Punch argues that "the decisive criteria for development were not the public good or social regeneration but exchange value and economic viability (that is, profitability)."[25] Despite the much-reported wealth of the Celtic Tiger and the huge developments that took place over that period, only one of Dublin's social housing estates — Fatima Mansions — actually underwent the regeneration process as agreed by the state and its private partners; when the property bubble collapsed, social housing projects were shut down. Regeneration consisted largely of the introduction of a middle-class population alongside penthouse apartments, high-end restaurants, and luxury shopping malls, "accompanied by a chorus of approval from the renewal authority, the development lobby and the property sections of the broadsheets."[26] As McDonough and Dundon argue, "the overall socio-spatial effect reflect[s] a class-divided city, with the division lines now clearly demarcated in the residential geography of gated private apartments and ghettoized public flats."[27]

Recession, Austerity, and the Crisis of Morality

When in September 2008 Ireland became the first Eurozone country to enter recession, the aggressive optimism that described the Celtic Tiger nation was replaced with popular expressions of anger, fear, disbelief, loss, and outrage. Following huge falls in bank shares on the Irish stock exchange, astoundingly and without public referendum the government announced a €400 billion guarantee scheme covering all six major Irish financial institutions, including Fitzpatrick's Anglo Irish. For a nation the size of Ireland with a then-GDP of minus 6.7 percent, the burden of this debt was impossible to manage, and in November 2010, the debt-ridden republic had to receive a bailout package amounting to €85 billion from the Troika—the collective name given to the International Monetary Fund, the European Central Bank, and the European Commission.

On November 18, 2010, an *Irish Times* editorial responded to the international bailout by evoking Irish nationalism's mythical moment of genesis, the 1916 Easter Rising:

> It may seem strange to some that The Irish Times would ask whether this is what the men of 1916 died for: a bailout from the German chancellor with a few shillings of sympathy from the British chancellor on the side. There is the shame of it all. Having obtained our political independence from Britain to be the masters of our own affairs, we have now surrendered our sovereignty to the European Commission, the European Central Bank, and the International Monetary Fund. Their representatives ride into Merrion Street today. . . . The true ignominy of our current situation is not that our sovereignty has been taken away from us, it is that we ourselves have squandered it. . . . It is the incompetence of the governments we ourselves elected that has so deeply compromised our capacity to make our own decisions.[28]

Prioritizing shame as the preeminent emotion of post–Celtic Tiger Ireland, the editorial frames the economic crisis as a crisis of morality and masculinity, mourning the lost ideals of patriarchal nationalism. By comparing the good choices or moral agency of the men of 1916 with the bad decisions of the contemporary Irish public, the editorial disregards the difference between personal and political sovereignty. Failing to address the inherent flaws and contradictions of the global capitalist system, the article instead espouses neoliberal notions of individual choice and agency but also evokes the contradictory neoliberal discourse of self-control and discipline.

Underlying moralizing explanations for the recession (such as the argument that "we all partied" during the Celtic Tiger) is a biopolitical discourse that functions to regulate those bodies whose agency threatens the social prosperity of global hegemonies.[29] For Berlant, "biopower operates when a hegemonic bloc organizes the reproduction of life in ways that allow political crises to be cast as conditions of specific bodies."[30] Rather than being discussed as a consequence of the ever-increasing Irish allegiance to American "free-market fundamentalism," the collapse of the Celtic Tiger is framed as a shameful example of Irish bodies' incompetent sovereignty.[31] In this way the editorial not only justifies the surrender of political sovereignty to a group of international institutions that instantiates "neoliberalism as a global set of rules" but actually frames this surrender as a necessary disciplinary measure.[32]

Since the Irish bailout, the nationalist myth of the risk-taking rebel has largely disappeared from political discourse, to be replaced by an emphasis on stability and promises to honor international commitments. Insisting that the country would pay back the bondholders of insolvent Irish banks (despite the fact that their losses were on private loans underwritten by banks across Europe), Taoiseach Enda Kenny's repeated statement that the people of Ireland will not have the "name defaulter across [their] foreheads" implies that for his government, shame is no longer equated with the loss of sovereignty, but with the failure to live up to the ideals of the neoliberal hegemony that have imposed austerity across Europe.[33] Described as a moral crisis, the recession affords conservative governments the opportunity to dismantle the social state; as Rosemary Meade argues, narratives of blame legitimize "reductions in the minimum wage, assaults on public sector spending and conditions, the broadening of the tax base to include the low-paid and the avoidance of more decisive redistribution from the summit of the earnings hierarchy."[34] In comparison to the unruly excesses of Celtic Tiger governments, Kenny's reinstatement of Irish pride through austerity measures reads like an oath of impoverishment for the Irish public.

In what follows, I analyze three contemporary Irish documentaries and their reception in post–Celtic Tiger Ireland in order to unpack the contradictions between idealized representations of female domesticity as the heart of the nation and embodied experiences of gendered and classed exclusion. The Irish Constitution describes the family as a "moral institution" and "the fundamental unit group of Society."[35] In this context the absent or disrupted family in His and Hers (dir. Ken Wardrop, 2010), The House (dir. Tanya Doyle,

2010), and *Pyjama Girls* (dir. Maya Derrington, 2010) can be read as a representational microcosm of the fractured recessionary nation. Inherent to imaginings of the family as the "fundamental unit group of Society" is the family home—a space that organizes physical and psychic boundaries around and between individuals who are otherwise disconnected and immoral. In the Constitution's description the home is constructed as an atavistic natural habitat and as a frame through which the normative good life of the nation is imagined. Not only is the house idealized as the cornerstone of the neoliberal fantasy, it is invested in as a signifier of gendered morality; the Irish Constitution states that "by her life within the home, woman gives to the State a support without which the common good cannot be achieved" and that "the State shall, therefore, endeavor to ensure that mothers shall not be obliged by economic necessity to engage in labour to the neglect of their duties in the home."[36] This conflation of house, femininity, and family presumes a heteronormative, middle-class nation; posited as "the common good," female domesticity is invested with moral status.

The three documentaries examined here are noteworthy for the heightened emotionality produced in response to representations of the classed female body. For Sara Ahmed, emotions like shame are not private, coming "from within and [moving] outward toward others" but are circulated between bodies and signs aligning "individuals with communities."[37] In the sense that representations of gender or class produce affective responses on bodies, in the form of red-faced shame, for example, or in the turning away of disgust, affect works to orient embodied performances of everyday life. In such a manner, I would argue, representations of gender and class in *His and Hers*, *Pyjama Girls*, and *The House* invoke affective responses that realign audiences with the hegemonic ideals of neoliberal nationalism.

Considered together, a number of factors illustrate some of the contradictions of contemporary capitalism in Ireland, namely, the Irish cultural infatuation with home ownership, which resembles that of the United States more than any other country in Europe; the property bubble that shaped Ireland's recent economic boom and subsequent bust; and the postboom phenomenon of "ghost estates"—the recession has seen over two thousand housing developments left unfinished across the Irish countryside. Although the recent boom was one of the few periods of Irish history wherein immigration was higher than emigration, much of the property built during that period is empty, unfinished, or derelict as mass emigration and unemployment once more become the reality of many families. Meanwhile, despite the marked increase of employed women during the Celtic Tiger, the performance of the Irish female as a domesticated consumer was ideologically privileged over her productivity in the workplace. During the economic boom, celebratory neo-liberal discourse formulated a country shaking off the shackles of a repressive Catholicism and the new era was given symbolic form in new tropes of sexually active postfeminst urbanites such as the fake-tanned Juicy Couture–wearing "D4 girl" and the "Drummy Mummy," Ireland's version of the "Yummy Mummy" named after the luxurious boom-time shopping mall, the Dundrum Town Centre. In what can be read as part of a larger discourse that attempts to manage the excesses of neoliberal capitalism by gendering consumption as a particularly female perversity, an October 2010 *Irish Independent* article titled "Sacred Cows" stated that "the boom years gave financial independence to Irish women and they spent it on investment properties, New York and Mini Coopers."[38] The "Sacred Cows" article warns against women's work outside the home, as if without the boundaries of housework to keep the Irish woman occupied, she loses all self-control in an orgy of consumer excess.

Although none of the award-winning 2010 documentaries that I deal with in this chapter overtly address the subject of recession, the way in which the house (or the lack of a house) is framed by the documentaries suggests different perspectives on the futurity of the neoliberal nation. The disconnect between idealizations of home and embodied experiences and material realities of housing in Ireland suggests that the affective value of house and home influences the reproduction of a way of life that can be inherently damaging to those who invest in it. Drawing on Berlant's concept of cruel optimism, I suggest that the neoliberal nation is a problematic object of desire, comprising a fantasy of Irishness that as a "life-building modality" is in fact "wearing out" the lives of the very subjects for whom the notion of the "Irish nation" provides a sense of "what it means to keep on living on and to look forward to being in the world."[39] The house is an affective commodity through which notions of futurity, family, and national belonging work to shape and regulate the gendered experience of everyday living. To think about the affective force of the idealized heteronormative middle-class family home is to confront the histories of encounter that mark bodies as belonging or not belonging.[40] The documentary lens's framing of bodies as housed or unhoused intimates how gender and class are discursively constructed, embodied, and challenged by contemporary Irish filmmakers and their (sometimes autobiographical) subjects.

The House, Slow Death, and Addiction

In the twenty-five-minute RTÉ documentary *The House*, the family of director Tanya Doyle discuss the life of their deceased mother as they prepare to move out of their childhood home in Clondalkin, West Dublin. At the outset, Doyle describes a history of community displacement and alienation: "Both my parents grew up in Ballyfermot in the early 1950s in West Dublin. . . . Families were relocated from the city centre out to the surrounding suburbs to deal with the housing crisis. They were given houses and promised that the support and infrastructure would follow, but it never did." When Doyle's sister Sarah takes up the narrative, her testimony is juxtaposed with archive footage of urban disenfranchisement:

> When my ma moved up to Clondalkin, there was no church, no school, no shop, no leisure centre, no bus stops, no trains, no nothing. They lived here for a good two years before they even got a little supermarket. They had to travel to Ballyfermot, and *walk* to Ballyfermot because there was no buses. So they built an estate just with a house and stuck you in it because they didn't think you had any prospects, because you'd a family and you weren't employed. They weren't giving you the chance to have any prospects because they didn't put schools in it for your children to go to.

The sea of red-roofed houses in the final wide shot of this particular sequence emphasizes the extensive human scale of the alienation described by Sarah and the ubiquity of this personal history. Notably, the titular house is not described possessively as "mine" or "ours"; rather, the use of the definite article "the" marks the dwelling (and by extension, its story) as generic, even mundane. In its excavation of personal history as national narrative, *The House* resonates not only with histories of social exclusion but also with the manifold forms of domestic disenfranchisement associated with the property bubble (negative-equity mortgages, ghost estates, unregulated and dangerous housing developments, and failed regeneration projects).

In the discourse of Irish nationalism, the house symbolizes the sovereignty of the Irish citizen and, by extension, of the nation itself. The house is not only the ultimate expression of the agency of the citizen as consumer, but an achievement on the heteronormative middle-class life trajectory; possession of the house stands for the self-control and disciplined decision making idealized by neoliberal discourse. In other words, the family home is an approved choice within a neoliberal economy. Yet in Doyle's documentary the house is not the space of sovereign life or empowered choice. Rather, the film's dismantling of the maternal home invokes the dead mother's absence as an exhaustion of free will and sovereignty:

> Patrice: Your da's off trying to make money, trying to supply the family with food, bring home the bread or whatever. And she's trying to take care of us. But the hard work is trying to take care of five other people

who are constantly going, "Ma, ma, ma, ma, will you do this, will you do that?" . . . When you don't . . . even feel like you're a person, because I don't think she looked at herself like she was a person. She was just a mother. And as we all got older, she was kind of going, "Well what am I supposed to do next?" . . . She was like, "Do not get yourself into this. . . . You should never be so unhappy that you don't want your kids to turn into you."

Berlant's notion of slow death can be used to explain Doyle's mother's alcoholism as "a kind of interruptive agency that aspires to detach from "the pressurized conditions" of her existence.[41] Doyle herself describes her mother's addiction as a response to the frustrations of everyday domestic motherhood: "When I think of my ma, like so many women of her generation, I think of a woman who was frustrated. Frustrated because she never had the chance to fulfill her potential, frustrated at the fact that she was on the dole trying to raise her children hand to mouth. Frustrated by her circumstances. She did try to rise above it, but this frustration, compounded by the drink, got the better of her." Although neoliberal discourse describes sovereignty as a life-building process of disciplined self-fashioning and agency, neoliberal politics bind populations to corrupt institutions that demand the ever-increasing attrition of life under the banner of austerity. In this situation, alcohol provides the relief of self-abeyance and meaninglessness from the exhaustion of trying to make the right choices under extremely constricted circumstances.

The documentary concludes with the director explaining that the house stopped being a home when her mother died. In this sense, the text explicates the spatiality of the body and the ideological imperatives that tie people to place. Gender and class are crucial factors in this scenario; whereas the father leaves the home and is able to give up drinking, the woman's agency is inhibited by the ideological conflation of "mother" and "home." This working-class mother's efforts to make a home for her children and "to rise above" constrictive social circumstances actually feeds her addiction; for her, slow death appears to be the only way of life.

His and Hers: Framing the Feminized Nation

The personal story detailed in *The House* resonates with contemporary and historical experiences of Irish domesticity as a situation of conflict, exclusion, and frustrated agency. In contrast, *His and Hers'* representation of domestic motherhood as the heart of the post–Celtic Tiger nation serves to realign bodies to the neoliberal agenda that constitutes the slow death of everyday Irish life. Released in Irish cinemas in June 2010, *His and Hers* soon became a

FIGURE 7.1. The *His and Hers* DVD cover (like the film itself) generates a heightened emotionality that works to bind people and communities together.

word-of-mouth success and one of the highest-grossing documentaries ever to be released in Ireland. The old Irish proverb that opens the film and which is printed above the title on the DVD (figure 7.1) provides a fairly concise summary of the narrative trajectory and affective nature of the documentary: "A man loves his girlfriend the most, his wife the best . . . but his mother the longest." The heightened emotionality of recessionary Ireland is seemingly refuted by the unapologetic and sentimental optimism of *His and Hers*. Ahmed's contention that "at times of crisis the language of happiness acquires an even more powerful hold" is vindicated by reviewer Gareth Naughton's description of the film as an affective break from the recession: "*His & Hers* is the kind of life-affirming film that everyone in this misery-sodden country could do with seeing right now."[42] For Ahmed, discourse describing crises of happiness works to reinvigorate social ideals, "as if what explains the crisis of happiness is not the failure of these ideals but our failure to follow them."[43] Against media characterizations of Celtic Tiger Ireland's hedonistic materialism, *His and Hers* posits happiness in heteronormativity, the institution of marriage, and in familiar, not to say traditional, configurations of domestic femininity.

His and Hers is inspired by the biography of director Ken Wardrop's mother, a self-designated farmer's wife. However, the film was made following the death of Wardrop's father, so though he describes the film as his mother's story, it could equally be read as that of his father. The film features seventy women of different ages who are interviewed about their relationship with a significant man in their life, whether that is father, boyfriend, husband, or son. It begins with a shot of a man's hands laying a baby girl down on a changing pad and ends with an old woman sitting in a nursing home as an elderly man with a walker moves slowly past the open door behind her. These two shots present the only visual representations of men in the film, yet since the interviews revolve entirely around the men in these seventy women's lives, the male figure is a remarkable and carefully structured absence nonetheless.

His and Hers moves chronologically through a life span of the Irish female, and the seamlessness of this biographical movement—the dissolving of one woman's story into another's—coincides with the smooth visual transition from one domestic place to another. The film's every shot is beautifully composed by a still camera, mirrors and windows functioning as additional frames to a carefully produced vision of Irish womanhood. The imagining of generational continuity is encapsulated by the DVD cover image of a young girl whose comically adult fashion accessories package her femininity as a gift to the futurity of the Irish nation. The image brings to mind Lee Edelman's description of "the function of the child as prop of the secular theology upon which our common reality rests—the secular theology that shapes at once the meaning of our collective narratives and our collective narratives of meaning."[44] For Edelman the figure of the child sustains a fantasy of the future and the "perpetuation of the same," a trope illustrated by a scene from *His and Hers* in which a newly married woman lays out her wedding dress for the camera, remarking that it will be made into a christening dress for her children.[45] In this film's account of femininity there is no room for historical change, no space for diversity, difference, or disruption. In its formal construction of Irish womanhood, the documentary frames an ordinary female body that achieves universality not by what it shows but by what it excludes, namely masculinity, sexual and class alterity, and the sociocultural histories of the public sphere. These absences shape a nostalgic vision of Irish femininity that invites the film's audience to invest in the collective "us" of the nation, by celebrating and mourning not the ups and downs of the Celtic Tiger but the love and loss of the patriarchal male.

The paraphernalia of Irish farmhouse domesticity organizes the film's sometimes comedic, sometimes tragic mise-en-scène; women and girls are positioned peeling potatoes at the sink, working out on an exercise machine, sitting on stairs, on couches, on tractors, speaking affectionately of their man in gleaming kitchens and in brightly colored bedrooms. Although there is no acknowledgment of age or epoch, the infatuation with the material house recalls the Celtic Tiger privileging of domesticity as a luxury in which all citizens should invest. *His and Hers* manages female domestic consumption (heralded by props such as exercise bikes, handbags, mobile phones, wedding dresses, and garden ponds) by framing it within the idealized heteronormative family structure of the rural middle-class home. The film's constricted focus denies woman's work outside of the home, implying that female consumption is not perverse as long as it is domestically focused and dependent on a male provider.[46]

The temporal trajectory of *His and Hers* is linear and progressive, but in the elision of generational difference the film also presents the rural domestic female as somehow out of time and ageless: a mode of Irishness that cannot be disrupted by the traumatic effect of the current recession. Explicit directorial interventions such as the fastidiously structured cinematography and narrow plot focus ensure that generational and historical differences are completely elided by *His and Hers*; it is extraordinary that a film made in 2010 purportedly describing the lives of the ordinary women of Ireland allows for no sense of social change despite the upheaval of both boom and bust. Sally Munt explains that while "nationalism preaches a historical continuity with the past . . . it operates using a form of nostalgia which is intrinsically new and commensurate with the demands to amalgamate and reformulate 'the nation' according to contemporary criteria."[47] In this sense, the film's timelessness operates as a detour around the exigencies of the present.

Although *His and Hers* occludes social and political history in favor of an incessantly personalized story, it is still very much the product of the post–Celtic Tiger epoch; in a period of massive national uncertainty the film stabilizes notions of Irishness through a highly stylized artistic frame that reproduces pride in a nation embodied by the domestic female — the ordinary Irish woman. Meanwhile, the coincidental structuring absence of the male figure alongside the determined elision of history operates as a confirmation of the gendered norm of the male as the subject of history and of the gendered dichotomy of the public and private spheres; the film's female subjectivities and their comfortable, naturalized domesticity are entirely dependent on the idealized, absent male.

Pyjama Girls and the Production of Class Difference

Behind the child on the cover of the *His and Hers* DVD is a diaphanous montage of the documentary's other female subjects that situates the young girl within a genealogy of Irish womanhood, a history of gendered sameness. In comparison, the anonymous white interior depicted on the *Pyjama Girls* DVD cover

FIGURE 7.2. *Pyjama Girls'* promotional imagery emphasizes a disruption of gender norms through the display of aggressively unfeminine stances and facial expressions.

(figure 7.2) serves to displace the film's two main subjects—Lauren Dempsey and Tara Salinger—from any recognizable place, culture, or history.[48] Clearly posing for the camera, the teenage girls' stances are defiant, even threatening, and their facial expressions are hostile. Tara's body is turned slightly away from the camera, and the arm on her hip protrudes as a warning against intimacy. Inverting gendered spatial norms, the colorful nightwear worn by the girls—usually associated with the private domestic sphere—is teamed with the fashion paraphernalia of public femininity: leather jacket, sneakers, hair band, earrings, and a black handbag. However, the power of the girls' subversive fashion statement is undermined by the film's framing of them as other; although Lauren and Tara explain their subversive uniform as an expression of belonging to the inner-city flat complexes where much of the documentary was filmed, this image represents the teenagers as disturbingly and dangerously out of place. If the affect of the emotive representation of domestic womanhood in *His and Hers* works to realign disenfranchised recessionary subjects to the ideals of neoliberal nationalism, by manipulating the life story of its teenage subjects the contemporaneous *Pyjama Girls* produces the working-class female body as a site of shame.

Pyjama Girls was initially conceived as a documentary exploring the phenomenon of urban working-class girls who change into pyjamas to go into public space. As an inversion of the Yummy Mummy's high-end leisure wear, the pyjama girl phenomenon—which began during the economic boom— interrupted Celtic Tiger fantasies of blissful suburban female domesticity.[49] Director Maya Derrington explains her initial interest in the phenomenon: "It brought out a surprise reaction in me, I was surprised that I was so shocked by this, I started asking myself why it shocked me so much."[50] By this account, the subversive uniform of the pyjama girls challenged Derrington's sense of self, the director constantly returning in interview to her own feelings of shock, intrigue, desire, and incompetence when confronted with overtly classed bodies and architecture: "I did begin with a fascination for this pyjama phenomenon. . . . But then, on another level, I was genuinely fascinated with life in the flats. I used to walk past Charlemont Street flats and wonder about the contrast between me walking to work in TV and these snippets of life that I would catch. I wanted to step over this boundary that frightened me. I wanted them to think of me as a person also."[51] The documentary's emphasis on visual and aural themes and motifs are more reflective of the affective experience of the middle-class filmmaker herself than that of the documentary's young teenage subjects.

Although *Pyjama Girls'* experimental style privileges the symbolic function of art, the positioning of the film as an observational work disguises some crucial directorial interventions, such as the purposeful omission of Lauren's mother from the film. Derrington explains, "It was important to me that she was an invisible character. She represents a missing generation of parents— my generation, really—that is, the much-documented drug generation. It was important to me that she was notable by her absence."[52] For Jenny Knell, "these editorial decisions powerfully underscore the impact of drugs upon Dublin's working-class communities, but they also distort the lived reality of the documentary's subjects and subordinate their individual experiences to the film's thematic coherence."[53] Concurrently, Derrington's explanation of her decision to exclude men from the film again reflects a prioritization of theme and aesthetic style over the lives of the documentary's subjects:

> It was quite a late stage in the edit when me and Paul who edited the film said, "Hang on, men are absent in this film." And it was at that point we decided to snip out the last remaining male characters because it seemed to give the film greater cohesiveness and speak more honestly and truly of what we had witnessed while filming. Which happened to be an environment where men did not seem to be hugely present, basically. Now Tara's father is very present in her life, but in terms of the theme, which emerged

from the film, that didn't seem to have a strong relevance. So it ended up being a film almost entirely peopled by women.[54]

This somewhat contradictory explanation arguably reflects Derrington's conflicting emotional responses to working-class bodies and spaces. Ultimately, the film manages this emotional conflict by presenting the pyjama girls through a voyeuristic middle-class frame that reasserts a dominant class relation of pride and shame.

In many ways, *Pyjama Girls* is concerned with the stories of those who did not experience any economic boom. To some extent, then, the absence of men and masculinity from the film reflects the alienation of Dublin's working-class communities from the patriarchal state's systems of power. Two scenes from *Pyjama Girls* suggest how the current ideology of neoliberal individualism disowns, alienates, pathologizes, and makes abject those on the margins of society. In a scene that indicates how reliant the hierarchical knowledge system is on caring work undertaken at home, the main protagonist, Lauren Dempsey, helps her sister with her homework. Although Lauren has been expelled from school, we see her very capably frame a sentence about snowmen in the Irish language.[55] Later in the film, Lauren shows her best friend Tara work sheets from an anger management class. Brightly colored childish writing spells out an alphabet of expletives and Lauren sings them out to Tara, laughing at their obsolescence. These scenes reveal how the decline of supportive structures, such as education, parallels the rise of diagnostic ones. The replacement of ideologically approved language with taboo words reveals Lauren's total alienation and abjection within the dominant value system.

Following *Pyjama Girls'* television screening by state broadcaster RTÉ in March 2012, Lauren Dempsey took part in RTÉ's *Liveline* radio phone-in show, intimating that important scenes were, if not staged, then highly contrived: the documentary subjects were asked to wear pyjamas on particular occasions and a city bus was hired out by the production company to film their journeys into town. In one particular bus scene, Lauren and Tara threaten another group of young girls with violent language, a seeming escalation of the aggressive language and delight in recounting street battles portrayed earlier in the film. This violent teenage posturing asserts a shamelessness that rejects bourgeois notions of female propriety. Indeed, callers to *Liveline* repeatedly emphasized the shame they felt watching the documentary on TV: "I thought it was absolutely disgraceful. I was ashamed of my life to be from Ballyfermot." "I was watching it last night with my husband. Not only was I disgusted, I was quite frightened . . . particularly with the girls. . . . For girls, their language was just awful. . . . Pyjamas are just so slovenly looking."[56] In response, a beleaguered Lauren explained, "That was years ago. Me and Tara are nothing like that now. . . . It is disgusting. I know meself it's disgusting."[57] Lauren's grandmother Peggy explained, "Lauren is terrified at the moment. . . . She's a bit nervous. She's ashamed of herself as well, for the cursing. . . . She's a completely different girl now."[58] This transformation of apparent pyjama-clad shamelessness into shame took place on a radio program often construed as lowbrow, hysterical, and working class. That this was the only platform that made a space for Lauren to speak without the guidance of director Derrington suggests that without historical distanciation, working-class concerns are almost always already positioned as a site of shame within Ireland's media landscape.

Conclusion: Receiving Representations of Class

Approaching the Irish Film Institute for the premiere of *Pyjama Girls*, which opened the Stranger Than Fiction Documentary Film Festival in April 2010, my entrance was blocked by a group of young girls who, dolled up in bright red heels and short skirts, dragged on cigarettes and flirted with the doorman. "So they're not wearing pyjamas," I noted disappointedly as I squeezed in. Their feminine presence was definite and unyielding; there was no concessional shimmy to one side to let me in the door. The girls stood out as extraordinary in that environment, and I wondered if on any other day of the year they would have been allowed to hang around the institute's entrance in such a dominating group.

As the cinema began to fill up, a group of the documentary's leading ladies came in, loud and laughing. Dublin's cultural, artistic, and academic elite smiled at their youth and at their accents. Festival programmer Niall Macpherson's introductory speech was welcomed with loud whoops and cheers from the group of girls in the front rows (and uncertain giggling from the crowd). When he passed the microphone to other officials, speeches were adapted in order to facilitate the girls' behavior and there were some awkward silences when the girls did not cheer as expected or failed to whoop on cue. However, when the screening started, the awkward feeling was magnified by the fact that the Dublin accents of the protagonists were subtitled. As Knell argues, "The subtitling of *Pyjama Girls* delegitimizes its subjects' working class culture, quite literally through the appropriation of their voices, and accommodates their marginalized identities only through the process of bringing them closer to the mainstream. In this sense, Derrington's attempt to traverse Dublin's class boundaries through the filmmaking process unwittingly replicates the larger power structures fundamentally implicated in society's marginalisation of the 'pyjama girls.'"[59] The implication that they "could not be understood in their own city" intimates how working-class females are positioned outside of the boundaries of the ordinary nation.[60] Director Maya Derrington acknowledged that "there is an offensive element to subtitling" and that "the film works a whole lot better without it" but said that the company could only afford one print, and to reach an international audience, it had to be subtitled.[61] While budgetary problems are inevitable, the privileging of middle-class economics over working-class voice seems to reenact the disaffections that the film attempts to critique. Notably, although the female voices in *His and Hers* are as accented as those of *Pyjama Girls* (but with a midlands rather than a Dublin twang), no subtitles were used to translate the middle-class accents for any audience, either at home or internationally.

And so the opening night of the Stranger Than Fiction festival turned into an event of both working-class and middle-class performance, the voyeuristic nature of the documentary disrupted by the very presence and returned gaze of the program's subjects. The film turned out to be much grittier and the girls themselves more violent and angry than the innocence of pyjamas would suggest. During the question-and-answer session, the teenagers' filmic performance of violence held the middle-class audience to ransom, and questions directed at the girls were soft and guarded rather than challenging. The juxtaposition of classes sullied and confused the atmosphere of this hallowed cultural space in which mere popcorn is seen as irreverent. The very real threat of the working-class other left most of the audience speechless and silent. There was the feeling that if the girls had not been present, the audience could have comfortably discussed and opined upon the social problems highlighted by the film. As it was, the girls and their friends in the audience inadvertently controlled the room through their presence and otherness. Tame questions such as "What did you think of the film?" and "How did you feel watching it with so many others?" skirted around what we all clearly wanted to know: "Are you embarrassed at all at your antisocial behavior?" When asked, "What will you do now?" Lauren turned the question on the audience: "If any of you want me to be in your next movie, I'll do it." This answer inspired collective nervous titters, a response emphasizing that this was the last thing the audience wanted.

In comparison, on June 26, 2010, the appearance of three of the cast of *His and Hers* on *Saturday Night with Miriam* led to a very different discussion of Irish womanhood than the timid Q&A in the Irish Film Institute or the fraught discussion on Joe Duffy's *Liveline*. Despite their unprecedented successes, the reception of these documentaries by cinema and television audiences and by the national media could not be more different, offering insight into the affective value of class in configurations of the feminized nation. Whereas the

Liveline debate focused on the problem of the pyjama girls, O'Callaghan introduced her guests as "ordinary" women who had "won the hearts of people all over the world." [62] Like the documentary, the feel-good interview focused mainly on the women's relationships with their husbands and partners; the piece featured plenty of laughter about household chores, compliments from the women's husbands inspiring "aws" from the audience, and sentimental thoughts on the secret to romantic success. Coming between more serious interviews with a prominent entrepreneur and survivors of road traffic accidents, the *His and Hers* segment clearly operated as the heart of the Saturday night program, intimating how constructions of Irish maternal domesticity as ordinary not only underpin contemporary social structures but also stabilize notions of national identity, especially in periods when the nation itself is seen to be in crisis. However, as *The House* suggests, although hegemonic discourse idealizes domestic femininity as a national good, very often this gendered identity functions to constrain women to subaltern positions so exhausting that the efforts of ordinary living result in the slow attrition of life. Under the current austerity regime, Ireland has seen an increase in emigration and suicide and the emergence of a "new poor," as the neoliberal class divides become ever more distinct. As welfare-dependent parents are the first to fall under the axe of austerity, the idealization of maternal domesticity is "a fantasy bribe" justifying exploitation and the "structurally motivated attrition of persons . . . because of their membership in certain populations." [63] In the various encounters between filmmakers, subjects, and spectators, the underpinning truth of *His and Hers*, *Pyjama Girls*, and *The House* is the chronic rigidity of Irish class relations despite the economic upheaval of the last three decades.

Notes

1. McDonough and Dundon, "Thatcherism Delayed?," 550–51, emphasis in original.

2. Brennan, "The Mingling of Business Models"; O'Toole, *Ship of Fools*, 10.

3. Smyth, "Irish National Identity after the Celtic Tiger," 133.

4. Writing about twentieth-century Ireland, critic Fredric Jameson described a "national situation which reproduces the appearance of First World social reality and social relationships . . . but whose underlying structure is in fact much closer to that of the Third World, or of colonised daily life." Jameson, *Nationalism, Colonialism and Literature*, 60.

5. Moore, "Rejuvenating Docklands," 140.

6. Punch, "Problem Drug Use and the Political Economy of Urban Restructuring," 764.

7. O'Gorman, "Illicit Drug Use in Ireland," 157.

8. Moore, "Rejuvenating Docklands," 136.

9. Rafferty, "Gregory Deal Would Have Had Huge Impact if Fulfilled," 14.

10. Rafferty, "Gregory Deal Would Have Had Huge Impact if Fulfilled," 14.

11. Rafferty, "Gregory Deal Would Have Had Huge Impact if Fulfilled," 14.

12. Mullally, "Heroin," 3.

13. Berlant, "Slow Death," 754, 756.

14. Guthman and DuPuis, "Embodying Neoliberalism," 443.

15. Berlant, "Slow Death," 754.

16. For Henry A. Giroux, austerity is "neoliberal code for making the working and middle classes bear the burden of a financial crisis caused by hedge fund operators, banking and investment houses, and the mega-rich." Giroux, "Neoliberalism and the Death of the Social State," 589.

17. McDonough and Dundon, "Thatcherism Delayed?," 548.

18. Quoted in O'Toole, "Liechtenstein on the Liffey," 36.

19. Quoted in O'Toole, *Ship of Fools*, 196. In October 2009, explaining the collapse of Lehman Brothers, former Taoiseach Bertie Ahern described the investment bank as having "testicles everywhere." Although quotes such as these are subject to popular ridicule, they do reveal how Irish elites imagined the world of global economics in terms of competitive masculinity. In July 2007, Ahern attacked commentators who warned that the Celtic Tiger property bubble could not last: "Sitting on the sidelines, cribbing and moaning is a lost opportunity. I don't know how people who engage in that don't commit suicide because frankly the only thing that motivates me is being able to actively change something" ("Ahern Apologises for Suicide Remark"). Five years later, Ahern's statement read like a sentencing; in 2009 Ireland's suicide rate was announced to be "the highest in its history," an increase attributable to recession-related factors such as unemployment (O'Regan, "Suicide Rate at an All-Time High, Says Minister," 10).

20. McDonough and Dundon, "Thatcherism Delayed?," 552.

21. McDonough and Dundon, "Thatcherism Delayed?," 553.

22. McDonough and Dundon, "Thatcherism Delayed?," 555.

23. Punch, "Contested Urban Environments," 99.

24. Punch, "Contested Urban Environments," 99.

25. Punch, "Contested Urban Environments," 100.

26. Punch, "Problem Drug Use and the Political Economy of Urban Restructuring," 768.

27. McDonough and Dundon, "Thatcherism Delayed?," 769.

28. "Was It for This?," 17.

29. Speaking on November 24, 2010, on RTÉ's *Prime Time* program, former finance minister Brian Lenihan said, "Let's be fair about it, we all partied" (Meade, " 'Our Country's *Calling Card*,' " 33). Similarly, on January 26, 2012, current Taoiseach Enda Kenny told the World Economic Forum, "What happened in our country was that people simply went mad borrowing" (Burke-Kennedy and Scally, "Taoiseach Blames Crash on 'Mad Borrowing' Frenzy").

30. Berlant, "Slow Death," 765.

31. Harvey, "Neoliberalism as Creative Destruction," 24.

32. Harvey, "Neoliberalism as Creative Destruction," 23.

33. "Taoiseach: We Will Not 'Have the Name Defaulter across Our Foreheads.'"

34. Meade, "'Our Country's *Calling Card*,'" 1.

35. Bunreacht na hÉireann/Irish Constitution, Article 41.1.1.

36. Bunreacht na hÉireann/Irish Constitution, Articles 41.2.1 and 41.2.2.

37. Ahmed, "Affective Economies," 117, 119.

38. Fitzpatrick, "Sacred Cows," 98.

39. Berlant, "Cruel Optimism," 21.

40. For more on "histories of encounter," see Ahmed, *Strange Encounters*.

41. Berlant, "Slow Death," 759.

42. Ahmed, *The Promise of Happiness*, 7; Naughton, "His and Hers."

43. Ahmed, *The Promise of Happiness*, 7.

44. Edelman, "The Future Is Kid Stuff," 21.

45. Edelman, "The Future Is Kid Stuff," 25.

46. One young woman mentions that she is a teacher, but apart from that, woman's work is presumed to be in the home or helping the husband on the farm.

47. Munt, *Queer Attachments*, 58.

48. Thanks to Anne Mulhall, Noreen Giffney, Emilie Pine, and Jenny Knell for their helpful discussions about *Pyjama Girls*.

49. In this sense, the phenomenon can be read as the opposite of the postfeminist retreatism outlined by Diane Negra in *What a Girl Wants?*

50. Derrington quoted in IFTN, "'Pyjama Girls,' an Observational Documentary."

51. Derrington quoted in Clarke, "So, What Are Pyjama Girls Really Like?," 8.

52. Derrington quoted in Clarke, "So, What Are Pyjama Girls Really Like?," 8.

53. Knell, "Pyjama Girls."

54. "Volta Speaks to Pyjama Girls Director Maya Derrington."

55. Although a vast majority of the population does not speak Irish, it is a compulsory exam subject for all students in primary and secondary school.

56. *Liveline*, RTÉ Radio One, March 14, 2012.

57. *Liveline*, RTÉ Radio One, March 14, 2012.

58. *Liveline*, RTÉ Radio One, March 14, 2012.

59. Knell, "Pyjama Girls."

60. Knell, "Pyjama Girls."

61. Clarke, "So, What Are Pyjama Girls Really Like?," 8.

62. *Saturday Night with Miriam*, RTÉ Television, June 26, 2010.

63. Berlant, "Slow Death," 765, 761.

"Stuck between Meanings"

RECESSION-ERA PRINT FICTIONS OF CRISIS MASCULINITY

If the phenomenon of masculinity in crisis that is a constitutive feature of cultural discourse in the contemporary United States serves primarily as a ruse or lure through which (predominantly white) masculinity has been able to secure and maintain privilege, the global recession has put pressure on the typical narrative tropes of masculine empowerment enabled by such crisis discourse. At the same time, economic contraction has provided an opportunity for their reinvigoration and renewal.[1] In this essay, I consider how the recessionary imaginaries of contemporary masculinist discourse function in order to critically account for the ways in which contemporary gender inequalities play out in popular culture. In particular, I ask how the financial crisis and the attendant pressures it has placed on contemporary life have been represented in recent popular fiction by and about men. Specifically, I focus on a pair of male-authored recession-era novels, *The Financial Lives of the Poets* (2009, Jess Walter) and *The Ask* (2010, Sam Lipsyte), which instantiate one epiphenomenon of the global financial collapse: an explosion of finance-related literary fiction.[2] The critical and commercial success of some of this literature highlights the fact that popular print fiction, both literary and genre, has been one of the privileged locations through which the public has attempted to make sense of the economic crisis. Other recent literary fiction that takes the world of finance as its subject includes Adam Haslett's *Union Atlantic* (2009), Jonathan Dee's *The Privileges* (2010), and Alex Preston's *This Bleeding City* (2010).[3] The economic collapse has also produced a cycle of financial thrillers, including Henry Sutton's *American Psycho*–esque *Get Me Out of Here* (2010), Cyrus Moore's *City of Thieves* (2009), and John Gubert's *One Step to Danger* (2007) and *The Financial Terrorist* (2010).[4] While much of this work is by—and about—men, female-authored (and female-centered) recession literature has also figured prominently in best-seller lists and the tributary media over the last few years. Fiction texts such as Erin Duffy's *Bond Girl* (2012) and Kimberly S. Lin's *Recession Proof* (2011) have appeared alongside nonfiction texts such as Jen Lancaster's autobiographical *Bitter Is the New Black: Confessions of a Condescending, Egomaniacal, Self-Centered Smartass, Or, Why You Should Never Carry a Prada Bag to the Unemployment Office* (2006). The range and quantity of these texts—just a few examples from a veritable avalanche of titles—suggest that publishers and the general public alike turned to print as they sought to understand the economic crisis.[5]

The two novels that I discuss in this essay are of particular interest because they both examine the financial crisis through male-centered, gender-conscious, and highly self-aware narratives of masculine disempowerment. Each of these novels offers a post–financial collapse narrative of fractured domesticity in which men are no longer able to rely on the family and the home as sites of security, stability, and recuperation. As such, the family and the bourgeois home no longer function in these texts as what Christopher Lasch famously called a "haven in a heartless world," but instead have become sites of anxiety in which that world repeatedly intrudes.[6] Creditors, sexual rivals, aging and infirm parents, and the police all invade and disrupt the space of the home in these novels. At the same time, the protagonist of each is ultimately forced to leave the home and the family unit, unsure whether or not he will be allowed to return. In both novels, moreover, the protagonist is fighting the pressures of time and anxiety is understood to be a pervasive feature of contemporary middle-class life: in *Poets* the protagonist, Matt Prior, has six days to save his house from repossession; in *The Ask*, Milo Burke must secure a sizeable donation from an old friend in order to keep his job. In each case, what the protagonist must save—if only in order to save himself—is his family, a feat that can be achieved only through the recuperation of the self and the restoration of the logic of men as primary breadwinners and the guarantors of domestic security.[7] In neither case are the protagonists entirely successful, and both must account for their failures as they attempt to extract viable domestic and economic futures from them.

Failure, in both of these novels, is understood to be constitutive. It is by admitting defeat, by narrating lives of missed opportunities, poor financial decisions, and failures of commitment, that the protagonists of these novels are able to develop a tenuous form of success. Unable—and crucially unwilling—to rely on outmoded forms of masculine self-empowerment, these men are able to secure potential futures, for both themselves and their families, by admitting that traditional gender roles were pernicious to both men and women. How, this essay asks, do contemporary formations of white masculinity imagine themselves to have been transformed in the face of the global financial collapse? What effect has the financial crisis, and the attendant transformations of working life, had on dominant narratives of white male privilege? How does white masculinity account for its own current (mis)fortunes? How, in the specific instances of these novels, are men understood to have failed? What forms does that failure take? Who does it affect? How can it be overcome? How, moreover, does failure become not only constitutive but also recuperative? In addressing these questions, I offer a broader understanding of masculinity as it is represented in contemporary recessionary print culture and link those literary representations to the larger sociocultural conditions that they reflect and work through.

Home Invasion: Domestic Capital, Adultery, and Gender Competition

A central aspect of the plots of both *Poets* and *The Ask* is the risk of the loss of the family home and the attendant transformation of the home from a place of well-being and comfort to a site of profound anxiety. Matt Prior, the protagonist of *Poets* who has recently been laid off from his job as a financial reporter for a provincial newspaper, has seven days to find the money to cover a $30,000 balloon payment to his mortgage provider or risk losing the family home. He has kept the details and the extent of their financial problems from his wife, Lisa, who struggles with her own shopping addiction. Matt suffers the burden of their financial obligations in silence and, following a chance meeting with a pair of small-time dealers outside a 7-Eleven convenience store, turns to drug dealing in an attempt to cover the family's debts. In its depiction of a middle-class family overly burdened with debt and at risk of home foreclosure, *Poets* represents the very real upheaval faced by many homeowners in the aftermath of the financial crisis, who found themselves unable to make monthly mortgage payments on properties whose value had plummeted.[8] While a great deal has been made of the subprime mortgage fiasco and the working poor who have been disproportionately affected by it, middle-class homeowners, many of whom had leveraged their homes to finance home improvements and other living expenses, have also found themselves at risk. Plunging stock market values and dwindling pension portfolios have placed many previously comfortable middle-class families at risk of foreclosure and, in some cases, homelessness. With everything invested in the home, and with savings and stock portfolios wiped out, members of the middle classes, whose precrisis prosperity was founded on a now-crumbling bedrock of easy consumer credit, find themselves unable to meet their debts (which were not wiped out alongside their savings and stocks).[9] As such, recovery becomes an uphill struggle and bankruptcy a real risk. It is precisely this scenario of middle-class disenfranchisement that *Poets* represents. And this, in fact, is one of the strengths of both *Poets* and *The Ask*: in their representations of middle-class white male anxiety, they steer clear of the moneyed classes represented in many other examples of finance literature, such as *Union Atlantic* and *The Privileges*. This allows them to chart more effectively the terrain of postcollapse middle-class life, in which the presumed financial benefits of membership in the middle classes, such as easy access to consumer credit and the ability to leverage home equity, have been transformed into its biggest burdens.

In *Poets*, Matt describes his own fall into insolvency in just such a fashion. The reader first hears about the Priors' financial problems when he describes a now foolish-seeming car purchase. "With the winter floor mats, taxes and redundant two-year service contract," Matt complains, "the car set me back $31,256." He goes on to position the car as just one among a series of interrelated financial problems that have precipitated the family's current crisis: "And because of several other *setbacks*—missed payments, ensuing penalties, house refi's, debt consolidations, various family crises and my untimely job loss—after two years of payments I still somehow owe $31,000. On a car worth eighteen. This is my life now: set as far back as it will go."[10] This calculus of mounting debts and of assets with negative value is precisely the situation described by Randy Martin in his discussion of the effects of the financial crisis on middle-class families: "Multiple credit cards per family and increasing mortgages added to vehicle financing to generate historically unprecedented levels of total consumer debt across the last 25 years—and especially since 2000." As Martin further suggests, "the promotion of a credit economy through direct and indirect government policy accompanied all manner of initiatives that replaced welfare state security with individuals' capacity to assume and sustain financial risk."[11] Before the rising of the subprime lending practices that helped precipitate the collapse, these risks were taken on most readily (and most easily) by the middle classes, who had easy access to the sorts of credit necessary to sustain the forms of risk Martin and Walter describe. In *Poets* such a calculus is also applied to the dream house that Matt and Lisa are soon to lose, a 1917 Tudor that has become the "third party" in their marriage (97). "I wonder," Matt asks, "if a house has ever represented as much as it does now, for people like Lisa and me." He continues:

It has been the full measure and symbol of our wealth and security over the last few years; every cent we threw into it and every cent we took out, seemed so smart, like such a good bet. Every time we got ahead, we borrowed against the thing to remodel, and every time we remodeled the thing we congratulated ourselves on our wisdom, and every time we saw a house go up for sale on our block . . . we became like derivative-crazed brokers; we stopped thinking of the value of our home as a place of shelter and occupancy and family . . . but as a kind of faith equation, theoretical construct, mechanism of wealth-generation, salvation function on a calculator, its value no longer *what it's worth* but some compound value that might exist given the continued upward tick of the market, because this was the only direction housing markets could ever go: up. (97–98, italics in original)

What Matt describes in this passage is a dream predicated on a seemingly secure present in which the housing bubble will never burst and a brighter future, while always deferred, is assured. In this way, the house ceases to be a home that the family inhabits in the present but becomes a sign of future prosperity. As both the engine and the outcome of financial security, its symbol and its guarantor, the family home stands as a sign of the transformation in the United States from a manufacturing to a credit-based economy, on the one hand, and from the era of the welfare state to the privatizations of civic and social responsibility that subtend neoliberalism, on the other.[12] Always taking place in its shadow, life is lived in relation to a possible future to which the present is always subordinated. What *Poets* describes through Matt's attempts to free himself from the burdens of middle-class debt is a loss of faith in the founding myth of social and economic mobility most commonly referred to as the American Dream and enabled in the later decades of the twentieth century by consumer credit.

If one of the most deleterious features of contemporary neoliberal society is the increasing focus on individual self-fashioning through the twinned mechanisms of consumer choice and the surveillance of the self, *Poets* describes the pernicious effects of neoliberalism's refashioning of the subject in some detail. The transition from a welfare society to one driven by the imperatives of finance, what Martin refers to as the "financialization of everyday life," not only affects how people live and their relationships with money and with one another, but also their conceptions of self.[13] Activities that were previously carried out in the workplace and in the bank, for example, have become the direct responsibility of the individual citizen and, as a result, have come increasingly to permeate the space of the home. Consumer choice has replaced political action and, having been both farmed out to private corporations and made the responsibility of the individual citizen, all manner of previously public services have been privatized. As finance has entered the private space of the home in the form of online banking and private, individually managed pension portfolios, that space has become susceptible to all manner of external pressures.[14] Not only have homes been remortgaged again and again, as in Poets, making the home itself a source of financial anxiety, but the inhabitants of that home increasingly have come to see themselves as defined by their possessions and their capacity to attract the consumer credit that makes the purchase of those possessions possible. Finance and ownership, Martin contends elsewhere, provide a "mode of self-possession" through which the contemporary middle-class subject can be constituted.[15] As a result, the inability to successfully manage the home, and the multiple lines of credit and debt associated with it, constitutes a manifest failure; the risk of losing the family home means not only the loss of shelter but also the loss of self-worth. Moreover, because the individual is denied other avenues for the accrual of self-worth (such as traditional forms of work and of social and familial obligation), the sociosymbolic value of the home becomes everything while, at the same time, it becomes increasingly vulnerable because it has become invested with immense value in the face of excessive risk. As Martin contends in An Empire of Indifference, "The perverse effect of financialization in daily life is to exchange security for volatility, to recast the recently revered ideals of middle-class stability in terms of risk."[16] And this is what the home symbolizes in Poets: a credit-based point of access into middle-class security.

As a result of the financial collapse, however, the home that once stood as the symbol of affluence has been transformed into a powerful sign of debilitating failure. Unable to successfully manage the home, Matt is also unable to manage its inhabitants and, in both Poets and The Ask, the putative heads of household are required to renegotiate their relationships with their wives and children. In both of these novels, men's shifting fortunes are charted against the economic, social, and reproductive empowerment of women, who are understood to be more capable of withstanding the post–financial crisis than men. Therefore, and despite their representations of male characters that hold middle-class liberal values, each of these novels still measures male disempowerment in relation to the forms of female success celebrated under postfeminism. As such, they offer a rich location through which post-recessionary masculinist culture's engagements with gender can be critically evaluated. In both novels, women are understood to be more adaptable and, as a result, better able to cope with the pressures of contemporary life.[17] For example, both Lisa and Milo Burke's wife, Maura, use social networking sites on the Internet and are shown to be competent users of contemporary informational and communicational technologies. For their husbands, these women's facility with the Internet and the mobile smartphone is a threat. In *The Ask*, Milo laments that he is "one of those people who hadn't caught up with the latest social networking site." "When it came to locating people," he continues, "I was still an old-timey search engine man."[18] Maura, on the other hand, "belonged to most [social networks]. She passed most evenings befriending men who had tried to date-rape her in high school" (154). Likewise, in *Poets*, Matt discovers that Lisa has been conducting an affair, largely via the Internet and text message, with Chuck Stehne, an old high school boyfriend with whom she had reconnected through a social networking site. While Lisa is Internet savvy and knowledgeable about the latest social sites, Matt's inability to master the latest online technologies, and to understand their transformative natures, is signaled most clearly by a recent failed business venture (from which the novel gets its title), a financial advice website in which stock tips were offered to customers in the form of poems.

As these men struggle to find work, or to successfully carry out the jobs they have, their wives have found the time, and have found it necessary, to seek emotional sustenance outside the family unit and have done so using the same technologies that have also brought home banking and the new financialized lifestyles of the middle classes into the home. The invasion of the home by modern communication technologies is understood to bring with it concomitant pressures that threaten to destabilize the bourgeois family and, as such, the well-being of the family's primary beneficiary. As the home has become a site of competition rather than comfort, husbands are shown to be in competition not only with the suitors of their spouses, who are gaining access to the master bedroom through the vehicles of online chat and the text message, but also with their wives.[19] In both of these novels, wives have become adversaries.

Poets and *The Ask* each offer different takes on the effects of the financial crisis on their female characters. In *Poets*, Lisa is understood to have been negatively affected not only by the hiatus from work she took in order to raise the couple's two children (both boys), but also by the altered labor landscape she encountered when she attempted to return to the workplace. After discovering Lisa's online affair with Chuck—which may or may not have been consummated—Matt mulls over the recent transformations in her character and the events that may have led her to commit adultery. She was, he tells the reader, a previously confident and successful businesswoman transformed by the trials of motherhood: "If I had to trace Lisa's current malaise (and if I didn't trace it to the moment she accepted my marriage proposal) I would say that it began when her confidence was battered by leaving her career to birth those two boys eleven years ago. Before that, Lisa was a world-beating, self-assured businesswoman, in charge of marketing a doctors' group that specialized in sports medicine, and she ventured out every day in curvy business suits that made me want to coax her into elevators for inappropriate workplace contact" (26). Once their two sons have been placed in school full time, Lisa attempts to return to work, only to discover that her business knowledge is out of date (she "doesn't even know Powerpoint," 26) and the best she can find is a job as a receptionist for an optometrist "who calls the women in his office *gals*, and whose idea of a Christmas bonus is twenty-five bucks at a craft store" (27). Having exchanged the world of work for the domestic realm of motherhood, Lisa is unable to reclaim her previous performance-based status as a successful businesswoman: an optometrist is not a doctor; a receptionist is not a marketing manager. Upon her return to work, Lisa is relegated to the confines of a job that is decidedly not a career, a shift that is signified by the demeaning Christmas bonus that takes the form of a financially meaningless and insulting gift, and not of performance-based remuneration. Having given up her job to raise their children, Lisa finds herself unmoored from the forms of social and work-based interaction that provided her life with meaning and validated her sense of self-worth.[20]

While he laments his wife's situation, Matt suspects not only that he bears some responsibility for her situation, but that he might also be secretly relieved by her failure to find the sort of job she wanted. "I hated seeing the woman I loved lose her confidence that way," he tells the reader. "And yet, in the deepest reaches of my psyche, I wonder if there wasn't a part of me that was glad she didn't go back to the gym-toned guys at the sports medicine clinic. . . . In the last few months—with things around her deteriorating—I've even asked myself if I didn't take some pleasure *keeping my wife* at home, that maybe I subconsciously preferred a depleted Lisa because I was threatened by the sexy, confident one, the one I couldn't control, the one I could lose" (27, italics in original). As this passage makes clear, Matt understands himself to have been an agent in his wife's loss of confidence, admitting that his own security may well be predicated on her confinement in the home. Unable to compete with her outside the home, and lacking her facility with the technologies that allow her some partial relief from the pressures contained within it, Matt relies on Lisa's failure to recalibrate his own.[21] Pressured from both within and outside the home, men such as Matt are trapped in a space in which the putative gains of feminism have not yet been fully realized but the privileges of patriarchy have nevertheless been eroded. One result of this neither-nor situation has been a retreat into prior modes of masculine behavior and the desire for a concomitant recalibration of gender roles.

Home Improvement: Labor, Patriarchy, and Male Sociality

If men such as Matt and Milo are required to endure unstable domestic relations, in which they are no longer able to perform their traditional domestic roles satisfactorily and in which their wives and partners have begun to seek alternative sources of emotional and financial stability, they also suffer from a crisis of patriarchal affiliation. As fathers and as sons, these men are deeply troubled. In both *The Ask* and *Poets*, masculinity is understood to have undergone a series of transformations over the course of the twentieth century that have put pressure on the traditional roles and responsibilities of patriarchal authority and on the availability of proper outlets for the release of male affectivity. In "The Economic Crisis and After," Mark Hayward argues that the "contemporary crisis has also given rise to a variety of forms of nostalgia."[22] While it is important to bear in mind that nostalgia and memory cultures of many sorts were a significant feature of contemporary life before the financial crisis, the particular nostalgic turns that have been taken since the recession are important to consider, and none have been more pervasive than the renewed cultural resonances of the figure of embattled masculinity. In both *Poets* and *The Ask*, nostalgia underscores depictions of paternal relationships, working life, and the now-tenuous bonds of working men. As prior forms of work are represented as being more natural and more fulfilling, traditional forms of male sociality are understood to have been lost, thereby disabling male characters who have no access to emotional fulfillment outside the home, and who are being denied it within the home. These issues are addressed most readily in both novels in relation to fatherhood and manual labor.

In *The Ask*, Milo Burke finds himself haunted by the memory of a father who died when he was young but who, in any case, had long been an absent presence in his life. Raised almost exclusively by his mother, Milo still harbors deep-seated regrets about the attenuated relationship he had with his father and worries that it has affected his relationship with his own young son, Bernie. Milo's father was a man of the old school, a traveling salesman and inveterate liar whose parting gift to his son upon his departure for college to study fine art (to become the first in his family to earn a bachelor's degree) was an ornate Spanish dueling knife he claimed to have won in a card game in a cathouse in El Paso. After his father's death two years later, the knife becomes for Milo a "talisman of bereavement" (50) as he confronts his father's absence and places what he calls "the final touches on the permanent exhibition—*Father, Fucker, Human: The Dreamtime of Roger Burke*—I was mounting in my heart" (51). Toward the end of the novel, Milo has the knife (which he had lost after college) returned to him. He wraps it in brown paper, intending to mail it to Don Charboneau, the illegitimate and unacknowledged son of his friend and erstwhile employer, Purdy Stuart. "I knew I had to get the knife out of my family for good" (294), Milo tells the reader in the novel's closing pages, acknowledging the talisman-like status the knife holds in his psychic life. Matt Prior's father is an equally troubling absent presence. Suffering from increasingly debilitating Alzheimer's and robbed of all his possessions by a stripper named Charity with whom he briefly cohabits, Matt's father comes to live with the family and provides Matt with a constant and foreboding glimpse of his own future. In both novels, the declension from fathers to sons charts a concomitant transformation of male endeavor in which the younger generations are found lacking at the same time as they are understood to have been abandoned, denied adequate male role models and outlets for masculine self-expression.

In The Ask, Milo describes the by now commonplace narrative about the end of history and the unmooring of men from social and political action that has dominated contemporary understandings of white male disenfranchisement. Discussing his wealthy friend Purdy's "slumming with the middle and upper-middle classes," Milo says, "I suppose there was a certain glory in it . . . not the glory of rushing a Nazi mortar position, or braving municipal billy bats to stop a war in Indochina, but the privileged of our generation did what they could, like the rest of us. We were stuck between meanings. Or we were the last dribbles of something. It was hard to figure. The fall of the Soviet Union, this was, the death of analog. The beginning of aggressively marketed nachos" (31). Without meaningful and fulfilling work, without a world war to fight in, or a war of imperialism to protest against, men of Milo's generation—both rich and otherwise—are caught without meaning, victims of marketing and the transformation from a creating to a consuming culture in which who you are is determined by what you can buy rather than what you believe in.

Poets contains its own version of this narrative of generational disenfranchisement. Finding himself, at the novel's beginning, in line at a 7-Eleven with a group of stoned youths whom he has met and fallen in with earlier in the evening, Matt describes his fellow shoppers: "I pat Skeet's shoulder, grab my steaming burrito and get in line to pay—take my place with the starving and the sorry, the paranoid, yawning with fear, the hungry lonely lost children let down by their unemployed fathers, men zapped by history's microwave, a generation of hapless, luckless, feckless fathers with no idea how to fix anything, no clue what to do except go home to face the incubated babies staring at their dry bowls of Crispix and confess" (11). In this twinned pair of observations about the status of masculine endeavor in the late twentieth century, Lipsyte and Walter each echo (probably consciously) the very similar claims made about the attenuated nature of historical agency for contemporary men in Chuck Palahniuk's cult novel *Fight Club* (1996) and David Fincher's 1999 film adaptation of it. In both book and film the unnamed protagonist's alter ego, Tyler Durden, makes a series of claims about the status of men in the contemporary United States. In Fincher's film, these statements are condensed into a single rousing speech in which Durden claims that the young men of his generation have been failed by historical circumstances:

> God damn it, an entire generation pumping gas, waiting tables—slaves with white collars. Advertising has us chasing cars and clothes, working jobs we hate so we can buy shit we don't need. We're the middle children of history, man. No purpose or place. We have no Great War. No Great Depression. Our great war is a spiritual war. Our great depression is our lives. We've all been raised on television to believe that one day we'd all be millionaires, and movie gods, and rock stars, but we won't. We're slowly learning that fact. And we're very, very pissed off.[23]

"Stuck between meanings," as Lipsyte puts it, the men of *Fight Club* and the protagonists of *The Ask* and *Poets* have been denied the putatively heroic feats of accomplishment that defined their fathers' and grandfathers' generations. The "end of history" has left the children of the postwar generation rudderless and unable to define their own identities through traditional forms of labor and masculine activity. Raised on television, but also, as Palahniuk and Lipsyte both have it, by women, these men lack the male role models their fathers should have been for them and can only define their worth through the metrics of consumption. Once access to money, through reliable employment or easily available credit, runs out, these men have nothing by which to either assess or signify their own value. The global financial collapse has rendered consumption as a way of life untenable for all but the most wealthy and has burst the bubble of middle-class complacency. This is where Milo and Matt find themselves at novels' end: with nothing to show for their labors—labors that themselves evidence nothing because they produce nothing.

In *The Ask*, Milo ponders his own attenuated masculinity when he sees a man on the street with visibly work-worn hands: "The man's hands looked ruined," Milo observes, "rheumatoid, nicked and pinched by gruesome machinery. I'd done many odd jobs in my life, but hardly any heavy lifting. I stared at my own hands, soft, expressive things, gifted, even, like specially bred, lovingly shaved gerbils" (79). The man, whom Milo originally takes to be of retirement age and then realizes is more likely only in his midforties, signifies the difference between manual and mental labor, only one of which becomes inscribed on the body.[24] Having lost his job, and about to lose his wife and his place in the family home, Milo has nothing to show for his "many odd jobs," his aborted artistic career, or his years working in the college alumni office. This man, in distinction, wears the visible markers of his life's labors on his body, indelible, irrefutable, and unimpeachable. Milo's observation of the man comes just after he has found himself remembering a "postmodern feminism class" he took at college in which he read "cyborg liberation essays" and ran home to masturbate after class each week (79). The inference is clear: young men who take postmodern feminism courses in college don't go on to become manual laborers and possibly end up losing something as a result.[25] Milo does not bear the signs of labor, of a worthwhile life, on his body, which is, as a result, coded as feminine—soft and expressive, more like a small animal than a man. Moreover, encouraged by his engagements with feminism only to masturbate, Milo at once fails to learn the lessons about gender such a class might otherwise have taught him and proves himself to be both onanistic, thereby incapable of productive forms of sexual outlet, and insufficiently in control of his own impulses, thereby incapable of the forms of self-control necessary for a productive life.

Poets makes a similar set of claims about the relationship between masculine self-worth and manual labor. Matt gives the reader the story of his father's working life, a career spent "with a good job at Sears, working his way up to manager of the automotive department" (86).[26] For Matt, his father occupies a middle position, neither manual laborer nor service worker, but an evolutionary stage between the two. He describes his father's pride at wearing a tie to work and links it to the generational transition from his grandfather, to his father, and via himself to his own sons: "It was important that his necktie peer out of his shop clothes like that but I don't think it was something he consciously thought about; it was more like an innate Darwinian drive, a man in a tie and coveralls being the missing link in the evolution of my family's male drive from *lower-middle-class, rural blue collar* (Dad's dad worked on cattle ranches and in lumber mills) to *upper-middle class urban white collar*. (I've never worn a pair of coveralls; my private-school kids have never seen them.)" (86, italics in original). Such sartorial markers of competing forms of masculine endeavor as neckties and coveralls are related here, as they are in *The Ask*, to the ability of contemporary men to engage in manual labor. As Milo has never done any heavy lifting, Matt can do little more than change lightbulbs (86). In both instances, the ability to perform manual work is linked to self-sufficiency, self-control, and the ability of men to appropriately manage their households, to maintain control over, and to extract benefit from, domestic space.

Manual labor commands a form of respect that the office-based, finance-related work of these men does not. It is significant, then, that these self-described urban white-collar men with soft hands each end up performing manual labor: Milo takes a job building decks with the brother of his son's day care provider; with the help of his father, Matt builds his own sons a tree fort with lumber he has purchased from Chuck Stehne, his wife's high school boyfriend and current fling. In each case, these moments of manual labor provide the opportunity for self-fulfillment and the potential development of masculine kudos. In postrecessionary culture, as it has at other moments in the history of postwar labor, blue-collar work provides a route to self-fulfillment for disenfranchised white-collar workers.[27] To take Matt's attempt at manual labor as an example, having discovered that his wife might be having an affair with an ex-boyfriend, Matt tracks the man down to the lumber store where he works. Matt mistakenly believes the man to be an employee of the store but soon discovers that he is the son of its owner and, therefore, a future owner himself, thereby situated in a different relationship to manual labor than the one in which Matt initially places him. As Matt points out, "*dude who stacks lumber for a living is not the same as dude who works for a hugely profitable family business, which he stands to inherit*" (45, italics in original). Not only has Matt underestimated the status of his rival, he has also flattened contemporary forms of manual labor into a single sphere of valueless work (in this case, lumber stacking). He is better than Chuck, he mistakenly believes, because he works not with his hands but with his mind.

In his attempts to get under Chuck's skin, Matt orders a thousand dollars worth of wood (that he can ill afford) to build a tree fort for his sons. Once it has been delivered, he then demands that the wood be collected and he be refunded his money. Before this can happen, however, Matt's father takes the construction of the tree fort into his own hands and refuses to let Chuck take the wood away. And thus, in the novel's penultimate chapter, Matt finds himself in the odd position of realizing his fantasy of engaging in manual labor with his father. As the facsimile of a proper form of labor, one that produces visible and tangible results, the building of the tree fort places Matt, if only for an instant and only in a radically attenuated way, into a different register of masculine identity. He becomes a man and is justly rewarded. During his feat of manual labor, Matt goes into the house to make a pot of coffee, only to find that Lisa has already done so. Rewarded for his labors, Matt can—for what seems to be the only time in the novel—rely on his wife to perform the proper domestic duty: prepare refreshments for the men who are working on the house. This moment of domestic felicity is undercut, however, by the fact that when Matt discovers the freshly brewed pot of coffee, Lisa is upstairs packing to leave the house, which is days away from being repossessed by the mortgage company in any case, and Lieutenant Reese (who, following Matt's arrest for selling marijuana, used him as a confidential informant) has come to take him to the police station to give a statement. While it comes too late and is thoroughly undercut by the context within which it takes place, this moment signals the significance of manual labor as a form of male socialization and offers a hint of its putative benefits for masculine self-worth and the cementing of proper gender roles. It suggests, moreover, the anxiety felt by the middle-class male over the distance modern life has carried him from visibly useful work.[28]

Matt's too little, too late treeless tree fort stands as a symbol of his failure to properly control the domestic realm and, thus, of his failure to reap its rewards. Literally standing in the shadow of the house he no longer owns, and then in the communal yard of the apartment building he moves into following his family's eviction, the fort is a sign of failure. Neither a proper home nor a plaything for his children, who are too old for it and are, in any case, not accustomed to the sort of play a fort requires, raised as they have been on electronic games and the Internet, the fort signifies Matt's failure to provide for his family. As a facsimile of a prior form of domestic structure, the frontier homestead, the tree fort further signals Matt's failures in the distance it represents between the copy and the original. That the domestic structure the fort replicates is obsolete and harkens back to an earlier era of putatively stable gendered relations further suggests the profundity of the failure it connotes. As Matt fails it—he builds it too late and it is an obsolete form in any case—it fails to provide him with the security of stable family life that he so strongly desires.

Milo also engages in manual labor, and also too little and too late. As it does in *Poets*, manual labor in *The Ask* stands as the representative sign of masculinity's sociocultural transformations. Having been persuaded by Nick, the brother of his son's day care provider, to work for him as an apprentice deck builder, Milo is subject to the obligatory hazing that is the tribulation of any new employee. Milo, on his first morning at work, is forced by Nick to load singlehandedly a truck's worth of lumber, and suffers the physical consequences on his soft body and his gerbil-like hands:

> I hopped out of the cab, barked my shin on the runner. I limped over to the woodpile, looked back at Nick, shrugged, yanked the lightest-looking beam to my shoulder. My knees buckled. I staggered to the truck bed. Nick sat bent over the steering wheel, heaving. For a moment I thought it might be a coronary. Then I saw him wipe the tears from his eyes, roll down the window.

"Hurry up, you prick!" he said, his voice breaking.

I rushed back to the pallet. It took me an hour to load the truck. My hands peeled and bled. My shoulders burned, my legs quivered, my vision grew blurry. I puked on Nick's grill.

It was time to go to work. (84–85)

As in *Poets*, Milo's encounter with physical labor does little more than highlight his inadequacies. Too weak, out of shape, inexperienced, Milo represents the nadir of male physicality. Too far removed from manual work, from the manipulation and control of physical objects, he is incapable of properly contributing to the development of the domestic space of the home: he cannot even build a deck. Like Matt, though, Milo comes tantalizingly close to benefiting from his labor in ways that go beyond the financial benefits of the paycheck he receives. Returning home after his first day of work, Milo is rewarded for his physical feats with the promise of sexual intimacy and a back and neck massage from his wife that reminds him of a childhood fantasy of manual labor and its rewards derived from a television advertisement for a muscle rub he remembers watching as a child. Unfortunately for Milo, the smell of the rub makes him nauseous and he falls asleep before the ultimate reward for his hard work can be realized. In his narrative, Milo euphemistically wonders whether Maura "kept the appointment with herself" (86). He provides an answer of sorts in the next passage when he describes awakening in the night to find his young son, who has been weaned for some time, nursing. Passing it off as regression, Maura reassures him that she is no longer producing milk and that Bernie's suckling is merely for comfort—an admission that renders the moment even more troubling for Milo. Emasculated by his failure to perform in either the work or the sexual arenas, the man becomes, and is then replaced by, the child. Supplanted by his son in his wife's emotional and physical affections, Milo's moment of blue-collar work comes too late to save him from his own failures and he cannot reap the rewards of a job done, if not well, then at some physical cost to the self. In both of these novels, the putative ability of blue-collar labor to provide meaning for men is recognized while its effects are radically undercut. Like the myth of economic and social self-making, manual labor's recuperative powers are taken to be equally enervated.

Conclusion: Redemption, Irony, and Narrative Voice

Deeply ironic, and richly satirical, both of the novels under discussion in this essay hold a mirror up to contemporary articulations of white male injury, commenting on it as much as they seem to engage in it. Each of these texts evidences an investment in the recuperation of the myth of possessive individualism that undergirds both contemporary American social life and the forms of masculine identity most empowered by it and, as such, should be understood in relation to the post–identity politics discourse in which masculinity is most empowered by its self-presentation as powerless. With protagonists who are on the verge of losing (or have already lost) jobs, wives, homes, children, and savings, each of these texts represents male crisis as an epiphenomenon of the collapse of the middle-class American family; each novel offers the reader a protagonist who seems to have failed. Representing husbands as primary breadwinners, holders of debt, and the public face of family finances, these texts represent traditional beliefs about domestic gender roles at the same time as they evidence profound anxieties about men's continued ability to fulfill them. Positioned in contrast to the relative success and independence of their wives and partners, the failure of these men to function as the heads of households marks a broader construction of failure in which men are understood to have been failed as much as they themselves fail.[29] Unmoored from traditional forms of male socialization, denied the benefits of patriarchal authority, incapable of maintaining control of the family home, Matt and Milo are taken to be typical, not exceptional.

In both *The Ask* and *The Financial Lives of the Poets*, however, masculinity's failures are constitutive. Milo Burke and Matt Prior are, after all, both the protagonists and the narrators of their own stories. While the future is unwritten for the men who occupy the centers of each of these novels (both of which end with the protagonist separated from his wife yet hopeful of reviving his failing marriage), they each describe only—and by necessity—the opinions, thoughts, and feelings of their first-person narrators. While women are understood to have taken control of their own lives and of the fortunes of family, they do not have voices in these texts. Everything is mediated through the male conscience and, perhaps as a consequence, the tones of these texts are ironic and rich with black humor. By making their protagonists their narrators, these novels restage a primal scene of home and family in which men are called upon to account for—and are therefore able to excuse—their own failings. Irony, moreover, installs a distance through which these men's actions are seen from a remove, refracted as they are through the occlusions of irony's distorting lens. The reader can laugh with these men as she is also allowed to laugh at them.

The protagonists of these novels, despite their manifest failings, have stories to tell. Financial downturn is represented as an opportunity to reassess lives and to recalibrate expectations. Admitting their failings, these men ask for another opportunity to prove their worth. Even if this does not result necessarily in family reunions, it does result in a return to masculine pride and—within a series of recalibrated and downsized expectations—the glimmer of future masculine success. In each of these first-person narratives of masculine disempowerment, domestic upheaval, and social failure, the men who stand at their centers—and who tell their own stories—reclaim agency through the representation of its loss. Fighting off creditors, battling to reclaim the love of their wives, struggling to regain a sense of self-worth and the respect of their children, each of these men is depicted as heroic. Wry, ironic, self-deprecating, they are men to whom the reader is encouraged to give a second chance.

Notes

1. I have discussed at length elsewhere the presumption that, despite a wealth of evidence to the contrary, economic downturns affect white men more than men of color or women. See Carroll, *Affirmative Reaction*, particularly the introduction.

2. I am using the term "literary fiction" here not as a marker of quality but as a definition of genre. As I will go on to discuss, it is significant that these texts are novels and that they inhabit a (broadly defined) genre of recessionary-era cultural production that is distinct from other recent literary cycles such as the concomitant flurry of nonfiction accounts of the financial collapse (briefly discussed in note 4 below) or the 1990s-era cycle of financially oriented self-help books.

3. While neither novel deals with the financial collapse directly, Joshua Ferris's *Then We Came to the End* (2007) and David Foster Wallace's *The Pale King* (2010) both take the world of office work as their milieus and evidence a focus on the world of white-collar labor in recent literary fiction.

4. Moore, Gubert, and Preston, moreover, all have professional connections to the world of global finance in which their novels are set, suggesting a popular interest in the insider perspective, offered by their novels, on a world that many members of the public consider to be opaque and impenetrable to outsiders. The concurrent publishing boom in explanatory nonfiction texts and insider accounts, evidenced by titles such as Michael Lewis's *The Big Short* (2010), Andrew Ross Sorkin's *Too Big to Fail* (2009), Gregory Zuckerman's *The Greatest Trade Ever* (2009), John Lanchester's *Whoops!* (2010), and Vicky Ward's *The Devil's Casino* (2010), also suggests that the general public had an almost insatiable appetite to understand what had happened to the world around them—to know who had so radically transformed the world in which they lived, and how—and a vested interest in knowing the answers to such questions.

5. While I do not have the space to discuss it here, it is also interesting to note how quickly such texts began to appear. While some of these texts (Gubert's *One Step to Danger*, for example) were published just before the crisis had reached the forefront of public consciousness, and were therefore understood to provide prescient foretelling of a coming event, many of them appeared very quickly in its aftermath. This is in distinction to literature about the events of September 11 and their aftermath, which was comparatively slower to appear in print, suggesting that the ethical questions

about representation that still haunt post–September 11 culture did not arise after the financial collapse. This is interesting because a number of these texts (*Poets* and *The Ask* included) understand the events of September 11 to be directly related, both to the financial crisis itself and to the lived experiences of their protagonists. Adding an interesting wrinkle to this connection, Doug Fanning, the protagonist of Haslett's *Union Atlantic*, is a veteran of the first Gulf War, thereby extending the connection between geopolitics and global finance further into the recent past of the nation.

6. Lasch, *Haven in a Heartless World*. In their focus on the failed or failing bourgeois family, these novels mirror the concerns of many post–September 11 novels that also focus primarily on affluent, white, middle-class male subjects. See, for example, Don DeLillo's *Falling Man* (2007), Ken Kalfus's *A Disorder Peculiar to the Country* (2007), Joseph O'Neill's *Netherland* (2007), and Jay McInerney's *The Good Life* (2007).

7. It is interesting that in both novels the work that is no longer available for these men is related to the arts and culture industries. Matt Prior is an ex-journalist specializing in business and finance and a would-be poet; Milo Burke is a failed artist who is desperately trying to hold onto a job as a fund-raiser for the arts programs of a fictitious university in New York. Each is highly educated and is invested in the capacity for visual or literary art to serve as an outlet for male self-expression. For the protagonists of both novels, the arts provide a valuable form of cultural capital, yet one with which they are not entirely comfortable. They have both, after all, failed to secure prosperous livings as artists. Milo raises money to allow others to fulfill their artistic dreams; Matt offers up financial advice in the form of poetry. For both men, therefore, their livelihoods are supplemental, not intrinsic, to the arts. As such, these novels mobilize models of success that at once seem to stand outside the realms of finance capitalism and consumer culture and to be reliant on them. (Which is, on one level, just another way of saying that they both work with money but not in a socially or morally reprehensible way.)

8. Randy Martin observes that, after the financial collapse, "some nine million US households (more than one in ten) owe more on their single family home than it is worth." Martin, "The Good, the Bad, and the Ugly," 425.

9. On the post–financial collapse fortunes of communities with high levels of home-related debt, see "Where Housing Once Boomed, Recovery Lags."

10. Walter, *The Financial Lives of the Poets*, 4–5, italics in original. All further references given parenthetically in the text.

11. Martin, "The Good, the Bad, and the Ugly," 424.

12. For more on this subject, particularly in relation to the erosion of the Protestant work ethic, see Sennett, *The Culture of the New Capitalism*, particularly 72–81.

13. See Martin, *The Financialization of Everyday Life*.

14. "The self-managerial entailments and exclusions that finance sets in motion," Martin argues, "reveal a fuller extension of labor into many habits of life. People are to ponder their financial security into the wee hours and work their investment portfolios, consumer debt, and accruals for their retirement and their children's college tuition accordingly." Martin, *An Empire of Indifference*, 5.

15. Martin, *The Financialization of Everyday Life*, 79. Martin further suggests that

"finance, the management of money's ebbs and flows, is not simply in the service of accessible wealth, but presents itself as a merger of business and life cycles, as a means for the acquisition of self" (3). "How individuals come to think about themselves," Martin continues at a later point, "take stock of how they are doing and what they have accomplished, and how they know themselves to be moving forward through the measured paces of finance, yields a particular subjectivity" (9).

16. Martin, *An Empire of Indifference*, 15.

17. For another example of this perceived shift in gender roles as it has been represented in popular print journalism, see Mundy, *The Richer Sex*.

18. Lipsyte, *The Ask*, 154. All further references given parenthetically in the text.

19. For a wide-ranging discussion of gender and social media, see "Roundtable," 185–243.

20. Matt, on the other hand, has turned to small-time drug dealing in an attempt to transform his financial situation. As in the successful television drama *Weeds* (2005–12), marijuana is represented in *Poets* as a vehicle of nostalgia in which white, suburban men (mostly) are able to return to a prior, prelapsarian moment of youth, thereby avoiding, rather than facing, crisis and change. Cinematic comedies such as *The 40-Year-Old Virgin* (2005) and *Knocked Up* (2007) present similarly nostalgic fantasies of the white male adolescent's retreat from the world of adult responsibility and serve as a counterpoint to these narratives of the pressures of adult responsibility. Such representations of the necessity for heads of households to turn to the illicit world of drug dealing suggests much about the perceived failures of the contemporary labor market to effectively enable the lives of middle-class white homeowners. While it does not present drug use in relation to nostalgia, Showtime's hit series *Breaking Bad* (2008–present) is a further example of this central plot device.

21. In *The Ask*, Milo is also forced to confront the fact that his wife is conducting an affair, in this instance with a coworker. If Matt's failure is made apparent in Lisa's turn to a former lover and, thereby, in the fact of her attempted retreat into a nostalgic past, Milo's failure is codified by the fact that Maura's lover is an ostensibly gay man. But as Maura laments when Milo asks her about Paul's sexual preferences, "you're like from another century. Nobody cares what anybody is" (214).

22. Hayward, "The Economic Crisis and After," 286.

23. Fincher, *Fight Club*. In Palahniuk's novel, the nearest approximation of this speech comes in the following passage: "We are God's middle children according to Tyler Durden, with no special place in History and no special attention. Unless we get God's attention, we have no hope of damnation or redemption. Which is worse, hell or nothing? Only if we're caught and punished can we be saved." Palahniuk, *Fight Club*, 141.

24. For a discussion of the embodiment of manual labor, see Zandy, *Hands*. See also chapter 3 of Carroll, *Affirmative Reaction*, 77–100.

25. At an earlier point, Milo confesses that his mother "was a second-wave feminist" and that, as a result, he "wasn't comfortable saying 'cunt' until he was twenty-three" (9).

26. It is worth noting that the sort of solid, middle-American values embodied in

the Sears brand have, like Matt's father, failed to live up to expectations in the face of financial downturn. In December 2011, the company announced that it was to close upward of 100 stores as a result of poor holiday sales. See "Sears to Close 100–120 Stores after Poor Holiday Sales."

27. The recuperative power of manual labor for white-collar workers is (as it has long been) a common trope in contemporary culture. In the postrecession film *The Company Men* (2010), for example, an event takes place similar to the one described in *The Ask*. In the film, one of the protagonists, Bobby Walker (Ben Affleck) loses his job as a high-flying financier and is persuaded by his wife, Maggie (Rosemarie DeWitt), to take a construction job working for her successful brother Jack (Kevin Costner). Reluctantly, and after his repeated failure to secure another job in finance, Bobby agrees to take the job. Like Milo, he is shown to be unsuited to manual labor and suffers not only the physical consequences of a life of leisure, but also the ribbing of his employer and fellow employees. Nevertheless, Bobby grows from the experience and is shown to benefit from it in ways that go beyond the remuneration of a much-needed paycheck. Although it is brief, Bobby's short career as a construction worker reinstalls a sense of confidence and masculine pride in him, and he is then able to secure another job in finance.

28. For more on the relationship between mental and manual labor in contemporary culture, see Carroll, "Men's Soaps," 263–83.

29. In a discussion of this phenomenon as it can be seen in contemporary U.S. labor, which he calls the "spectre of uselessness," Richard Sennett suggests, "the most afflicted subjects . . . are middle-class, middle-aged men who, cut out of the old corporate culture, are having trouble finding a place in the new. It's important not to sentimentalize their condition in order to understand their problems. . . . But in their communities these men have become invisible." Sennett, *The Culture of the New Capitalism*, 101. See also, Peck, *Pinched*; and, from a different perspective (and written in an earlier moment), Faludi, *Stiffed*.

NINE   *HANNAH HAMAD*

Fairy Jobmother to the Rescue
POSTFEMINISM AND THE RECESSIONARY CULTURES OF REALITY TV

> There *are* jobs out there. . . . There is something out there
> for everyone if they search hard enough.
>
> HAYLEY TAYLOR, *THE FAIRY JOBMOTHER*, JULY 27, 2010

> There is not one of you that cannot go out and
> get a job today, and that is a fact.
>
> HAYLEY TAYLOR, *BENEFIT BUSTERS*, AUGUST 20, 2009

The global financial crisis and its aftermath have given rise to a recession-ary culture that has inflected numerous media forms. The recurrent thema-tization of downsizing, unemployment, thrift, austerity, poverty, and other recession-related issues across the spectrum of media content evidences the scale of this trend. Since its dramatic rise to prominence as one of the domi-nant forms of television in the early twenty-first century, reality TV has been a significant site for the playing out of topical anxieties and concerns. Through its emphasis on individualism and empowerment, and via its overriding inter-est in the management, governance, labor, and transformation of the self, reality TV has been instrumental in popular culture's negotiation of neolib-eral discourse, consistently speaking to the related concerns of postfeminist culture.[1] Frequently held up, then, as a cultural form that particularly visibly typifies the discursive intersection between postfeminism and neoliberalism, the genre's reliance on expertise to guide participants through periods of uncertainty echoes a wider cultural yearning for trustworthy figures that has arguably been heightened in recession.[2]

Of particular concern to me in these regards is the U.K. reality TV series *The Fairy Jobmother* (Channel 4, 2010–), which is notable for its continued reliance on the figure of the celebrity expert.[3] This is at a time when the currency of expertise is being called into question, amid a larger context in which expertise has repeatedly been proven fallible, with revelations of corruption, incompetence, and dishonesty on the part of public authority figures spanning the spheres of politics, finance, and the media. The cultural capital of expertise is therefore in flux, with some commentators lamenting what they have prophesied to be "the end of expertise."[4] This growing cynicism toward the figure of the expert has also begun to permeate popular media, including reality TV. For example, in April 2011 one British TV critic questioned whether it was "time for a rain check" on celebrity expertise.[5] Nonetheless, and notwithstanding Helen Powell and Sylvie Prasad's contention that the form and function of the celebrity lifestyle expert has become problematic in light of the transformed post-2008 economic environment, which they suggest ought to negate the cultural viability of these figureheads of neoliberalism, the reality TV expert has proved remarkably resilient to the emergent rhetoric of backlash against expertise and authority.[6] Seemingly impervious to the challenges posed by recessionary social realities to their advocacy of the preeminence of personal responsibility in effecting upward economic mobility and improved social health and power, celebrity lifestyle experts like *The Fairy Jobmother*'s central figure, "employment expert" Hayley Taylor, have instead been given renewed license to operate. They have done so on more or less the same terms of reference as prerecession iterations of this figure; if anything, the necessity of their work is negotiated with a greater sense of urgency, as the recessionary stakes of their instructions in self-governance are shown to be raised.

All of this is indicative of what recessionary reality TV like *The Fairy Jobmother* brings into view, which is that despite economic and social developments seemingly at odds with the continued viability of neoliberal postfeminist discourse, its hegemony is entrenched in cultural consciousness, and this can be seen in popular culture's persistent recourse to celebrity expertise in addressing pressing social and economic problems. Disparities of social health and economic power along lines of gender, race, and class, which should come into sharper view as they become increasingly stark in recessionary times, instead continue to be veiled beneath the work of reality TV experts, who are some of the most practiced agents of neoliberal postfeminism. Their disingenuous focus on personal responsibility, the disciplined practice of selfhood, and the ability of individuals to determine the outcome of their own endeavors, irrespective of structural inequalities and severely strained economic conditions, denies the impact on the individual of systemic and institutionalized inequity. Their emphasis on the transformative power of self-governance similarly refuses solutions that require social change, rather than individual transcendence of one's environment. And they endear themselves to recessionary audiences otherwise primed to reject their expertise and deny their authority by appearing to advocate for their interests. In this way, British celebrity chef Jamie Oliver deploys his clout to campaign against obesity, but denies it is a problem with a particularly classed dimension, in shows like *Jamie's School Dinners* (Channel 4, 2005), *Jamie's Return to School Dinners* (Channel 4, 2006), and *Jamie's American Food Revolution* (Channel 4, 2010–11).[7] Mary Portas's celebrity expertise, garnered in shows like *Mary Queen of Shops* (BBC, 2007–10) and *Mary Portas: Secret Shopper* (Channel 4, 2011), trumpets the cause of the small business owner, with a view to fostering consumer spending on moribund U.K. high streets, in such striking accordance with the coalition government's aims that she was appointed as its advisor, on account of her retail knowledge. And Hayley Taylor in *Benefit Busters* (Channel 4, 2009) and *The Fairy Jobmother*, as this chapter elaborates, presents herself as cognizant of the barriers and disincentives that stop the unemployed from working, but rejects the notion that such hurdles cannot be surmounted by individual willpower regardless of any social inequities or power imbalances in play. So, even as scandal frequently undercuts the reliability of experts, whether in politics, finance, or the markets, reality TV continues to look to the figure of the celebrity lifestyle expert to tutor citizens in selfhood.

Reality TV has been remarkably quick to accommodate recessionary discourse, proving shrewdly adaptable and responsive to the social changes wrought by the economic downturn. In turn this has necessitated shifts in tone and a reordering of thematic priorities, evident in the widespread recession-oriented reformulations of tried and tested formats. In the face of major economic shifts, postboom reality TV has deftly retained the discursive remit of neoliberal postfeminism, the viability of which it continues to negotiate. As I have suggested, it has done this by thematizing the recession in a manner congruent with the gender mores of postfeminism, as well as the allied politics of the self propounded by neoliberalism. *The Fairy Jobmother* particularly epitomizes this discursive intersection between neoliberal postfeminism and the new cultures of recession and is symptomatic of the recessionary turn in cultures of reality TV. Tropes of postfeminism, neoliberalism, celebrity culture, and recessionary discourse coalesce in *The Fairy Jobmother* to offer a pointedly gendered, politically evasive, and ideologically disingenuous popular cultural text.

The show's aforementioned central figure, "employment expert" Hayley Taylor, is tasked with life coaching members of the long-term unemployed into a state of what she calls "job readiness," facilitating their reentry into the public-sphere workforce, a process that signifies intertextually in relation to numerous tropes and archetypes of what Diane Negra terms "the [postfeminist] female labor market."[8] In various ways Taylor embodies domestically located and emotionally charged work germane to that market, connecting to a number of recognizable postfeminist femininities grounded in trends and tropes such as the affective laborer, the fairy godmother, and the female authority figure, the last of which she performs as a postfeminist take on the popular cultural figure of the "bossy woman."[9] By signified association, this can be seen in her adoption of "flight attendant chic," as she sports her signature neckerchief: a fetishized connotative marker of the emotional labor and feminized authority that symbolically places the affective labor of flight attendants as a point of comparison alongside her own.[10] Additionally, Taylor exemplifies what Negra terms the "enchantment effect" through her performance as a fairy godmother, a persona or role that imbues her interventions into the job seeking of the subject participants with a magical air, commensurate with what Negra argues to be the ideological evasiveness of this trope of postfeminist culture.[11] In enacting "magical" transformations on her subject participants that involve the acts of consumption germane to the makeover, *The Fairy Jobmother* aligns itself with the discourse of magically transformative consumerism, entrenched in postfeminist culture, and familiar from female-oriented film and television of the early twenty-first century in particular.[12] However, *The Fairy Jobmother* amends this discourse, deploying it as interventionist action addressing the problem of recessionary unemployment, and thus purporting to raise the stakes of this aspect of postfeminism. Further, here the "enchantment" trope also uses humor and whimsy to lighten both the characterization of an authority figure that has elsewhere been maligned as petty and hectoring, as well as the gloomy economic scenario that necessitates her magically charged interventions, which cheerily enact solutions for the participants, while brightening the picture for audiences. All of these types and tropes have characterized cultural manifestations of women's work in postfeminism, and are employed in *The Fairy Jobmother* to center its gender discourse on Taylor's overdeterminedly postfeminist signification.

It is through Taylor that *The Fairy Jobmother* is able to wave the neoliberal banners of choice, empowerment, and self-help in its shepherding of participants into employment, while negotiating rigid gendered subject positioning through seemingly commonsense appeals to what are positioned as the

FIGURES 9.1 AND 9.2. A rigidly gendered bifurcation of labor and the public sphere workplace characterizes postintervention outcomes in *The Fairy Jobmother*.

larger and more urgent imperatives of the U.K.'s unemployment crisis. Taylor's empowerment rhetoric and self-help strategizing are therefore shown to facilitate and negotiate the recidivism of workplace gender bifurcation. The normative gendering of separate-spheres employment scenarios is naturalized at the end of each episode through a three-month flash-forward to the happy smiling faces of employed subject participants, who are shown to be thriving in their gender-appropriate jobs (figures 9.1 and 9.2).[13] Thus Taylor's male subject participants are relatively unproblematically placed in the dwindling fields of semiskilled manual labor and heavy machinery operation, as she shepherds them into suitably manly blue-collar work contexts such as joinery, refuse collection, kitchen remodeling, security, and warehouse management. Meanwhile, female subject participants are placed in equally feminized occupational milieus, such as beauty parlors, retail outlets, makeup and cosmetics counters, cafés, and child care facilities, all of which enable them to transfer their hitherto domestically located affective labor into feminized public-sphere "emotion work."[14]

This chapter interrogates postfeminist and recessionary discourse in *The Fairy Jobmother*, offering a feminist critique of its articulation of this discursive intersection, mapping the terrain of emergent recessionary cultures of reality TV, and conceptualizing its tropes for gendering the recession. It aims to understand some of the ways in which the disingenuous rhetoric of choice and empowerment that has so starkly characterized neoliberal postfeminist culture persists in recessionary culture. It does so in the face of strong contextual forces that ought to belie the credibility of this discourse, making manifest and bringing into sharper focus the structural social inequalities it willfully glosses over, and forcing a cultural reevaluation of its viability. *The Fairy Jobmother* perpetuates illusory paradigms of individualism, choice, and self-governance, suggesting that it is possible to self-manage, self-empower, and consume one's way out of crisis. Notwithstanding its differently gendered token gestures toward the respective impacts of the recession and its consequences for the United Kingdom's men and women, *The Fairy Jobmother* sidesteps any imperative to confront the entrenched inequalities of gender, class, and race that give rise to the grim realities of the U.K. benefits culture.[15] As Gareth Palmer writes, "The economic crash of 2008 and the more aggressive flows of capital have entailed more insecure conditions for all workers but it is working-class women, ethnic minorities, and the poor who are left most susceptible to changes in economic circumstances, who live more closely with risk, and whose 'options' are more limited by holding less educational, symbolic and cultural capital."[16]

Recessionary Culture on Television

The recession-oriented sensibility of a show such as *The Fairy Jobmother* emerged as part of a broader turn in both U.K. and U.S. television cultures toward making sense of the 2008 economic crisis and its consequences. While the synergy between the recessionary television cultures of the United Kingdom and the United States is, up to a point, commensurate with the "discursive harmony" between their respective cultures of postfeminism,[17] it is nevertheless the case that exportable recessionary formats, including *The Fairy Jobmother*, which was reconceived for U.S. audiences via an abortive remake for the Lifetime network, must necessarily speak to their localities in order to meaningfully chime with audiences' lived experiences of the recession.

An indicative example of how the respectively culturally located iterations of *The Fairy Jobmother* have spoken to their localities is the second episode of the U.S. version, in which the doubly impacted unemployment status of Louisianans Paul and Melissa Bethe is attributed both to the recessionary economic context and to the fact of their having been displaced from their former home by Hurricane Katrina. More broadly though, while part of the agenda of the U.K. version appears to be to combat the benefits culture supposedly enabled by the British welfare state, which itself was under attack by the coalition government's recessionary program of public spending cuts while the show was in production, the U.S. version instead emphasizes the victims of corporate downsizing. Hence, a greater proportion of subject participants come from the middle rather than working classes. Thus, while the majority of Taylor's U.K. participants are entry-level, minimum wage, trainee, or apprentice workers, her U.S. participants are much more likely to be laid-off skilled, salaried, or professional workers. In this way, the different iterations of the series approach class quite differently, commensurate both with culturally specific priorities and proclivities and with particular recessionary issues germane to each national locality. The ways that the differently located iterations of the format thus speak to their audiences similarly entails an equally culturally specific relationship to both recessionary culture and postfeminist discourse, both of which necessarily unfold in discursive accord with the cultural imperatives of their national contexts.

Elsewhere, early responses to the onset of recession could be seen on U.S. television in numerous midrun shows, such as *Nip/Tuck* (FX, 2003–2010), *Entourage* (HBO, 2004–11), *Desperate Housewives* (ABC, 2004–12), *The Office* (NBC, 2005–13), *Ugly Betty* (ABC, 2006–10), *30 Rock* (NBC, 2006–13), and *Friday Night Lights* (NBC, 2006–11). All responded to the onset of recession by adapting their resident discourse to accommodate its thematic topicality. In most cases the address to altered economic circumstances was episodic and relatively superficial. For example, from early 2009 the worsening economy and related topical events were intermittently used to stage the situation comedy in *30 Rock*, notably the season 3 episode "Generalissimo," originally aired in February 2009, in which newly redundant Lehman Brothers brokers are recruited as interns at NBC; in the sixth season of *The Office*, the straitened times impact upon the salaries of Dunder Mifflin employees to set up a scenario that runs across the October 2009 episode "The Promotion," in which bride-to-be Pam (Jenna Fischer) circulates the office soliciting wedding gifts of cash from her colleagues. The recession was thematized with greater solemnity and longevity in *Friday Night Lights*, which more candidly and melodramatically depicted the economic strife of its small-town community, especially in its 2009 fourth season, across narrative threads dealing with unemployment, teenage pregnancy, university tuition fees, de facto racial segregation, and economically driven inequalities of access to education. Notwithstanding the varying degrees of gravitas with which the economic crisis was treated, and the sometimes cursory extent to which ongoing narratives were affected by the adoption of recessionary themes, it is clear that over the course of 2009, television, along with other forms and modes of cultural expression, attuned to the recessionary moods of audiences, and began to speak to and through discourses of recession.[18]

The term "recession television" entered journalistic rhetoric as early as October 2008 when, for example, Adam Buckman in the *New York Post* used it in reference to NBC's developmental turn toward programming "featuring working class heroes,"[19] showing such characters being developed in series such as Fox's *Two Dollar Beer* (2009), in which a group of young people resist relocating from their hometown of Detroit as the state of the economy worsens. Autumn of the following year bore witness to a flurry of overtly recession-oriented pilots, such as Canadian cable network Global's *The Dealership* (2009), about a family-run used car dealership plunged into crisis when the bottom drops out of the market; ABC's *Canned* (2009), a comedy featuring Amanda Bynes in which a group of investment banker friends all lose their jobs on the same day; *This Little Piggy* (ABC, 2009), in which financially disenfranchised siblings hit by the tough economic times move in together in their deceased parents' old house; and *Hank* (ABC, 2009–10), which ran for a season, in which Kelsey Grammer is a laid-off CEO who downshifts from New York to small-town Virginia with his family. The premise of *Hank* thus offered up a noteworthy gender reversal of retreatism, commensurate with the cultural tendency to frame the economic crisis as masculine, and the tendency of postfeminist culture to recuperate derogated masculinities through fatherhood.[20] In line with the industrial realities of U.S. television's pilot system, only a small number of shows from this manifestly recessionary-themed season were picked up, or survived beyond one season. Nonetheless, the expedience with which the recession was thematized at that time does speak to the extent to which cultural producers were determined to keep pace with concerns and anxieties arising from this major social and economic shift. Further, 2009 also saw the premieres of more successful, long-running, and resonant examples of recessionary television drama and, notably, dramas that manifested the tendency of recessionary culture to highlight masculine subjectivities. This can be seen in serial dramas *White Collar* (USA Network, 2009–), centered on the apprehension of white-collar criminals, and *Hung* (HBO, 2009–11), in which the financially struggling protagonist (Thomas Jane) turns to prostitution.

The U.K. television film *Freefall* (BBC, 2009) charted the buildup to the onset of the financial crisis and its subsequent aftermath over the course of 2007 and 2008. It too gendered the economic situation as pointedly white and masculine, notwithstanding an advance press release for the film, which highlighted the extent to which the financial collapse was "an issue . . . destined to impact everyone in the UK."[21] *Freefall* narrativizes the events depicted according to their impact on three white men, and their respective resulting social and economic disenfranchisement: a city banker (Aidan Gillen), a discount mortgage salesman (Dominic Cooper), and a defaulting homeowner (Joseph Mawle).

A notable development in contrast to this trend was NBC's commissioning of *Downwardly Mobile*, a Roseanne Barr–scripted sitcom in which she is the proprietor of a mobile home park. This is significant not only in terms of the recessionary resonance of Barr's 1990s television persona, as the matriarchal working-class media figurehead of an earlier recession, in *Roseanne* (ABC, 1988–97). The show additionally promises to privilege those American subjectivities most socially marginalized by the recession, especially in light of what Barbara Ehrenreich has lamented as the invisibility of the working classes and the abjectly poor in media depictions of the recession's social impact.[22] In some of the aforementioned ways therefore, U.S. and U.K. television have fostered emergent recessionary cultures of television drama and situation comedy through narratives of downward mobility, masculinity in crisis, and white-collar crime.[23]

Reimagining Reality TV in Response to the Global Financial Crisis

In his recuperative retrospective of 1980s popular culture, Toby Litt highlights that "TV shows about the unemployed" were a major preoccupation of television producers in Thatcher's Britain, and that the preferred prism through which 1980s British recession television thematized the unemployment spikes of the time was the serial drama.[24] The Thatcher-era recession thus gave rise to highly revered and canonized U.K. series that addressed the experience of mass unemployment, such as *Boys from the Blackstuff* (BBC, 1980–82) and *Auf Wiedersehen, Pet* (ITV, 1983–86), both of which, unsurprisingly given the extent to which so-called quality TV tends to be gendered, largely privileged masculine subjectivities in their respective treatments of unemployment. Commensurate with its latter-day prevalence in contemporary television cultures, it is now reality TV, a "low" cultural form hence customarily viewed as feminine, that is the major site for British television's responses to the current recession.

All of the examples of television drama and situation comedy mentioned in the previous section are symptomatic of this turn toward austerity-themed shows in the recessionary cultures of contemporary television. But reality TV iterations of this trend are particularly noteworthy both for the extent to which they manage to accommodate recessionary discourse at no, or little, expense to their neoliberal postfeminism, and for their transatlantic (and beyond) exportability, albeit with varying levels of success. Recessionary culture and its emergent tropes have thus inflected several generic forms of reality TV, which was probably an inevitable development given "the public narrativisation of traumatic events or experiences" that Anita Biressi and Heather Nunn describe as germane to this television genre.[25] A number of recession-themed reality TV shows have adapted the premise and amended the discourse of an extant conceptual forerunner to accommodate the topicality and currency of recessionary culture.

For example, *Undercover Boss* (Channel 4, 2009–), a U.K. series that now has a number of nationally specific iterations, adapts the secret identity premise of conceptual forerunners *Faking It* (Channel 4, 2000–2006) and *The Secret Millionaire* (Channel 4, 2006–12) for an explicitly recessionary context. *Undercover Boss* features the CEOs of enterprises and corporations negatively impacted by the recession, who go undercover (following a "make under") with a camera crew. They pose as prospective entry-level employees, in order to identify work and employment practices at a grassroots level that require intervention and the enactment of a makeover from upper management. Meanwhile, examples of good practice identified in their employees are rewarded with isolated gestures of generosity and disingenuous good will, subsequent to their "big reveal" as the eponymous undercover boss.[26] In the face of recessionary contextual forces, the CEOs profiled maintain the neoliberal ethos of individual empowerment and the credo of self-managing one's way out of crisis; moreover, they are able to positively reframe themselves, ameliorating their own images to convey paternalistic benevolence at a time when the figure of the greedy self-interested corporate CEO or financier is frequently demonized.[27]

Famous, Rich and Jobless (BBC, 2010) puts a recession spin on the celebrity slumming or tourism reality TV subgenre exemplified by *The Simple Life* (Fox, 2003–5; E!, 2005–7). The show featured wealthy and privileged minor U.K. celebrities Larry Lamb, Meg Matthews, Diarmuid Gavin, and Emma Parker-Bowles looking for employment while living on a restricted budget (equivalent to the U.K. job seeker's allowance) and housed in correspondingly low-rent accommodations. New Zealand Television's *Would Like to Work* (TVNZ, 2010) invokes the premise, format, and tropes of earlier postfeminist culture's dating and makeover series *Would Like to Meet* (BBC, 2001–4) and *What Not to Wear* (BBC, 2001–7). British psychologist Dr. Duncan Thomson attempts to counsel New Zealand's unemployed back to work, with the help of two female sidekicks responsible for making the subject participants over, and helping them shop their way back to work, in a premise not dissimilar to that of *The Fairy Jobmother*, but with an added element of "colonial cringe" via the culturally demarcated empowered-disempowered dynamic between Thomson and his participants.[28] *How the Other Half Live* (Channel 4, 2009–10) reworks the life switch device that, as Laurie Ouellette and James Hay state, "temporarily move[s] subjects into environments that test their ethics and their commitment to a certain lifestyle," and that found great prerecession success in *Wife Swap* (Channel 4, 2003–9), as each episode sees a rich family and a poor family host one another, and gain snippet views of one another's lives.[29] This culminates in the bestowment by the rich family onto the poor family of a life (or lifestyle)-changing gift of money. The obligation, which is built into the show's format, for the rich family to provide financial aid to the poor family, constitutes a recessionary reality TV continuation of state devolution of social work and welfare. In this case wealthy families take up the mantle of individualized welfare and thus, with their social consciences assuaged, are complicit in perpetuating a blinkered approach to confronting poverty in Britain that suggests it can be combated at an individual level, on a case-by-case basis, through isolated acts of paternalistic benevolence. This approach declines to interrogate poverty's structural entrenchment and the inequalities that are fostered as a result. Even the celebrity gourmet dining expert Gregg Wallace of reality TV cooking show *Masterchef* (BBC, 2005–), whose associations with gastronomy might otherwise seem out of step with the austerity imperatives of recessionary culture, was granted renewed relevance with *Gregg Wallace's Recession Bites* (BBC, 2009), which undertook to explore the impact of the recession on the nation's food shopping habits, and thereby on the larger food economy of the United Kingdom, identifying an expected turn toward thrift on the part of British grocery shoppers.

In this way, as we can see, dominant modes and tropes of reality TV such as the life swap, the makeover, the secret identity, the celebrity expert, and the lifestyle intervention are reframed and reoriented to accommodate recessionary culture. *The Fairy Jobmother* similarly makes use of celebrity lifestyle expertise, the "life intervention" device, and the makeover for its postrecession adaptation of an existing reality TV format. Thus, the use of preexisting formats renders the downturn in some fundamental sense familiar. As a consequence, the economic challenges of the recession are reworked as a set of problems to be addressed in terms analogous to reality TV's approach to relationships, the home, or management of the body.

Writing in July 2010, during the lead-up to the U.K. television premiere of *The Fairy Jobmother*, Decca Aitkenhead of the *Guardian* profiled Hayley Taylor, noting, "If something really matters to us, we turn it into a reality television show . . . so it was probably inevitable that the recession would inspire its own age of austerity star."[30] Aitkenhead thus points to the efficacy of turning to thematic and tonal developments in reality TV in order to assess the cultural mood with regard to anxieties and concerns arising from altered economic circumstances and social issues, like unemployment, that resultantly present themselves as urgent. She also highlights the pathway to celebrity that reality genres provide for media-savvy lifestyle experts with relevant knowledge or skill bases understood to be germane or instructive to issues with cultural currency and social resonance. Concerns on the radar of media producers and audiences in 2010, in recessionary Britain, included spiking unemployment and the concomitantly overburdened benefits system, opening the door for Taylor's emergence as a media personality.

Taylor's celebrity status intensified as the United Kingdom's unemployment and benefits system became the focus of political scrutiny. Her initial television appearance in August 2009 was as part of the Channel 4 documentary series *Benefit Busters*, which profiled her work for the Sheffield-based organization A4e (Action for Employment), a body working under contract to the government's Department for Work and Pensions in a bid to help the jobless into employment. Here Taylor was shown specializing in working with jobless single mothers, a group that would be particularly impacted by the government's program of austerity.[31] The following year *Benefit Busters* was reimagined as a star vehicle for Taylor, reframed as a "life intervention" reality TV series of the type defined by Ouellette and Hay, which "mobilize[d] professional motivators and lifestyle experts, from financial advisors to life coaches, to help people overcome hurdles in their personal, professional, and domestic lives."[32]

Taylor is thus called upon to enable her subject participants to transcend the barriers (always internal, and never external, commensurate with the cultural logic of neoliberalism) preventing them from gaining employment.[33] She deploys her employment expertise in a manner that is as much therapeutic and affective as it is instructive. Taylor counsels participants in emotional and psychological terms, typically providing an empathetic tactile affective display in response to a solicited tearful breakdown (when an epiphany is reached as to the root cause of the inability to work: childhood bullying, paternal abandonment, spousal abandonment, bereavement, etc.). She further requires participants to implement domestic regimes and financial management plans, making over their outward appearances, instructing them on attire, personal hygiene, grooming, comportment, and public speaking, and ultimately taking interventionist action to secure them work experience and job interviews when she deems them "job ready."

Brenda Weber observes that reality TV shows "seem aware of their like-mindedness [speaking] through the same idioms, [and] deploying similar imagery."[34] The Fairy Jobmother borrows liberally from the format, premise, and textual and discursive terms of reference of a prerecession Channel 4 "life intervention" reality TV series, Supernanny (2004–11). In this iconically post-feminist conceptual forerunner to The Fairy Jobmother, celebrity child care expert Jo Frost intervenes in and makes over the parenting strategies of her subject participants, a process that follows time spent observing them in their homes, surveilling their flawed parenting.[35] The format of Supernanny was closely followed for the run of the first series of The Fairy Jobmother, in which Taylor sets up camp in the homes of her unemployed subject participants, in order to monitor them, pass censorious judgment on their improper domestic self-governance (what Weber terms "affective domination"[36]), stage the aforementioned "life intervention," and make over both their interior and exterior selves, to the point that they are, in her view, fit for public-sphere employment.

Taylor is therefore made knowable to audiences by her placement within familiar frames of reference, and via the exploitation of formats with proven commercial success. The transparent similarities between the two series in terms of format, iconography, and the symbolically maternal emotional labor of their respective female celebrity lifestyle experts did not go unremarked upon by critics, who dubbed The Fairy Jobmother "Supernanny for the unemployed."[37] In this way, Taylor's maternal mode of address similarly veers between stern and sympathetic but is always officiously matriarchal. Her unemployed subject participants, whose behavior she is required to manage, in a scenario equivalent to Frost's management of the behavior of unruly children and the practices of their ineffectual parents, are thereby infantilized. This infantilization of the unemployed is compounded in the second series by a format change that shifts the locus of the show, and Taylor's work, from the homes of her subject participants to a classroom, and the dynamic between them shifts from one-to-one, or a sustained focus on a particular family, to one-to-many, in line with the group dynamic of the classroom. Correspondingly, and in an amended continuation of her symbolically maternal affective labor, this sees her at times adopt the persona of a schoolmistress. She ejects participants from the room, enforcing time-outs ("you're going to have to have five minutes"), and chastising them for their unruliness and immaturity ("That behavior . . . is totally inappropriate"). Thus, there is clear discursive overlap with the nanny persona of Jo Frost, and her comparably maternally signified "affective domination" of her own similarly infantilized (whether literally in the case of the children, or figuratively in the case of their parents) subject participants.

In *The Fairy Jobmother* Taylor is presented as at once an employment expert, life coach, lifestyle guru, and makeover facilitator, with the goal of enabling self-help and improvement in subjects socially derogated by long periods of joblessness (and poverty in many cases). The intended outcome is to move subjects out of a state of unemployment and into a work environment, and thereby to improved economic status, social health, and quality of life. The premise, format, and execution of *The Fairy Jobmother* thus interoperate to fulfill what has elsewhere been either gestured toward or argued directly by scholars to be the wider social role of reality TV in the neoliberal economy, which is for it to stand in for state, government, and welfare intervention into contemporary social ills, including, in this case, unemployment, a problem of marked and acute significance in a period of sustained recession.[38] In this way, *The Fairy Jobmother* makes relatively explicit what is usually only implicit in this genre of interventionist reality TV. In this case, the employment crisis brought on by the dissolution of the welfare state and the acute onset of recession has enabled *The Fairy Jobmother* to transfer or devolve responsibility for the enactment of their own social care and upward mobility onto individuals, delegating the role of facilitator to Taylor, a celebrity figurehead framed as an expert. The ideologically charged disingenuousness of this is boldly underscored by the crisis-ridden economic context in which *The Fairy Jobmother*'s discourse of self-governance continues to be negotiated, and in which these preselected individuals are shown to quickly and successfully find public-sphere work, and sometimes of a kind that belies the realities of the present-day labor market. For example, in the second series, Taylor helps a homeless nineteen-year-old British Army dropout to be appointed to a joinery apprenticeship from a highly competitive field. This takes place in a social, economic, and historical context in which such modes of employment barely exist. Thus, the ease by which a change in the job seeker's attitude, combined with his acceptance of help, is shown to enable him to secure this opportunity perpetuates the neoliberal illusion that external forces such as the recession, the attendant construction industry crisis, the decline in skilled manual labor, a globalized and technologized labor market, and the rise of the service economy, can all be surmounted if a job seeker "feels" he can achieve. As Taylor insists, "there *are* jobs out there." This observation is discordant given the rising unemployment levels of the time, and in the face of austerity-driven welfare reforms being implemented by U.K. Prime Minister David Cameron's coalition government, in a more aggressive and punitive repackaged continuation of the welfare reforms instigated by the previous Labour government. The cultural efficacy of reality TV series like *The Fairy Jobmother*, as well as comparable examples that purvey a similar discourse, such as the aforementioned *How the Other Half Live* and *Undercover Boss*, thus illustrate the continuation of what Ouellette and Hay call the "neoliberalization of social work through television."[39] This devolution of social work to producers of popular culture remains steadfast, even in the context of a recessionary culture in which it is ripe to be debunked.

The Fairy Jobmother negotiates recessionary cultural priorities alongside and in discursive tandem with some of the extant cultural priorities of neoliberal postfeminism. The series anchors its related discourses of gender and recession to the momentum of a thriving culture of reality TV. Specifically, it rigidly adheres to a number of extant tropes and devices of the format, already engaged in politically evasive social work. In this way, the potential for the discursive coherence of neoliberal postfeminism to be destabilized, by recessionary concerns that shed light on its political evasiveness, is offset by the sense of familiarity provided to the audiences by these well-worn tropes and devices.

As indicated earlier, *The Fairy Jobmother* is organized around the reality TV device of the "life intervention." The show conforms to Ouellette and Hay's outline of this reality TV template, which they break down into a series of stages. First the lifestyle expert (here Taylor) "arrives at the home, observes the family in their natural habitat, [and] diagnoses their problems."[40] Through its first season Taylor beds down in the homes of her job seekers so she can scrutinize them in their own environments, and thereafter find fault with anything and everything to do with their domestic self-governance: from pet care to grocery shopping habits, parenting styles, personal finances, hours kept, and, of course, job-seeking strategies. Following these initial observations, the lifestyle expert "introduces a set of rules, and sums up their new and improved lifestyle with a list of easy to memorise slogans."[41] For example, in an early episode Taylor bans the family dog from living areas, insisting that he be confined to the kitchen, and restricts the video gaming of twenty-year-old Stephen (who has never worked) to set times of the day and to a specific location in the home. Subject participants are encouraged to view their path to employment as a "Drive to Life," to believe that "positivity is the key to everything," and to buoy themselves up with self-empowerment rhetoric ("I am the man that *can*!"). Subsequently, the template involves the presentation of resistance as "cameras capture initial resentments."[42] Thus the job seekers resist Taylor's help; nineteen-year-old single mother Tammy, for example, rejects Taylor's proffered suggestions that work for which she is overqualified (as a crew member at McDonald's) is preferable to unemployment and state benefits: "I'm worth a lot more than that!" Tammy's adherence to a particular form of empowerment rhetoric is shown to have been misappropriated as a work avoidance strategy, ringing hollow in the context of reordered recessionary cultural priorities.

Gendering Recessionary Culture in *The Fairy Jobmother*

In one second-season episode, fifty-four-year-old Liverpudlian Dave jokingly dismisses Taylor's advice as the nagging of a "bossy woman." In this way, he speaks directly to the overdetermined gendered construction of her persona as a female authority figure elsewhere in the series, such as through camerawork and editing that fragments her body, emphasizing signifiers of her feminized authoritarianism (her high heels and neckerchief) and gendering the authority of her employment expertise, rendering her, to augment Weber's term, an affective dominatrix.

This signifies intertextually, not only in relation to Jo Frost's comparable *Supernanny* persona, as outlined above, but also via intertextual references to comparable popular cultural constructions of derogated female authority figureheads of politically evasive neoliberal social work, that situate Taylor and make her knowable in relation to a familiar frame of reference. Specifically, in the U.K. context the expert female self-help enabler is rendered grotesque, largely through the cross-dressing antics of male British sketch comedians Steve Pemberton as employment adviser "Pauline," and Matt Lucas as weight loss guru "Marjorie" in, respectively, the job seekers sketch in *The League of Gentlemen* (BBC, 1999–2002) and the fat fighters sketch in *Little Britain* (BBC, 2003–6). Both comically lampooned this figure prior to her reality TV manifestation as *The Fairy Jobmother*, which itself seems to knowingly deploy similar iconography and framing in its construction of Taylor's persona.

It is therefore possible that through this knowing wink to its U.K. audience, *The Fairy Jobmother* incorporates an element of veiled critique of its own problematic discourse of politically evasive neoliberal self-help, by ambivalently positioning the expert adviser as its mouthpiece, commensurate with Weber's argument that in makeover reality TV, "overbearing" figures of expert authority "are often subject to ridicule . . . turning viewers into advocates against authority, even as those viewers are eager to see subjects change."[43] This is certainly borne out in Internet user comments posted about Taylor, which read her as grotesque, one poster, for instance, referring to her as "a cow."[44]

Viewers might sympathize, up to a point, with the desire to use satire to demystify and disempower these figureheads of politically evasive neoliberal social work. However, it is nevertheless highly problematic, and symptomatic of the troublingly persistent misogyny that colors feelings about female authority in the British popular cultural imaginary, that dissatisfaction with the social and cultural impact of these figures is articulated in the form of grotesque caricatures of femininity. These figures are placed in superior socioeconomic positions to symbolically and literally disempowered men, commensurate with media framing of the economic downturn as a crisis of masculinity. These comedic takes on this figure perpetuate a cultural determinant to gender her as female, in line with the gendering of affective labor of the kind performed by Hayley Taylor, in culture and society more broadly.

Another way in which gendered recessionary culture is articulated in *The Fairy Jobmother* is via the discursive, if not quantitative, emphasis on the derogated masculinities of Taylor's male subject participants, which the series suggests have been compromised by the emasculating experience of unemployment. For example, Taylor requires twenty-year-old Stephen to find his masculinity before she is prepared to deem him "job ready," so she enrolls him in classes at a boxing gym; the aforementioned Dave's appeals to victim status place the blame for his long-term unemployment at the foot of the most maligned of female authority figures in the British cultural imaginary: Margaret Thatcher ("she ruined this country"). Dave's disdain for female authority is then transposed onto Taylor, as illustrated at the outset of this section. However, the most vivid example can be seen in Taylor's elicitation from subject participant Shakil Safir of an admission that he equates his state of unemployment with deficient masculinity, especially having ceded the role of principal breadwinner to his wife. He views his gendered self as a paterfamilias ("It's my responsibility to provide. . . . That's the biggest responsibility for any man") and his unemployment as a failure of his masculinity. The series overdetermines its framing of Shakil's unemployment as an abject emasculation by depicting him engaged in domestic labor, specifically cooking and ironing, the suggestion of course being that his joblessness has resulted in an obligation to perform women's work, which typifies how domestic sphere affective labor, notwithstanding feminist attempts to recuperate and equalize it, and postfeminist culture's tendency to fetishize or entrepreneurialize it, remains devalued. This is compounded in recessionary culture when labor must be seen to feed the economy at as little cost to it as possible, in the spirit of austerity. This accounts both for the workplace gender bifurcation that characterizes the subject participants' endpoints, and for the fact that Taylor frequently forces her male subject participants to stoically confront the possibility of performing service economy "women's work" in the public sphere, before they are granted the reward of a normatively gendered job. In this way Shakil, for example, must interview for a position as a receptionist before being granted his payoff: a normatively gendered position as a warehouse supervisor.

Notwithstanding the cultural tendency to gender the recession as a masculine crisis, one in which *The Fairy Jobmother* is complicit up to a point through its differently gendered treatments of its male and female subject participants, it is nevertheless the case that the series does at times tacitly flag the disproportionate impact of the recession on women. One way in which it does so is through its intermittent focus on jobless single motherhood, and its gestures toward the entrenched reactionary discourse circulating in the United Kingdom around single mothers as benefits claimants, that chime with the normalization of cultural disparagement of working-class femininities more broadly.[45] From her first appearance on *Benefit Busters*, Taylor forced her single mother subject participants to confront stereotypes that they "can't be bothered to work" and that they "stay at home using the kids as an excuse." She juxtaposes the perceptions they hold about themselves as benefits claimants with equally charged stereotypes of hoodie-wearing Staffordshire bull terrier dog owners smoking outside the United Kingdom's job centers, and this juxtaposition is reflected in the editing of this segment, which situates the women alongside the hoodies. She thus aligns these two differently culturally demarcated, but similarly vilified groups (single mothers and underclass youth) as comparable, amid protests of disavowal by the subject participants. She also makes direct references to the particular impact of new government welfare reform on single mothers, repeatedly reminding them of the new imperative to actively seek work when their youngest child turns seven. In this way *The Fairy Jobmother*'s treatment of unemployment points to particular cultural identity intersections of class and gender. More recently, the show has articulated such intersections with a bent toward profiling working-class women, seemingly acknowledging the extent to which the social power of jobless single mothers is doubly derogated. However, this ostensible focus on the plight of this particular demographic is a continuation of Taylor's strategies of "affective domination," deployed with a view to eliciting fear to spur these jobless single mothers into proactive self-governance, and not to unpack the inherent gender inequalities of welfare reform.

The fourth episode of the second season, first broadcast in June 2011, takes a more direct approach to pinpointing this demographic particularly affected by spiking unemployment, focusing exclusively on unemployed women and profiling an all-female group of subject participants. It points out that having risen sharply in the preceding year (to 1.04 million), unemployment among women in the United Kingdom was then the highest it had been in twenty years (since the early 1990s recession). Using voice-over narration, it cites these figures in an apparent concession to some of the gendered ramifications of recessionary unemployment, and seemingly with a view to highlighting the impact of the economic crisis on women. Nonetheless, in the long term it remains to be seen whether this acknowledgment of some of the gender-specific impacts of the recession is tokenistic and politically evasive. It seems telling that within the episode, the show reverted to the apolitical stance previously taken by Taylor. Typically, she dismissed the significance of contextual forces in favor of her individualistic empowerment rhetoric and neoliberal self-help strategizing in a way that appositely intersected with postfeminist discourse, when she urged the all-female group of subject participants in this episode to "empower" themselves. Thereafter, one of them, twenty-three-year-old Leanne, compliantly professed to feeling "like Superwoman now."

To summarize then, *The Fairy Jobmother* genders recessionary culture in a number of ways. It commodifies hitherto domestically located affective labor. Most prominently, this takes place through the figure of Taylor herself, whose overdetermined gendered authoritarianism is at once mobilized in efficacious service to neoliberal postfeminism and derogated for its hectoring of beleaguered masculinities. This gendering takes place further through the shepherding of stay-at-home mothers out of the domestic sphere and into public-sphere employment. The series frames the recessionary unemployment crisis as masculine through a discursive, if not quantitative, emphasis on the impact of unemployment on the masculine psyche, and it makes tacit and tokenistic gestures toward its impact on women. It facilitates the recuperation of masculinities that have been downtrodden by unemployment, by enabling the acquisition by subject participants of normatively masculine public-sphere employment, often having first required male subject participants to confront the possibility of symbolically feminine employment, in ultimately evasive gestures toward a labor market dominated by the service economy. All of this culminates in a vision of the contemporary British workplace characterized by recidivist gender bifurcation, where women clean, serve, and care for children, and men operate machinery, lift heavy loads, and build things.

At times, Taylor presents herself as openly complicit in the show's depoliticization of postrecession U.K. unemployment. In an online chat with viewers, she offers up the politically evasive statement, "I like work with the people and for the people. I don't have any political view other than look at the people and not the policys [sic]."[46] However, notwithstanding the apolitical stance she professes to take, it is nevertheless the case that, seemingly in a bid to play devil's advocate, she uses inflammatory headlines from the United Kingdom's most conservative newspapers to force her subject participants to respond to reactionary rhetoric that paints them as "work shy" malingerers.

According to the neoliberal cultural logic of lifestyle intervention reality TV, the dependency of the long-term unemployed on the state to provide benefits and thus extend social care can be transcended by willpower, choice, effort, determination, and positive thinking, as reflected in one of Taylor's favorite aphorisms: "Positivity is the key to everything." In the face of strong contextual socioeconomic forces, and manifest and mounting evidence to the contrary, she continues to willfully ignore the impact of the recession on employability and the job market with her mantras: "There *are* jobs out there" and "There is something out there for everyone if they search hard enough." The onus is thus on the subject participant to transcend the obstacles germane to the recessionary context and its intensified social inequalities. As Ouellette and Hay state, "there is no imperative within the 'can-do' political rationality of [lifestyle intervention reality TV] to move beyond individualized work on the self to strategize about structural and institutionalized experiences of sexism, racism, and economic exploitation."[47] *The Fairy Jobmother* thus contrives the necessity of Taylor's magically charged enactment of makeovers on the homes and exterior selves of her subject participants in a recession-era continuation of neoliberal postfeminist strategies of individuation, transformation, and processes of self-governance as disingenuously apolitical cure-alls for social derogation, subjugation, and marginalization.

The Fairy Jobmother presents itself as responding proactively to government interventions in state policy on unemployment benefits, but it proposes no solutions to U.K. unemployment, beyond the manifest inadequacy and ideological disingenuousness of individual self-governance. Nor does it imagine a scenario in which wider socioeconomic forces have the power to trounce either the individual's corrective self-governing actions or the efficacy of Taylor's affective labor in enabling them. Taylor herself attests to her belief that "the biggest barrier" preventing people from gaining employment "is a lack of self-belief," and if job seekers believe they can achieve, then they will, "without a shadow of a doubt."[48] She therefore openly disavows the impact of the recessionary contextual forces that caused rising rates of unemployment, enabling her cultural viability.

Neoliberal postfeminist reality TV like *The Fairy Jobmother* perpetuates and intensifies the extant discursive function of its format to deny the causal relationship between socioeconomic context, cultural identity, and the agency of the self, even in a recessionary culture that highlights the limitations of self-determination discourses. It recontextualizes familiar scenarios of makeover, consumption, and individual empowerment for a drastically different economic environment, enabling the perpetuation of a neoliberal discourse that views no contextual force or external factor as insurmountable, thus sidestepping any imperative to address the entrenched structural social inequalities of recession. Correspondingly, such reality television forms negotiate and qualify the renewed relevance of elements of postfeminist culture. In this way, tropes that might otherwise appear unattuned to shifted priorities in an age of austerity, such as acts of consumption and enactments of the makeover, are presented as means for individual transcendence of economic dire straits.

Notes

1. Some noteworthy examples of scholarship that interrogates articulations of postfeminism through reality TV include Banet-Weiser and Portwood-Stacer, "'I Just Want to Be Me Again'"; Cohan, "Queer Eye for the Straight Guise"; Taylor, *Single Women in Popular Culture*, 105–41; Weber, *Makeover TV*.

2. Discursive intersections between postfeminism and neoliberalism in reality TV are addressed in, for example, essays in Gill and Scharff, *New Femininities*, including Tincknell, "Scourging the Abject Body," and Press, "'Feminism? That's So Seventies'"; Ouellette and Hay, *Better Living through Reality TV*, 119–21; Doyle and Karl, "Shame on You," 86–88; Roberts, "The Fashion Police"; Taylor, *Single Women in Popular Culture*, 6–32; Weber, *Makeover TV*.

3. For discussions of reality TV's ubiquitous intersections of lifestyle media and celebrity expertise see, for example, Taylor, "From Ways of Life to Lifestyle"; Bonner, *Ordinary Television*, 83–88; Bell and Hollows, "Making Sense of Ordinary Lifestyles," 12–15; Weber, *Makeover TV*, 115–24; Powell and Prasad, "Life Swap"; Powell and Prasad, "'As Seen on TV'"; Lewis, *Smart Living*; Lewis, "Branding, Celebritization and the Lifestyle Expert"; Bennett, *Television Personalities*, 153–56.

4. Sullivan, "The End of Expertise?"

5. Raeside, "Celebrity Experts."

6. Powell and Prasad, "'As Seen on TV,'" 121.

7. Powell and Prasad, "'As Seen on TV,'" 121.

8. Negra, *What a Girl Wants?*, 86.

9. Negra, *What a Girl Wants?*, 102–7. On the bossy woman, Brunsdon, "Television Crime Series, Women Police, and Fuddy-Duddy Feminism," 18. Further, this figure is seen elsewhere in postfeminist media culture through the figure of the dominating female boss (or "bosszilla"), Levenson, *The Noughtie Girl's Guide to Feminism*, 70–72.

10. Negra, *What a Girl Wants?*, 107.

11. Negra, *What a Girl Wants?*, 14.

12. Tasker, "*Enchanted* (2007) by Postfeminism," 77.

13. As well as compulsorily gendering the outcome of Taylor's process, these flashforwards also do further ideological work to insist on the inherent resolvability of the hardships heretofore engendered by the participants' failures to self-govern. Taylor's process is thus almost always shown to have a successful outcome, and its success is generally made clear with respect both to participants' socioeconomic health and at

the level of affect, as they are shown to be better off financially and to be happier in employment than out of it. This neatly sidesteps the possibility that The Fairy Jobmother might be exposed as an example of what Anna McCarthy, in her theorization of governmentality and trauma in reality television, calls the "neoliberal theater of suffering," in which hardship is shown to be insurmountable. In this way, McCarthy argues, the participant's trauma is ongoing, beyond the disingenuously neat line drawn beneath it following the staged intervention of the reality TV producers. McCarthy, "Reality Television," 19–21.

14. Hochschild, The Managed Heart, x. Affective labor is characterized by Melissa Gregg as "work with an emotional, communicative or symbolic dimension" (Gregg, Work's Intimacy, 175); by Angela McRobbie as "work which requires high levels of intimacy, care, or emotions" (McRobbie, "Reflections on Feminism, Immaterial Labour and the Post-Fordist Regime," 62–63); and exemplified by Leopoldina Fortunati as "care labor, affection, consolation, psychological support . . . and communication" (Fortunati, "Immaterial Labor and Its Machinization," 140). What this reveals of course is the extent to which Taylor herself is an affective laborer, as each definition and explication of the concept corresponds to the work she does with her subject participants in the capacity of the Fairy Jobmother.

15. See for example, Allen, "Female Employment Hit by Public Sector Cuts and Childcare Costs"; Stewart, "More Women Join Dole Queue as Public Sector Cuts Bite"; Ball, Milmo, and Ferguson, "Half of UK's Young Black Males Are Unemployed"; UK Women's Budget Group, "The Impact on Women of the Coalition Spending Review 2010"; and Donald, "The Feminisation of Poverty and the Myth of the Welfare Queen," who highlights that in the postrecession U.K., "women are shouldering 70% of the budget cuts."

16. Palmer, "Governing Bodies," 69.

17. Tasker and Negra, "Introduction," 13.

18. Barbara Ehrenreich identified this turn in media culture in 2009, when she pointed to "the new media genre that's been called 'recession porn.'" Ehrenreich, "Too Poor to Make the News."

19. Buckman, "Recession TV."

20. Negra, What a Girl Wants?, 15–46. Fatherhood similarly recuperates the maligned masculinity of Gordon Gekko (Michael Douglas), popular culture's most iconic bogeyman of corporate greed in Wall Street's (1987) recessionary sequel Wall Street: Money Never Sleeps (2010).

21. BBC Press Office, "Stellar Cast in Freefall for Savage Drama from Origin Pictures for BBC Two."

22. Ehrenreich, "Too Poor to Make the News."

23. The extent to which downward mobility, in particular, has become an entrenched situational device in U.S. situation comedy since the recession was lampooned in the second episode of the second season of U.S./U.K. coproduction Episodes (BBC/Showtime, 2011–), in which a team of sitcom writers struggles to pitch a new idea that deviates from this recessionary premise.

24. Litt, "The 80s."

25. Biressi and Nunn, *Reality TV*, 95.

26. Weber, *Makeover TV*, 30.

27. As in the case of characters played by Ted Danson, Len Cariou, and John Goodman in the series *Damages* (FX, 2007–10; Audience Network, 2011–12) and Alan Alda in the film *Tower Heist* (2011).

28. "Colonial cringe" refers to postcolonial settler nations' cultural deference to an internalized perception, conscious or not, of the supposed superiority of the culture of colonial forebears.

29. Ouellette and Hay, *Better Living through Reality TV*, 194.

30. Aitkenhead, "Hayley Taylor."

31. Sands, "Single Mothers."

32. Ouellette and Hay, *Better Living through Reality TV*, 63.

33. Evaluating the British coalition government's welfare-to-work policy, which similarly subscribes to this neoliberal cultural logic, one journalist summarized it as follows: "The subtext is that external economic factors can never be the cause of someone's unemployment: the problem must somehow lie with the individual." Gentleman, "Rising Unemployment Puts Cameron's Work Programme in the Spotlight."

34. Weber, *Makeover TV*, 28.

35. For interrogations of neoliberal discourse and the "life intervention" format at work in *Supernanny* see, for example, Becker, " 'Help Is on the Way!' "; and Ouellette and Hay, *Better Living through Reality TV*, 93–98.

36. Weber, *Makeover TV*, 30.

37. Aitkenhead, "Hayley Taylor."

38. See, for example, Palmer, *Discipline and Liberty*; Becker; " 'Help Is on the Way!' "; Roberts, "The Fashion Police"; Ouellette and Hay, *Better Living through Reality TV*; Lewis, *Smart Living*; Hay and Ouellette, "Makeover Television, Governmentality and the 'Good' Citizen"; Weber, *Makeover TV*.

39. Ouellette and Hay, *Better Living through Reality TV*, 89.

40. Ouellette and Hay, *Better Living through Reality TV*, 89.

41. Ouellette and Hay, *Better Living through Reality TV*, 89.

42. Ouellette and Hay, *Better Living through Reality TV*, 89.

43. Weber, *Makeover TV*, 116.

44. Channel 4, "Fairy Jobmother/Interview Techniques/Channel 4."

45. See Skeggs, *Formations of Class and Gender*, 3; and Skeggs, *Class, Self, Culture*, 88–89.

46. Taylor, "Hayley's Advice."

47. Ouellette and Hay, *Better Living through Reality TV*, 84.

48. Taylor, "Live Chat with Hayley."

How Long Can the Party Last?
GENDERING THE EUROPEAN CRISIS ON REALITY TV

Europe's *Jersey Shore*

The U.K. reality program *My Big Fat Gypsy Wedding* aired in January 2011 to record ratings: the 6.4 million viewers of the first week increased to 8.7 million by the second, making the five-part series Channel 4's highest-rated factual program ever. The program's opening voice-over promised to take the audience behind the (wedding) veils of a hidden community, whose customs and secrets would finally be revealed. The teaser shown during the voice-over, however, portrayed a semitribal, fringe ethnic group, where girls are only interested in bizarre, gigantic wedding dresses and where boys have the right to grab girls and force them to yield to groping and kissing. Jes Wilkins, executive producer for Firecracker Films, who created the program, described the show as part of a documentary tradition with an educational purpose: "Eight million people are watching a quite serious documentary about women, domestic abuse," he said. "People are talking about things that would normally be seen by a tiny fraction of that audience."[1] The general effect of the show has been less one of enlightenment than of ethnophobia and class contempt, however. For the most part, it has confirmed audiences' already demeaning views of the group the title sums up as "Gypsies," who are mostly Irish Travellers and occasional Roma families on the show. According to a review of the first few episodes in the *Guardian*, racial slurs such as "pikeys" and "gypos" abounded in post-broadcast tweets. Typical responses ranged from mocking the Traveller girls' dresses to explicitly racist comments about lazy, thieving, irresponsible Gypsies.[2] Tina Flintoff, who commissioned the show for Channel 4, was baffled by these comments: "Some of the things we've seen on Twitter are absolutely terrible. But they're not to do with the programme. They're almost separate from the programme. These are people who have got axes to grind with Travellers and Gypsies."[3]

My starting point here is the contradiction that underscores media executives' statements about the show: they imply that the majority's views about a minority group are both untouched and heavily influenced by popular media. More specifically, negative views about Roma and Travellers are assumed already to exist separately from the groups' media representations. At the same time, Channel 4 supposedly creates accurate representations of this otherwise unknown and unseen community, which then actively influence the public's allegedly unchangeable views. Unpacking this contradiction is not a question of the naïveté or cynicism of television executives. After all, it does not take much persuasion to see that television programs, particularly reality shows that purport to document the lives of actual people, are social texts that tend to confirm existing sociopolitical relations. In fact, as Diane Negra and Yvonne Tasker argue, most of us gather what we know about economic and social change from a wide range of popular media forms that reach far beyond the news media commonly entrusted with providing objective information. Fictional media forms have been particularly effective at rationalizing the logic of inequality that propels neoliberal economies.[4]

Reality programs are especially important to scrutinize for the way in which they frame economic and political issues. *My Big Fat Gypsy Wedding* and popular reality programs like it activate a gendered synergy between the political management of the European debt crisis and its symbolic management in popular culture. They visualize the reasons and solutions for the current crisis of European identity and economy in ethnoracial, gendered, and class terms. They are particularly effective at justifying inequality from the allegedly neutral position of the observational documentary, in this case fortified by the educational remit of public service broadcasting.

More broadly, reality programs such as *My Big Fat Gypsy Wedding* participate in the large-scale culturalization of politics that has occurred since the late 1970s. Neoliberal states have gradually expanded the space of identity politics and multiculturalism to increasingly fragmented minority and marginal groups. Such cultural recognition has of course been one of the goals of the groups concerned, and is undoubtedly one of the positive outcomes of the civil rights and women's movements. However, such recognition has also been incorporated within neoliberal rhetoric. In the process, what Nancy

Fraser terms the politics of recognition has authorized a "post" thinking; if equality has been achieved, then antiracist and feminist politics are rendered unnecessary.[5] In turn, during the global neoliberal economy's recurring crises, the multicultural politics of recognition—seemingly the only available framework for politics—has been reassessed as indulgent, used as a platform to blame marginal groups for their own economic failure. As Alana Lentin and Gavan Titley claim in their analysis of the failure of European multiculturalism, "In an era of crisis, culture is all."[6] The recalibration of multiculturalism "as a dominant framework for understanding and responding to problems of power that were once considered political" accrues governmental power to culture.[7] For Stuart Hall this recalibration even extends to mobilizing nationalism in the service of market rationality. It engenders a contradictory alliance between neoliberal market rationality and the archaic emotional attachment to nationalism, justifying the "free market / strong state" model successfully implemented by Britain's Margaret Thatcher in the 1970s and 1980s. "Even today, the market / free enterprise / private property discourse persists cheek by jowl with older conservative attachments to nation, racial homogeneity, Empire and tradition."[8]

As I explore in the next two sections, *My Big Fat Gypsy Wedding* exemplifies how the culturalization of politics is reinforced at different, interconnected geopolitical levels. Most obviously, it has a specific national grounding in Britain in the context of official and popular discourses about "chav" classes, a British version of white trash.[9] The program's techniques of presentation and management are recognizable and translatable on a transnational scale as well, which is evidenced by the format's export to the United States, where TLC successfully adopted it with an American voice-over. The American adaptation—*My Big Fat American Gypsy Wedding*—was launched in the spring of 2012. Reality programs such as *My Big Fat Gypsy Wedding* effectively participate in confirming the global norms of consumer citizenship through marking out normative tastes and behaviors.

My main focus here is on a third, European geopolitical level. I analyze the way the program's apparent obsession with gender roles and fashion distracts from the politics of redistribution and contributes to the culturalization of politics through what Shannon Jones and Jelena Subotic call "everyday practices of Europeanization."[10] The Roma, a diverse European minority without a territorial state and thus without a legitimate national history, are the ideal scapegoats for representing and symbolically managing the economic and political crisis of the Eurozone. But the designation "Gypsy" has a more general reach than the European Roma. The show itself is only one of the most ambivalent and popular examples of recent European reality programming that "documents" the lives of working-class or underclass "trash," "chav," migrant, and immigrant Muslim or Eastern and Southern European groups. Rather than being the subjects of an educational ethnographic documentary, as Channel 4 would have it, "Gypsies" on the show act as placeholders for the European ethnic and class poor. The program is not interested in why the "Gypsies" are poor, why they feel the need to protect their ethnic identities from the national majority, or why they migrate when they do. Predictably, the reaction to My Big Fat Gypsy Wedding from Roma viewers and organizations has been outrage and protest.[11] It is not simply that the show confirms superficial views about "Gypsies," a term that most Roma groups find derogatory; more fundamentally, it shows no interest in who these people are. Ignoring the diversity of groups under this ethnic umbrella, the show focuses primarily on ethnically Irish Travellers whose mobile lifestyles differ significantly from those of most Roma, a diverse and transnational ethnic group, most of whom have been settled for centuries.

My Big Fat Gypsy Wedding's reality format offers a community-forming exercise of self-affirmation to the supposedly postracist European majority based on their shared distaste at the spectacle of the racialized, premodern underclass. At a time when the multicultural fantasy of Europe has been considered fulfilled—thanks to what Alain Badiou terms an "official politics of recognition"[12]—the flare-ups of the neoliberal free market's crisis justify as rightful crisis management exposing and symbolically expelling the unworthy "Gypsy" from the European family. Cultural representations align with a policy direction in the EU and within its member state governments that points to too much tolerance for the "Gypsies" as the problem of Europe. In contrast to the wasteful and excessive ways of "Gypsy" populations, "common European values"—framed as a unifying Christian heritage and national integrity—have reemerged without irony or much criticism. Those who do not share the newly recovered and neutralized "European way of life" are viewed as suspect.[13]

Gypsy Wedding serves as an eminent case study in which interlinked national, European, and global patterns of managing the economic crisis in the cultural realm manifest themselves simultaneously, foregrounding both the specificities and the mutual imbrication of these different registers. Its capacity to provide such a complex lesson rests on the shared element of crisis within neoliberal free-market economics and the anti-makeover reality format the show exemplifies. One of the most evident manifestations of the Europe-wide recession is the way crisis links economic and aesthetic patterns across national, regional, and global scales. Neoliberalism's diverse history is punctuated by cyclical economic crisis. Rather than marking the failure of free-market rationality, crisis is its sustaining element, the motor for its expansion and transformation.[14] Reality programs that revolve around a social cohort's failure have their own built-in "crisis structure," a pattern that maximizes entertainment value based on the generation of *Schadenfreude* and a corresponding audience sense of superiority and middle-class normativity.[15] In their introduction to this volume, Negra and Tasker reference the notorious reality series *Weg van Nederlands* (2011), which tests failed asylum seekers on their knowledge of Dutch culture. Similarly, Mattias Frey discusses Schadenfreude in relation to a slew of recent German reality shows that feature German families who emigrate to faraway countries. Such programs externalize a Europe-wide anxiety about *Überfremdung*, that is, the perceived dwindling of native, white, national populations and the proliferation of foreigners—an anxiety that is disproportionate to actual patterns of immigration. Drawing on John Portmann's work, Frey explains the consumption of Schadenfreude in economic terms: "At an historical point where another sort of credit has proved overdrawn . . . *Schadenfreude* is a symptom of the hopelessness that flourishes in times when the gap between the most and least successful is widest—and when the reminders of this disparity are most stark."[16]

While, as I elaborate in the next section, the ethnic and national implications of the European recession and the global financial meltdown are more evident and have been more consistently addressed, I want to uncover the largely unspoken gendered dimension that frames the ethnic poor's media depiction. In the central part of this chapter I discuss *Gypsy Wedding*'s and the entire reality format's obsession with weddings, girls' First Communions, and other highly gendered family rituals that are presented as pivots of ethnic tradition. As I show, the gendered focus of such programs is crucial to depoliticizing their justification of neoliberal inequality. I highlight the significant work that postfeminist assumptions do in generating Schadenfreude in the everyday mediating practices of establishing national and European standards of belonging.

Nancy Fraser's notion of "misframing," through which she explores the post–Cold War theoretical and political paralysis of feminism, is central to my argument here.[17] In the immediate post–World War II decades, feminists joined the New Left's radical efforts to transform the reigning economistic political imaginary and expose male dominance within the hidden personal realm. These efforts were resignified and incorporated into a culturalist imaginary in the following decades. Feminism's gradual reduction to identity politics was further facilitated by the decline of nation-based social democracy under pressure from global neoliberalism. Under these conditions, a culture-centered politics of recognition proved not only limited but also counterproductive. Much like other progressive social movements, feminism fell prey to a "tragic historical irony" by inadvertently trading attention to distribution for attention to recognition.[18] It neglected issues of political economy and geopolitical developments exactly at the time when free-market policies were normalized and fortified by right-wing chauvinism and nationalism in the wake of the fall of communism and the terrorist attacks of September 11, 2001.[19] "Effectively mesmerized by the politics of recognition, we unwittingly diverted feminist theory into culturalist channels at precisely the moment when circumstances required redoubled attention to the politics of redistribution," Fraser writes.[20]

The challenge and hope for feminism now is to change the frames that have limited feminist struggles. Besides reuniting recognition with redistribution and the politics of identity with struggles for social equality, feminists also need to shift attention from the geopolitical frame of the territorial nation-state. For Fraser the nation-state is "a major vehicle of injustice," which "partitions political space in ways that block many women from challenging the forces that oppress them. Channeling their claims into the domestic political spaces of relatively powerless, if not wholly failed, states, this frame insulates offshore powers from critique and control. Among those shielded from the reach of justice are more powerful predator states and transnational private powers, including foreign investors and creditors, international currency speculators, and transnational corporations. Also protected are the governance structures of the global economy, which set exploitative terms of interaction and then exempt them from democratic control."[21] The struggle against maldistribution and misrecognition can only succeed, then, if it is coupled with a struggle against misframing, which "arises when the state-territorial frame is imposed on transnational sources of injustice" and whose effect is to "gerrymander political space at the expense of the poor and despised, who are denied the chance to press transnational claims."[22] Changing the frame from the nation-state to the transnational politics of recognition and distribution is particularly relevant in the transnational space of the European Union, Fraser argues.

Many commentators and critics have identified at the core of Europe's ongoing crisis of identity and the EU's recent financial instability a "democratic deficit" that arises from misframing. Nation-states are no longer nodal points of the economy but are embedded in global markets; they are charged with offsetting the adverse social effects of a deregulated transnational economy on their populations despite efforts to transfer decision making from nation-states to intergovernmental commissions based in Brussels. Perhaps most famously, Jürgen Habermas has assessed the three major European responses that have been proposed to overcome this democratic deficit: the first one is a proglobalization route following the Chicago School's neoliberal orthodoxy of a self-regulating market. Such a direction would leave a "trail of tears" and present a grave danger to democratic self-determination, with "many marginalized lives [to] be cast by the wayside" and "many precious achievements of civilization [to] fall victim to 'creative destruction.'"[23] The second option is to fall back on democracy within the framework of the nation-state, lending "grist to the mill of ethnocentric reactions against diversity, xenophobic reactions against others, and antimodern reactions against the complexity of contemporary living conditions."[24] The third, in-between way, increasingly embraced by the EU and its national governments, is to apply social politics proactively, not so much to provide a safety net from the exploitative conditions of the globalized labor market as to train citizens to be entrepreneurial, competitive players. As Habermas summarizes: "The familiar maxim 'helping people to help themselves' still preserves the economistic sense of a fitness program designed to whip everyone into shape for assuming personal responsibility and developing the initiative for competent self-assertion in the market. 'Failures' can no longer count on help from the government."[25]

It is this in-between directive to "help people to help themselves" that *My Big Fat Gypsy Wedding* and European programs like it reinforce by telling the stories of groups who don't deserve help because they are unwilling to help themselves. If the program is an educational tool in any sense, it is one only insofar as it operates as a cautionary tale of what happens when people, or entire communities, refuse to get with the (fitness) program. My goal is not so much to criticize the show but to analyze how it foregrounds three major, paradigmatic misframing mechanisms within the sphere of popular media culture: First of all, it dismisses the need for a politics of redistribution by focusing on subjects undeserving of cultural recognition because they are unfit to form properly gendered families. Second, the transnational reality TV format allows the political and economic framework in which "Gypsies" are embedded to be left strategically vague. The "Gypsies" are no longer the state's responsibility and, since they are only to be blamed for their own failure, are rightly cast out as scapegoats for the economic crisis in the national, European, and global contexts at once. Third, the pretense of ethnographic observation directed at an ethnic community covers up the very gendered frame that makes the show function as a fitness program. Refocusing on this frame also brings into relief the extent to which a depoliticized, postfeminist culturalism is used, in a "tragic irony," precisely to justify inclusion and exclusion on an ethnicized class basis.

The PIGS and GIPS(I)s of Europe

As I write in the spring of 2013, the future of the European Union is uncertain. My purpose is not to engage in predictions or even to analyze the causes and consequences of the current recession. Rather, I consider the financial crisis an extraordinary historical event only to the extent that it crystallizes the cultural logic of the neoliberal economy and symptoms of Europe's much more enduring identity crisis, which also forces a reassessment of Europe's suppressed postcolonial baggage.

It is more than a coincidence in this regard that the television series considered here references in its title *My Big Fat Greek Wedding* (dir. Joel Zwick, 2002), a controversial film that celebrates the essentialized ethnonational characteristics of a Greek family in the guise of gentle mockery. Europe's monetary crisis has reopened the divide within the Eurozone between the core northwestern countries and the peripheral southeastern region. This division has been seized on by some European politicians pandering to their national constituencies in strikingly essentialist, ethnoracial terms, which construct a moral hierarchy between the two regions. Greece, the first country to threaten to default on its debt despite the €110 billion EU bailout package it received in 2010, has been blamed for excessive government spending, failing to meet the budget targets set as a condition of the bailout. In the summer of 2011, Italian, Spanish, and Irish debt spiked to the highest levels since the introduction of the euro. These once-booming economies are now threatened by default and forced by the EU to impose austerity measures. By contrast, countries such as Germany and France have reemerged as mature, responsible planners, who must reluctantly foot the bill to bail out their irresponsible peripheral Euro-partners.

One of the more radical proposals to put an end to the recession has been to shrink the Eurozone to include only the "surplus" countries and let go of Greece, Italy, Portugal, Spain, and Ireland, the debt-based states also collectively referred to as the PIGS or GIPSIs.[26] It is not a stretch to read into these acronyms: CNBC has also used the variation "GIPSI" precisely to mimic the word "Gypsy."[27] The widening continental rift between the "surplus" and "GIPSI" countries also maps onto and reinforces the long-term divide between Western and Eastern Europe, confirming the division between the core of Europe and its expanding, shifting peripheries that now incorporate post-socialist Gypsy states and crisis-ridden GIPSI states. When it comes to the latter, the Cold War only redrew a hierarchy that harks back to the Enlightenment, one which established Europe as the bedrock of rationality and democracy and generated tropes that linked Eastern Europe with Africa, Southeast Asia, and Latin America.[28] Larry Wolff famously retraced the history of Eastern Europe as a discursive construct whose roots go back two hundred years before the Cold War and Churchill's infamous Iron Curtain speech.[29] While civilization was firmly tied to the West, Eastern Europe shifted to an imaginary location somewhere in between civilization and barbarism, serving as the West's immediate and intermediary other. Although Eastern European cultures did not directly participate in actual territorial imperialism, the hierarchical division between the two Europes qualifies as an imperial order sustained through mutually constituting Eastern and Western discourses.[30]

The fall of the Iron Curtain renewed the discursive hierarchy between East and West under the guise of neoliberal free-market ideology. The majority of postsocialist populations have been designated the losers of capitalism, who are themselves to be blamed for their immobility and incapacity.[31] The EU expansion in the mid-2000s has not eliminated an ensuing sense of inferiority and resentment, further whipped up by right-wing nationalistic regimes. Nativist nationalism festers beneath the official European rhetoric of a swift generational change, which supposedly creates brand-new postsocialist citizens for whom democracy and market rationality are second nature.[32] József Böröcz claims that, despite the EU's pledge to extend the four freedoms (of labor, capital, goods, and services) to all its citizens, the hierarchy between the former imperial powers and the peripheral newcomers is unmistakable; unequal and unidirectional economic flows have characterized the privatization of postsocialist government assets. Tax incentives have been created to lure foreign direct investment, and new policies have allowed the draining of national wealth from new member states. EU-based corporations are the most prominent investors in the newly accessed states while Eastern companies have very small investment portfolios. Geopolitical power remains concentrated in the Western center, and technologies of Foucauldian governmentality are being deployed to normalize, standardize, and control the operation of postsocialist states. The EU's eastern expansion thus combines state coloniality with a civilizing mission that features low-level violence.[33] Negative stereotypes and discourses of backwardness flourish, not despite, but because of the absence of a fully processed intra-European colonial history.[34] The financial crisis has only deepened what has been described as mutual disappointment in this encounter: the EU core sought to "normalize" and discipline the postsocialist countries, to turn them into functioning neoliberal democracies by external control, on condition of a promise to "behave." Instead, the new democracies refused to be disciplined, proved skeptical of the EU's intentions to open them up as new markets, and fell back on populist nationalisms. Conversely, postsocialist populations wanted prosperity, access to markets, and general welfare instead of another imposed rule of law.[35]

Thus, the crisis of the Eurozone—from which most postsocialist EU members are actually excluded—is managed on well-cultivated ideological soil, where the PIGS or GIPSIs have simply drifted farther east, away from the civilized, fiscally responsible Euro-core. Fear of default within the Eurozone has only compounded existing anxieties about immigrants and job seekers from postsocialist countries, and has led to the erection of walls around a Fortress Europe of ethnic nationalisms in the West. The integration of the union in economic terms has not been paralleled by a political integration, evident in the core states' repeated refusal to ratify a European constitution. Worse, politicians are compelled to appeal to their national voters in order to get elected, which they often do by exploiting the national-supranational divide and supporting popular nationalistic positions against the EU.[36]

The recession has shifted Europe to the right, in the process lending support to ultranationalist movements; a similar shift has taken place in the United States, notably with the emergence of the Tea Party movement. Predictably, nationalist parties and other political groups have consistently blamed immigrants and ethnic "aliens" for siphoning off jobs and welfare. The Roma, the largest European minority and the only one officially designated as such, consists of the poorest and most despised populations, who have been prime targets of intimidation, discrimination, violent expulsion, terror attacks, and murder across Europe. In some areas of Eastern and Central Europe, Roma populations have experienced 100 percent unemployment after the loss of heavy-industry jobs and the consolidation of the political right. Anti-Roma attacks, increasingly frequent since the early 1990s, grew into paramilitary mobilization as the economic crisis deepened in the 2000s. Political parties such as Jobbik in Hungary, Ataka in Bulgaria, Delnicka Strana in the Czech Republic, Jörg Haider's para-Nazist "Freedom Party" in Austria, and Lega Nord in Italy have organized armed groups, supposedly to "curb Gypsy crime" by patroling Roma neighborhoods and staging threatening military marches. In 2004, for the first time since the end of communism, the Slovak government deployed its army against "Gypsy unrest." The populist Hungarian Jobbik (literally, "more right") party describes the country as "torn by Hungarian-Gypsy civil war."[37] In Italy, Roma refugee camps (*campi nomadi*) have been targets of increasing mob violence. In 2007, several large Italian cities signed a security pact to deal with the "public emergency" presented by Roma "nomads."[38] In an incident that made international news, in the summer of 2010 French President Nicolas Sarkozy engaged in a systematic campaign to expel Bulgarian and Romanian Roma as a national security threat.[39]

The "Roma issue" has become entangled in the shuffle between national and supranational governance. As a transnational minority group with no nation-state to speak for them, the Roma have been fair game. Their elevation to "European" status has also brought mixed results for the Roma. It is true, as Huub van Baar suggests, that neoliberal governmentality practices have at times produced what Foucault calls "counter products," which often reverse power relations. These have strengthened Roma self-governance and energized activism in local communities. Acknowledgment as a European minority has also given various Roma actors agency to contribute to and even contest European master narratives.[40] Since the 1990s, the Roma have been targeted by the inclusion programs of various organizations, including the Open Society Institute's Decade Action Plans, the World Bank, and the Organization for Security and Cooperation in Europe, as well as by nongovernmental organizations and by governments.[41] Of course, the ambition to manage the Roma at several levels at once did not come out of the blue. Rather, such initiatives follow previous assimilation programs, which have been on European imperial and national agendas since the seventeenth century. Socialist governments also engaged in reeducation, health, "antinomadism," resettlement, and other programs, paralleled by Western governments' efforts to improve the lives of the Roma during the Cold War. But the EU only developed specific minority policies in the 1990s, in advance of its eastward expansion. As I have suggested, this was also the decade that saw the reemergence of Europe-wide violence against the Roma, when the "Roma problem" began to be framed as a problem of security within Europe.[42]

Van Baar writes that "Roma governmentality" as part of wider practices that involve private-public partnerships that depoliticize issues, that is, "remove [them] from the legitimate domain of politics and render them subjects of 'problematization' by experts."[43] At the heart of Roma governmentality is the notion of "good governance" introduced by the World Bank in the 1990s, which, ideally, promotes the horizontalization and dispersion of governance.[44] In reality, practices of neoliberal governmentality tend to reduce democratic participation to individual responsibility and consumer action. They promote a social inclusion agenda instead of a participatory democratic inclusion. Historically ingrained problems of marginalization are reduced to questions of decency and morality, to be resolved by the Roma themselves.[45]

Far from "educating" the public about Gypsy ways, *My Big Fat Gypsy Wedding* uses the dual cover of public service broadcasting and factual programming to legitimize ethnophobic and racist views in a way that is at once national and European in scale but is also easily translated into a global neoliberal rhetoric of proper consumer values and behavior. In Eastern Europe the Roma have long played a central role in symbolically bridging the political-economic and cultural spheres, a role often downplayed or disavowed by politicians, economists, and media professionals alike. The fact that "Gypsies" have been discovered by the British broadcaster Channel 4 as well as other channels in both the United Kingdom and Ireland (see introduction, this volume) signals a new stage in the crisis of the European economic zone and the EU's efforts to build supranational European identities in the face of increasing ethnic nationalisms. While several successful and controversial reality programs have been launched in Eastern Europe about Roma characters and lifestyles, *My Big Fat Gypsy Wedding* is the first widely available, English-speaking program to do so, affirming in the realm of popular culture that the "Roma problem" is a problem of Europe.[46]

Rather than "discovering" a formerly unknown community, however, the show's creators have rediscovered and reproduced the full set of racist and orientalist discourses that have accumulated around the "Gypsy" in the past three hundred years: a suspiciously mobile, secretive, parasitic community keeping to premodern traditions, prone to waste, excessive reproduction, and crime, and resistant to education, self-improvement, and nation-forming.[47] Reality television, more than any other form of popular media, has been instrumental in recalibrating this underlying racist-imperialist discourse in the updated, ethically neutralizing language of market rationality. As I elaborate in the rest of the chapter, zooming in on gendered family rituals that isolate and attach to the "Gypsies" of Europe the excesses of postfeminist consumerism is key to erecting an essentialist wall around proper European family membership within popular culture.

This larger European context charges with ominous significance the question with which the voice-over of *My Big Fat Gypsy Wedding*'s first episode ends the promo sequence: "How long can the party last?" The question comes after a teaser sequence of highlights from the show: absurdly large, overdecorated dresses, a group of stocky men hovering threateningly in undershirts, teen boys forcing themselves on girls and then brutally kicking someone in a fight, an old lady being dragged through the mud while a woman screams, and finally girls with bare midriffs and short shorts jumping merrily into a pool. Each image adds a piece of the mosaic that neoliberal rhetoric, in the context of both nation-states and the EU, insistently identifies as the problem that led to the crisis: the giant (overdetermined) bridal dress itself, around which much of the show revolves, operates as a material representation of feminized waste and of living on borrowed money. The blatant inequality of the sexes evokes a semitribal condition, where men are unreformed sexists and women have been untouched by the advances of feminism and are therefore unworthy of the benefits of postfeminism.

Gypsy Postfeminists

The first episode of *My Big Fat Gypsy Wedding*, "Born to Be Wed" (January 18, 2011), follows Josie, a sixteen-year-old Traveller girl, who is to marry her fiancé of four months, a burly farm laborer (figure 10.1). During the days leading up to her wedding, Josie is seen going out with her girlfriends and mother, all in highly revealing outfits, and gyrating provocatively to music in a bar. Most girls, the voice-over narrator (Barbara Flynn) explains to us, drop out of school early to care for the household and their "enormous families." Josie, the eldest of nine siblings, left school at age eleven. The program's in-show expert is dressmaker Thelma Madine, qualified as an ethnographic guide by virtue of making the Travellers' wedding and First Communion dresses. Madine reveals early on that she thought at first that the teen brides were prostitutes. She later establishes that Travellers in fact have strict morals, which keep the girls and boys separate until they marry. Madine's assessment of this apparent contradiction is that they are "stuck in a time warp."

The show sustains the illusion of political neutrality and educational intent by wrapping itself quite literally in wedding dresses and gendered domestic affairs that stand in for tradition. "Gypsy ways" are reduced to the curious ways of being men and women, roles around which "Gypsy" lives entirely revolve, according to the program's selective attention. This attention spills into the media hype about the program's real-life participants, which is characterized by the same sarcastic tone applied to the Kardashian sisters or Snooki from *Jersey Shore*: viewers and commentators share a wink about the clueless reality starlet, who alone doesn't realize the emperor has no clothes — or, in this case, that her clothes are too large. The *Daily Mirror* comments that Josie and husband Swanley appeared at the National Television Awards ceremony in January 2012, where they were "one of the most dressed up couples . . . looking a little alarmed with all the attention they were getting on the red carpet." According to the "awkward interview" Josie gave, her dress "was custom made by 'some lady in Finchley' — not the nice blonde one off the telly who always cries." She has also "gone on to have a baby (which she called, um, Josie)."[48] The *Sun*, among other tabloids, followed up with a piece on baby Josie, who apparently "has a wardrobe to rival Harper Seven Beckham's, and she already wears diamond bling ear-rings plus lipgloss and mascara."[49]

The "Gypsies" featured on the show fail as national and European subjects in the first place because they fail as gendered consumers. When it comes to

FIGURE 10.1. Sixteen-year-old Traveller girl Josie and her new husband Swanley, the couple in the center of the first episode of Channel 4's *My Big Fat Gypsy Wedding*, were to become returning tabloid personalities in the following months.

wedding or other party dresses, the only principle is "the bigger the better." Every episode's centerpiece is a Christmas tree–like wedding dress adorned with frills and bling, whose value is measured by its size, weight, and the battle scars it leaves on the body. Often, the dresses and the stories of the brides' wedding preparations are intercut with young Traveller girls' preparations for their First Communions or birthday parties. Foregrounding the parallels between these alternating storylines makes the teen brides appear childish and immature while it makes the younger girls appear as oversexualized miniature adults. Both age groups wear two distinct kinds of clothing for much of the series: the enormous, blinged-out wedding dresses and skimpy party outfits that leave little to the imagination (figure 10.2).

What a commentator calls the "Munchkin strip club" of young girls, in particular, while bracketed on the show as "tradition," plays on existing public alarm about the sexualization of young and teen girls, who are routinely treated as victims in government and media reports, routinely ignoring feminist ethnographic research on media.[50] Drawing a consistent parallel between the unwholesome gender training of precocious girls and teen brides also isolates two of the most criticized aspects of postfeminism: its frequent collapsing of female empowerment into consumer choices and sexuality; and its simultaneous push for women to return to the home. On the program, these controversial dimensions of postfeminism are magnified into allegorical images of absurd clothing: the gigantic wedding dress and the provocative party outfit, respectively. The affective reactions elicited by the relentless focus on these two different kinds of attire crystallize a misunderstanding of

FIGURE 10.2. Preteen Traveller and Gypsy girls are regularly featured on *My Big Fat Gypsy Wedding* in skimpy party outfits, implying a grotesque misappropriation of postfeminist empowerment on the part of ethnicized families.

both wedded domesticity and empowering sexuality on the part of "Gypsy" women. What are in fact the very problems with postfeminist politics are thus recalibrated as grotesque misappropriations of postfeminism and deferred to ethnicized, migrant women and their alien "tradition."

My Big Fat Gypsy Wedding provides ample evidence of Madine's evaluation that (female) Travellers are "stuck in a time warp": on the one hand, they are apparently left behind in a prefeminist era, willingly sacrificing their intellectual potential and labor in the service of ne'er-do-well boy-men. On the other hand, when they do engage in self-care and self-improvement, they do so in a tasteless, voracious fashion, with disastrous results. In essence, their excess makes a mockery of the careful balance within postfeminist female selfhood between a sacrificial return to traditional female roles and the ongoing display of narcissistic self-care. Rather than exposing the contradiction at the core of the postfeminist mantra of "having it all," its failure is blamed on the "Gypsy way of life" and on "Gypsy" women's failure to "choose" more enlightened ways of being women.[51]

Within the British context, such a coding of failed femininity is also readable within the more specific interpretive framework of "celebrity chav" discourses. Imogen Tyler and Bruce Bennett show that such discourses have circulated pathologized femininities around the grotesque, carnivalesque figures of reality TV celetoids such as Kerry Katona and Jade Goody. The so-called celebrity chav has released, justified, and mobilized middle-class community forming around hatred for the bad object that is the chav, who is primarily identified by her excessive and vulgar consumer choices.[52] Tyler argues that chav femininity is read as a drag act marked by an inability to pass and a failure to perform femininity appropriately. She traces the trajectory of the chav female back to the Edwardian notion of the great unwashed, the libidinal excess of the dirty underclass:

> The emergence of these figures is always expressive of an underlying social crisis or anxiety: these figures are mobilised in ways that attribute superior forms of social capital to the subject positions and social groups they are explicitly or implicitly differentiated from. In terms of classed identities, we can understand the emergence of the chav figure as an intrinsic part of the larger process of "class making" which attempts to distinguish the white upper and middle classes from the white poor. These processes of class differentiation are particularly fraught within a social and political present in which some of the traditional markers of class difference, such as access to branded consumer goods and access to higher education, have been eroded. . . . The chav figure should also be understood in the context of deepening economic inequality and class polarization in Britain.[53]

The disgust that motivates "class making" as the chav figure moves through various media representations also authorizes overt "class naming" in media accounts, in which "class differences are not seen as irrelevant, outmoded or shameful to articulate but are openly and aggressively explored through virulent unapologetic stereotyping."[54] Such widespread accounts openly celebrate the new class snobbery as a socially necessary release and a compensation for middle-class injury, in what Tyler calls a "perverse appropriation of identity politics."[55]

At the same time, the abject figure of the British "chav" easily morphs into the European "Gypsy" character on a shared transnational platform saturated with discourses of social racism or what Lentin and Titley call "race talk," conjuring up a long history of constructing undeserving welfare recipients and illegal immigrants as threats to society.[56] In the second episode of *Gypsy Wedding*, seventeen-year-old barmaid Sam, a non-Traveller girl, prepares for her wedding to twenty-year-old Traveller with a mullet haircut, Pat. Dressmaker Madine explains, "If an outsider is married into the Gypsy community, they are expected to discard their own lifestyles and adopt Gypsy ways." As before, these Gypsy ways evidently consist of layers of makeup, spray-on tan, and an electric "frock horror" of a dress described by a commentator thus: "Walking down the aisle, Sam looked like a day-glo cross between a Christmas tree and a crochet toilet-roll holder."[57]

Unlike other bridal reality shows, the ritual moment of the big reveal, when the bride and her mother Linda view the larger-than-life dress for the first time, is set up to evoke mocking disgust. With her platinum blonde hair, unnaturally darkened skin hue, prominent tattoos, and an oversized cross hanging from her neck, Linda looks like she is in drag. When Sam tries on the gown and is finally revealed as a bride for the first time, Linda's reaction, "Sam is gorgeous," sounds like a joke since her daughter is barely visible in what looks like a grotesque, fluffy, illuminated pink cloud in the middle of the darkened room. Through the excess produced in the wrong hands, the wedding dress, which is a crucial instrument in proving one's normative middle-class femininity as both a memorable and individualized consumer item and a symbol of entry into marriage, is turned into a sign of failure, a desperate attempt at passing as a woman.

In another rite of passage that is supposed to transform Sam into a proper Gypsy bride, she and Pat go shopping for a mobile home. The godlike voice of the narrator explains, as if this were a neutral piece of information, that they are looking for a very specific caravan, one without a toilet. Pat comments that Gypsies consider a flush toilet unclean and prefer to use one outside. Clearly, what Sam is demonstrating here is a regression away from rather than progression toward middle-class femininity: from education to domestic slavery, from taste to kitsch, from living in a house to shifty mobility, and, most disgusting of all, from modern sanitation to squalor. Sam and Linda are crossover figures who highlight the continuity between white chavs and Gypsies by their failure to behave like proper women.

To hammer home the point, throughout the episode, the invisible male interviewer keeps pressing Sam to confess to fears of being judged for "going Traveller." During one of these interrogations, while her bridesmaids are trying on corsets, Sam declares, "I don't care because, at the end of the day, I love him and he loves me." The camera cuts to Pat sitting next to Sam in apparent discomfort. Since they are both depicted as young, uneducated, and generally clueless, the insistence on love as the glue to their marriage rings hollow and intimates eventual disaster.

The effect is enhanced by the fact that, unlike on other reality shows that revolve around families, no effort is made to observe the couple and their broader communities in the course of everyday practices that would create a sense of intimacy. For instance, the program contrasts sharply with another one of Channel 4's shows, The Family, an update of sorts of a twelve-part 1974 BBC One program of the same title, which is about the everyday life of a working-class family, itself inspired by the American PBS series An American Family (1973). In the contemporary Channel 4 series, the Hughes family's everyday activities model "the new social family of late modernity."[58] While the Hugheses display a fairly traditional family structure, in their everyday lives relationships and gendered domestic roles are more fluid and permeated by moments of love and intimacy, which gives the show a fly-on-the-wall authenticity and produces a "loose definition of what it is to be family."[59] All three of these white-family shows follow the observational documentary method, employing increasingly sophisticated surveillance technologies.

My Big Fat Gypsy Wedding, by contrast, is meticulously choreographed, suggestively edited, and framed by the voice of a godlike narrator. One gets the impression that all of "Gypsy" life is made up of life-changing family events defined by strict rules of gendered behavior. "Gypsies" are enwrapped in "Gypsy tradition" all the time.

However, the invisible narrator's sanctimonious commentary about Traveller tradition can only be read ironically as the images that are supposed to conjure up something as venerable as "tradition" reveal very familiar "chav" and "Gypsy" class behavior. Tradition seems to equal lower-class speech habits, caked-on makeup, spray tans, breast implants, inappropriate dressing, general lack of style and taste, suspicious mobility with an implied lack of work ethic and reliability, criminal behavior among the men—horse cart races, bare-knuckle fights, and violent family mafias—and an absolute gender hierarchy within the household. To enhance the ironic effect, most of the shocking stories are introduced by whimsical music on the soundtrack, as if to undercut empathy and suggest that one is not supposed to take any of it seriously.

The maintenance of an ironic distance between commentary and spectacle is particularly apparent in the show's token efforts at drawing an actual socioeconomic context around Traveller and Roma lives. In the second episode, which features Pat and Sam's wedding, the narrator touches on the Dale Farm evictions, the British government's 2011 initiative to dismantle the largest Traveller community in a protracted legal battle that involved state as well as local authorities.[60] But rather than spending any time discussing the history of Dale Farm, the storyline turns toward the "last party" held there as the residents wait for the eviction notice. The party is organized by Margaret in honor of her six-year-old granddaughter Mary Ann's First Communion. Dale Farm is then swiftly reduced to a background to the usual scenario: the little girl's preparation for the event, including her first ritual spray tan, a brief glimpse of the church ceremony itself, where the Traveller girls' over-the-top outfits shock the regular middle-class Catholic crowd, and a postceremony reveal of Mary Ann's injuries from wearing the heavy dress, followed by the little girls' transformation into miniature strippers. The segment ends with a wild party held while the group is allegedly waiting for the bailiff to deliver the eviction notice, significantly tipping the balance back from sympathy to Schadenfreude.

As a reality show that pivots around dresses, reveals, and life-changing rituals, *Gypsy Wedding* exhibits a strong structural affinity with the makeover subgenre. It has been argued that the televisual makeover paradigm show-cases how government has been dispersed into practices of governmentality and has featured prominently in discussions about class, gender, and emotional labor within "postwelfare" states.[61] Makeovers have been said to demonstrate neoliberal "responsibilization," in Nikolas Rose's famous phrase, by adopting a normative middle-class viewpoint and making abnormal subjects endure a set of disciplining rituals supervised by an army of experts, at the end of which they emerge trained and transformed.[62] Makeover television offers a "decentralized network of entrepreneurial ventures" purporting to teach personal responsibility and demonstrate how to acquire economic and cultural capital.[63] Makeover formats specialize in identifying good middle-class subjects and disciplining, transforming, shaming, and punishing those whose refusal to improve their own behavior incurs costs to the nation.[64]

But the makeover paradigm is also recast ironically here as a formula that the participants fail to perform. On regular makeover formats such as *What Not to Wear* (BBC Two, 2001), *Wife Swap* (ABC, 2004), or *Extreme Makeover* (ABC, 2002), participants reach an emotionally charged turning point that at least promises a lifestyle change, whose evidence is often revisited and confirmed in "after-the-show" segments. The network TLC embeds *My Big Fat Gypsy Wedding* and *My Big Fat American Gypsy Wedding* in a programming block of female lifestyle programs including wedding shows. But even on programs such as *Brides of Beverly Hills* (TLC, 2011), the initial dramatic roadblocks, mostly disagreements among the key players about style choices, are resolved by the time of the wedding, which delivers a fashion-show-like display bursting with the promise of a happy middle-class marriage. By contrast, Gypsy weddings are too "fat," too excessive to succeed from the start. They spell disaster instead of a makeover. Gypsies are unfit for training and improvement.

This fixed condition, being stuck in tradition, is confirmed through the impermeable gender roles that form iron fences around the community. The narrator promises in her introductory monologue to the third episode of *Gypsy Wedding*, called "Desperate Housewives," "Today we're going to reveal what it's really like to be a Traveller woman before, during and after her wedding day." A cut to a teen bride follows, who comments with conviction, "We ain't going to be doctors or lawyers. Housewives: that's what we're going to be." The final snippet of the sequence features boys forcefully dragging girls away from the house, and an interview sound bite describing how they force a kiss from girls. As the show begins, over playful tango music, the narrator ominously announces, "But behind the petticoats lies a *very* different story." Expert Thelma Madine affirms this by declaring that Traveller girls are second-class citizens. The ensuing storyline sets up a contrast between two teens: eighteen-year-old Lizzie, who was removed from school at thirteen so that she could take care of her four siblings and the household and has to ask for permission for every little thing while her male siblings roam free; and sixteen-year-old Martin, who lives in his own caravan next to his parents' chalet while his mother and sister do the cooking and cleaning for him. He is featured among male buddies, playing a video game.

In effect, rather than offering hope for improvement, *My Big Fat Gypsy Wedding* is an "anti-makeover" show. Instead of eliciting empathy for its subjects to complement the inevitable Schadenfreude, the pleasure of the show is in shared disgust and horror about the failure to transform. Beverly Skeggs and Helen Wood's explanation of the anti-makeover show's mechanism applies here precisely:

> There are also programmes where the potential for redemption is not available. In opposition to the ethical self that can transform, tell and show its moral worth, is the self that does not know how to tell or display itself correctly and cannot claim or profess propriety. Instead it displays "diseases of the will" . . . failures of responsible self-control by those who do not know how to behave and provide a spectacle of subjectivity turned sour. . . . Rather, an ethnographic display of unmediated, unknowing, bad choice culture is displayed to demonstrate working-class limits to propriety whilst providing visual sexual images for voyeurs. The selfhood displayed is not part of the individual reflexive biography project identified by Giddens; it cannot be rationalised by the ethical scenarios of good choice and transformation. Excessive behaviour and ways of telling and displaying oneself inappropriately are not reflected-on or transformative, but rather reflect the lack of taste, pathological culture and "bad choice" in which the subjects are displayed with no possibility of redemption.[65]

But, as June Deery shows, while anti-makeover programs typically individualize and decontextualize failed bodies, in this case the bodies are locked in the essentialized cage of tradition without much individual agency.[66] When they do break out of the "Gypsy" tradition, they are simply reduced to "chav" status. This is demonstrated in episode thirteen, "Reputation Is Everything," in the story of twenty-six-year-old unwed Traveller mother Pricilla, who had four children with two different men, the latter of whom, her fiancé, is a non-

Traveller. In the course of the episode, she goes out with girlfriends, all fully corseted and high heeled, for a bachelorette party. Then, to complete her wedding preparation, she travels to Poland for what turns out to be her second discounted breast enlargement and tummy tuck, leaving her fiancé in charge of her young children. When we next see her after the commercial, the fiancé has left her and she has moved out of her house and into a hotel with the kids.

Although it deserves a separate discussion, it is instructive briefly to compare the original Channel 4 version of the show with its run on TLC (2011) and the format's American spinoff, *My Big Fat American Gypsy Wedding* (2012). That the program can travel with such ease and generate similar viewer reactions along its journey confirms the fact that the economic crisis and the neoliberal management techniques it has engendered are global in scale. Even though Gypsies are mostly known from movies and fairy tales in the United States, the postfeminist management of the crisis resonates as a crucial element of neutralizing and rendering transparent the links between neoliberal governmentality and popular media entertainment. The allegedly neutral terrain of "factual" entertainment allows for assigning blame to the "lazy," "useless," "criminal," "fringe," "immigrant" element, who are racially and culturally distinguished from the desirable middle class and its morality. The analogy was recognized by viewers of the TLC version. Many have compared the show to the MTV reality program *Jersey Shore* (2009–12), which stirred controversy for perpetuating negative stereotypes of Italian Americans. A reviewer writes,

> To watch *My Big Fat Gypsy Wedding* is to see Travellers and Roma as uneducated, flashy, and closed-minded people who live in mobile-home parks and throw enormous parties. This was easily confirmed on Twitter Sunday night, as viewers called the show "crazy" and "a trainwreck," and referred to the women on it as "whores" and "hookers." The show's representation of its subjects was best summarized by one viewer who tweeted, "So far they get married @ 16, live in trailers & dress like sluts." The truth about Travellers and Roma, however, is infinitely complex—and both Channel 4 and TLC have wronged these communities, as well as the show's viewers, by failing to tell it. As a tweet summed up the educational import of the show about "the Roma's plight," "I now understand why all of Europe hates gypsys [sic]."[67]

However, the comparison also highlights the European, as well as the specifically British, aspects of crisis management. *Jersey Shore* has been argued to provide not so much a portrayal of working-class Italian Americans as a "fantasy of ethnicity" transplanted to New Jersey, a place where the housing crisis has, in fact, chased away even the last token members of the working class and where property values and taxes are some of the highest in the United States.[68]

The same fantasy of ethnicity also underscores *My Big Fat American Gypsy Wedding*, where the "Romany" families seem to be produced by the performative force of the television format itself. The creators even managed to locate a local Thelma Madine, a dressmaker in Boston who is called upon to create the giant dresses. If it weren't for the format established by the original series, the families on the show would be recognized as quite ordinary "white trash" from poor Southeastern regions of the United States. This performativity is different from that associated with the socioeconomic charge of the term "Gypsy" in post–Cold War Europe. It also returns us to the specifically European role of nationalism and the nation-state in misframing the feminist politics of redistribution as the politics of identity.

Misframing and Representation

The family rituals featured on *Gypsy Wedding* signify beyond the Gypsy families: they prove the failure of certain groups to become part of the British national family and the European Union's multicultural family. The "Gypsies" of the show, in fact, act as scapegoats who are blamed for the friction between national and European families, which have so far failed to integrate. Despite the European Union's efforts to manufacture a European identity and sense of belonging, an EU-level public sphere has not materialized. The deepening of the economic recession has further jeopardized the European public sphere, the very notion of which tends to make citizens "bored and angry."[69] European politicians are reluctant to risk their jobs by throwing support behind integration. At the same time, just like during the Weimar Republic in 1920s Germany, states have fallen back on nationalism, the "next-door neighbour of selfishness and self-interest."[70] Nationalism is fostered by political ineffectiveness and an economically strapped middle class who, even in the "surplus" countries, "no longer think solidarity is something they can afford."[71] The compression of the public sphere as a medium for dialogue and compromise leads to political fragmentation and extremism, which is evident in the rise of xenophobia and chauvinism in Europe and the United States alike.[72]

In the absence of European-level television beyond top-down efforts that most Europeans regard as feeble and inorganic Brussels propaganda, national, television-mediated public spheres have taken on the role of "speaking honestly" about Euro-citizens' actual frustrations. These frustrations are projected onto Gypsies and Travellers, who live in premodern family structures, are wasteful, drain public resources, and refuse to integrate. I have discussed *My Big Fat Gypsy Wedding* as a particularly revealing case study that demonstrates instances of misframing that characterize the neoliberal politics of the "post."

Analyzing popular media representations may be seen as a limited enterprise or even as part of the problem since the "representational turn" that so enriched academic cultural studies was also instrumental in the co-optation of identity politics by neoliberal states and corporations. Yet I believe that it is crucial to understand how the politics of representation operates in an era when popular culture is one of the main conduits of politics. Moreover, I want to align my efforts with Nancy Fraser's revised feminist understanding of representation, in which "feminist claims for redistribution and recognition are linked increasingly to struggles to change the frame."[73] As she explains, "By confronting misframing, this phase of feminist politics is making visible a third dimension of gender justice, beyond redistribution and recognition. I call this third dimension representation. As I understand it, representation is not only a matter of ensuring equal political voice for women in already constituted political communities. In addition, it requires reframing disputes about justice that cannot be properly contained within established polities. In contesting misframing, therefore, transnational feminism is reconfiguring gender justice as a three-dimensional problem, in which redistribution, recognition, and representation must be integrated in a balanced way."[74] For Fraser, this notion of representation, in which problems of recognition and redistribution receive equal attention, is particularly relevant to the "developing transnational political space surrounding the European Union." In her geography of feminism's three major phases, the first phase, social movements, encompassed North American and Western European feminisms, while the second one, identity politics, flourished in the United States. The third, transnational phase is emerging in the most pertinent and promising way in Europe, where the task is to do three things at once: "First, feminists must work with other progressive forces to create egalitarian, gender-sensitive social-welfare protections at the transnational level. In addition, they must join with allies to integrate such redistributive policies with egalitarian, gender-sensitive recognition policies that can do justice to European cultural multiplicity. Finally, they must do all that without hardening external borders, ensuring that transnational Europe does not become fortress Europe, so as not to replicate injustices of misframing on a broader scale."[75]

The crucial work that popular media products perform in misframing tends to remain caught up in discussions that reduce representation to female images and their postfeminist pleasures. In the case of a program like *My Big Fat Gypsy Wedding*, a feminist representational analysis in Fraser's revised sense of reconnecting the economic and cultural spheres reveals how the program's alleged educational goal, the aesthetic of public service broadcasting, and the entertaining format jointly replace redistributive with cultural politics. The putative pedagogical mandate of the show wraps the representation of "Gypsy weddings" within a pseudoconcern with social realism and, by extension, social justice. The key ingredient of this false concern with social justice is the stance of pseudofeminism projected over the show. The narrator speaks from the vantage point of those who have already achieved feminist consciousness, which is made evident by visualizing its constitutive absence among "Gypsy" women. If there is an entire community that lives within a prefeminist world, then, by contrast, postfeminism must be a vital force that continues to provide empowerment for women—rather than an inherently contradictory set of ideas that converges precisely on the assumption that feminism is "past" and redundant. According to this logic, problems are introduced only when postfeminist tools are misused by insufficiently enlightened subjects. If Gypsy women stubbornly refuse to choose education, continue to live as domestic slaves and baby factories, and are easily seduced by large dresses and excessive makeup, that is their fault. Cultural representations that zoom in on the dresses, propped up by a pseudoconcern with social issues, actually eliminate structural socioeconomic factors, or the redistributive angle, from the politics of representation.

Travellers and Gypsies fascinate producers and viewers of programs such as *My Big Fat Gypsy Wedding* precisely because they allow this pernicious postfeminist logic of self-exclusion to solidify around what is portrayed as an entire ethnic tradition, rather than around individual subjects. "Gypsies" refuse to choose proper postfeminism because they are ethnically different. This contradiction is embedded within the media executives' disavowals about the program, with which I began this essay: the show reveals the truth about an ethnic community but has no role to play in perpetuating vicious stereotypes. It simply displays traditional domestic gendered rituals, which in turn authorizes an ethnonational class disgust further reinforced within an interlinked European and global neoliberal common sense. Such programs' postfeminist obsession with clothes and rituals is thus the lynchpin, the neutralizing platform that at once enables and distracts from a broad pattern of neoliberal exclusion. Depriving those unable and unwilling to dress with restraint of the moral value of personhood is in synergy with and perpetuates the exclusion from the free market's moral order of entire communities, even countries, that are unwilling to act frugally and responsibly. In both cases, a predetermined order defines the outcome, whose failure is then represented as simply a bad choice.

Notes

1. Frost, "Channel 4's Big Fat Gypsy Ratings Winner."

2. Tracey Jensen and Jessica Ringrose describe the "post-documentary" effect created by the show, evident in a massive outpouring of responses in social networking sites, as "anthropological voyeurism." Jensen and Ringrose, "Sluts That Choose vs. Doormat Gypsies," 2.

3. Frost, "Channel 4's Big Fat Gypsy Ratings Winner."

4. Negra and Tasker, "Neoliberal Frames and Genres of Inequality."

5. Fraser, "Mapping the Feminist Imagination."

6. Lentin and Titley, "The Crisis of 'Multiculturalism' in Europe," 133.

7. Lentin and Titley, "The Crisis of 'Multiculturalism' in Europe," 128.

8. Hall, "The Neo-liberal Revolution," 713.

9. Jensen and Ringrose explain that "chav" was introduced in the U.K. as a buzzword in 2004 and gained currency as panic increased about Britain's "infestation" by an "uneducated, lazy, promiscuous workshy . . . lumpenproletariat, or 'underclass.'" Jensen and Ringrose, "Sluts That Choose vs. Doormat Gypsies," 5.

10. Jones and Subotic, "Fantasies of Power."

11. See "Big Fat Gypsy Reaction"; "Gypsy Weddings Show Has Outraged Us."

12. Lentin and Titley, "The Crisis of 'Multiculturalism' in Europe," 127. While my focus is on the overlap between Badiou's and Fraser's uses of the term, Badiou's "politics of recognition" is more specific to institutional practices of multiculturalism, while Fraser's is closer to the terrain covered by "identity politics."

13. Lentin and Titley, "The Crisis of 'Multiculturalism' in Europe."

14. See Hall, "The Neo-liberal Revolution," 705; Klein, *The Shock Doctrine*; Harvey, *A Brief History of Neoliberalism*, 162–63.

15. Bruzzi, *New Documentary*, 127–28.

16. Frey, "Good Bye Germany."

17. Fraser, "Mapping the Feminist Imagination."

18. Fraser, "Mapping the Feminist Imagination," 299.

19. Fraser, "Mapping the Feminist Imagination," 296.

20. Fraser, "Mapping the Feminist Imagination," 299.

21. Fraser, "Mapping the Feminist Imagination," 304.

22. Fraser, "Mapping the Feminist Imagination," 304.

23. Habermas, "Toward a Cosmopolitan Europe," 92.

24. Habermas, "Toward a Cosmopolitan Europe," 92.

25. Habermas, "Toward a Cosmopolitan Europe," 93.

26. Dalton, Radowitz, and Horobin, "EU Ends Talks with Little Progress in Overcoming Divisions."

27. See Wikipedia, "PIGS (Economics)," http://en.wikipedia.org/wiki/PIGS_(economics). Thanks to Diane Negra for calling my attention to this.

28. Korek, "Central and Eastern Europe from a Postcolonial Perspective"; Buchowski, "The Specter of Orientalism in Europe."

29. Wolff, *Inventing Eastern Europe*.

30. See Verdery, "Whither Postsocialism?"; Böröcz, "Introduction."

31. Buchowski, "The Specter of Orientalism in Europe."

32. Sztompka, "The Trauma of Social Change."

33. Böröcz, "Introduction."

34. See Imre and Bardan, "Vampire Branding."

35. Kaufman, "The EU," an interview with Ivan Krasteve, Claus Offe, Sonja Puntscher-Riekmann, and Martin M. Simecka.

36. As Nobel Prize–winning economist Paul Krugman wrote in the *New York Times*, unlike the U.S. dollar area, the Eurozone lacks a federal government, common language, and shared political culture, which, "from the beginning, made the prospects of the single currency dubious" (Krugman, "Can Europe Be Saved?"). In a similar vein, a conversation among European intellectuals in the online pan-European magazine *Eurozone* identifies the EU as "the sick man of Europe" (Kaufman, "The EU"). Simon Jenkins in the *Guardian* notes the biting irony of the situation that Germany is spearheading the Euro bailout, since it was redesigned to operate after World War II to prevent it from taking on European leadership. Yet it is the European country with the largest surplus and the only one that did not indulge in the housing bubble. Jenkins, "Europe Is Turning Back to National Identity."

37. Van Baar, "The European Roma," 332.

38. Van Baar, "The European Roma," 320.

39. Imre and Tremlett, "Reality TV without Class," 92.

40. Quoted in van Baar, "The European Roma," 13.

41. Van Baar, "The European Roma," 1–2.

42. Van Baar, "The European Roma," 324.

43. Van Baar, "The European Roma," 13.

44. Van Baar, "The European Roma," 7.

45. Van Baar, "The European Roma," 18.

46. Imre, "Love to Hate."

47. Bogdal, "Europe Invents the Gypsies."

48. Wheeler, "Watch Our Awkward Chat with Josie and Swanley Smith off *My Big Fat Gypsy Wedding* at the NTAs."

49. Lazzeri, "Blinging Up Baby."

50. "My Big Fat Gypsy Wedding"; Duits and van Zoonen, "Coming to Terms with Sexualization."

51. Jensen and Ringrose make a similar argument in their article "Sluts That Choose vs. Doormat Gypsies."

52. See Tyler and Bennett, "'Celebrity Chav'"; Tyler, "'Chav Mum Chav Scum,'" 21.

53. Tyler, "'Chav Mum Chav Scum,'" 18.

54. Tyler, "'Chav Mum Chav Scum,'" 22.

55. Tyler, "'Chav Mum Chav Scum,'" 23.

56. Lentin and Titley, "The Crisis of 'Multiculturalism' in Europe," 388.

57. "My Big Fat Gypsy Wedding."

58. Holohan, "'We're a Very Normal Family,'" 32.

59. Holohan, "'We're a Very Normal Family,'" 32.

60. See Okely and Houtman, "The Dale Farm Eviction."

61. See, for instance, Ouellette and Hay, *Better Living through Reality* TV.

62. Rose, *Powers of Freedom*.

63. Ouellette and Hay, *Better Living through Reality* TV, 471; also see Palmer, "'The New You.'"

64. Skeggs, Wood, and Thumin, "Making Class through Moral Extension on Reality TV." See also Skeggs and Wood, "The Moral Economy of Person Production."

65. Skeggs and Wood, "Notes on Ethical Scenarios of Self on British Reality TV," 207.

66. Deery, "Trading Faces."

67. Darby, "Big Fat Disgrace."

68. Kraszewski, "Coming to a Beach Near You."

69. Lauristin, "The European Public Sphere and the Social Imaginary of the 'New Europe,'" 398.

70. Elmbrant, "Whose Europe?"

71. Elmbrant, "Whose Europe?"

72. Daianu, "Markets and Society."

73. Fraser, "Mapping the Feminist Imagination," 304.

74. Fraser, "Mapping the Feminist Imagination," 304.

75. Fraser, "Mapping the Feminist Imagination," 304.

BIBLIOGRAPHY

Abramsky, Sasha. "Look Ahead in Anger." *Chronicle Review*, July 16, 2010.

"Ahern Apologises for Suicide Remark." RTÉ News, July 4, 2007. www.rte.ie/news /2007/0704/economy.html.

Ahmed, Sara. "Affective Economies." *Social Text* 22, no. 2 (2004): 117–39.

———. *The Promise of Happiness*. Durham, NC: Duke University Press, 2011.

———. *Strange Encounters: Embodied Others in Post-coloniality*. London: Routledge, 2000.

Aitkenhead, Decca. "Hayley Taylor: 'I've Felt What the Unemployed Feel: Losing Confidence, Staring at the Four Walls': The Star of the New Reality TV Show *The Fairy Jobmother* on Getting the Long-Term Unemployed Back to Work." *Guardian*, July 12, 2010.

Alilunas, Peter. "Male Masculinity as the Celebration of Failure: The Frat Pack, Women and the Trauma of Victimization in the 'Dude Flick.'" *Mediascape* (spring 2008).

Allen, Katie. "Female Unemployment Hit by Public Sector Cuts and Childcare Costs." *Guardian*, December 14, 2011.

Annesley, Claire, and Alexandra Scheele. "Gender, Capitalism and Economic Crisis: Impact and Responses." *Journal of Contemporary European Studies* 19, no. 3 (2011): 335–47.

Aparicio, Frances. "Jennifer as Selena: Rethinking Latinidad in Media and Popular Culture." *Latino Studies* 1, no. 1 (2003): 90–105.

Appelbaum, Binyamin. "As Men Lose Economic Ground, Clues in the Family." *New York Times*, March 20, 2013.

Armour, Stephanie. "Foreclosures Take Toll on Mental Health; Crisis Hotlines, Therapists See a Surge in Anxiety over Housing." *USA Today*, May 15, 2008.

Arthurs, Jane. "*Sex and the City* and Consumer Culture: Remediating Postfeminist Drama." *Feminist Media Studies* 3, no. 1 (2003): 83–98.

Báez, Jillian M. "Speaking of Jennifer Lopez: Discourses of Iconicity and Identity Formation among Latina Audiences." *Media Report to Women* 35, no. 1 (2007).

Baker, Peter, and Jeff Zeleny. "Obama Chooses Hispanic Judge for Supreme Court Seat." *New York Times*, May 27, 2009.

Ball, James, Dan Milmo, and Ben Ferguson. "Half of UK's Young Black Males Are Unemployed." *Guardian*, March 9, 2012.

Banet-Weiser, Sarah. *Authentic™: The Politics of Ambivalence in a Brand Culture*. New York: New York University Press, 2012.

———. "Branding the Crisis." In *Aftermath: The Cultures of the Economic Crisis*, ed. Manuel Castells, João Caraça, and Gustavo Cardoso. London: Oxford University Press, 2012.

———. "Elian Gonzalez and 'The Purpose of America': Nation, Family, and the Child-Citizen." *American Quarterly* 55, no. 2 (2003): 149–78.

Banet-Weiser, Sarah, and Inna Arzumanova. "Creative Authorship: Self-Actualizing Individuals and the Self-Brand." In *Media Authorship*, ed. Cynthia Chris and David Gerstner. New York: Routledge, 2012.

Banet-Weiser, Sarah, and Laura Portwood-Stacer. "'I Just Want to Be Me Again': Beauty Pageants, Reality Television and Post-feminism." *Feminist Theory* 7, no. 2 (2006): 255–72.

Banks, Ralph Richard. *Is Marriage for White People?* New York: Penguin, 2011.

Barker, Drucilla K., and Susan F. Feiner. *Liberating Economics: Feminist Perspectives on Families, Work, and Globalization*. Ann Arbor: University of Michigan Press, 2004.

Barnett, Roslind C., and Caryl Rivers. "Don't Call Women the Richer Sex!" *Daily Beast*, April 28, 2012.

Bartels, Larry. *Unequal Democracy: The Political Economy of the New Gilded Age*. Princeton, NJ: Princeton University Press, 2008.

BBC Press Office. "Stellar Cast in *Freefall* for Savage Drama from Origin Pictures for BBC Two." October 24, 2008. http://www.bbc.co.uk/pressoffice/pressreleases /stories/2008/10_october/24/freefall.shtml.

Becker, Ron. "'Help Is on the Way!': *Supernanny*, *Nanny 911*, and the Neoliberal Politics of the Family." In *The Great American Makeover: Television, History, Nation*, ed. Dana Heller. Basingstoke: Palgrave Macmillan, 2006.

Bell, David, and Joanne Hollows. "Making Sense of Ordinary Lifestyles." In *Ordinary Lifestyles: Popular Media, Consumption and Taste*, ed. David Bell and Joanne Hollows. Maidenhead: Open University Press, 2005.

Beltrán, Mary. *Latina/o Stars in U.S. Eyes: The Making and Meanings of Film and TV Stardom*. Chicago: University of Illinois Press, 2010.

Bennett, Catherine. "Go On. Buy Yourself an It Bag. It's Your Duty to Your Nation." *Observer*, March 21, 2010. www.guardian.co.uk/commentisfree/2010/mar/21 /catherine-bennett-recession-spending.

Bennett, James. *Television Personalities: Stardom and the Small Screen*. London: Routledge, 2011.

Bennhold, Katrin. "Recession Seen Taking Toll on Gender Equality." *New York Times*, August 26, 2011.

Benson-Allott, Caetlin. *Killer Tapes and Shattered Screens: Video Spectatorship from VHS to File Sharing*. Berkeley: University of California Press, 2013.

Berlant, Lauren. "Cruel Optimism." *differences: A Journal of Feminist Cultural Studies* 17, no. 3 (2006): 20–36.

———. *Cruel Optimism*. Durham, NC: Duke University Press, 2011.

———. "Slow Death (Sovereignty, Obesity, Lateral Agency)." *Critical Inquiry* 33 (summer 2007): 754–80.

"Big Fat Gypsy Reaction: Warwickshire Travellers' Views." BBC, February 1, 2011.

Bingham, Dennis. *Whose Lives Are They Anyway? The Biopic as Contemporary Film Genre*. New Brunswick, NJ: Rutgers University Press, 2010.

Biressi, Anita, and Heather Nunn. *Reality TV: Realism and Revelation*. London: Wall-flower, 2005.

Blume, Lesley. "High Styles for Low Times: How Fashion and Luxury Firms Will Ride Out a Recession." *Slate*, May 14, 2008. www.slate.com/id/2191398.

Bobo, Kim. *Wage Theft in America: Why Millions of Americans Are Not Getting Paid—and What We Can Do about It*. New York: New Press, 2009.

Bode, Lisa. "Transitional Tastes: Teen Girls and Genre in the Critical Reception of *Twilight*." *Continuum: Journal of Media and Cultural Studies* 24, no. 5 (2010): 707–19.

Bogdal, Klaus-Michael. "Europe Invents the Gypsies: The Dark Side of Modernity." *Eurozine*, February 24, 2012. www.eurozine.com/articles/2012-02-24-bogdal-en.html.

Bolick, Kate. "All the Single Ladies." *Atlantic* (November 2011): 116–36.

Bonner, Frances. *Ordinary Television: Analyzing Popular TV*. London: Sage, 2003.

Böröcz, József. "Introduction: Empire and Coloniality in the 'Eastern Enlargement' of the European Union." *Central Europe Review* (2001): 4–50. http://aei.pitt.edu/144/01/Empire.pdf.

Bose, Purnima, and Laura E. Lyons, eds. *Cultural Critique and the Global Corporation*. Bloomington: Indiana University Press, 2010.

Boushey, Heather. "Jobs Returning, Slowly." Center for American Progress, March 4, 2011. http://www.americanprogress.org/issues/labor/news/2011/03/04/9319/jobs-returning-slowly/.

Bravo, Ellen. "'Having It All?'—The Wrong Question for Most Women." *Women's Media Center*, June 26, 2012. http://www.womensmediacenter.com/feature/entry/having-it-allthe-wrong-question-for-most-women.

Brennan, Donagh. "The Mingling of Business Models: Ireland, China and Apple." Irish Left Review.org, May 2, 2012. www.irishleftreview.org/2012/05/02/mingling-business-models-ireland-china-apple.

Brown, Mark. "Recession Era Movie." *Guardian*, May 21, 2009.

Brown, Wendy. *Edgework: Critical Essays on Knowledge and Politics*. Princeton, NJ: Princeton University Press, 2006.

———. *Politics out of History*. Princeton, NJ: Princeton University Press, 2001.

Brunsdon, Charlotte. "Feminism, Postfeminism, Martha, Martha, and Nigella." *Cinema Journal* 44, no. 2 (2005): 110–16.

———. "Television Crime Series, Women Police, and Fuddy-Duddy Feminism." *Feminist Media Studies* (2012): 1–20.

Brush, Lisa. *Poverty, Battered Women and Work in U.S. Public Policy*. New York: Oxford University Press, 2011.

Bruzzi, Stella. *New Documentary*. 2nd rev. ed. London: Routledge, 2006.

Buchheit, Paul. "Three Ways the Rich and Powerful Have Cheated Young Americans." Nation of Change, July 14, 2012. http://www.nationofchange.org/three-ways-rich -and-powerful-have-cheated-young-americans-1341846413.

Buchowski, Michael. "The Specter of Orientalism in Europe: From Exotic Other to Stigmatized Brother." *Anthropological Quarterly* (2006): 463–82.

Buckman, Adam. "Recession TV." *New York Post*, October 8, 2008.

Bunreacht na hÉireann / Constitution of Ireland. Dublin: Government Publications, 1937.

Burgess, Jean. "Hearing Ordinary Voices: Cultural Studies, Vernacular Creativity and Digital Storytelling." *Continuum: Journal of Media and Culture Studies* 20, no. 2 (2006): 201–14.

Burgess, Jean, and Joshua Green. *YouTube: Online Video and Participatory Culture*. Cambridge, MA: Polity, 2009.

Burke-Kennedy, Eoin, and Derek Scally. "Taoiseach Blames Crash on 'Mad Borrowing' Frenzy." Irish Times.com, 26 January 2012. www.irishtimes.com/newspaper /breaking/2012/0126/breaking27.html.

Cabot, Meg. *Boy Meets Girl*. New York: Avon, 2004.

Calla, Lindsey. "FAQ—Saucy Glossie," Saucy Glossie. Accessed June 6, 2012. www .saucyglossie.com/faq.

Carroll, Hamilton. *Affirmative Reaction: New Formations of White Masculinity*. Durham, NC: Duke University Press, 2011.

———. "Men's Soaps: Automotive Television Programming and Contemporary Working-Class Masculinities." *Television and New Media* 9, no. 4 (2008): 263–83.

Carroll, Rory. "Is HBO's New Hit Show a *Sex and the City* for Recession-Era America?" *Guardian*, April 21, 2012.

Casserly, Meghan. "The New Celebrity Money Makers." *Forbes*, June 6, 2011, 66–74.

Castells, Manuel. *Communication Power*. London: Oxford University Press, 2009.

Castells, Manuel, João Caraça, and Gustavo Cardoso, eds. *Aftermath: The Cultures of the Economic Crisis*. London: Oxford University Press, 2012.

Cauchon, Dennis. "Tough Times for Older Male Workers: Older White Males Hurt More by This Recession." *USA Today*, July 29, 2009. www.usatoday.com/money /economy/employment/2009-07-29-oldermales_N.htm.

Cepeda, Maria Elena. *Musical ImagiNation: US Colombian Identity and the Latin Music Boom*. New York: New York University Press, 2010.

Channel 4. "Fairy Jobmother/Interview Techniques/Channel 4." YouTube, June 22, 2011. http://www.youtube.com/watch?v=e-Shxz4UyPM.

Chavez, Leo. *Covering Immigration: Popular Images and the Politics of the Nation*. Berkeley: University of California Press, 2008.

Cherlin, Andrew. *The Marriage-Go-Round: The State of Marriage and the Family in America Today*. New York: Knopf, 2009.

Child, Julia, Simone Beck, and Louisette Bertholle. *Mastering the Art of French Cooking, Volume I: The 40th Anniversary Edition*. New York: Knopf, 2004.

Child, Julia, with Alex Prud'homme. *My Life in France*. New York: Alfred A. Knopf, 2006.

Clark, Kameri Maxine, and Deborah Thomas. *Globalization and Race: Transformations in the Cultural Production of Blackness*. Durham, NC: Duke University Press, 2006.

Clarke, Donald. "So, What Are Pyjama Girls Really Like?" *Irish Times*, August 14, 2010.

Clifford, Stephanie. "High Fashion Relents to Web's Pull." *New York Times*, July 11, 2010.

———. "Sites That Pay the Shopper for Being a Seller." *New York Times*, October 2, 2012.

Cohan, Steven. "Queer Eye for the Straight Guise: Camp, Postfeminism, and the Fab Five's Makeovers of Masculinity." In *Interrogating Postfeminism: Gender and the Politics of Popular Culture*, ed. Yvonne Tasker and Diane Negra. Durham, NC: Duke University Press, 2007.

Cohn, Carol. "War, Wimps and Women: Talking Gender and Thinking War." In *Gendering War Talk*, ed. Miriam Cooke and Angela Woolacott. Princeton, NJ: Princeton University Press, 1993.

Collins, Jim. *Bring on the Books for Everybody: How Literary Culture became Popular Culture*. Durham, NC: Duke University Press, 2010.

Collins, Katherine. *Watching What We Eat: The Evolution of Television Cooking Shows*. New York: Continuum, 2009.

Connell, Raewyn. "Inside the Glass Tower: The Construction of Masculinities in Financial Capital." *Feminist Studies: Journal of Interdisciplinary Women's and Gender Studies* 28, no. 1 (2010): 8–24.

Connell, Robert. *Masculinities*. Berkeley: University of California Press, 1995.

Considine, Austin. "For Asian Stars, Many Web Fans." *New York Times*, July 31, 2011.

Cook, Nancy. "What Mancession?" *Newsweek*, July 16, 2009.

Coontz, Stephanie. "The M.R.S. and the Ph.D." *New York Times*, February 11, 2012.

Cooper, James. "Where Have All the High Paying Jobs Gone?" *Fiscal Times*, May 23, 2011.

Cunningham, Tessa. "I Was Little Miss No Mates: Now I've Made 250,000 Friends by Showing Them How to Put Lippy On." *Daily Mail*, October 15, 2009.

Dabbous, Yasmine, and Amy Ladley. "A Spine of Steel and a Heart of Gold: Newspaper Coverage of the First Female Speaker of the House." *Journal of Gender Studies* 19, no. 2 (2010): 181–94.

Daianu, Daniel. "Markets and Society: When High Finance Cripples the Economy and Corrodes Democracy." *Eurozine*, July 21, 2011. www.eurozine.com/articles/2011-07-21-daianu-en.html.

Dalton, Matthew, Bernd Radowitz, and William Horobin. "EU Ends Talks with Little Progress in Overcoming Divisions." *Wall Street Journal*, September 17, 2011. http://online.wsj.com/article/SB10001424053111903927204576576633002950972.html.

Darby, Seyward. "Big Fat Disgrace: TLC's 'My Big Fat Gypsy Wedding' Is Wildly Misleading." *New Republic*, May 31, 2001. www.tnr.com/article/books-and-arts/89173/my-big-fat-gypsy-wedding-tlc-traveller-roma.

Davies, Lord M. "Women on Boards." Department for Business Innovation and

Skills, 2011. Accessed June 10, 2011. http://www.bis.gov.uk//assets/biscore
/business-law/docs/w/11-745-women-on-boards.pdf.

Dávila, Arlene. *Latinos, Inc.: The Marketing and Making of a People.* Berkeley: University of California Press, 2001.

———. *Latino Spin: Public Image and the Whitewashing of Race.* New York: New York University Press, 2008.

Day, Elizabeth. "True Confessions in New Women's Lit." *Guardian,* September 22, 2010.

Dayan, Daniel, and Elihu Katz. *Media Events: The Live Broadcasting of History.* Cambridge, MA: Harvard University Press, 1994.

de Beauvoir, Simone. *Ethics of Ambiguity.* Translated by B. Frechtman. New York: Citadel, 1976.

DeCarvalho, Lauren J. "Hannah and Her Entitled Sisters: (Post)Feminism, (Post)Recession, and Girls." *Feminist Media Studies* 13, no. 2 (2013): 367–69.

"The Decline of Marriage and the Rise of New Families." Pew Research Center, November 18, 2010. http://www.pewsocialtrends.org/files/2010/11/pew-social -trends-2010-families.pdf.

Deery, June. "Trading Faces: The Makeover Show as Prime-Time 'Infomercial.'" *Feminist Media Studies* 4, no. 2 (2004): 211–14.

De Goede, Marieke. *Virtue, Fortune and Faith: A Genealogy of Finance.* Minneapolis: University of Minnesota Press, 2005.

Dell'Antonia, K. J. "Single Parents: Unsupported and Feeling the Blame." *New York Times,* March 20, 2013.

Denby, David. "A Fine Romance." *New Yorker,* July 23, 2007.

de Vise, Daniel. "More Women Than Men Got PhDs Last Year." *Washington Post,* September 14, 2010.

De Vries, Hilary. "Tinseltown, Ghost Town." *New York Times,* February 22, 2012.

Dewan, Shaila, and Robert Gebeloff. "More Men Enter Fields Dominated by Women." *New York Times,* May 20, 2012.

Donald, Kate. "The Feminisation of Poverty and the Myth of the Welfare Queen." Open Democracy, March 6, 2012. www.opendemocracy.net/5050/kate-donald /feminisation-of-poverty-and-myth-of-welfare-queen.

Douthat, Ross. "No Mystique about Feminism." *New York Times,* June 13, 2010. www .nytimes.com/2010/06/14/opinion/14douthat.html?emc=eta1.

Dow, Bonnie. "The Traffic in Men and the Fatal Attraction of Postfeminist Masculinity." *Women's Studies in Communication* 29, no. 1 (2006): 113–19.

Doyle, Julie, and Irmi Karl. "Shame on You: Cosmetic Surgery and Class Transformation in *10 Years Younger.*" In *Exposing Lifestyle Television: The Big Reveal,* ed. Gareth Palmer. Aldershot: Ashgate, 2008.

Duggan, Lisa. *The Twilight of Equality? Neoliberalism, Cultural Politics, and the Attack on Democracy.* Boston: Beacon, 2003.

Duits, Linda, and Liesbet van Zoonen. "Coming to Terms with Sexualization." *European Journal of Cultural Studies* 14, no. 5 (2011): 491–506.

Dunn, Jancee. "Sofia Vergara Spills All." *Redbook*, September 2011. www.redbookmag
.com/fun-contests/celebrity/sofia-vergara-interview.

Dyer, Richard. *Stars*. London: British Film Institute, 1979.

Edelman, Lee. "The Future Is Kid Stuff: Queer Theory, Disidentification, and the
Death Drive." *Narrative* 6, no. 1 (1998): 18–30.

Edelman, Peter. *So Rich, So Poor: Why It's So Hard to End Poverty in America*. New York:
New Press, 2012.

Edin, Kathryn, and Maria J. Kefalas. *Promises I Can Keep: Why Poor Women Put Motherhood
before Marriage*. Berkeley: University of California Press, 2005.

Edin, Kathryn, and Laura Lein. *Making Ends Meet: How Single Mothers Survive Welfare and
Low-Wage Work*. New York: Russell Sage, 1997.

Ehrenreich, Barbara. "The Suicide Solution." *Nation*, August 4, 2008.

———. "Too Poor to Make the News." *New York Times*, June 14, 2009.

"Ellen to Sofia Vergara: Who Has More Fun Blondes or Brunettes?" VOXXI, January 12, 2012. voxxi.com/ellen-to-sofia-vergara-who-has-more-fun-blondes-or
-brunettes.

Elliott, Stuart. "In TV Pilots, Paranormal Is the New Normal." *New York Times*, May 22,
2011.

Elmbrant, Björn. "Whose Europe?" *Eurozine*, January 17, 2012. www.eurozine.com
/articles/2012-01-17-elmbrant-en.html.

Emerson, Newton. "Working Women Almost Certainly Caused the Credit Crunch."
Irish Times, February 2, 2009.

Esposito, Jennifer. "What Does Race Have to Do with Ugly Betty? An Analysis of Privilege and Postracial Representations on a Television Sitcom." *Television and New
Media* 10, no. 6 (2009): 551–67.

Ewen, Stuart. *Captains of Consciousness: Advertising and the Social Roots of the Consumer Culture*. New York: Basic Books, 2001.

Faludi, Susan. *Stiffed: The Betrayal of the American Man*. New York: Perennial, 1999.

Farrell, Kirby. *Berserk Style in American Culture*. New York: Palgrave, 2011.

Ferguson, Michaele L., and Lori Jo Marso. "Introduction: Feminism, Gender, and
Security in the Bush Presidency." In *W Stands for Women: How the George W. Bush Presi-
dency Shaped a New Politics of Gender*, ed. Michaele L. Ferguson and Lori Jo Marso.
Durham, NC: Duke University Press, 2007.

Ferriss, Suzanne. "Fashioning Femininity in the Makeover Chick Flick." *Chick Lit: The
New Woman's Fiction*, ed. Suzanne Ferriss and Mallory Young. New York: Routledge,
2006.

Ferriss, Suzanne, and Mallory Young, eds. *Chick Lit: The New Woman's Fiction*. New York:
Routledge, 2006.

Fitzpatrick, Pat. "Sacred Cows: Irish Women." *Sunday Independent: Life Supplement*,
October 3, 2010.

Folbre, Nancy. "Economix: Risks, Radiation, and Regulation." *New York Times*, March
18, 2011.

Fortunati, Leopoldina. "Immaterial Labor and Its Machinization." *Ephemera* 7, no. 1
(2007): 139–57.

Foster, Peter. "No End to Capitalism." *Financial Post*, September 18, 2009.

Foucault, Michel. *The Birth of Biopolitics: Lectures at the Collége de France 1978–1979*. New York: Palgrave, 2010.

———. *Madness and Civilisation: A History of Insanity in the Age of Reason*. London: Routledge, 1999.

Fraad, Harriet. "The Great Recession and Gender Marriage Transformation." *Journal of Psychohistory* 39, no. 2 (2011): 129–32.

Frank, Thomas. *The Conquest of Cool: Business Culture, Counterculture, and the Rise of Hip Consumerism*. Chicago: University of Chicago Press, 1998.

Fraser, Nancy. "Mapping the Feminist Imagination: From Redistribution to Recognition to Representation." *Constellations* 12, no. 3 (2005): 295–307.

Freeland, Chrystia. *Plutocrats: The Rise of the New Global Super-Rich and the Fall of Everyone Else*. New York: Penguin, 2012.

Fregoso, Rosa Linda. *MeXicana Encounters: The Making of Social Identities on the Borderlands*. Berkeley: University of California Press, 2003.

Frey, Mattias. "Good Bye Germany: Emigration, Reality TV and Schadenfreude." *Jump Cut Online* 52 (summer 2010). http://www.ejumpcut.org/archive/jc52.2010/freyEmi.

Friedberg, Anne. *Window Shopping: Cinema and the Postmodern*. Berkeley: University of California Press, 1993.

Frost, Vicki. "Channel 4's Big Fat Gypsy Ratings Winner." *Guardian*, February 6, 2011. http://www.theguardian.com/media/2011/feb/07/bigf.

Fuller, Andrea. "Female Undergraduates Continue to Outnumber Men, but Gap Holds Steady." *Chronicle of Higher Education*, January 26, 2010.

Gamble, Sarah. "Postfeminism." In *The Routledge Critical Dictionary of Feminism and Postfeminism*, ed. Sarah Gamble. London: Routledge, 2001.

Gans, Joshua. "Hard Times Are Harder for Women." *New York Times*, January 11, 2012.

Gant, Charles. "Mother's Day." *Variety*, June 10, 2011.

Gentleman, Amelia. "Rising Unemployment Puts Cameron's Work Programme in the Spotlight." *Guardian*, January 31, 2012.

———. "Women's Groups Struggle Amid Funding Cuts." *Guardian Online*, February 2, 2011.

———. "Women's Refuge Chief Returns OBE in Protest over Cuts." *Guardian*, February 15, 2011.

Georgia Department of Labor. "Georgia Men Hit Hardest by Recession December 2007–May 2009." July 2009. assets.bizjournals.com/cms_media/atlanta/pdf /georgia_men_hit_hardest_whitepaper.pdf.

Gerhard, Jane. "*Sex and the City*: Carrie Bradshaw's Queer Postfeminism." *Feminist Media Studies* 5, no. 1 (2005): 37–49.

Gilbert, Elizabeth. *Eat, Pray, Love: One Woman's Search for Everything across Italy, India, and Indonesia*. New York: Viking, 2006.

Gill, Rosalind. "Culture and Subjectivity in Neoliberal and Postfeminist Times." *Subjectivity* 25 (2008): 432–45.

———. "Postfeminist Media Culture: Elements of a Sensibility." *European Journal of Cultural Studies* 10, no. 2 (2007): 147–66.

Gill, Rosalind, and Elena Herdieckerhoff. "Rewriting the Romance: New Femininities in Chick Lit." *Feminist Media Studies* 6, no. 4 (2006): 487–517.

Gill, Rosalind, and Christina Scharff, eds. *New Femininities: Postfeminism, Neoliberalism and Subjectivity*. Basingstoke: Palgrave Macmillan, 2011.

Gilligan, Paula. "Flexicurity/Insecurity: New Managerial Cultures and Academic Freedom." Paper presented in New Realities: The Politics of Representation, Education and Culture seminar series, UCD Clinton Institute for American Studies, Dublin, February 15, 2010.

Gilmore, Ruth Wilson. *Golden Gulag: Prisons, Surplus, Crisis and Opposition in Globalizing California*. Berkeley: University of California Press, 2007.

Giroux, Henry. "Neoliberalism and the Death of the Social State: Remembering Walter Benjamin's Angel of History." *Social Identities* 17, no. 4 (2011): 587–601.

Giroux, Henry A., and Imre Szeman. "Ikea Boy Fights Back: *Fight Club*, Consumerism and the Political Limits of Nineties Cinema." In *The End of Cinema as We Know It: American Film in the Nineties*, ed. Jon Lewis. New York: New York University Press, 2001.

Glenn, Evelyn Nakano. "From Servitude to Service Work: Historical Continuities in the Racial Division of Paid Reproductive Labor." *Signs: Journal of Women in Culture and Society* 18, no. 1 (1992): 1–43.

Glink, Ilyce. "*American Horror Story* Home for Sale." CBS *Money Watch*, January 17, 2012.

Goldman, Robert, and Stephen Papson. *Sign Wars: The Cluttered Landscape of Advertising*. New York: Guilford, 1996.

Goodman, Michelle. "Recession Ethics: Dealing with Morally Bankrupt Bosses." ABC *News*, June 25, 2009. abcnews.go.com/Business/Economy/story?id=7919449 &page=1#.T32IfKt8C8A.25.

Gordon, Avery, and Christopher Newfield. "Introduction." In *Mapping Multiculturalism*, ed. Avery Gordon and Christopher Newfield. Minneapolis: University of Minnesota Press, 1996.

Gottlieb, Lori. *Marry Him: The Case for Settling for Mr. Good Enough*. New York: Dutton, 2010.

Graser, Marc, and Andrew Stewart. "Fright Plan for All Seasons." *Variety*, October 18–24, 2010.

Gregg, Melissa. *Work's Intimacy*. Cambridge, MA: Polity, 2011.

Groeneveld, Elizabeth. " 'Be a Feminist or Just Dress Like One': BUST, Fashion and Feminism as Lifestyle." *Journal of Gender Studies* 18, no. 2 (2009): 179–90.

Gurian, Michael. *The Minds of Boys: Saving Our Sons from Falling Behind in School and Life*. San Francisco: Jossey-Bass, 2005.

Guthman, Julie, and Melanie DuPuis. "Embodying Neoliberalism: Economy, Culture and the Politics of Fat." *Environment and Planning D: Society and Space* 24 (2006): 427–48.

"Gypsy Weddings Show Has Outraged Us." *Peterlee Mail*, February 6, 2011.

Habell-Pallán, Michelle. *Loca Motion: The Travels of Chicana and Latina Popular Culture*. New York: New York University Press, 2005.

Habell-Pallán, Michelle, and Mary Romero, eds. *Latino/a Popular Culture*. New York: New York University Press, 2002.

Habermas, Jürgen. "Toward a Cosmopolitan Europe." *Journal of Democracy* 14, no. 4 (2003): 86–100.

Halberstam, Judith. *In a Queer Time and Place: Transgender Bodies, Subcultural Lives*. New York: New York University Press, 2005.

Hale, Elizabeth. "Long Suffering Professional Females: The Case of Nanny Lit." In *Chick Lit: The New Woman's Fiction*, ed. Mallory Young and Suzanne Ferris. New York: Routledge, 2006.

Hale, Mike. "They Said It Had Good Bones." *New York Times*, October 4, 2011.

Hall, Stuart. "The Neo-liberal Revolution." *Cultural Studies* 25, no. 6 (2011): 705–28.

Halpern, Sue. "Mayor of Rust." *New York Times*, Magazine section, February 11, 2011.

Hamad, Hannah. "Dad TV: Postfeminism and the Paternalization of US Television Drama." *Flow Online* 11, no. 2 (2009).

———. " 'My Wife Calls Him My Boyfriend': Gary Barlow and Robbie Williams' Reconciliatory Bromance." *Flow Online* 13, no. 9 (2011).

Hancock, Jay. "He-Cession Has More Men Looking at Once 'Female' Jobs." *Baltimore Sun*, July 17, 2009.

Harris, John. "Back to the Workhouse." *Guardian*, June 8, 2012.

Hartmann, Heidi. "Women, the Recession and the Stimulus Package." *Dissent* 56, no. 4 (2009): 42–47.

———. "The Unhappy Marriage of Marxism and Feminism: Towards a More Progressive Union." *Capital and Class* 3, no. 2 (1979): 1–33.

Harvey, David. *A Brief History of Neoliberalism*. Oxford: Oxford University Press, 2005.

———. "Neoliberalism as Creative Destruction." *Annals of the American Academy of Political and Social Science* 610, no. 21 (2007): 21–44.

Harzewski, Stephanie. *Chick Lit and Postfeminism*. Charlottesville: University of Virginia Press, 2011.

Hay, James, and Laurie Ouellette. "Makeover Television, Governmentality and the 'Good' Citizen." In *TV Transformations: Revealing the Makeover Show*, ed. Tania Lewis. London: Routledge, 2008.

Hayes, Stephanie. "Modern Makeover." *St. Petersburg Times*, August 23, 2009.

Hays, Sharon. *Flat Broke with Children: Women in the Age of Welfare Reform*. Oxford: Oxford University Press, 2003.

Hayward, Mark. "The Economic Crisis and After: Recovery, Reconstruction and Cultural Studies." *Cultural Studies* 24, no. 3 (2010): 283–94.

Heath, Stephen, and Andrew Potter. *Nation of Rebels: Why Counterculture became Consumer Culture*. New York: Harper, 2004.

Hegewisch, Ariane, Hannah Liepmann, Jeffrey Hayes, and Heidi Hartmann. "Separate and Not Equal? Gender Segregation in the Labor Market and the Gender Wage Gap." Institute for Women's Policy Research, September 2010. http://www.iwpr.org/.

Hendershot, Heather. "Belabored Reality: Making It Work on *The Simple Life* and *Project*

Runway." In *Reality TV: Remaking Television Culture*, 2nd ed., ed. Susan Murray and Laurie Ouellette. New York: New York University Press, 2009.

Henig, Robin Marantz. "What Is It about 20-Somethings?" *New York Times*, August 18, 2010.

Heritage, Stuart. "*Paranormal Activity 3*: Is There a Demon in the House?" *Guardian* Film Blog, July 27, 2011. www.guardian.co.uk/film/filmblog/2011/jul/27/paranormal-activity-3.

———. "*Paranormal Activity 4* Is Haunted by the Sequel Problem." *Guardian* Film Blog, January 6, 2012. www.guardian.co.uk/film/filmblog/2012/jan/06/paranormal-activity-4-sequel.

Hildebrand, Elin. *Silver Girl*. New York: Regan Arthur, 2011.

Hill, Annette. *Paranormal Media: Audiences, Spirits and Magic in Popular Culture*. London: Routledge, 2010.

Hilton, Perez. "Dylan McDermott Is Nekkid and Seksi in *American Horror Story*." Perez Hilton.com, October 6, 2011. perezhilton.com/2011-10-06-dylan-mcdermott-is-naked-and-sexy-on-american-horror-story#.T32vpqt8C8A.

Ho, Karen. *Liquidated: An Ethnography of Wall Street*. Durham, NC: Duke University Press, 2009.

Hochschild, Arlie Russell. *The Managed Heart: The Commercialization of Human Feeling*. Berkeley: University of California Press, 1983.

Hollows, Joanne. "Can I Go Home Yet? Feminism, Post-feminism and Domesticity." In *Feminism in Popular Culture*, ed. Joanne Hollows and Rachel Moseley. Oxford: Berg, 2006.

———. *Feminism, Femininity and Popular Culture*. Manchester: Manchester University Press, 2000.

Holohan, Siobhan. "'We're a Very Normal Family': Representing the Mundane in Channel 4's *The Family*." *Media Culture and Society* 34, no. 1 (2002): 21–35.

Huggan, Graham. *The Postcolonial Exotic: Marketing the Margins*. New York: Routledge, 2001.

Hugo Lopez, Mark, and Gabriel Velasco. "The Toll of the Great Recession: Childhood Poverty among Hispanics Sets Record, Leads Nation." Pew Hispanic Center, September 28, 2011. www.pewhispanic.org/2011/09/28/childhood-poverty-among-hispanics-sets-record-leads-nation.

Hymowitz, Kay. *Manning Up: How the Rise of Women Has Turned Men into Boys*. New York: Basic Books, 2011.

IFTN. "'Pyjama Girls,' an Observational Documentary." August 20, 2009. www.iftn.ie/?act1=record&only=1&aid=73&rid=4282424&tpl=archnewshome&force=1.

Illouz, Eva. *Cold Intimacies: The Making of Emotional Capitalism*. London: Polity, 2007.

Imre, Anikó. "Love to Hate: National Intimacy and Racial Intimacy on Reality TV in the New Europe." *Television and New Media*, published online May 27, 2011. doi: 10.1177/1527476411408121.

Imre, Anikó, and Alice Bardan. "Vampire Branding: Romania's Dark Destinations." In *Branding Post-Communist Nations: Marketizing Identities in the "New" Europe*, ed. Nadia Kaneva. London: Routledge, 2011.

Imre, Anikó, and Annabel Tremlett. "Reality TV without Class: The Postsocialist Anti-celebrity Docusoap." In *Real Class: Ordinary People and Reality Television across National Spaces*, ed. Beverly Skeggs and Helen Wood. London: BFI, 2011.

Jacob, Jennine. "Blogger Compensation: To Charge or Not to Charge." Independent Fashion Bloggers. http://heartifb.com/2012/06/13/blogger-compensation-to -charge-or-not-to-charge/.

———. "Perfect White Button Down Blouse." The Coveted, August 26, 2011. the-coveted.com/blog/2011/08/26/perfect-white-button-down-blouse.

———. "Yellow Jeans for Work." The Coveted, March 6, 2012. the-coveted.com /blog/2012/03/06/yellow-jeans.

Jameson, Fredric. *Nationalism, Colonialism and Literature: Modernism and Imperialism.* Field Day Pamphlet no. 14. Derry, 1988.

Jancovich, Mark. "The Critical Reception of the Twilight Saga." In *Screening Twilight: Critical Approaches to a Cinematic Phenomenon*, ed. Wickham Clayton and Sarah Harman. London: I. B. Tauris, 2013.

Jeffords, Susan. *Hard Bodies: Hollywood Masculinity in the Reagan Era.* New Brunswick, NJ: Rutgers University Press, 1993.

Jenkins, Henry. *Convergence Culture: Where Old and New Media Collide.* New York: New York University Press, 2008.

Jenkins, Simon. "Europe Is Turning Back to National Identity—and It's Exhilarating." *Guardian*, September 15, 2011. www.guardian.co.uk/commentisfree/2011 /sep/15/europe-national-identity-debt-crisis.

Jensen, Tracey, and Jessica Ringrose. "Sluts That Choose vs. Doormat Gypsies: Exploring Affect in the Postfeminist, Visual Moral Economy of *My Big Fat Gypsy Wedding*." *Feminist Media Studies*. doi: 10.1080/14680777.2012.756820.

Jones, Jonathan. "From Hockney to *Downton Abbey*: Have Our Cultural Tastes Gone Conservative?" *Guardian Blog*, January 23, 2012. www.guardian.co.uk /artanddesign/jonathanjonesblog/2012/jan/23/hockney-downton-abbey-culture -conservative.

Jones, Shannon, and Jelena Subotic. "Fantasies of Power: Performing Europeanization on the European Periphery." *European Journal of Cultural Studies* 14, no. 5 (2011): 542–57.

Joseph, Ralina L. " 'Tyra Banks Is Fat': Reading (Post-)Racism and (Post-)Feminism in the New Millennium." *Critical Studies in Media Communication* 26, no. 3 (2009): 237–54.

Kaufman, Therese. "The EU: The Real Sick Man of Europe?" *Eurozine*, August 5, 2011. www.eurozine.com/articles/2011-08-05-vienna-en.html.

Kellner, Douglas. "*Poltergeist*, Gender and Class in the Age of Bush and Reagan." In *Media Culture: Cultural Studies, Identity and Politics between the Modern and the Postmodern*, 127–39. London: Routledge, 1995.

Kennedy, John F. "The Soft American." *Sports Illustrated*, December 26, 1960.

Kershaw, Sarah. "Google Tells Sites for 'Cougars' to Go Prowl Elsewhere." *New York Times*, May 14, 2010.

Kiefaber, David. "Walt Whitman Is Reborn. To Sell Jeans." *Adweek*, July 6, 2009.

King, Stephen. "Why We Crave Horror Movies." *Playboy*, January 1981.

Kissell, Rick. "Cable Dramas Win Key Demo." *Variety*, November 28–December 4, 2011.

Klein, Naomi. *No Logo: No Space, No Choice, No Jobs*. New York: Picador, 2000.

———. *The Shock Doctrine: The Rise of Disaster Capitalism*. New York: Metropolitan, 2007.

Knell, Jenny. "Pyjama Girls." *Estudios Irlandeses*, no. 6 (2011): 207–10. www .estudiosirlandeses.org/Issue6/FilmIssue6/Film&TVIssue6.htm#Pyjama_Girl.

Kochhar, Rakesh. "The Demographics of the Jobs Recovery: Employment Gains by Race, Ethnicity, Gender and Nativity." Pew Research Hispanic Trends Project, March 21, 2012, http://www.pewhispanic.org/2012/03/21/the-demographics-of -the-jobs-recovery/4/.

———. "A Recovery No Better Than the Recession: Median Household Income, 2007– 2011." Pew Research Center, September 12, 2012. http://www.pewsocialtrends.org /2012/09/12/a-recovery-no-better-than-the-recession/.

Koeher, Robert. "Dream House." *Variety*, October 16, 2011.

Korek, Janusz. "Central and Eastern Europe from a Postcolonial Perspective." In *From Sovietology to Postcoloniality*, vol. 32, ed. J. Korek. Stockholm: Södertörn Academic Studies, 2007.

Kraszewski, Jon. "Coming to a Beach Near You: Examinations of Ethnic and State Identity in *Jersey Shore*." *Flow Online* 11, no. 8 (2010).

Krieder, Rose, and Diana Elliot. "Historical Changes in Stay-at-Home Mothers." Paper presented at the American Sociological Association, Atlanta, GA, 2010.

Krugman, Paul. "Can Europe Be Saved?" *New York Times*, January 12, 2011. www .nytimes.com/2011/01/16/magazine/16Europe-t.html?_r=2&pagewanted=all.

Kuehn, Kathleen M. "Home/Work or Hope Labor? Social Media Pedagogy and the Future Worker." Paper presented at Society for Cinema and Media Studies Annual Conference, Chicago, March 9, 2013.

Kurutz, Steven. "Fashion Bloggers, Posted and Represented." *New York Times*, September 28, 2011.

La Ferla, Ruth. "An Everywoman as Beauty Queen." *New York Times*, August 6, 2009.

———. "The New Icons of Fashion." *New York Times*, November 11, 2010.

———. "Who Am I Wearing? Funny You Should Ask." *New York Times*, September 12, 2012.

Larasati, R. Diyah. "Eat, Pray, Love, Mimic: Female Citizenship and Otherness." *South Asian Popular Culture* 8, no. 1 (2010): 89–95.

Lasch, Christopher. *Haven in a Heartless World: The Family Besieged*. New ed. New York: Norton, 1995.

Lauristin, Marju. "The European Public Sphere and the Social Imaginary of the 'New Europe.'" *European Journal of Communication* 22, no. 4 (2007): 397–412.

Lazar, Michelle. "Entitled to Consume: Postfeminist Femininity and a Culture of Post-critique." *Discourse and Communication* 3, no. 4 (2009): 371–400.

Lazzeri, Antonella. "Blinging Up Baby," *Sun*, February 16, 2012. www.thesun.co.uk /sol/homepage/features/4130372/Gypsy-Weddings-couple-are-blinging-up-baby .html.

Lears, T. J. Jackson. *No Place of Grace: Antimodernism and the Transformation of American Culture, 1880–1920.* Chicago: University of Chicago Press, 1981.

Leland, John. "In Housing Fall, Breaking Up Is Harder to Do." *New York Times,* December 30, 2008.

Lentin, Alana, and Gavan Titley. "The Crisis of 'Multiculturalism' in Europe: Mediated Minarets, Intolerable Subjects." *European Journal of Cultural Studies* 15, no. 2 (2012): 123–38.

Leonard, Suzanne. *Fatal Attraction.* West Sussex: Wiley-Blackwell, 2009.

Levenson, Ellie. *The Noughtie Girl's Guide to Feminism.* Oxford: One World, 2009.

Levin, Peter. "Gender, Work, and Time: Gender at Work and at Play and in Futures Trading." In *Fighting for Time: Shifting Boundaries of Work and Social Life,* ed. Cynthia Fuchs Epstein and Arne Kalleberg. New York: Russell Sage, 2004.

Levy, Ariel. *Female Chauvinist Pigs: Women and the Rise of Raunch Culture.* New York: Free Press, 2005.

Lewis, Michael. "Shorting Reform." *New York Times,* May 28, 2010.

Lewis, Tania. "Branding, Celebritization and the Lifestyle Expert." *Cultural Studies* 24, no. 4 (2010): 580–98.

———. *Smart Living: Lifestyle Media and Popular Expertise.* New York: Peter Lang, 2008.

Leyda, Julia, Nicholas Rombes, Steven Shaviro, and Theresa Grisham. "Roundtable Discussion: The Post-cinematic in *Paranormal Activity* and *Paranormal Activity 2.*" *La Furia Umana.* Accessed May 19, 2012. www.lafuriaumana.it/index.php/locchio-che-uccide/385-roundtable-discussion-about-post-cinematic.

Lipsitz, George. *The Possessive Investment in Whiteness: How White People Profit from Identity Politics.* Philadelphia: Temple University Press, 1998.

———. *Time Passages: Collective Memory and American Popular Culture.* Minneapolis: University of Minnesota Press, 1990.

Lipsyte, Sam. *The Ask.* New York: Farrar, Straus and Giroux, 2010.

Litt, Toby. "The 80s: The Best of Times, the Worst of Times." *Guardian,* July 29, 2010.

Littler, Jo. *Radical Consumption: Shopping for Change in Contemporary Culture.* Berkshire: Open University Press, 2008.

Liveline. RTÉ Radio One, March 14, 2012. http://www.rte.ie/radio1/liveline/programmes/2012/0314/350648-2012-03-143/.

López, Ana. "Are All Latins from Manhattan? Hollywood, Ethnography, and Cultural Colonialiam." In *Unspeakable Images: Ethnicity and the American Cinema,* ed. Lester Friedman, 404–24. Urbana: University of Illinois Press, 1991.

Lopez, Mark Hugo, and Gabriel Velasco. "The Toll of the Great Recession: Childhood Poverty among Hispanics Sets Record, Leads Nation." Pew Hispanic Center, September 28, 2011. www.pewhispanic.org.

Lotz, Amanda D. "Postfeminist Television Criticism: Rehabilitating Critical Terms and Identifying Postfeminist Attributes." *Feminist Media Studies* 1, no. 1 (2001): 105–21.

Luke, Lauren. "Kelly Clarkson Stronger Make Up Look." YouTube, February 19, 2012. www.youtube.com/watch?v=n2qsYHIO6iQ.

———. "LEONA LEWIS Bleeding Love Inspired Make Up Look." YouTube, December 14, 2007. youtu.be/T6QH4AKhOFk.

———. "My Vintage Glams Make Up Tutorial." YouTube, April 27, 2009. www.youtube.com/watch?v=dvodbogykWc.

Lury, Celia. *Brands: The Logos of the Global Economy.* London: Routledge, 2004.

Luscombe, Belinda. "Workplace Salaries: At Last, Women on Top." *Time,* September 1, 2010. http://www.time.com/time/business/article/0,8599,2015274,00.html.

Lynch, Kathleen. "Women, Class and Gender: New Discriminations." UCD School of Social Justice, Dublin, September 10, 2010.

Lyons, James. "Miami Slice: Surgical Shockings in *Nip/Tuck.*" *Journal of Popular Film and Television* 35, no. 1 (2007): 2–11.

Manning, Joy. "I Will Make You Hurt." *Inked,* December 10, 2009. Accessed August 25, 2010. http://www.inkedmag.com/features/article/i-will-make-you-hurt/page/1/.

Mannur, Anita. "Eat, Dwell, Orient: Food Networks and Asian/American Cooking Communities." *Cultural Studies,* published online September 24, 2012. doi: 10.1080/09502386.2012.725060.

Marages, Kelly. "I'm Not Buying Recession Chic." *Washington Post,* March 15, 2009.

Marshall, Kelli. "Bromance and the Boys of *Boston Legal.*" *Flow Online* 13, no. 14 (2011).

Martin, Randy. *An Empire of Indifference: American War and the Financial Logic of Risk Management.* Durham, NC: Duke University Press, 2009.

———. *The Financialization of Everyday Life.* Pittsburgh: Temple University Press, 2006.

———. "The Good, the Bad, and the Ugly: Economies of Parable." *Cultural Studies* 24, no. 3 (2010).

Marx, Karl. *Das Kapital.* London: Gateway, 1996.

Matheson, Peter. "What Horror Movies Can Teach Economic Policy Makers." *Wall Street Journal,* October 28, 2011.

Matrix. "Obama Appoints Stone Cold Racist to US Supreme Court." Neocon Express blog, May 26, 2009. http://neoconexpress.blogspot.com/2009/05/obama-appoints-hardcore-racist-to-us.html.

Mattioli, Dana. "Few Gender Differences in a Recession." *Wall Street Journal,* August 18, 2009.

McAbbe, Sarah. "He-Cession, She-Cession." *Bitch: Feminist Response to Pop Culture* 44 (winter 2009): 21–23.

McCarthy, Anna. "Reality Television: A Neoliberal Theatre of Suffering." *Social Text* 4, no. 93 (2007): 17–42.

McCarthy, Cameron, and Gregory Dimitriadis. "Governmentality and the Sociology of Education: Media, Educational Policy and the Politics of Resentment." In *Race, Identity, and Representation in Education,* ed. Cameron McCarthy and William Crichlow. New York: Routledge, 2005.

McDonough, Terrence, and Dundon, Tony. "Thatcherism Delayed? The Irish Crisis and the Paradox of Social Partnership." *Industrial Relations Journal* 41, no. 6 (2010): 544–62.

McGee, Micki. *Self-Help, Inc.: Makeover Culture in American Life*. Oxford: Oxford University Press, 2005.

McNeill, Laurie. "Teaching an Old Genre New Tricks: The Diary on the Internet." *Biography* 26, no. 1 (2003): 24–47.

McRobbie, Angela. *The Aftermath of Feminism: Gender, Culture and Social Change*. London: Sage, 2009.

———. "Notes on Postfeminism and Popular Culture: Bridget Jones and the New Gender Regime." In *All about the Girl: Culture, Power and Identity*, ed. Anita Harris. New York: Routledge, 2004.

———. "Reflections on Feminism, Immaterial Labour and the Post-Fordist Regime." *New Formations* 70 (2010): 60–76.

Meade, Rosemary. " 'Our Country's Calling Card': Culture as the Brand in Recessionary Ireland." *Variant* 43 (spring 2012): 33–35. www.variant.org.uk/43texts /RosemaryMeade43.html.

Mendible, Myra. "Introduction." In *From Bananas to Buttocks: The Latina Body in Popular Film and Culture*, ed. Myra Mendible. Austin: University of Texas Press, 2010.

Messner, Michael A., and Jeffrey Montez de Oca. "The Male Consumer as Loser: Beer and Liquor Ads in Mega Sports Media Events." *Signs: Journal of Women in Culture and Society* 30, no. 3 (2005): 1879–1909.

Miller, Michelle. "Fashion Week's Runway Recession." CBS *Evening News*, September 12, 2008. www.cbsnews.com/stories/2008/09/12/eveningnews/main4446292 .shtml.

Mock, Brentin. "Hate Crimes against Latinos Rising Nationwide." *Intelligence Report*, no. 128 (winter 2007). www.splcenter.org/get-informed/intelligence-report /browse-all-issues/2007/winter/immigration-backlash.

Modleski, Tania. *Loving with a Vengeance: Mass-Produced Fantasies for Women*. 2nd ed. London: Routledge, 2008.

Molina-Guzmán, Isabel. *Dangerous Curves: Latina Bodies in the Media*. New York: New York University Press, 2010.

———. "Gendering Latinidad in the Elián News Discourse about Cuban Women." *Latino Studies* 3 (2005): 179–204.

———. "Mediating Frida: Negotiating Discourses of Latina/o Authenticity in Global Media Representations of Ethnic Identity." *Critical Studies in Media Communication* 23, no. 3 (2006): 232–51.

———. "Salma Hayek's Celebrity Activism: Constructing Race, Ethnicity, and Gender as Mainstream Global Commodities." In *Commodity Activism: Cultural Resistance in Neoliberal Times*, ed. Roopali Mukherjee and Sarah Banet-Weiser. New York: New York University Press, 2012.

Molina-Guzmán, Isabel, and Angharad Valdivia. "Brain, Brow or Bootie: Iconic Latinas in Contemporary Popular Culture." *Communication Review* 7, no. 2 (2004): 205–21.

Moore, Niamh. "Rejuvenating Docklands: The Irish Context." *Irish Geography* 32, no. 2 (1999): 135–49.

Mosco, Vincent. *The Political Economy of Communication*. London: Sage, 2009.

Mothel, Seth, and Eileen Patten. "Hispanics of Colombian Origin in the United States, 2010." Pew Hispanic Center Report, June 27, 2012. www.pewhispanic.org.

Muhlke, Christine. "Video Artist." *New York Times Women's Fashion Magazine*, August 22, 2010.

Mukherjee, Roopali, and Sarah Banet-Weiser, eds. *Commodity Activism: Cultural Resistance in Neoliberal Times*. New York: New York University Press, 2012.

Mullally, Una. "Heroin: The Next Generation." *Irish Times*, May 14, 2011.

Mulvey, Laura. "Visual Pleasure and Narrative Cinema." *Screen* 16, no. 3 (1975): 6–18.

Mundy, Liza. *The Richer Sex: How the New Majority of Female Breadwinners Is Transforming Sex, Love and Family*. New York: Simon and Schuster, 2012.

Munt, Sally. *Queer Attachments: The Cultural Politics of Shame*. Hampshire, U.K.: Ashgate, 2008.

"My Big Fat Gypsy Wedding: Why Is It a Hit?" BBC News Magazine. www.bbc.co.uk/news/magazine-12311604, January 28, 2011.

Nagel, Joane. "Masculinity and Nationalism: Gender and Sexuality in the Making of Nations." *Ethnic and Racial Studies* 21, no. 2 (1998): 242–69.

Nakamura, Lisa. "The Comfort Women of the Digital Industries: Asian Women in David Fincher's *The Social Network*." *In Media Res*, January 17, 2011.

———. *Digitizing Race: Visual Cultures of the Internet*. Minneapolis: University of Minnesota Press, 2007.

National Institute of Justice. "Research Briefing: Understanding Trends in Hate Crimes against Immigrants and Hispanic-Americans." http://www.nij.gov/topics/crime/hate-crime/immigrants-hispanics.htm#stateselection.

Naughton, Gareth. "*His and Hers*." For Your Consideration, June 18, 2010. http://garethnaughton.blogspot.ie/search?q=his+and+hers.

Neate, Rupert. "YouTube to Allow Its Users to Cash In." *Daily Telegraph*, August 27, 2009.

Nederdog, Jethro. "*American Horror Story*'s Dylan McDermott on Nude Scenes: 'It's All Me.'" *Hollywood Reporter*, November 16, 2011.

Negra, Diane. "Structural Integrity, Historical Reversion, and the Post 9/11 Chick Flick." *Feminist Media Studies* 8, no. 1 (2008): 51–68.

———. *What a Girl Wants? Fantasizing the Reclamation of Self in Postfeminism*. New York: Routledge, 2009.

———. "Where the Boys Are: Postfeminism and the New Single Man." *Flow* 4, no. 3 (2006). flowtv.org/2006/04/wedding-crashers-failure-to-launch-feminism-postfeminism-masculinity.

Negra, Diane, and Yvonne Tasker. "Neoliberal Frames and Genres of Inequality: Recessionary Chick Flicks and Male-Centered Corporate Melodrama." *European Journal of Cultural Studies* 16, no. 3 (June 2013): 344–61.

Negrin, Llewellyn. "The Self as Image: A Critical Appraisal of Postmodern Theories of Fashion." *Theory Culture Society* 16, no. 3 (1999): 99–118.

Negrón-Muntaner, Frances. *Boricua Pop: Puerto Ricans and the Latinization of American Culture*. New York: New York University Press, 2004.

Newton, Matthew. "Levi's Attempts to Salvage 'Go Forth' Campaign with Sincerity."

June 24, 2010. www.trueslant.com/matthewnewton/2010/06/24/levis-attempts-to -salvage-go-forth-campaign-with-sincerity/.

Nichols, Michelle. "Recession Creates New Trend in Fashion Shopping." Reuters, September 9, 2010. www.reuters.com/article/2010/09/09/us-newyork-fashion -idUSTRE6882OZ20100909.

Noah, Timothy. *The Great Divergence: American's Growing Inequality Crisis and What We Can Do about It.* New York: Bloomsbury, 2012.

Norris, Floyd. "In This Recession, More Men Are Losing Jobs." *New York Times*, March 13, 2009.

NPR. "Levi's Gives Struggling Town Cinderella Treatment." *All Things Considered*, October 10, 2010.

Odell, Amy. "The Recession Has Forced High-Fashion Companies to Use the Internet." *New York*, July 12, 2010.

O'Gorman, Aileen. "Illicit Drug Use in Ireland: An Overview of the Problem and Policy Responses." *Journal of Drug Issues* 28, no. 1 (1998): 155–66.

Okely, Judith, and Gustav Houtman. "The Dale Farm Eviction: Interview with Judith Okely on Gypsies and Travellers." *Anthropology Today* 27, no. 6 (2011): 24–27.

O'Leary, Amy. "In Virtual Play, Sex Harassment Is All Too Real." *New York Times*, August 1, 2012.

Oler, Tammy. "Pinned Down: Is Pinterest as Girly as the Media Paints It? And If So, Who Cares?" *Bitch* (fall 2012).

Ong, Aihwa. *Neoliberalism as Exception: Mutations in Citizenship and Sovereignty.* Durham, NC: Duke University Press, 2006.

O'Regan, Michael. "Suicide Rate at an All-Time High, Says Minister." *Irish Times*, April 28, 2011.

O'Toole, Fintan. "Liechtenstein on the Liffey." *Guardian*, February 27, 2009.

———. *Ship of Fools: How Stupidity and Corruption Sank the Celtic Tiger.* London: Faber and Faber, 2009.

Ouellette, Laurie. "Branding the Right: The Affective Economy of Sarah Palin." *Cinema Journal* 51, no. 4 (2012): 185–91.

———. "'Take Responsibility for Yourself': Judge Judy and the Neoliberal Citizen." *Reality TV: Remaking Television Culture.* 2nd ed. New York: New York University Press, 2009.

Ouellette, Laurie, and James Hay. *Better Living through Reality TV: Television and Postwelfare Citizenship.* Oxford: Blackwell, 2008.

Palahniuk, Chuck. *Fight Club.* New York: Vintage, 2006.

Palmer, Gareth. *Discipline and Liberty: Television and Governance.* Manchester: Manchester University Press, 2003.

———. "Governing Bodies." In *The Politics of Reality Television*, ed. Marwan M. Kraidy and Katherine Sender. London: Routledge, 2011.

———. "'The New You': Class and Transformation on Lifestyle Television." In *Understanding Reality Television*, ed. Susan Holmes and Deborah Jermyn. London: Routledge, 2004.

Passel, Jeffrey, D'Vera Cohn, and Ana Gonzaléz-Barrera. "Net Migration from Mexico

Falls to Zero—and Perhaps Less." Pew Hispanic Center, May 3, 2012. www
.pewhispanic.org/2010/04/23/net-migration-from-mexico-falls-to-zero-and
-perhaps-less.

Peck, Don. "How a New Jobless Era Will Transform America." *Atlantic*, March 2010.

———. *Pinched: How the Great Recession Has Narrowed Our Futures and What We Can Do about It*. New York: Crown, 2011.

Peiss, Kathy. *Cheap Amusements: Working Women and Leisure in Turn-of-the-Century New York*. Philadelphia: Temple University Press, 1986.

Pentney, Beth. " 'We're Still Blaming Mothers': Postfeminist Mother Blame in *We Need to Talk about Kevin* and *American Horror Story*." Paper presented at Console-ing Passions International Conference on Television, Video, Audio, New Media and Feminism, Suffolk University, Boston, July 19–21, 2012.

Pesch, Kimberly. "Bold + Bright." eat.sleep.wear, September 28, 2011. www
.eatsleepwear.com/2011/09/28/bold-bright.

———. "A Pretty Woman Moment." eat.sleep.wear, August 8, 2011. www
.eatsleepwear.com/2011/08/08/a-pretty-woman-moment/.

Petrella, Christopher. "Recovery for the 1%, Recession for the Rest." Nation of Change, March 15, 2012. http://www.nationofchange.org/recovery-1-recession
-rest-1331826118.

Pfeiffer, Alice. "Young Bloggers Have Ear of Fashion Heavyweights." *New York Times*, Financial Desk, September 14, 2009.

Phan, Michelle. "Mulan Bride." YouTube, June 18, 2011. youtu.be/ebcc1WXJS6A.

———. "Perfect Red Lips." YouTube, February 24, 2011. youtu.be/jd_Qgcue3lU.

———. "Seductive Smokey Eyes Tutorial." YouTube, July 30, 2008. youtu.be
/zupy7R4uR2g.

Polan, Dana. *Julia Child's "The French Chef."* Durham, NC: Duke University Press, 2011.

Pou, Claudia-Teresa. " 'Recessionista' Talks about the Success of Recession-Friendly Blog." Medill Money Mavens, February 23, 2009. medillmoneymavens.com/2009
/02/23/recessionista-talks-about-the-success-of-recession-friendly-blog.

Powell, Helen, and Sylvie Prasad. " 'As Seen on TV': The Celebrity Expert; How Taste Is Shaped by Lifestyle Media." *Cultural Politics: An International Journal* 6, no. 1 (2010): 111–24.

———. "Life Swap: Celebrity Expert as Style Adviser." In *The Great American Makeover: Television, History, Nation*, ed. Dana Heller. Basingstoke: Palgrave Macmillan, 2006.

Powell, Julie. *Julie and Julia: 365 Days, 524 Recipes, 1 Tiny Apartment Kitchen; How One Girl Risked Her Marriage, Her Job, and Her Sanity to Master the Art of Living*. New York: Little, Brown, 2005.

Pozner, Jennifer L. *Reality Bites Back: The Troubling Truth about Guilty Pleasure TV*. Berkeley, CA: Seal Press, 2010.

Press, Andrea L. " 'Feminism? That's So Seventies': Girls and Young Women Discuss Femininity and Feminism in *America's Next Top Model*." In *New Femininities: Postfeminism, Neoliberalism and Subjectivity*, ed. Rosalind Gill and Christina Scharff. Basingstoke: Palgrave Macmillan, 2011.

Projansky, Sarah. *Watching Rape: Film and Television in Postfeminist Culture.* New York: New York University Press, 2001.

Punch, Michael. "Contested Urban Environments: Perspectives on the Place and Meaning of Community Action in Central Dublin, Ireland." *Interface* 1, no. 2 (2009): 83–107.

———. "Problem Drug Use and the Political Economy of Urban Restructuring: Heroin, Class and Governance in Dublin." *Antipode* 37, no. 4 (2005): 754–74.

Radner, Hilary. *Neo-feminist Cinema: Girly Films, Chick Flicks and Consumer Culture.* New York: Routledge, 2011.

Raeside, Julia. "Celebrity Experts: Time for a Rain Check." *Guardian*, April 8, 2011. www.guardian.co.uk/tv-and-radio/tvandradioblog/2011/apr/08/celebrity-vacation-vacation-vacation.

Rafferty, Mick. "Gregory Deal Would Have Had Huge Impact if Fulfilled." *Irish Times*, March 9, 2012.

Ramirez Berg, Charles. *Latino Images in Film: Stereotypes, Subversion, Resistance.* Austin: University of Texas Press, 2002.

"Recession Harder on Men Than Women, Study Says." Fox News.com, March 11, 2009. http://www.foxnews.com/story/2009/03/11/recession-harder-on-men-than-women-study-says/.

Remnick, David. "We Are Alive: Bruce Springsteen at 62." *New Yorker*, July 30, 2012.

Roberts, Martin. "The Fashion Police: Governing the Self in *What Not to Wear*." In *Interrogating Postfeminism: Gender and the Politics of Popular Culture*, ed. Yvonne Tasker and Diane Negra. Durham, NC: Duke University Press, 2007.

Roberts, Michael. "The Five Hottest Money Honeys to Break the News about Economic Catastrophe." *Denver Westword*, September 30, 2008.

Roberts, Sam. "Birth Rate Is Said to Fall as a Result of Recession." *New York Times*, August 6, 2009.

Rose, Nikolas. "Governing 'Advanced' Liberal Democracies." In *Foucault and Political Reason: Liberalism, Neo-liberalism, and Rationalities of Government*, ed. Andrew Barry, Thomas Osborne, and Nikolas Rose. Chicago: University of Chicago Press, 1996.

———. *Powers of Freedom: Reframing Political Thought.* Cambridge: Cambridge University Press, 1999.

Rosin, Hanna. "The End of Men." *Atlantic*, July–August 2010, 56–72. http://www.theatlantic.com/magazine/archive/2010/07/the-end-of-men/308135/.

———. *The End of Men: And the Rise of Women.* New York: Riverhead, 2012.

———. "Primetime's Looming Male Identity Crisis." *Atlantic*, September 2011.

———. "Who Wears the Pants in This Economy?" *New York Times Magazine*, August 30, 2012.

Ross, Steven J. *Working-Class Hollywood: Silent Film and the Shaping of Class in America.* Princeton, NJ: Princeton University Press, 1998.

"Roundtable: Women Gone Wild: Reflections on the Feminist Blogosphere." *Journal of Women's History* 22, no. 4 (2010): 185–243.

Rowlands, Penelope, and Christine Berrie. "OP-ART; on the Heels of a Recession." *New York Times*, July 15, 2010.

Safire, William. "The Way We Live Now: 11-23-08: Frugalista." *New York Times Magazine*, November 23, 2008.

Salam, Reihan. "The Death of Macho." *Foreign Policy* (July–August 2009): 65–70.

Sandberg, Sheryl. *Lean In: Women, Work and the Will to Lead*. New York: Alfred A. Knopf, 2013.

Sanders, Joshunda, and Diana Barnes-Brown. "Eat, Pray, Spend: Priv-Lit and the New Enlightened American Dream." *Bitch* 47 (summer 2010): 29–33.

Sands, Daisy. "Single Mothers: Singled Out." Fawcett Society, June 2011. http://www.fawcettsociety.org.uk/.

Saturday Night with Miriam. RTÉ Television, June 26, 2010. www.rte.ie/tv/miriam/video.html.

Sax, Leonard. *Boys Adrift: The Five Factors Driving the Growing Epidemic of Unmotivated Boys and Underachieving Young Men*. New York: Basic Books, 2009.

Scanlon, Jennifer. "Making Shopping Safe for the Rest of Us: Sophie Kinsella's Shopaholic Series and Its Readers." *Americana: The Journal of American Popular Culture 1900–Present* 4, no. 2 (2005): 1–14.

Schneider, Steven. *Horror Film and Psychoanalysis: Freud's Worst Nightmare*. Cambridge, MA: Cambridge University Press, 2004.

Schudson, Michael. *Advertising, the Uneasy Persuasion: Its Dubious Impact on American Society*. New York: Basic Books, 1986.

Schuman, Emily. "FAQ—Cupcakes and Cashmere." Cupcakes and Cashmere. cupcakesandcashmere.com/faq.

Schwarz, Ori. "On Friendship, Boobs and the Logic of the Catalogue: Online Self-Portraits as a Means for the Exchange of Capital." *Convergence: The International Journal of Research into New Media Technologies* 16, no. 2 (2010): 163–83.

Scott, A. O. "Ghostbusters on a Budget: If Things Go Bump in the Night, Grab a Camera." *New York Times*, October 9, 2009.

"Sears to Close 100–120 Stores after Poor Holiday Sales." *Guardian*, December 27, 2011.

Sennett, Richard. *The Culture of the New Capitalism*. New Haven, CT: Yale University Press, 2006.

Sharkey, Betsy. "Drag Me to Hell." *Los Angeles Times*, May 29, 2009.

Sheffield, Rob. "*American Horror Story* Will Restore Your Faith in Ryan Murphy's Dark Side." *Rolling Stone*, November 10, 2011.

Shohat, Ella, and Robert Stam. *Unthinking Eurocentrism: Multiculturalism and the Media*. London: Routledge, 1994.

"Shopper: And with All That Money I Saved." *Washington Post*, August 28, 2008.

Silva, Jennifer M. *Coming Up Short: Working-Class Adulthood in an Age of Uncertainty*. Oxford: Oxford University Press, 2013.

Singer, Natasha. "A Label for a Pleather Economy." *New York Times*, October 26, 2008.

Skeggs, Beverley. *Class, Self, Culture*. London: Routledge, 2004.

———. *Formations of Class and Gender*. London: Routledge, 1997.

Skeggs, Beverley, and Helen Wood. "The Moral Economy of Person Production: The Class Relations of Self-Performance on Reality TV." *Sociological Review* 57, no. 4 (2009): 626–44.

———. "Notes on Ethical Scenarios of Self on British Reality TV." *Feminist Media Studies* 4, no. 2 (2004): 205–8.

Skeggs, Beverley, Helen Wood, and Helen Thumin. "Making Class through Moral Extension on Reality TV." 2007. www.sprak.umu.se/digitalAssets/29/29326 _workshop_intimacy_ahorarkop.pdf.

Slaughter, Anne-Marie. "Why Women Still Can't Have It All." *Atlantic*, July–August 2012, 84–102.

Smith, Caroline J. *Cosmopolitan Culture and Consumerism in Chick Lit.* London: Routledge, 2009.

Smith, Christopher Holmes. "Bling Was a Bubble." *International Journal of Communication* 3 (2009).

———. "We Have Armageddon! Media Ritual, Moral Panic, and Market Meltdown." Annenberg Research Seminar, Annenberg School for Communication and Journalism, University of Southern California, Los Angeles, August 29, 2011.

Smith, Erin Copple. "Pinning Postfeminism." *Antenna*, August 21, 2012.

Smolinski, Julieanne. "*American Horror Story* Recap: I Love the Eighties (Murders)!" Vulture.com, October 20, 2011. www.vulture.com/2011/10/american_horror_story _murder_h.html.

Smyth, Gerry. "Irish National Identity after the Celtic Tiger." *Estudios Irlandeses* 7 (2012): 132–37.

Snelson, Tim. "The Ghost in the Machine: World War Two, Popular Occultism and Hollywood's 'Serious' Ghost Films." *Media History* 17, no. 1 (2011): 16–32.

Sommers, Christina Hoff. *The War against Boys: How Misguided Feminism Is Harming Our Young Men.* New York: Simon and Schuster, 2001.

Sotomayor, Sonia. "A Latina Judge's Voice." *Berkeley La Raza Law Journal* (spring 2002). www.nytimes.com/2009/05/15/us/politics/15judge.text.html?pagewanted=all.

Springsteen, Bruce. *Wrecking Ball.* Columbia Records, 2012.

Stapleton, Christine. "New Rules Aim for Smoother Defaults." *Palm Beach Post* (Florida), October 12, 2008.

Stein, Catherine, et al. "Family Ties in Tough Times: How Young Adults and Their Parents View the U.S. Economic Crisis." *Journal of Family Psychology* 25, no. 3 (2011): 449–54.

Stephenson, Correy E. "Breaking Up Is Even Harder to Do: Divorce Becoming Increasingly Complicated." *Lawyers Weekly USA*, May 5, 2008.

Stevenson, Seth. "Levi's Commercials, Now Starring Walt Whitman." *Adweek*, October 26, 2009.

Stewart, Dodai. "Black Women: Wise Best Friend to White Women Everywhere." *Jezebel*, August 27, 2007.

Stewart, Heather. "More Women Join Dole Queue as Public Sector Cuts Bite." *Guardian*, May 18, 2011.

Stolberg, Sheryl Gay. "Sotomayor's Opponents and Allies Prepare Strategies." *New York Times*, May 27, 2009.

Stratton, Allegra. "Women Will Bear Brunt of Budget Cuts, Says Yvette Cooper." *Guardian*, July 4, 2010.

Streitfeld, David. "Rock Bottom for Decades, but Showing Signs of Life." *New York Times*, January 31, 2009.

Strugatz, Rachel. "To Pay or Not to Pay: A Closer Look at the Business of Blogging." *Women's Wear Daily*, June 5, 2012.

Sturken, Marita. *Tourists of History: Memory, Kitsch and Consumerism from Oklahoma City to Ground Zero*. Durham, NC: Duke University Press, 2007.

Sturken, Marita, and Lisa Cartwright. *Practices of Looking: An Introduction to Visual Culture*. 2nd ed. Oxford: Oxford University Press, 2009.

Suarez, Natalie. "Rooftop Breeze." Natalie Off Duty, October 6, 2011. natalieoffduty .blogspot.com.

Sue, Derald Wing, Christina M. Capodilupo, Gina C. Torino, Jennifer M. Bucceri, Aisha M. B. Holder, Kevin L. Nadal, and Marta Esquilin. "Racial Microaggressions in Everyday Life: Implications for Clinical Practice." *American Psychologist* 62, no. 4 (2007): 271–86.

Sullivan, Andrew. "The End of Expertise?" *Atlantic*, September 6, 2008. www .theatlantic.com/daily-dish/archive/2008/09/the-end-of-expertise/211907.

Sztompka, Piotr. "The Trauma of Social Change: A Case of Postcommunist Societies." In *Cultural Trauma and Collective Identity*, ed. Jeffrey C. Alexander et al. Berkeley: University of California Press, 2004.

"Taoiseach: We Will Not 'Have the Name Defaulter across Our Foreheads.'" *Irish Examiner*, January 24, 2012. www.irishexaminer.com/breakingnews/ireland /taoiseach-we-will-not-have-name-of-defaulter-across-our-foreheads-537162 .html.

Tasker, Yvonne. "Enchanted (2007) by Postfeminism." In *Feminism at the Movies: Understanding Gender in Contemporary Popular Cinema*, ed. Hilary Radner and Rebecca Stringer. London: Routledge, 2011.

———. *Working Girls: Gender and Sexuality in Popular Culture*. London: Routledge, 1998.

Tasker, Yvonne, and Diane Negra, eds. *Interrogating Postfeminism: Gender and the Politics of Popular Culture*. Durham, NC: Duke University Press, 2007.

———. "Introduction: Feminist Politics and Postfeminist Culture." In *Interrogating Postfeminism: Gender and the Politics of Popular Culture*, ed. Yvonne Tasker and Diane Negra. Durham, NC: Duke University Press, 2007.

Tavernise, Sabrina. "Gains Made in Equality of Income in Downturn." *New York Times*, September 30, 2011.

Taylor, Anthea. *Single Women in Popular Culture: The Limits of Postfeminism*. Basingstoke: Palgrave Macmillan, 2012.

———. "The Urge towards Love Is an Urge towards (Un)death: Romance, Masochistic Desire and Postfeminism in the *Twilight* Novels." *International Journal of Cultural Studies* 15 (2012): 31–46.

Taylor, Hayley. "Hayley's Advice." Channel4.com, July 14, 2010. www.channel4.com /programmes/the-fairy-jobmother/articles/hayleys-advice.

———. "Live Chat with Hayley." Channel4.com, July 14, 2010. www.channel4.com /programmes/the-fairy-jobmother/articles/live-chat-with-hayley.

Taylor, Lisa. "From Ways of Life to Lifestyle: The Ordinari-ization of British Gardening Lifestyle Television." *European Journal of Communication* 17, no. 4 (2002): 479–93.

Thorne, Deborah. "Extreme Financial Strain: Emergent Chores, Gender Inequality and Emotional Distress." *Journal of Family and Economic Issues* 31 (2010): 185–97.

Tincknell, Estella. "Scourging the Abject Body: *Ten Years Younger* and Fragmented Femininity under Neoliberalism." In *New Femininities: Postfeminism, Neoliberalism and Subjectivity*, ed. Rosalind Gill and Christina Scharff. Basingstoke: Palgrave Macmillan, 2011.

Torres-Saillant, Silvio. "Inventing the Race: Latinos in the Ethnoracial Pentagon." *Latino Studies* 1, no. 1 (2003): 123–51.

Traister, Rebecca. "Sarah Palin's Grab for Feminism." Salon.com, June 1, 2010.

Traube, Elizabeth. *Dreaming Identities: Class, Gender and Generation in 1980s Hollywood Movies.* Boulder, CO: Westview, 1992.

Tudor, Deborah. "Twenty-First Century Neoliberal Man." In *Neoliberalism and Global Cinema*, ed. Jyostna Kapur and Keith B. Wagner. London: Routledge, 2011.

Turse, Nick. "The Body Count on Main Street." In *These Times*, December 19, 2008.

Tyler, Imogen. "'Chav Mum Chav Scum': Class Disgust in Contemporary Britain." *Feminist Media Studies* 8, no. 1 (2008): 17–34.

Tyler, Imogen, and Bruce Bennett. "'Celebrity Chav': Fame, Femininity and Social Class." *European Journal of Cultural Studies* 13, no. 3 (2010): 375–93.

Tyre, Peg. *The Trouble with Boys: A Surprising Report Card on Our Sons, Their Problems at School, and What Parents and Educators Must Do.* New York: Random House, 2008.

UK Women's Budget Group. "The Impact on Women of the Coalition Spending Review 2010." November 2010. www.wbg.org.uk/RRB_Reports_4_1653541019.pdf.

United States Census Bureau. "Mother's Day: May 8, 2011." March 17, 2011. www.census.gov/newsroom/releases/archives/facts_for_features_special_editions/cb11-ff07.html.

Valdivia, Angharad. *Latina/o Communication Studies Today.* New York: Peter Lang, 2008.

van Baar, Huub. "The European Roma: Minority Representation, Memory, and the Limits of Transnational Governmentality." PhD diss., University of Amsterdam, 2011.

Van Slooten, Jessica Lyn. "A Marriage Made in the Kitchen: Amanda Hesser's *Cooking for Mr. Latte* and Julie Powell's *Julie and Julia* as Foodie Romance." In *You Are What You Eat: Literary Probes into the Palate*, ed. Annette M. Magid. Newcastle upon Tyne, U.K.: Cambridge Scholars, 2008.

Vargas, Lucilla. "Genderizing Latino News: An Analysis of a Local Newspaper's Coverage of Latino Current Affairs." *Critical Studies in Media Communication* 17, no. 3 (2000): 261–93.

Verdery, Katherine. "Whither Postsocialism?" In *Postsocialism: Ideals, Ideologies and Practices in Eurasia*, ed. C. Hann. London: Routledge, 2002.

Vinnicombe, S., R. Sealy, J. Graham, J. Doldor, and E. Doldor. "The Female FTSE Board Report 2010: Opening up the Appointment Process." Cranfield University School of Management, 2010. www.som.cranfield.ac.uk/som/dinamic-content/research/documents/FemaleFTSEReport2010.pdf.

"Volta Speaks to Pyjama Girls Director Maya Derrington" [video]. Volta. www.volta
.ie/clips-and-trailers/volta-speaks-to-pyjama-girls-director-maya-derrington.

Walter, Jess. *The Financial Lives of the Poets*. New York: HarperCollins, 2009.

Walters, Natasha. "Why Is There So Much Movie Violence against Women?" *Guardian*,
June 3, 2010.

Wanzer, Darrel Enck. "Barack Obama, the Tea Party, and the Threat of Race: On
Racial Neoliberalism and Born again Racism." *Communication, Culture, Critique* 4,
no. 1 (2011).

Warner, Michael. *The Trouble with Normal: Sex, Politics, and the Ethics of Queer Life*. Cambridge, MA: Harvard University Press, 1999.

"Was It for This?" *Irish Times*, November 18, 2010.

Weber, Brenda. *Makeover TV: Selfhood, Citizenship and Celebrity*. Durham, NC: Duke University Press, 2009.

———. "Puerile Pillars of the Frat Pack: Jack Black, Will Ferrell, Adam Sandler, and
Ben Stiller." In *Shining in the Shadows: Movie Stars of the 2000s*, ed. Murray Pomerance.
New Brunswick, NJ: Rutgers University Press, 2012.

Weeks, Kathi. *The Problem with Work: Feminism, Marxism, Antiwork Politics, and Postwork
Imaginaries*. Durham, NC: Duke University Press, 2011.

Weigel, D. "Sotomayor, Enemy of the White Male." Center for Media_and_Democ-
racy, May 26, 2009. http://www.sourcewatch.org/index.php/Center_for_Media
_and_Democracy.

West, Kelly. "ABC 2012 Midseason Premiere: Work It." Television Blend, May 17,
2011. http://www.cinemablend.com/television/ABC-2012-Midseason-Premiere
-Work-It-32109.html.

Wheeler, Rachael. "Watch Our Awkward Chat with Josie and Swanley Smith off *My
Big Fat Gypsy Wedding* at the NTAs." *Mirror Online*, January 26, 2012. www.mirror
.co.uk/3am/tv-film-news/my-big-fat-gypsy-weddings-josie-190701.

"Where Housing Once Boomed, Recovery Lags." *New York Times*, April 3, 2012.

"Where to Find High Style at Penny-Pinching Prices." *Washington Post* (Style), August 7, 2008.

Whitman, Walt. "America." In *Leaves of Grass*, 1891–92. Boston: James R. Osgood,
1892.

———. "Pioneers! O Pioneers." In *Leaves of Grass*, 1871–72. New York: J. S. Redfield,
1872.

Wilcox, Bradley. "Marriage Haves and Have-Nots." *New York Times*, July 3, 2011. http://
www.nytimes.com/roomfordebate/2011/07/03/marriage-the-next-chapter/marriage
-havesand-have-nots.

———. "When Marriage Disappears: The Retreat from Marriage in Middle
America." In *When Marriage Disappears: The New Middle America*, 13–61. Charlottesville,
VA: National Marriage Project.

Wilkinson, Amy. "Entrepreneurial Nation: Our Enduring Prosperity Depends on
Innovation, Which Is Truly American." *USA Today*, July 16, 2009.

Williams, Joan C. *Reshaping the Work-Family Debate*. Cambridge, MA: Harvard University Press, 2010.

Williams, Linda. "Melodrama Revised." In *Refiguring American Film Genres: Theory and History*, ed. Nick Browne. Berkeley: University of California Press, 1998.

Williams, Raymond. *The Long Revolution*. Peterborough, ON: Broadview, 1961.

Williams, Rosalind. *Dream Worlds: Mass Consumption in Late Nineteenth-Century France*. Berkeley: University of California Press, 1991.

Williams, Ruth. "*Eat, Pray, Love*: Producing the Female Neoliberal Spiritual Subject." *Journal of Popular Culture* (September 21, 2011): 1–21.

Williams, Tony. "*Poltergeist* and Freddy's Nightmares." In *Hearths of Darkness: The Family in the American Horror Film*. Madison, NJ: Fairleigh Dickinson University Press, 1996.

Wilson, Elizabeth. *Adorned in Dreams: Fashion and Modernity*. New Brunswick, NJ: Rutgers University Press, 2003.

Wilson, Eric. "Bloggers Crashed Fashion's Front Row." *New York Times*, December 27, 2009.

Wiltz, Teresa. "Shopper: And with All That Money I Saved." *Washington Post*, August 28, 2008.

Wolff, Larry. *Inventing Eastern Europe: The Map of Civilization on the Mind of Enlightenment*. Palo Alto, CA: Stanford University Press, 1994.

Wong, Jocelyn, and Grace Yip. "Guru Faces Global Appeal: Michelle Phan's Cosmetic Tips on YouTube Have Made Her a Huge Star." *South China Morning Post*, July 11, 2011.

Wood, Robin. *Hollywood from Vietnam to Reagan*. New York: Columbia University Press, 1986.

Yen, Hope. "Recession Rips at U.S. Marriages, Expands Income Gap." Associated Press, September 28, 2010.

Yochim, Emily, and Julie Wilson. "Mommy Media: Productivity, Pleasure and Politics." Paper presented at Society for Cinema and Media Studies Annual Meeting, Boston, March 21, 2012.

"YouTube Stars." *Observer*, August 21, 2011.

Zandy, Janet. *Hands: Physical Labor, Class, and Cultural Work*. New Brunswick, NJ: Rutgers University Press, 2004.

Zelizer, Viviana. *Economic Lives: How Culture Shapes the Economy*. Princeton, NJ: Princeton University Press, 2011.

Zimbardo, Philip G., and Nikita Duncan. *The Demise of Guys: Why Boys Are Struggling and What We Can Do about It* [e-book]. TED Conferences, 2012.

CONTRIBUTORS

Sarah Banet-Weiser is professor at the Annenberg School for Communication and Journalism and the Department of American Studies and Ethnicity at the University of Southern California. She is the author of *The Most Beautiful Girl in the World: Beauty Pageants and National Identity* (1999), *Kids Rule! Nickelodeon and Consumer Citizenship* (2007), and *Authentic™: The Politics of Ambivalence in a Brand Culture* (2012). She is the coeditor of *Cable Visions: Television beyond Broadcasting* (2007) and *Commodity Activism: Cultural Resistance in Neoliberal Times* (2012). She has published in journals such as *Feminist Theory, Critical Studies, Media Studies*, and the *International Journal of Communication*, among others, and she is the current editor of *American Quarterly* (2010–14).

Hamilton Carroll is lecturer in American literature and culture at the University of Leeds. He is the author of *Affirmative Reaction: New Formations of White Masculinity* (Duke, 2011). He has also published various articles on whiteness, masculinity, American literature, film, and literary and cultural responses to the events of September 11, 2001. He is currently completing work on a monograph on September 11 and the narrative imaginary.

Hannah Hamad is lecturer in film studies at King's College London. Her principal research interests are postfeminist cultures of popular film and television, Hollywood stardom and celebrity culture, and the cultural politics of contemporary Hollywood. She has taught in the areas of gender and race in film and media, popular culture, and stardom and celebrity. She is the author of articles on contemporary popular media culture and Hollywood stardom, and her monograph *Postfeminism and Paternity in Contemporary US Film: Framing Fatherhood* was published in 2013.

Anikó Imre is associate professor of critical studies at the School of Cinematic Arts of the University of Southern California. Her publications include *Identity Games: Globalization and the Transformation of Post-Communist Media Cultures* (2009), *East European Cinemas* (2005), *The Blackwell Companion to East European Cinemas* (2012), *Transnational*

Feminism in Film and Media (2007), and *Popular Television in Eastern Europe during and since Socialism* (2012).

Suzanne Leonard is associate professor of English at Simmons College and author of *Fatal Attraction* (2009), the inaugural text in Wiley-Blackwell's series Studies in Film and Television. Her published articles have appeared in *Signs, Genders, Women's Studies Quarterly*, and in various anthologies including *Interrogating Postfeminism: Gender and the Politics of Popular Culture* (Duke, 2007) and *Reclaiming the Archive: Feminism and Film History* (2010).

Isabel Molina-Guzmán is associate professor of Latina/Latino studies and media and cinema studies and chair of the Department of Latina/Latino Studies at the University of Illinois at Urbana-Champaign. Her book *Dangerous Curves: Latina Bodies in the Media* (2010) reflects her long-standing interest in the intersections between gender, race, and Latina/o identity. Molina-Guzmán's work has appeared in numerous edited collections and scholarly journals such as *Critical Media Communication Studies, Journalism*, and *Latino Studies*.

Sinéad Molony is a PhD candidate in the School of English, Drama and Film at University College Dublin. Her dissertation, "Where the Girls Are So Pretty: Literary, Visual and Material Configurations of Femininity in Dublin," examines the production of Dublin City as a gendered space and draws on women's self-representations to examine the interrelation between bodies and the city with a particular focus on genealogies of exclusion and dislocation as well as women's performances of dissent and subversion.

Elizabeth Nathanson is assistant professor in the Department of Media and Communication at Muhlenberg College. She received her PhD in screen cultures from Northwestern University. Her research examines representations of housework in contemporary American popular culture and considers the changing temporality of postfeminist domesticity. Her articles have been published in *Television and New Media* and *Framework*, and she is author of *Television and Postfeminist Housekeeping: No Time for Mother* (2013).

Diane Negra is professor of film studies and screen culture and head of film studies at University College Dublin. She is the author, editor, or coeditor of eight books, one of which, *Interrogating Postfeminism: Gender and the Politics of Popular Culture*, was edited with Yvonne Tasker. Her current project is *Extreme Weather and Global Media*.

Tim Snelson is lecturer in media history at the University of East Anglia. His research addresses the relationship between media and social history, focusing particularly on gender, media consumption, and the politics of taste in relation to popular film and television genres and cycles. He has published in journals including *Cultural Studies, Media History*, and *New Review of Film and Television Studies*.

Yvonne Tasker is executive dean of arts and humanities at the University of East Anglia. She is the author, editor, or coeditor of nine books, one of which, *Interrogating Postfeminism: Gender and the Politics of Popular Culture*, was edited with Diane Negra.

Pamela Thoma is associate professor of women's studies in the Department of Critical Culture, Gender, and Race Studies at Washington State University. With teaching and research interests in feminist theory, popular film and media studies, and literary studies, she has published articles in *Feminist Media Studies*, *Frontiers*, and *Genders*. She is the author of *Asian American Women's Popular Literature: Feminizing Genres and Neoliberal Belonging* (2013). She is currently completing a book about fertility, family, and domesticity in postfeminist popular culture.

INDEX